Lineages of the Present

Lineages of the Present

Ideology and Politics in Contemporary South Asia

———◆———

AIJAZ AHMAD

VERSO

London • New York

First published by Verso 2000
© Aijaz Ahmad 2000
All rights reserved

Verso
UK: 6 Meard Street, London, W1V 3HR
US: 180 Varick Street, New York, NY 10014–4606

Verso is the imprint of New Left Books

ISBN 1–85984–765–X

British Library Cataloguing in Publication Data
A catalogue record for this book is available from the British Library

Library of Congress Cataloging-in-Publication Data
A catalog record for this book is available from the Library of Congress

Typeset in 11/13pt Stempel Garamond by
SetSystems Ltd, Saffron Walden, Essex
Printed by Biddles Ltd, Guildford and King's Lynn

To Michael, a gift beyond the silence

Contents

Preface

Lineages of the Present was first published in 1996 by Tulika, Delhi. The present edition is substantially different. Five texts, amounting to over one-third of that volume, have been dropped and a number of new ones have been added.[1] That earlier edition was conceived as a selection of political essays I had published over some fifteen years, on sundry topics. The present volume has been made much tighter in focus, to include only a selection from a series of interlocking essays that I have been writing on the politics of the South Asian subcontinent. With the exception of the one essay on Pakistan, which was published some twenty years ago, all the rest deal with modern, mainly contemporary, India. Written within the last eight years, the texts on India now include several recent pieces that did not appear in the 1996 volume and were published in various Indian journals only more recently. In the last two chapters I have sought to bring the narrative up to the Indian General Elections of September–October 1999 and the most recent of the military takeovers in Pakistan that coincided so perfectly with the formation of a new BJP-led government in India, which is likely to be more stable – and therefore even more damaging – than the previous one. The unity of the book, however, is thematic and analytical rather than narrative. More than telling the story of a sequence of events, I try to make sense of some enduring structures.

The essay on Pakistan is the only one in this volume that was written expressly for publication in a European journal. It was drafted in the aftermath of Zia ul Haq's coup of 1977 and then extended after the subsequent, judicially sanctioned assassination of Zulfiqar Ali Bhutto. That was a major turning point in the history of contemporary Pakistan as we now know it and the essay is included here not only to recall the decisive importance of the years following the separation of Bangladesh, but also as a backdrop to the discussion of Pakistan that resurfaces much later in chapters 8 (in 'The Many Roads to Kargil', pp. 253–70) and 9, where I analyse more recent events. With the exception of 'Democracy and Dictatorship in Pakistan, 1971–80', in other words, all the other texts that are included in the present edition, whether in their original or revised form, were drafted, delivered as lectures,

and/or published in the context of specific debates within the Indian
Left and have never before been published outside India. This has
introduced what from some points of view may appear as distortions of
a specific kind. Since several of these essays try to deal with overlapping
themes, though for different audiences and with changing analytic
accents and configurations, I have been unable to remove all repetition,
which, in the reading now, should be treated simply as implying special
emphasis and reiteration. Several of these began as lectures and some
were quick commentaries on current events for a mass-circulation
magazine. The commentaries on the nuclear explosions and the Kargil
war, initially published in *Frontline*, appear here without any revisions,
as does the opening essay on the politics of the 1947 Partition, '"Tryst
with Destiny"', which was written for a special issue of *The Hindu* on
the fiftieth anniversary of Indian Independence. The lectures have been
revised, but here too I have been able to eliminate only a part of the
informality. The spoken voice intrudes time and again, grounding even
the theoretical reflections in the ephemeral. The conjunctural nature of
the original composition is thus frequently evident in the texture of the
prose and relative lightness of the scholarly apparatus. Finally, since the
texts were addressed to specifically Indian audiences and readers, I felt
free to write without explaining much of the specific detail with
reference to Indian history and politics. This I have tried to modify as
much as possible but some difficulty for the non-specialist Western
reader may yet remain, in whom the opacity of Indian politics, combined with the hermetic intricacy of argument within the Indian Left,
may induce the sort of sensation I felt when I first tried to comprehend
the beauties of the sonnet form.

I did think of changing even the title of the book when its scope and
design were altered so very substantially. Retaining the same title seemed
appropriate, however, not only because some two-thirds of the book
(and the crux of the argument) is the same but also because the title
seemed even more appropriate here than it was for the earlier, Indian
edition. This title, *Lineages of the Present*, has had for me, from the
beginning, not one resonance but two. There is an obvious sense in
which no present is ever *sui generis*, no lives ever lived merely in the
present tense; the lineages of historical time that went into the making
of a present remain a sedimented part – often a *fatal* part – of that
present. As I look back on these essays, each of them served, at the time
of its writing, as a way of coming to terms with some aspect of our
political and social present. None of these essays observes the protocols
that are proper to History as an academic discipline. Even so, the effort
in virtually each case seems to have been to try and make the opacity of
the present less unintelligible by reflecting on the *making* of that present.

This engagement with the present significance of a past that refuses simply to recede into history is there not only in the essays on the historical project of the Hindu far Right with which much of the book is so centrally concerned but also in those essays which appear to be reflections on events and personalities of several decades ago, such as the one on Maulana Azad where I trace the many detours in that fragmented career, not to write yet another of those hagiographies that are the norm in Azad studies, nor mindlessly to celebrate a past that has bequeathed us so catastrophic a present, which is also the norm in contemporary liberal accounts of the Indian National Movement, but to illustrate how limited was the achievement of nationalist Muslims even at their best, and how meagre are the resources – intellectual, political, historical resources – that they have left behind for succeeding generations of those Muslim intellectuals of today who insist on drawing inspiration primarily from a Muslim past. It is a great paradox of modern Indian history that Jinnah, who at length became the chief spokesman for Muslim particularity, did not invoke the scripture to authenticate the claims of this particularist separatism, whereas men like the Deoband *ulema* or Maulana Azad, who affirmed the multi-denominational compositeness of the Indian polity, invoked the Prophetic tradition in support of their affirmation. One wonders whether or not a secularism that refuses to break with the necessity for scripturalist authorization is in any fundamental sense a secularism at all; it is perhaps best to treat it as a certain kind of multi-denominational tolerance and decency. This refusal to break with scripturalism is a regular feature of Indian Muslim modernism as formulated by the upper-class, north Indian Muslim intelligentsia and still punctuates such discussions as the ones on legal reform for Muslim women which are so palpable in contemporary India. This paradoxical will to inhabit simultaneously the scriptural and the modern worlds, so characteristic of Azad, is also connected, as both effect and cause, with the contemporary reality of a Muslim politics still dominated by the traditional religious personnel on the one hand, the *petite* intelligentsia on the other. I might add that I wrote that essay with the awareness that it would be read, if at all, by that socially conservative but politically liberal intelligentsia that currently partakes of the Azad iconography; the rhetorical arrangements in the essay have that pedagogical slant.

In '"Tryst with Destiny"', where I reflect upon that Partition of India which Azad had so valiantly opposed, I offer very condensed commentary not on the failures of the nationalist Muslims but on the culpability of the Indian National Congress as such, notably of the right wing of the party which drew such sustenance from Gandhi himself at crucial junctures. The Partition itself, though, I see neither simply as a point of terminus for colonial rule and the dawn of a rosy new day, nor only as a communal holocaust of half a century ago in which the present communal violences were so fatally prefigured. Rather, I have thought of the Partition as a key episode in that much longer historical process where structures of caste, class, colony, and denomination have combined to thwart the civilities of the politics of equality and thus paved the way, at every turn, for savageries of the politics of identity. Neither the high-caste Hindu nor the genteel and propertied Muslim, neither the fatefully colonial forms of our modernity nor the exclusivist practices of our anti-colonial reform movements, have been entirely free of cultivating those savageries.

That same sense of a past that remains a residual but intractable element even within the utter originality of the present has been there whenever I have sought to reflect upon histories of European fascisms or the more contemporary West Asian Islamisms. Thus, the 1996 edition of *Lineages* included a lengthy essay on Italian Fascism which served both as the factual account of the world in which Antonio Gramsci's thought is embedded, as I analyse some aspects of that thought in a related essay that does appear in the present edition; and also as part of a more intricate argument about fascism and about nationalism that runs, like a connecting thread, through much of this collection. That particular essay has been omitted from the present edition. Even so, I have long held that as revanchist and proto-fascist tendencies become more rampant in contemporary India, it is still useful, with all the necessary caveats, to reflect on what one might call the classic fascist experience of the inter-war years (roughly, 1919–39), not for exact analogy but for that kind of creative, complex, and comparatist reflection through which experiences of the past do sometimes illuminate the opacities of the present. And I have also believed that as we reflect on that past we may think more fruitfully not so much about the advanced capitalist society of Nazi Germany, the most industrialized in the Europe of that time, but about the Italy that got caught in the coils of Fascism, with its predominantly agrarian society, its regional diversities, its classical traditions of language and religion, and its weakly developed institutions of political democracy and the nation-state.

The latter point was part of my concern in the essay entitled 'Fascism and National Culture: Reading Gramsci in the Days of *Hindutva*' which has been retained in the present edition. There, I had sought to deal not so much with that powerful conceptual apparatus – 'hegemony', 'war of position', 'national-popular', etc. – for which Gramsci is now best remembered in the Anglophone countries, but that other, though related, line of thought in his work which negotiates the issues of *tradition, classicism,* and imperial *religions,* to suggest that semi-industrialized societies which have inherited such powerful traditions but have nevertheless made no social revolution in the present or the immediate past may be more rather than less prone to fascistic movements, thanks to the intrinsically conservative, authoritarian, and national-chauvinist pressure of such traditions and the corresponding organizational forms upon what he felicitously called 'common sense' – a key conceptual category through which Gramsci sought to capture the fragmentary and sedimented nature of popular consciousness and thus to render intelligible the intricate weaves of belief, cognition, and practical reason. In something of an allegorical move, this essay on Gramsci was drafted as an indirect reflection on that deeply disorientating moment of 6 December 1992 in which a spectacle of the classical fascist type was staged at Ayodhya, a little pilgrimage town in northern India, to destroy Mir Baqi's antique mosque – officially and even popularly known as 'Babri Masjid' – in the name of Hindu national redemption in the present. In India, far too many of us are rather too proud of our classicism and of the great religious traditions. I found it useful to remind myself what Gramsci, an Italian communist living in an altogether different context, had to say about the disabling imprint of classical linguistic and religious traditions on modern but moribund societies, as he reflected on the politics of his time in the catastrophic loneliness of a Fascist prison.

Antonio Gramsci's thought has been discussed around the world mainly in relation to the European experience. My own essay was written under the impact of the destruction of the Ayodhya mosque and was presented in Calcutta three weeks after that event. It had seemed to me then that the ghost of fascism, laid to rest in the flames of the Second World War, had risen again to inhabit our own present. It was an unpleasant lineage about which I had sought to write with some degree of composure. A year later, I drafted the essay 'On the Ruins of Ayodhya' for a conference held in Hyderabad, in December 1993, to commemorate the anniversary of that day of national shame. On this latter occasion, I was able to drop the indirection of the earlier essay and spoke directly of what we quaintly call 'communalism', and of the beleaguered category of 'secularism'. In this essay, then, I sought to clarify for myself, in brief, three obscurities: (1) the centuries-old and still very unfinished struggle in what we now call our 'nation' for the creation of a denominationally pluralist society, which has been at the root of the struggles that came later, for democratic politics and socialist equality; (2) the crisis of the modern Indian polity which has led to the peculiar and dangerous circumstance that the Rashtraiya Swameksevak Sangh (RSS), which had remained a marginal political force from its inception in the 1920s up to the mid-1970s, has been gaining respectability and indeed something resembling hegemony over the cultural imaginary of this country, certainly in the Hindi heartlands but much beyond those regions as well, over the past two decades; and (3) the idea, the contours of which are still not entirely clear in my own mind, that a developing market economy in the age of imperialist dominance *needs* a nationalist ideology that would serve as the cement of society as it gets riven by competing interests, and that with the decline of the anti-imperialist nationalism which was dominant in India during the Independence struggle and for a decade or so thereafter, it is quite logical that a rightwing, quasi-fascist, obscurantist, market-friendly ideology would seek to serve as a nationalist ideology, considering that a national cement of one kind or another is an *objective* necessity in such a society. In other words, the struggle in contemporary India is not merely between universalism and a politics of identity, or between communalism and secularism as abstract cultural values, but, more specifically on the terrain of nationalism, between socialist anti-imperialism and fascistoid projects of the far Right. In this struggle, secularism is a necessary basis but an insufficient one; fascistic communalism can be defeated in the long run only if we build that national community of radical equalities for which my word continues to be 'communism'. I might add that the reader here would be faced with a deafening litany of at least three words – 'we', 'us', 'our' – and several other related ones. I have been subjected enough to the pathologies of many a nationalism and could hardly be a nationalist myself, in most senses of that word. Yet, I do live a politics of common possession, common resource, common project, and therefore with rather a sharp sense of 'us' and 'them': Left and Right, the imperialist and the imperialized, that which conjoins and that which divides. In this age of imperialism, I believe, it is simply not possible to bypass the politics of anti-imperialist nationalism; one has to go through it, as if through a darkness in which only the stars can be the reliable guide, and find oneself on the other side. To that extent, the vocabulary of 'we' and 'us' is, in my sights, neither sentimental nor spurious.

*

But this phrase, 'lineages of the present', also has an autobiographical resonance, in the sense that these few essays which I have selected for inclusion in this book have for me the status of some traces left by a prolonged and arduous apprenticeship. General Zia made his coup in July 1977 and, in consequence of a great many changes that need not detain us here, I bade farewell to Pakistan some two years later, never to return there for prolonged residence after the summer of 1984 when even indirect political connections were severed. This had two sizeable consequences for my publications. English now became the predominant, almost exclusive language of my political and theoretical writings. Since publishing a book of translations in 1971,[2] I had really not written much in English except in a couple of transient publications of Pakistani exiles and émigrés – essays, moreover, that I today regard, for the most part, as juvenilia, at times useful but at other times misguided. This renunciation of Urdu as the primary language of intellectual discourse has been a painful cultural price I have paid for not returning to Pakistan, the country that had provisionally become mine as a result of migration after finishing my schooling in India. That this price should become all the more exacting after my return to India and in the course of my residence in Delhi, the historic home of the language, is an irony of unspeakable proportions, traceable to the recompositions of classes and communities in northern India, in the aftermath of the Partition, a matter on which I offer some comment in the essay 'In the Mirror of Urdu'. Within the text of that essay, however, I have sought to avoid the kind of self-display that is now so much the norm in contemporary cultural criticism and have attempted, instead, to tell the tale of the tribe as it were, objectifying what is at another level a deeply felt personal loss.

The other consequence of that break with my political past in Pakistan was more complex. Certitudes were easier to maintain during the phase of the expansion, during roughly the ten years after 1967, of that very sizeable – in my opinion, the central – current of the Pakistani Left with which I had been quite intimately involved. The next ten years, 1977 onwards, were momentous and, for someone with my modest theoretical understanding, very bewildering. The declaration of the Emergency in India had already signalled one kind of ending for the sort of world which one had until then taken for granted. Then, in a matter of two years, the region to the west of India witnessed the rightwing coup of General Zia in Pakistan, the leftwing coup inspired by PDPA in Afghanistan, and an *Islamicist* revolution in Iran which was not only supported by much of the Irani Left but, more bewilderingly, was the culmination of a proletarian uprising and a General Strike that brought to mind – very incongruously, under the circumstances – Lenin and Rosa Luxemburg. The time had clearly come for me to *read*. Neither my academic training, nor my self-education, nor the education I had received in the course of my political involvements had prepared me to understand the history that was taking such fearsome and fateful shapes all around me. So began that intellectual restlessness, that encounter with theory and history, which is now likely to remain forever unsettled, despite the few cracks that one may occasionally succeed in making in this cloud of unknowing. The essays in this book are among the traces of that restlessness in which I recognize the lineages of my own intellectual present. These are of course not the only traces. During this same period, I have published much else, notably *In Theory: Classes, Nations, Literatures*, which has been my way of settling accounts with my erstwhile literary-critical conscience; even there, though, the entire argument hinges on an understanding, developed most sharply in the Introduction,[3] of the mid-1970s as a defining moment in modern

history, not only of South Asia but on a global scale, when the tide
turns against the Left, the victory in Vietnam notwithstanding. And, I
have written much more than I have published; most should of course
be left, in Marx's eloquent phrase, 'to the gnawing criticism of mice',
and the rest gets published as the occasion arises. I have chosen the title
of this book, in any case, as a way of indicating what Gramsci once
called an 'inventory of traces' that the larger history leaves upon an
individual consciousness.

*

All these writings have appeared previously and appropriate acknowl-
edgements can be found elsewhere in the book. Many of these essays
have been revised to a lesser or greater extent, but none so much that it
becomes in any basic way different from what had been published
previously. Most revisions have been small, for stylistic improvement,
textual reference, or factual correction. In some essays, however, revisions have been substantial, for editorial reasons certainly but also for
refining the argument. On the whole, I have resisted the temptation of
extensive rewriting to make everything conform to my present views.
Much that I no longer find acceptable has been left as I formulated it at
the time of initial publication.

These essays were written over so many years and have involved so
many debts that it is impossible now for me to enumerate all the
kindnesses I have received in the process. May all those who have been
kind in the past be generous yet again and simply understand that I am
entirely mindful of their generosities! But for the coaxing by Rajendra
Prasad and the patient work of Indira Chandrashekhar and Sudhanva
Deshpande, I would not have thought of assembling a collection of this
kind. Most of these essays were written in the course of my Professorial
Fellowship at the Centre of Contemporary Studies, Nehru Memorial
Museum and Library, New Delhi. Association with that fine institution
had been my pride and privilege, until the BJP took it over. The
dedication of the 1996 edition to Ravinder Kumar was in some oblique
way an acknowledgement of that fact but it referred mainly to a
cherished personal friendship. The present edition I have dedicated to
my friend, Michael Sprinker, who kept insisting for some two years that
I let Verso publish this book. He received the manuscript of the present
edition barely a week before his sudden death but he did edit all the
fresh materials for me within that very brief time – as a parting gift, it
now appears.

Aijaz Ahmad
March 2000

PART I

Intertwined Genealogies

1

'Tryst with Destiny':
Free and Divided

Historiography of the Partition in India, and of communalism generally, is dominated by a self-congratulatory narrative prepared by Congress-inspired scholars in which the Indian National Congress is represented as being synonymous with the Independence Movement as such, and denominational communalisms, of Hindus and Muslims alike, are said to have been merely discreet and pathological epiphenomena that arose on the fringes of Indian society. In this narrative, Congress is portrayed as always having been secular, splendidly free of the communal virus, and increasingly representative of the national interest as such. Independence is said to be the practical realization of this Secular National Spirit embodied in the Congress, while the Partition is seen as the point of culmination of separatist tendencies that had been growing among Muslims since the 1880s and had come to hegemonize the Muslim masses by the time the elections of 1946 were held. Hagiographies are prepared for the Nationalist pantheon, from Tilak to Gandhi to Patel to Azad; Jinnah is equated with Savarkar, and the Muslim League becomes the other face of the RSS.

The night of 15 August then becomes that magical moment when the Indian people finally arrive at, in Nehru's famous phrase, their 'tryst with destiny'. This triumphalist account of a nationalism that failed to protect a fifth of the territorial nation that it claimed to represent is credible only if the creation of Pakistan is seen as the severance of 'the diseased limb', as Patel put it in 1946 while recommending the bloody surgery. This way of representing the politics of the Partition – the contrasting careers of Congress and the League – in binary metaphors of health and disease, is very popular among Hindu communalists but not entirely contrary to the way Congress nationalism tells its own story. In this one respect at least, the line between our canonical nationalism and full-bodied communalism is at times very thin indeed.

The factual situation was somewhat more complex. It is undoubtedly true that representatives of the Muslim elite, especially the north Indian landed elite, not to speak of sundry nawabs and khan bahadurs in places like Dhaka, had always been preoccupied with the defence of their sectional interests, even though they claimed to speak for Muslims in general. It is equally plausible that this elite was able to disseminate its own anxieties among some other sections of Muslims. That was all the more possible in a colonial society built along axes of caste, sect, and denomination, with no experience of universal suffrage or of institutions of secular, democratic, and denominationally pluralistic governance. Nor was the Indian polity free, from the last quarter of the nineteenth century onwards, of quite aggressive forms of Hindu communalism. That articulate sections among Indian Muslims would demand safe-guards against the possible tyranny of the denominational majority is hardly surprising. Syed Ahmed Khan's famous refusal to endorse the then newly formed Congress during the 1880s, which is often portrayed as the starting point of Muslim separatism, was indicative of those sectional anxieties of the Muslim upper classes and politically articulate strata, while the anxieties themselves had been greatly exacerbated by a distinct increase in the aggressivity of Hindu communalism at that time, notably in Bengal.

It is also true that the Muslim League, under Jinnah's leadership, won the great majority of Muslim reserved seats in the elections of 1946, thereby claiming to represent the Muslims of India: a claim that was quickly recognized by the British, and by the Congress as well. This recognition had come earlier, in fact. The British had already elevated Jinnah to the status of their main interlocutor in the wake of the resignation of the Congress ministries at the beginning of the Second World War, to the extent that he suddenly came to exercise a power of veto over all decisions pertaining to the issue of independence, well before the League had demonstrated any considerable following among the Muslim voters. Without that unilateral elevation by the British, Jinnah would never have had the temerity to play the high-stakes poker that he began with the Lahore Resolution of March 1940; his Address to the League that year more or less says so.

One might add that the elections of 1946, which were treated by all sides as the test of the Muslim League's claim to represent Indian Muslims in their generality, had been held on the basis of a franchise so narrow that the elections could hardly prove anything about mass sentiment. It is true that the League received almost two-thirds of the votes polled in the Muslim constituencies in 1946, but that amounted to barely half a million votes. The very large number of Muslims who lived in the princely states were not allowed to vote, and the League received a majority of votes only in the Muslim-minority provinces. In provinces where Muslims were in the majority, the plurality of votes went to other parties. It is only because we now forget the extremely narrow scale of the franchise during the colonial period, and because we have now grown into the habit of having a democracy based on universal suffrage, that we might think of elections of the colonial period as representing any kind of general will. Those elections had the status, at best, of a straw poll to gauge opinion among the propertied and professional elites. As Mushirul Hasan, on whose statistics I rely here, has commented: 'never before in South Asian history did so few divide so many, so needlessly'.

In short, then, the elections of 1946 did not provide any basis for the claim that the majority of Muslims had preferred the Partition or had given the League any sort of mandate. Nor is there a straight line between the events of 1880s and the elections of 1946. Even the making and unmaking of the Bengal Partition in the opening years of this century, which did so much to fan the communal flames on both sides of the divide, and which is often viewed as a prelude to the Partition of 1947, can hardly be so construed. There is a world of difference between the creation of new provincial units within a stable empire, at a time when virtually no one, certainly not the Muslim elite, was demanding independence, as was done in Bengal in 1906, and the carving out of separate nation-states from an existing country in the process of decolonization in 1947. And, except for the fact that it was achieved through machinations of small elite groupings and that the British partitioned Bengal in line with their 'divide and rule' policy, the Bengal Partition was qualitatively not very different from the reorganization of states in independent India on linguistic lines, or the separation of Haryana and Himachal Pradesh from Punjab, or, more to the point, the perfectly justified demand today that Kashmir be given a special constitutional status within the Indian Union. Between the Bengal Partition and the Partition of the country in 1947, there had been, furthermore, the Khilafat Movement and the Rowlatt satyagraha, which had brought together Hindus and Muslims in their millions, in the aftermath of World War I, while the League remained, until the late 1920s, a gathering of not much more than a thousand notables. So dispirited was Jinnah at that time that he withdrew to his London home for four years and returned to India only on the eve of the Act of 1935.

At no point before 1940 was the demand for a separate state for Muslims voiced by any significant number of individuals. Jinnah's Presidential Address to the Muslim League in March 1940, in which he first presented the idea of a full-scale division of India along denominational lines, was, despite its hair-raising communal vitriol, something of a surprise, one that he sprang with little prior preparation: neither a map nor a name for the new nation-state was given. In deed, the famous 'Lahore Resolution' which gave to the Address a programmatic form and which was later to be renamed as the 'Pakistan Resolution', did not use the term 'Pakistan' and was deliberately so vague that one could not tell whether the League was asking for one such state or two or several. Nor was it clear whether the state(s) would be 'sovereign' or 'independent' or 'autonomous'. The intent clearly was to keep the options open, to see whether he could get 'sovereign' state(s) or would have to settle for either a confederation of 'independent' ones or, even, merely 'autonomous' units in a federation with a weak centre. These options Jinnah seems to have kept open until the middle of 1946.

Thus it is that he continued to speak, for some six years, with a forked tongue. On the one hand was the insistent repetition of the so-called 'two-nation theory', with its equally insistent conjuring of spectres of bloodbaths and civil wars if Muslims were to be 'forced' to live with Hindus in one state. This was balanced, however, with elaborate disavowals. When the press kept reporting that Jinnah had demanded the creation of Pakistan, he retorted, in his Presidential Address to the League in 1943, that 'Pakistan is a word which is really foisted upon us and fathered on us by some sections of the Hindu press and also British press'. In such pronouncements – merely four years before the Partition and three years *after* he had presented the Lahore Resolution – he was clearly dissociating himself from the idea of Pakistan as such. 'Give the dog a bad name and then hang him', he said bitterly. Not surprisingly, the most astute among the British officials and observers continued to believe for quite a while that the Lahore Resolution was in reality a bargaining counter and, in Hugh Tinker's words, a 'deliberate overbid'. As late as June 1946, just a year before the actual Partition, the League did not wait for the Congress to give even its 'conditional' assent and announced its own acceptance of the Cabinet Mission Plan which had firmly excluded the possibility of partition while providing for a weak centre and regional regroupings of the Muslim majority areas in the north (Bengal and Assam were to be grouped in a separate category). This, too, Jinnah did with his characteristic brinkmanship; in accepting the plan he in effect withdrew the demand for a separate, sovereign state, but to his own constituency he presented this as a ploy to draw closer to the objective of a partition.

It was in any case only after the scuttling of that plan, mainly by the Congress, that a process was unleashed, starting with the communal conflagrations Jinnah now deliberately provoked, which paved the way for partition of the country, the division of its two largest provinces, and the division also of the Indian Muslim population so gigantic that if sixty-five million of them found themselves in a brand new country they had done little to make, another thirty-five million remained in the same old country which was not, according to the so-called 'two-nation theory' and the dispensation of the Partition itself, theirs any longer. It is very unlikely that, as Mr Nehru arose in the Parliament of newly independent India to speak so sonorously of a 'tryst with destiny', there were many who felt the stirrings of such a 'tryst' either in Bengal or in Punjab where much was going down that very instant in blood and flame.

The Congress-inspired nationalist mythology explains the Partition as an effect of three interlocking processes. There is, first, the separatism that begins to grow among Indian Muslims in the last quarter of the nineteenth century and keeps spreading, like a virus, despite valiant doctoring by the Congress as the guardian of India's 'composite culture', until it becomes incurable and grows to maturity in the shape of the Pakistan Movement. Second, there is the diabolical figure of Jinnah, a veritable Savarkar of the Muslim hue, and the League, the home of the rabid and the 'diseased', which cynically propagate communalist hysteria among the Muslim masses until a majority of them becomes infected, while the Congress leaders go in and out of jails, organize the Quit India Movement, and try to save the country's integrity while winning its freedom. Third, and finally, is the heartbreaking but resolute decision, in the service of the rest of the body politic, surgically to remove 'the diseased limb'. On the night of 15 August, then, the grandeur of Independence is symbolized by Nehru and his eloquence in Parliament, the tragedy of the Partition by Gandhi, who stays away from the Independence Day celebrations.

As nationalist mythologies go, this one is neither better nor worse than most. It fails, though, as mythologies frequently fail, to explain simple facts. For example: how is it that, fifty years after the severance of 'the diseased limb', Hindu majoritarian nationalism is more menacing today, and envelops a larger proportion of the country's population, than was ever possible in the case of Muslim separatist communalism prior to the Partition? Perhaps communalism is not so discreet a pathology after all, nor a pathology specific to a cross-section of the Muslims; perhaps it is not a matter of this limb or that, but a creeping failure of the immune system as a whole. After all, RSS, which was once seen as the Hindu equivalent of the Muslim League but an ignorable, fringe element in Hindu society, has by now 'fathered' what is the largest party in Parliament, not to speak of numerous such machineries of terror and hysteria as the Vishwa Hindu Parishad, the Bajrang Dal, the Durga Vahini. It is also more than arguable that RSS now dictates the agenda for much more than itself, its fronts, and the support base of those fronts. The proposition may well be entertained that the programmatic communalism of the RSS is matched to a very considerable extent by the pragmatic communalism of the Congress itself, not to speak of influences far beyond the two dominant political parties. One can no longer look forward to using the alibi of severing a limb; the body politic itself may have to be conceded.

Perhaps we need to turn around, therefore, and think of the Partition along a somewhat different explanatory axis. Here, too, we shall have to consider a long-term dynamic that will include much more than Muslim separatism, as if it occupied some discreet and autonomous space, unrelated to the larger contexts of colonial society; as well as a short-term dynamic, which also will include more than Jinnah and the League, as discreet political agents, and will have to consider the complex developments between the promulgation of the constitutional reforms of 1935 and the Independence that came some twelve years later. Viewed in this light, the Partition emerges not as the expression of a singular will, brought about by individual leaders or political parties, but as a catastrophic resolution of some objective processes that had been maturing over many decades but were then greatly accelerated after (1) the fateful decision of the Congress in 1936–37 to form provincial ministries within the overall structure of the colonial state, (2) the outbreak of the Second World War, (3) the equally fateful decision of the Congress to resign from those ministries, and (4) the drastically altered imperatives of British colonialism thanks to the exigencies of the war. These are complex matters and, owing to restrictions of space, we shall have to summarize them in rather telegraphic terms.

Any consideration of the long-term dynamic should include at least three things: the very structure of colonial polity, the peculiarities of Indian reformism during the colonial period, and some features of the anti-colonial mass movements themselves. We shall argue that these three elements constituted a very specific structure in which nationalism and communalism grew in tandem with each other, not just as contraries but also as different plants growing in the same soil. It is not accidental, for example, that the history of communal riots begins more or less in the 1890s precisely at the time when the first rudimentary forms of modern political organizations appear. Nor is it incidental that Gandhi kept a wide cross-section of Hindu communalists inside the Congress as long as he could; that the frequent convergence between the Congress Right and the Hindu Mahasabha was never portrayed by the Congress leaders as a sign of growing majoritarian sentiment within the Congress itself; that the Congress and its apologists always spoke of Jinnah and the League as opposing its secularism, without acknowledging that some of that opposition was aimed at elements of majoritarian communalism and paternalism within the Congress itself.

The key fact about India is that modern politics began here in the colonial context, and that no colonial society can be based on rights of common citizenship, which meant that conditions were exceptionally unfavourable for the growth of secular, democratic politics. That initial phase, lasting roughly until the First World War, had some distinct features. Except for the underground revolutionary groups which in India always remained very small, political organizations arose under severe legal restrictions and essentially as pressure groups. The absence of structures of popular representation, such as universal suffrage, meant that representatives were either appointed from above or claimed to represent 'the people' when no one had elected them to do so. In either case, such elite groupings arose, first of all, as supplicants in relation to the colonial state. Development of the classes of modern society itself remained weak, thanks to the colonial blockage of industrial development, which was then reflected in the weakness of class organizations and the proliferation of non-class pressure groups, organized from above; the proletariat remained small, and rather few among the numerically very small modern bourgeoisie were particularly bourgeois. In such circumstances, organizations of the modern type arose more in the social arena than in the political, and most such organizations arose along the fault lines already available in premodern society, such as denominational community, religious sect, caste association. Under colonial conditions, such entities lost much of their earlier amorphous character and gave to themselves, with no little encouragement by the colonial government, far greater solidity in social life and representational claim in the newly emergent political arena; prohibitions on the politics of equality, even in the simple juridical domain, served to enhance savageries in the politics of difference. Even the type of social organization that worked for reform, such as the educational society or philanthropic trust, arose mainly to serve caste and communal ends. If much 'modern' education was dispensed through caste societies and denominational schools and colleges, most of politics was similarly conducted in the form of deputations and conferences representing castes and denominations. In other words, the emergence of modern forms of power, in the shape of the state and of colonial capital, *required* the emergence of corresponding political forms through which the colonized could represent themselves; however, in blocking collective representation in the form of equal citizenship rights and universal suffrage, the colonial state fragmented the emergent nation into its social units and greatly accentuated the existing cleavages, even though the fact of being governed by the same colonial state gave to each of these units a certain investment in nationalist rhetoric and some rudimentary form of nationalist consciousness.

Such remained the structure of colonial polity until after the First World War. When the era of mass politics began, Indian colonial society was already organized, socially as well as politically, along the axes of caste, denomination, and region. The contribution of colonialism to the growth of communal and caste politics was thus not merely tactical ('divide and rule') but structural. This structure of colonial society was fully reflected in the type of social reform movements that arose during the formative period of Indian politics, up to the First World War, and which persisted, in great profusion, throughout the period of the mass politics of the Independence Movement.

The most striking feature of these reform movements was that they too were usually confined to denominational, caste, or regional boundaries, and to issues that were specific to these. When a Muslim reform movement began in northern India, specifically through the medium of Urdu, there was not even a trace of any consciousness that they might learn something from the earlier reform movements in Bengal or the contemporaneous ones in Maharashtra, which had been characteristically confined to non-Muslims. Similarly, from Rammohun to Phule to Periyar to Ambedkar, there is a rich history of radical reformers becoming heretics in relation to their own denominational origins, but there is not even a rudimentary tradition of Muslims participating in Hindu reform movements, or Hindus including Muslims in their reform projects; nor of multi-denominational reform movements working for the creation of non-denominational civic and political secularity, of the type that was already the object of the French Revolution some two hundred years ago. And, typically, most reform movements remained confined to specific regions. Most spoke of reforming 'the nation' but virtually all settled to reform that particular segment to which they were tied by birth. Modern consciousness in India was almost always a fractured consciousness, and those fractures have left an enduring mark on the non-revolutionary, divisive path that the Independence Movement took, as well as on structures of power and politics subsequently.

In this context, then, two more features of these reform movements are worthy of note. One is that atheists like Periyar were rare. Starting with Rammohun himself, authorization for modern reform was almost always sought in Shastric or Quranic knowledge, and, ironically enough, even Ambedkar's final transgression took him from one religion (Hinduism) to another (Buddhism). Second, cooperation among organized members of different denominational communities almost always took the form of mutual accommodation among exclusivist orthodoxies. In relation to the denomination of one's own birth one could be a radical reformer, even a heretic; about other denominations, one punctually uttered pieties and platitudes, at least in public.

Gandhi was characteristic in this regard. It is perhaps all to the good that he set out to reform Hindu society; unreformed, the society is likely to succumb to majoritarian communalism all the easier. And what he called his Sanatan Dharma was, by Sanatani standards, so novel and eccentric that, as Nehru was to chide him, it was incapable of converting a single true-blooded Sanatani. Beginning with *Hind Swaraj*, however, there is also in Gandhi a full-blown rhetoric of an idyllic Golden Age somewhere in the Hindu past which was casteless, classless, ungendered; hence the theme of the *recovery* of virtue by returning to the worldview of the forefathers. It is as if modern politics was in its own nature so sinful that it had to be anointed in some prior form of piety. One consequence of this pietistic notion of politics is specially relevant to the issue of the politics of Partition.

Gandhi seemed to have shared with far too many others, of various political stripes, the conviction that India was a conglomeration of discreet religious communities and that its 'composite culture' therefore required an organizational form in which each community shall be represented by its own members who will then speak from the common platform of the Congress. This led, then, to a stark duality of claims. In relation to the world outside itself, Congress alone had the right to represent the people of India, regardless of denominational differences among them; inside the Congress, however, only Muslims had the right to represent Muslims. In other words, Congress could claim to represent Indian Muslims not because it claimed to be a party fighting for a common, secular citizenship in an independent India, but because it included such eminent Muslim figures as Ansari, Azad, and the Deoband *ulema*. Jinnah claimed to represent Indian Muslims and described Azad as a 'showboy' of the Congress; Gandhi treated Azad as the true leader of Indian Muslims, ignored Jinnah while the latter had an insignificant following but then took to addressing him as *Qaid-e-Azam* (the great leader), in the fashion of the League itself, from 1944 onwards, once Jinnah had shown that the British had indeed recognized him as the 'sole spokesman' of Indian Muslims which had, in turn, helped him garner the support of provincial Muslim leaders. What is striking in all this is an agreement between Gandhi and Jinnah, in principle, that Muslims could be represented only by other Muslims; what remained to be settled was whether Jinnah or Azad had among them the greater legitimacy. That no Hindu, not even Gandhi himself, could truly represent Indian Muslims was something on which Gandhi, Jinnah, the British, the whole culture of the caste-ridden, denomination-bound colonial society appeared to be almost wholly agreed.

In the individual case of Gandhi, however, there was another complication. His pietistic view of the world, and surely of India, meant that he found it easier to deal with pious, or at least very traditional, Muslims, especially the ones who formally accepted his status as the Mahatma. Muslims were for him, first of all, Muslims; and that meant religion! With Muslims of a modern temper, such as Jinnah, he felt distinctly uncomfortable, more so, strangely, than with the likes of Nehru, who were undoubtedly no less modern but were of Hindu origin. Aside from his own pietistic bias, it was perhaps the Khilafat Movement, which broke out so soon after Gandhi's own entry into Indian mass politics, that may have left an enduring impression on him that Muslims could be led only by men of the Quran. It is significant that while Gandhi gave eloquent support to the Muslim *ulema* who were leading the agitation for restoration of the Turkish Caliphate, Jinnah described that Caliphate as an 'exploded bogey', refusing to endorse the unleashing of religious frenzy. Whatever its origins, that conviction of Gandhi had two demonstrable consequences.

People like Jinnah, who were Muslim but modern by temper and strong in their own opinions, though no less devoted to Indian nationhood in their early political formation, found themselves increasingly sidelined and alienated. The advocacy of Partition and Pakistan during the 1940s was, for one such as Jinnah, in part a furious reaction against frustrations accumulated through a lifetime in which he had sought to combine two prongs of his conviction: the generality of 'Hindu–Muslim unity' which he often described as his life's mission, and the specificity of what he used to call 'Muslim interest'. But then in losing commanding figures such as Jinnah, Gandhi's Congress also lost increasing proportions of the modern Muslim middle class, who came to believe that their career opportunities would be far greater in a brand new country of their own. Their mentality had been prepared already by a whole history of education and culture which had by no means been communal but, like the rest of colonial society, was deeply bound by a sense of denominational difference. The Aligarh muslim university, for example, suddenly began to provide the cadres for mass mobilization in the service of the Pakistan movement, even though its denominational character had not been until then, in any recognizable sense, politically communal. A slide from denominational assertions in the political arena to communal politics, in the accurate sense, was not inevitable but always possible.

The other consequence of Gandhi's proximity to the pietistic Muslims on the one hand and the Congress Right on the other was more complex. The majority of Muslims of a modern temper who gravitated towards the Congress were the ones who were not religious and were of a leftist inclination. They gravitated, therefore, not towards Gandhi or even Azad but Nehru. This was the fraction that could be called 'secular' in the proper sense, secularism being practised here as an ideology not of accommodation between orthodoxies but of non-denominational, common citizenship. The fraction was unfortunately, and under the circumstances inevitably, rather small. And most leaders of the Congress looked at them with suspicion. In other words, the Congress as it evolved under Gandhi, Azad, Patel, *et al.*, as an alliance of social conservatisms, valued Muslim nationalists very much but had little use for secular Muslims as such.

The fortunes of the Muslim Mass Contact Campaign that was organized in the mid-1930s, with the blessings of Nehru and seeming acquiescence of the Congress Right, were indicative in this regard. It was in initiatives of this kind that secular and Left-leaning Muslims, such as K.M. Ashraf, who had no roots in traditionalist Muslim politics, found their vocation within the Congress, fleetingly as it were. To the extent that Nehru was recognized as its real leader, this Campaign was the first, and in some senses the only, mass initiative undertaken by the Congress on the principle that a non-Muslim could lead the Muslims directly, without conceding this constituency to a Muslim even of the same party. To the extent that key organizers of the Campaign were not pietistic but drawn from the Muslim fraction of the middle class, it promised to give the Muslim League a fight on its own grounds. And, to the extent that it was designed to mobilize the Muslim *masses* on a platform of the Left, it promised to tap areas of society to which the League had no and the Congress very limited access.

The Campaign had, in other words, great potential and, in the short span of life that was allowed to it, very impressive numbers of Muslims were registered for membership in the Congress. Under the circumstances, however, the Campaign could only die. In the factional struggles within the Congress Nehru was expected to be the main beneficiary of this Campaign, as Gandhi had been of the Khilafat Movement; the Congress Right could not allow that. The proposition that a campaign designed to mobilize Muslims could bypass the Muslim leaders of the Congress and, worse still, would mobilize them on a non-denominational, secular, Left platform was little short of heresy. Those who organized it simply lost the patronage of the dominant Muslim leadership within the Congress while their linkages with traditional Muslim notables within and outside it were always minuscule. No wonder the Campaign died an orphan, neglected all the more because Congress by then had more pressing things to do, as it began to exercise the powers it had gained when it took up provincial ministries. Which brings us, then, to the the Act of 1935 and its aftermath.

When the Act was promulgated Nehru was still in his leftist phase. In his Presidential Address to the Congress in 1936, he warned that accepting office under the Act 'will be a pit from which it would be difficult for us to come out', and that formation of ministries under the circumstances 'would inevitably mean our cooperation in some measure with the repressive apparatus of imperialism, and we would become partners in this repression and in the exploitation of our people'. Prophetic words, indeed! Gandhi typically followed a two-track policy. He formally opposed the acceptance of office but, prodded by G.D. Birla, the powerful industrialist, and others, he encouraged the leaders of the Congress rightwing not to reject the idea of working within those reforms. Meanwhile, he also kept open a channel to the British through Birla, who assured them of eventual compromise. Birla also noted elsewhere, with much satisfaction, that the Congress Working Committee comprised overwhelmingly 'Mahatma's men'. After Nehru's proposal against taking office was rejected by these 'Mahatma's men', Purshotumdas Thakurdas, another industrial magnate, was to note that 'a good deal of nursing will have to be done to keep J[awahrlal] on the right rails all through'. In the event, 'nursing' worked: Nehru sulked but fell in line and Congress went into the elections in due course. After that Nehru was never again to have any sort of quasi-Marxist élan, preferring to settle into an Indian variant of Fabian socialism. It is also significant that when Congress came into office in March 1937, Jinnah proposed a 'united front', declaring that 'There is no difference between the ideals of the Muslim League and of the Congress'. But to no avail! The more the Congress prevailed, the less capable it became of flexibility or a long-term view.[1]

With benefit of hindsight, we can now say that three consequences of the formation of the 1937 provincial ministries exacerbated the configuration that eventually led to the Partition. First, Congress won so overwhelmingly and the League was cut to size so drastically that the Congress felt no need to accommodate the latter, while Jinnah's plea for a 'united front' appeared to be an attempt to gain a favour that the electoral results did not warrant. Few realized that such acts of generosity were necessary if the Congress was to win the confidence of those who felt threatened by the size of its victory; if Jinnah was capable of seeking a 'united front' he was also capable of whipping up hysteria on the charge that the 'Hindu party' which had taken over was refusing to share with the Muslims any part of its power. Second, the exercise of even limited governmental power revealed to the general run of Congress leaders how sweet the fruits of power could be. During the crisis years of the 1940s, there was not to be any significant opinion within the Congress that would favour postponing the day of Independence in order first to settle the communal problem. Full governmental powers, in the shape of Independence, were to be obtained as quickly as possible. Third, as the ministries went into action, the Congress had to bear the responsibility for acts of omission and commission by the combined force of its party machinery as well as the existing governmental machinery. In the past, acts of Hindu communalism could be ascribed to this local factor or that; now the responsibility for all kinds of hurt, real and imagined, lay with the Congress, as party and as government. Much of the Congress had no truck with communalism, but substantial numbers of it, especially at local levels, were complicit in what one could call the culture of the Hindu Mahasabha. As these elements gained more power than before, instances of their communalist conduct multiplied, which in turn fuelled the fear that Muslims would be unsafe in a Congress-ruled independent India. Having been denied its proposed 'united front', the League was to play havoc with such apprehensions, especially in Uttar Pradesh.

Then came the Second World War, the decision of the British authorities unilaterally to declare India a party to the war, the resignation of the Congress ministries on this issue, the imprisonments, the Quit India Movement, more imprisonments. It was virtually by British appointment that Jinnah got elevated as a counterweight to Gandhi, and it was this suddenly enhanced status, combined with grievances accumulated during the short-lived Congress ministries, which gave to Jinnah the opportunity to win over most of the provincial Muslim leaders as well as a substantial base among common Muslims. The story is well known and need not be detailed here.

As one reads the record now, one is struck by how early most Congress leaders got reconciled to the idea of Partition. Indicative of the drift was Nehru's own comment in April 1940, barely a month after Jinnah had initially tabled full-fledged Partition, to the effect that Partition was preferable to any postponement of the coming of Independence. The quicker the better, in other words, whatever the cost! In the course of the war, and especially as the war ended and the prospect of Independence loomed on the horizon, one leader after another, including such stalwarts of Congress conservatism as Rajagopalachari and Patel, went on record favouring the acceptance of the Lahore Resolution and cutting off 'the diseased limb'. Nor is there much evidence that either Gandhi or Azad, who were so saddened by the Partition, ever seriously contemplated the postponement of Independence so as to prevent the Partition. Nor did they, at the decisive moment, actively try to bloc the majority opinion in the Congress Working Committee in its favour.

We may now conclude with the perennial question of the historiography of the Partition: could the Partition have been averted, and at what point did it become inevitable? Our analysis would suggest (1) that the politics of caste and communalism was inherent in the structure of colonial society itself; (2) that our reform movements usually contributed to solidifying such identities rather than weakening them in favour of an ecumenical culture and non-denominational, secular politics; and (3) that the National Movement itself, including the majority of the Congress under Gandhi, was deeply complicit in a transactional mode of politics which involved bargaining among elites and a conception of 'secularism' which was little more than an accommodation of self-enclosed orthodoxies. Given the immensity of this historical weight, the wonder is not that there was a partition but that there was only one.

We have also suggested, however, that despite the great acceleration of events between the formation of the Congress ministries in 1937 and the coming of Independence ten years later, there was no one point when the Partition became inevitable. There is, in other words, no point zero at which this sorry tale begins. Instead, what we have is the clash of wills and the collapsing of wills; calculations and miscalculations; and different types of cynicism all around. The mode of British departure was as unprincipled as their rule had been. Jinnah got a country much smaller than he had desired; he called it a 'moth-eaten Pakistan'. But Congress too got much less than it had set out to obtain; what remained of India was not merely 'moth-eaten' but scarred for generations to come. The indecent haste to become rulers of some sort of country – no matter how truncated or bloodied or 'moth-eaten' – was by no means limited to Jinnah alone.

2

Democracy and Dictatorship in Pakistan, 1971–80

... despite Mr Bhutto's juggling with the command structure and his many rewards to Army and Police, there will still be a coup ... this type of regime is likely not to *start* in the tradition of Suharto or Pinochet; rather, it is likely to adopt a populist and puritanical stance ... In the name of an 'Islamic way of life', it will impose a medieval labour code in the factories; will weed out all remnants of intellectual life in the universities; and will seek to reverse all the marginal gains the peasantry has made during struggles of the past five years ... and terror under such a regime, if it comes about, is likely to reach a scale heretofore unknown and unimagined in our body politic.[1]

As the destabilization campaign against the government of Zulfikar Ali Bhutto got under way after the elections of March 1977, one got the impression that ground was being prepared covertly for a takeover by the ultra-Right, with the much publicized 'Democratic Movement' fitting into the scheme of things rather like the famous 'strikes' of truckowners, housewives, and some other elements of the middle strata in Allende's Chile.[2]

Coup of the Ultra-Right

This impression became unmistakable as one examined the political composition of the so-called 'Democratic Movement', led as it was by political parties of the extreme Right, viz. the Jama'at-e-Islami (henceforth Jama'at),[3] Jami'at-e-Ulema-e-lslam (JUI), the Muslim League (ML), and Tehrik-e-Istiqlal (Tehrik).[4] Moreover, the demands of this 'Movement' were indicative of its temper and purpose; significantly, the chief demand was that the army – the same army whose bloody deeds in Bangladesh and Baluchistan are well enough known – should form the government and ensure 'free and fair' elections. Meanwhile, the social base of this 'Movement' comprised the most retrograde sections of the petty bourgeoisie and the urban lumpen, while it was backed by a cluster of trade unions nurtured over the years by the American Institute of Labour and its affiliates. The tactic of colossal disruption, with losses in production and property calculated at $2 billion, not to speak of the countless dead, was itself a classic of prefascist upheavals. This massive disruption of the domestic economy was closely synchronized with cancellation of sale agreements for fighter aircraft by the Carter Administration, cancellation of loan agreements by the First National City Bank, and refusal of the Aid-to-Pakistan Consortium even to hold a meeting while the destabilization campaign raged in the country. In context, it became fairly clear that certain policies of the Bhutto regime – e.g. some concessions to the Soviet Union, the nationalization of agro-based factory units, the establishment of state monopoly in rice exports, the announcement of far-reaching land reforms in January 1977 – had led to a confluence of domestic and external determinations to oust the regime and to replace it with a regime of the ultra-Right. The coup of 5 July 1977, which did just that, was thus an altogether unsurprising denouement.

Upon taking power, the junta kept a predictable low profile, claiming 'no political ambitions' for itself and promising elections within ninety days. At the time of this writing, in October 1978, the military dictatorship has completed fifteen months in power, has created a so-called 'civilian' government by appointment, has set no date for elections, and has undertaken such far-reaching modifications in the established constitutional convenant, in the administrative and economic structures, and in the ideological perimeters of the state that one cannot now imagine the military returning to barracks in the near future.

The Constitution of 1973, we are told, still lives, although the Chief of the Army Staff has also said, on television, that he is answerable to none but Allah, and the country is governed through military courts and martial law regulations which violate the Constitution in letter and spirit. The Chief Justice of the Supreme Court, who was expected to resist, was dismissed at twenty-four hours' notice. All other judges of the Supreme Court and High Courts have been required to take a fresh oath of office, suitably rephrased to legitimize military rule. It is a measure of the bankruptcy of bourgeois institutions in Pakistan – where the *New York Times* perceived a 'sturdy and independent' judiciary after Bhutto was sentenced to death – that none of the judges refused to take the new oath, while the ceremony was supervised by Generals Zia and Chishti, in full military regalia. In turn, the same judges dutifully administered, with scant regard for legality, the oath of office to the Chief Martial Law Administrator when he later decided to usurp the presidency as well. Earlier, these judges had already upheld the imposi-

tion of martial law, itself altogether unconstitutional, as a '*necessary*
deviation from the law'.

This crisis of constitutional legitimacy and of judicial institutions is
combined further with unprecedented political repression and a steep
decline in social ethos. For instance, physical torture has of course
always been widespread in Pakistan, but no previous government has
been brazen enough to institutionalize it or even confess it; now
corporal punishments, such as amputation of limbs, have been made
part of the penal code; floggings have been staged in public places, so as
to brutalize national culture and terrorize the populace; and the regime
has even promised to televise executions in the future. Estimates of the
number of political prisoners apprehended by this regime range between
20,000 and 100,000. The truth must lie somewhere in between. Over a
thousand, we know, have been flogged inside prison walls and at least
ten have died as a result of these floggings. Bhutto's Pakistan Peoples
Party (PPP) is thus far the main target of this repression, but the scope
of intent is much wider; 'Everybody knows I'm a man of the Right,' the
Chief of the Army Staff exults, 'all these liberals and democrats better
move to the Centre.' In his lexicon, liberals are leftists and hence
dangerous. Scores, perhaps hundreds, of workers have been killed, as,
for example, in January when at least seventy were shot dead in the
streets of Multan. Groups of women have been beaten up inside the
High Court compounds, in full view of photographers, with the regime
not bothering even to institute an inquiry. Every time the Opposition
plans to mount a political rally, the police simply round up thousands
of young men (and now, increasingly, women as well) on the basis of
information gathered through covert organizations of the Jama'at. The
news media are gagged; dozens of journalists have been imprisoned at
various times; television workers have been flogged; some publications
are banned altogether, while others are functioning under strict censor-
ship codes. The armed forces, loudly committed to safeguarding the
'ideological frontiers' of the country, have been awarded a permanent
role in police and civil administration, while, in the ideological sphere,
Islamic pieties are in full bloom. Before being appointed Law Minister
in the illegitimate 'civilian government', Mr Brohi, the country's most
reactionary lawyer, had the audacity to argue in the Supreme Court that
the present regime needed no legal basis for its existence because it had
come into being in order to promulgate an Islamic social system – Islam,
and the military regime as its political expression, was *ipso facto* above
the law.

In short, the crisis that had erupted in March 1977 has now culminated in an Islamicist military dictatorship, and the chief author of this
story is Zia ul Haq, a man of kulak origins, Pakistan's Chief of the
Army Staff, Chief Martial Law Administrator, and now President by

self-appointment – a man who is well known for his role as a key advisor to King Hussein of Jordan during the Black September massacre of Palestinians in 1970.

That the repressive apparatus of the state should so blatantly assume once more the tasks of its political apparatus shows in no uncertain terms that the reformist model of the Bhutto era has failed. Conversely, the increased visibility of the repressive apparatus extends the very crises which its activity seeks to resolve. In this situation, two contrasting perspectives are developing among Left groups in Pakistan. Some have argued, implicitly in writing and explicitly in discussions, that (1) since the Bhutto regime was undoubtedly liberal and 'progressive' compared to the present military dictatorship, and (2) since Bhutto has already become the focus of the democratic upsurge in Pakistan, it is necessary for the combined Left to wage a struggle for the 'restoration' of democracy (i.e. the Bhutto government) in a broad united front led by the leftwing of Bhutto's party; they argue against developing a criticism of Bhutto at this time, and they go so far as to claim that Bhutto had actually fought to make Pakistan independent of imperialism and had contributed significantly to the revolutionary process in Pakistan.[5] At the other end of the spectrum, some others argue that Bhutto was a 'fascist' comparable to Hitler and Mussolini, and that the working class must struggle to prevent him from returning to power. They imply a degree of support for the junta which is said to have destroyed 'fascism'.[6] While the latter view is simply absurd, the former also needs modification. Our analysis will seek to demonstrate that the July coup was indeed arranged by the ultra-Right in opposition to the reformist aspects of the Bhutto regime; Bhutto was in no sense a fascist. However, it is also true that the apparatuses which carried out the coup were permitted to proliferate throughout the Bhutto period. We therefore need to examine carefully the crises of the economic base, of the dominant ideology, and of the institutions, and even the legitimacy of the existing state.

The present analysis will thus have two objectives. One, we shall examine the nature, the context, and also the limits of Bhutto's reformism. Second, we shall try to situate both strategies, the reformist and the Islamicist, in the matrix of concrete social crises. Throughout, we shall assume that mass struggle must take a broad democratic form but that the struggle nevertheless cannot be for 'restoration' of the 'democracy' which prepared the objective ground for the July coup by nurturing the repressive apparatus (not only General Zia, but the whole apparatus), and that the social bases for democracy cannot be secured without democratization of economic life, of the relations among nationalities in Pakistan, and of the state institutions. Here, we must begin by summarizing the history and limitations of the reformist model. Then we shall analyse the crises which led to the coup, as well as the class character of the present regime.

Bhutto and the PPP: General Background

Today, as some friends begin to portray Bhutto as an anti-imperialist and even a revolutionary, it is useful to recall that he is a scion of one of the biggest landlord families of Sindh and that his father was the Chief Minister of the feudal Junagadh state in British India and owner of extensive investments in commerce and urban real estate, hence closely aligned with the nascent Muslim bourgeoisie based in Bombay which later constituted the main nucleus of the Pakistani bourgeoisie in Karachi after Partition. Thanks to these class origins Bhutto himself was trained at Berkeley and Oxford. Upon returning to Pakistan, he quickly emerged as one of the two civilian ministers in the military cabinet which was formed after the *coup d'état* of 1958 and for seven years, he held a variety of portfolios in the regime of Field Marshal Ayub Khan. His subsequent experiments with 'Islamic socialism' cannot be separated from these basic facts.

As Ayub's minister, Bhutto carefully cultivated an image of himself which balanced his domestic location among the most reactionary elements with a radical stance in foreign affairs. Thus, he awarded a contract for a geological survey and oil exploration to the Soviet Union, normalized state relations with China, developed a close personal friendship with Sukarno, and professed to draw his inspiration from the leading non-aligned countries, such as Ben Bella's Algeria and Nasser's Egypt. Popular consciousness thus perceived in Bhutto a relatively enlightened element in Ayub's otherwise despotic regime. Then he quit the government, just in time, when popular discontent against Ayub had begun to manifest itself, and with enough fanfare to emerge later as the main beneficiary of the mass movement of 1968–69[7] which brought about Ayub's downfall.

The political party he then created, namely the Pakistan Peoples Party (PPP), was a classic formation of radical elements, on the one hand, drawn from the petty bourgeoisie of Punjab and Sindh, and on the other hand, substantial elements of the landlord class – the latter, however, consisted typically of those who (1) were hostile to the biggest landlords of Punjab (the top stratum of landlordist power in Pakistan) and (2) were committed to capitalization of agriculture, which involved restrictions on the *scale* of landholdings (hence the land reforms, discussed below). The dominant position of the radical petty bourgeoisie within the initial formation of this political party was evident in the original Manifesto of the PPP which was clearly anti-imperialist, anti-feudal and anti-monopolist. This same stratum played a key role in devising a propaganda machine suited to the Manifesto, in presenting it as a 'revolutionary' programme, and in using this programme to vulgarize the concept of socialism while simultaneously radicalizing mass consciousness in some respects.[8] In sum, the elections of December 1970, which culminated in the electoral victory of the PPP in (West) Pakistan, signified the emergence of the radical stratum in the petty bourgeoisie as an important force in the formation of power blocs which contended for dominance in the political apparatus of the state. (Other strata of the petty bourgeoisie, notably those which served in the repressive apparatus – the army, police, etc. – and the ideological apparatus – schools, colleges, media, etc. – had of course already established a place for themselves in state institutions, although in more mystified forms.)

This radical stratum was, however, drawn from diverse social origins, while different members of it held divergent political objectives and therefore connected themselves to Bhutto in separate groups. Their inability to transform themselves into a distinct bloc within the PPP greatly facilitated the purges which came later, from 1972 onwards, after Bhutto had consolidated his power and began actively to shift the balance of forces within the PPP in favour of the landlord group.[9] This shift in the class composition of the PPP, once it had formed the government, was neither accidental nor a *personal* betrayal on Bhutto's part, as it was subjectively experienced by the purged cadres. Changes in the internal class composition of the PPP were objectively determined by the changed position of the party in relation to the state. In other words, the PPP *had* to be an apparatus predominantly of the radical petty bourgeoisie in the pre-election phase when the main objective was to secure a mass base and an electoral majority against the entrenched ruling groups, particularly in the countryside. Once, however, the PPP had formed the government on the premise of seeking marginal reform within the predicates of the state as already constituted, thereby becoming the political apparatus of the reactionary state, its left wing was faced with the objective choice of either accepting the exigencies of the state or getting liquidated. In the event, the Left was of course liquidated. But what were the exigencies of the state? Here, we shall discuss only the most outstanding features, focusing first on some obvious permanent features of this state, and then on certain exigencies which were specific to the period immediately after the separation of Bangladesh.

First, coming to power in a country where external debt is almost half of the GNP, and a country, moreover, which relies on imperialism and its regional conduits not only for budgetary and balance-of-payments support but, most crucially, for replenishing the enormously parasitic armed forces, the PPP could restructure neither external relations nor the domestic structure. Second, the acute underdevelopment of the national bourgeoisie and the whole genesis of the state in Pakistan has led to the creation of a structure dominated by the military-bureaucratic apparatuses, which are, in turn, wholly dependent upon imperialism while retaining a degree of autonomy, especially at junctures of crisis, from the indigeous propertied classes. The PPP in power, committed already to stability of the state as constituted, could only become an instrument of these apparatuses. Third, with its independence sharply curtailed by imperialism and the military-bureaucratic apparatuses, the PPP could not possibly hope to survive in power without extensive compromises with the big landlords, who henceforth began joining the party in large numbers to occupy positions which the Left was vacating.[10] Bhutto was especially prone to these compromises, precisely because initially his links with the big landlords of Punjab and with the military-bureaucratic elite were rather weak, while his survival in government depended on these links. Fourth, in a multi-national state where economic, social, and military power was concentrated on power blocs drawn from Punjab and from among the Urdu-speaking minority, Bhutto, himself a member of the dominant landowning class of the oppressed Sindhi national minority, chose to refurbish his political position by acting on behalf of the ruling classes of the dominant nationalities, hence his chauvinistic and militarist stance in Bangladesh and Baluchistan geared to the ideological orientation of the dominant nationalities. Finally, the enormous economic crisis of the 1970s, which will be discussed below, left little room for the social and economic reforms advocated by the radical stratum of the petty bourgeoisie. For all these reasons, the stratum simply became a political liability and was therefore set aside.

All these factors obviously do not amount to any fatalism whereby Bhutto was doomed, by objective circumstance, merely to carry out the wishes of the metropolitan bourgeoisie, the military-bureaucratic elite and the big landlords of the dominant nationalities. As we argue in the following section, Bhutto had actually come to power at an extraordinary juncture in Pakistan's history, when the separation of Bangladesh had brought about a great crisis for the ruling classes in all spheres of society, while the PPP possessed immense authority and legitimacy, as well as an elaborate political apparatus, which *could* have been used for far-reaching social transformation. Thus, restrictions on the 'reformist model' stemmed as much from the class position of the PPP itself including Bhutto's own paradoxical political position, as from external determinations.

Bhutto and the Repressive Apparatus

Bhutto came to power as President and Chief Martial Law Administrator in December 1971, after the separation of Bangladesh, in an
extraordinary situation.

The Bangladesh War had cut the country to half its size, leading to
financial bankruptcy of the state, severe economic setbacks for its
bourgeoisie, and the collapse of the armed forces both militarily (as a
fighting force) and politically (as the leading factor in the political
apparatus of the state, actually in charge of government since 1958).
Meanwhile, the crisis of the dominant ideology was immense indeed,
since Pakistan, heretofore the 'national homeland' of Muslims in the
subcontinent, now had fewer Muslims living in it than in Bangladesh or
even India; it had simply lost its *raison d'être*. Quite apart from the
'nationalist' movement in Bangladesh, moreover the country had experienced continual and very intense militancy of the urban and rural
working classes since 1968, and the wave of factory occupations and
land seizures which followed Bhutto's accession to power was simply
the continuation of the politics which had been unfolding previously in
the wake of the mass movement of 1968–69. In some cases, such as the
occupation of Dawood Cotton Mills and Kohinoor Rayon Mills, many
workers took the initiative in the mistaken belief that their government,
i.e. the Bhutto regime, would be at least neutral, if not altogether
helpful, in the economic class struggle of the working class against the
monopolistic, comprador fraction of the capitalist class. In these circumstances, the PPP government commanded a vast scope for manoeuvre,
not only because it was the first elected government in the country's
history, nor simply because of its absolute majority in the National
Assembly, but mainly because the disarray of the ruling class and its
constituted state *at that juncture* gave the PPP unparalleled leverage. In
itself, the PPP was a new and raw political formation, without any
institutionalized collective leadership, and built from the outset around
the charismatic personality and articulations of Bhutto himself; moreover, it was a conglomerate of disparate political tendencies held
together by Bhutto's personal authority, which then defined, moment
to moment, whatever consensus existed within the PPP at given times.
These circumstances gave Bhutto a relatively autonomous stature in the
party and government.

This constellation of elements – the collapse of the armed forces, the
economic breakdown of the bourgeoisie, the extreme crisis of the dominant ideology, the existence of a popular government, and the concentration of unprecedented power in the hands of a man who was a
self-professed 'socialist' and who commanded the loyalty of a militant

mass movement – had created a classic prerevolutionary situation in Pakistan (not a revolutionary crisis, in so far as there was no proletarian party to make a bid for state power; but the situation was objectively revolutionary). In other words, the time of testing had arrived for Bhutto's 'socialism' precisely when he had the greatest power and opportunity to pass that test.

In the event, Bhutto did three things. First, he made an extensive compromise with imperialism, symbolized by his early acceptance of an IMF package which included: 130 per cent devaluation, lifting of import restrictions for over 300 commodities, exemption of foreign capital from nationalization, brutal suppression of the working class (resulting, for example, in the use of paramilitary forces against striking workers in June, and again in October, 1972), and inflow of foreign capital to the extent that Pakistan's debts doubled in the next four years. By 1976, debt servicing would have accounted for 36 per cent of the total foreign exchange earnings if rescheduling arrangements had not been obtained. Second, Bhutto used the opportunity presented by the exhaustion of alternative power blocs within the ruling classes (a) to enhance the autonomy of his own apparatus, and (b) to fortify the institutions of the state which had come to be dominated politically by his apparatus. Third, he undertook a number of reforms and even structural changes in the economy, though well within the predicates of the model of peripheral capitalism which Pakistan has pursued since its birth in 1947.

In order to revitalize the state-in-crisis and to establish the hegemony of his own apparatus, Bhutto moved on several fronts quite vigorously. In the armed forces, he conducted two purges in quick succession, first to get rid of the five top generals – 'fat and flabby', as he appropriately called them – who had dominated the government before and during the Bangladesh crisis, and then to purge the commanders, notably General Gul Hasan and Air Commodore Rahim, who had been instrumental in the transfer of power to Bhutto himself. Thus, he got rid of opponents and benefactors alike, to obtain maximum freedom of movement. Significantly, General Tikka Khan, the famous 'butcher' of Baluchistan and Bangladesh, escaped both purges, became Commander-in-Chief of the army and, upon retirement, Bhutto's Advisor on Military Affairs.[11] In the end Bhutto promoted Zia ul Haq, known even then for his ultra-Right connections, to Chief of the Army Staff, superseding four more senior generals. This last was obviously a miscalculation, as regards loyalty, for which Bhutto is now paying dearly. Meanwhile, he also instituted the Federal Security Force, a paramilitary organization – or, rather, a veritable political police – independent of the armed forces and responsible directly to the Prime Minister. Significantly, the star witness of the prosecution against Bhutto during his trial was none other than Masoud Mahmood, Bhutto's hand-picked chief of the FSF, who is now appearing under judicial immunity granted to him by the makers of the July coup. Thus, Bhutto's personal tragedy is one of betrayal by his associates of the ultra-Right whom he had trusted with too much power.

The case of the civil bureaucracy is more complex. Bhutto started, typically, by purging 1,300 officials, allegedly on grounds of corruption (which was undoubtedly evident in most cases, but then corruption was also rampant among most of those bureaucrats who were *not* purged), though the main purpose of the purge seems to have been the upgrading of bureaucrats loyal to Bhutto's regime. Second, Bhutto restricted the system of elite recruitment through the hierarchy of Civil Superior Services (CSS) and instituted the system of lateral entry, i.e. direct appointment at all levels of administrative and diplomatic services upon recommendation of his political machine. This measure brought certain advantages for the growing and newly influential stratum of technocrats over the traditional bureaucracy, but the main purpose was again to expand the loyalist base among the administrative elite. Third, the phenomenal growth of the public sector expanded the field of employment for an overgrown bureaucracy which was faced with a threat of retrenchments after the separation of Bangladesh (which this bureaucracy used to administer), and in practice, the public sector became yet another area of very lucrative collaboration between the bureaucrats and the PPP functionaries, for mutual benefit.

In the political domain, the main problem for the PPP was that while it commanded comfortable majorities at the federal level and in the more populous provinces of Punjab and Sindh, it had an insignificant following in Sarhad (NWFP) and Baluchistan, the two minority provinces with volatile electorates and militant mass movements. No political party had obtained a clear majority in either of those provinces, but the National Awami Party (NAP)[12] had won a plurality of votes in Baluchistan, and JUI[13] the largest number of seats in Sarhad; the NAP–JUI coalition had thus formed governments in both those provinces after the constitutional accord of 1972.[14] Bhutto resolved this problem two and a half years later by summarily dismissing those provincial governments, imposing a ban on NAP and imprisoning its leadership. Thereafter, money and coercion won many allies for the PPP in both those provinces, but not enough in Baluchistan to make it possible for the Provincial Assembly even to meet in session for the next two years. The insurgency this measure provoked in Baluchistan is of course well known. In brief, approximately 100,000 troops were deployed there at any given time over the next three years, on a rotating basis, so that the majority of Pakistan's armed forces had gained the Baluchistan experience, in order to apply it elsewhere in the country if and when the opportunity arose. This experience included the familiar pattern of garrison towns and freefire zones, heliborne troops and population transfers, air-dropped supplies and routine missions to bomb and napalm the rural and semi-nomadic communities. It was thus a classic counter-insurgency operation by an army eager to retrieve the 'honour' it had lost in Bangladesh. So we can see that, in Baluchistan, Bhutto's pursuit of dominance for his own apparatus converged with his actual subservience to the armed forces and the ruling classes of the dominant nationalities, who sought ferociously to suppress the movement of national rights by devising a military solution for a political problem. Moreover, once set into motion, the war began to take on its own logic, because prolonged warfare necessarily created the opportunity for the more militant nucleus to start assuming positions of leadership in the Baluch national movement as a whole, and the military action was henceforth deemed necessary to prevent further radicalization of an essentially regional movement.

Exigencies of this type led to a quasi-Bonapartism whereby the growing autonomy of the state from all spheres of 'civil society' was systematically reinforced by restricting parameters of action for all social classes and groups, including, to a certain extent, the propertied classes. The nationalizations, particularly of commercial banks and insurance companies which undoubtedly restricted the freedom of the monopoly houses and of private capital generally, will be discussed below, along with the land reforms which promised similar restrictions on the extent of large-scale agrarian property. Here, it should suffice to illustrate this quasi-Bonapartist aspect with a few examples.

Bhutto formed the government in December 1971. In January 1972, he announced a set of nationalizations, the first in the country's history, and got a few big industrialists handcuffed for television display. In March, he announced the first set of land reforms, hyperbolically described at the time as the 'liberation of the Pakistani peasantry'. This last aspect, namely the rhetoric which accompanied each reformist measure, undoubtedly terrified the propertied classes even more than the economic content of the reforms. These high-pitched flourishes reached a tremendous climax by May Day, which was declared a holiday, while Bhutto himself expounded on 'the spirit of the Paris Commune'.

Then came the turnabout. In June, while a visiting team of experts from the World Bank firmly linked the question of multilateral aid to control of the domestic labour situation, armed police shot down 30 workers in the streets of Karachi. In October, 15 more workers were killed in a joint operation of the police and the paramilitary forces, while over 4,000 workers were either arrested or driven into the underground which now extended beyond the city of Karachi. Over the next few years, far-reaching recession in domestic industry, combined with the sustained bid by the PPP to establish its dominance over organizations of the working class, led practically to a state of siege, and the working class suffered retrenchment by the thousands,[15] wholesale destruction of many trade unions' offices, occupation of factories (and even whole industrial areas) by armed police, and widespread arrests, tortures, and in some cases assassinations of militant labour leaders. The working class of course retaliated: in factory takeovers of Seven-Up and Kohinoor Rayon in 1972; in the prolonged strike by over 80,000 workers in SITE and Landhi–Korangi industrial areas of Karachi during the same year; in sustained agitations of the railway workers throughout 1974–75; in the sixty-day strike in all of Swat during the winter of 1974–75; in the militant trade union actions in Hyderabad in the spring and summer of 1975; in strikes and job actions in Hyderabad in the spring and summer of 1975; in a thousand acts of militancy throughout the country.[16] These heroic struggles of the proletariat had their equivalent in the countryside in similar struggles of the peasantry, notably in Sarhad, and in struggles of the oppressed nationalities, especially the Baluch struggle which combined a variety of political tendencies including a cluster of communist groupings. The history, or rather histories, of those struggles will have to be told elsewhere. It is important to remember, however, that the regime of the Peoples Party bequeathed to the working class a list of martyrs which is indeed painfully long.

Politics of the Reformist Model

The elaboration of the repressive apparatus during the Bhutto regime has led some to brand him as a 'fascist'. Quite apart from the theoretical problem of applying such a term to so contradictory a regime, the political line derived from this perspective seeks clearly to prepare the ground for collaboration with the military regime, in so far as it ignores the reformist aspect of Bhutto – precisely the aspect that sets off the PPP so sharply from the regime which now exists and which is reversing whatever gains the popular classes had made under Bhutto. It is necessary, therefore, to comment briefly on those gains

In the terrain of ideological class struggle, the permeation of some socialist ideas deep into the countryside, whatever their practical application or lack of it, constituted a very definite advance in a country which was born in religious bigotry, was dominated by semi-feudal social structures, was fed for two decades a very controlled diet of Dulles-style anti-communism, was ruled by the armed forces for thirteen years, and which therefore lacked any widespread culture of secular, democratic, progressive ideas. In co-opting the language of socialism, Bhutto himself became the chief propagandist of that language: 'socialism', heretofore an obscure and suspect word in Pakistan's political culture, now became a household word and a symbol for legitimate social aspiration. Thus, the opportunism itself served inadvertently to raise the level of political debate in the country. Moreover, just as the failure of the 'developmentalist' ideology of the Ayub period (1958–69) with its explicit commitment to capitalist enterprise had given birth to its opposite, namely the 'socialism' of the PPP, the adoption of such a programme by the Bhutto regime as its official programme, and its manifest failures, opened the way now for wide dissemination of straightforward Marxist ideas and critiques. Precisely because the political posture of the regime was already determined by the democratic, even libertarian, mass movement of 1968–69, of which the regime was an offspring, it was constrained to allow, even encourage, the publication, import, and distribution of revolutionary literature on a scale previously impossible and unimaginable in the country. This legalization of Marxism of course had its own pitfalls, but it is worth emphasizing that the progressive ideas which circulated freely during this period were not only the milder social democratic ideas approved by the regime but also the revolutionary Marxist ideas which were clearly opposed to the regime. Again, these gains in the terrain of ideological class struggle were not a freakish 'cultural phenomenon', grafted at random by a 'fascist' state. Rather, the ideological parameters were modified precisely to the extent that the Bhutto regime was forced by the mass movement (1) to make room for a radical stratum of the petty bourgeoisie inside the state structure, thereby introducing into that structure a significant leftist element, and (2) to seek social legitimacy for the regime on the basis of widespread political support among the popular masses. It was thus the political class struggle, in all its ramifications, which had brought forth the gains in the terrain of ideology.

This pursuit of social legitimacy among the popular masses was again paramount in the way Bhutto presented his foreign policy at home. In this period, as in the past, Pakistan's actual dependence on the United States continued to grow, as our economic analysis will demonstrate. Yet, aware that the question of imperialism was at the heart of all mass movements in Pakistan, Bhutto took a series of highly publicized actions which eventually had a cumulative impact on political consciousness in the country. For example, he moved quickly to recognize the Democratic People's Republic of Korea and the German Democratic Republic, and a little later, the revolutionary governments of Vietnam and Cambodia. Similarly, he developed close ties with China, Romania, the DPRK, and the PLO. Relations with the Soviet Union and other Eastern Bloc countries were normalized, and Pakistan's diplomatic corps were instructed to support a variety of liberation movements, notably in Mozambique, Zimbabwe, East Timor, and the Spanish Sahara. Bhutto personally denounced imperialism for the fascist coup in Chile, and he sought to play an influential role in the economic self-assertion of the Third World countries. Actions of this type are of course ordinary fare with co-optive regimes of Asia and Africa. In the concrete circumstances of Pakistan, however, where a series of military regimes, before Bhutto and after him, have sought to turn Pakistan into imperialism's 'most allied ally' in Asia, the impact on popular consciousness of these actions was very considerable, for it was the first time in Pakistan's history that the official media adopted a progressive idiom and presented a consistent image of the socialist countries and liberation movements as friends, not enemies, of Pakistani people.

In his policies regarding the labour movement and nationalization of industries, Bhutto again combined his pursuit of hegemony for his own apparatus with the parallel pursuit for social legitimacy among the broad masses. We have already indicated the brutal use of the repressive apparatus against the vanguard of the labour movement, and we must note also that wherever trade unions had a communist orientation, the PPP regime cooperated with mill-owners and with rightist parties to break them and to replace them with PPP-dominated unions. It is also true, however, that the first three years of the PPP government were a period of brisk unionization and that more trade unions were permitted to register in this period than in the two decades previously; moreover, some of the middle-level leadership of the PPP covertly cooperated with the most militant trade unions in numerous instances. And, although industrial employment declined absolutely owing to the overall economic crisis of industry, the employed section of the working class made substantial economic gains, in the way of revised wage scales, job security, and other benefits, especially in the expanding public sector, which then began to have an impact on the private sector as well. Because of these economic gains, workers in the public-sector industries were quick to form the first line of defence for the proletariat against the martial law regime, after the coup of July 1977. The policy of nationalization will be discussed below at some length. We should note, however, that although the nationalizations altered the structure of domestic monopolies only marginally and without concentrating industrial production significantly in the public sector, their social impact was far greater than their immediate economic relevance. Pakistan has a rich history of industrial plants being built with public monies and then being sold at cost, and on credit, to private investors, but, unlike India or certain countries of the Middle East, it had until then no history at all of nationalization of property already in the private sector. In context, the *idea*, however bureaucratized and within whatever narrow predicates, of the nationalization of the means of production was explosive, sending shock waves through the bourgeois class and raising the level of aspiration and demand in the workers' movement. When actual nationalization proved to be mere 'bureaucratization', the sentiment against the bureaucracy was of course strengthened. But the idea of nationalization continued to gain wider currency. Other reforms – such as the extension of the social security system, nationalization of educational institutions, distribution of some land among a fraction of the landless, and so on – had a similar social impact far beyond the actual economic gains. We cannot discuss all these measures in any great detail here. However, the nature of many of these reforms can be seen, quintessentially, in the land reforms of January 1977, the last such measure which Bhutto announced and which could not be implemented after the July coup.

These reforms should be seen from the perspective of the structure of landownership and revenue systems in Pakistan. Briefly stated, the statistics are as follows: as of 1959, on the eve of the first land reforms (announced then by the military regime of Ayub Khan), 6.8 per cent of all landowners owned 51.4 per cent of all agricultural land, with the top 1.2 per cent owning 30.4 per cent of the land.[17] Moreover, rates of land revenue were uniform for all owners, large and small. In the reforms of 1959, only 2 million acres out of the total of 48.6 million acres were taken over by the government; the landlords thus lost, for compensation, only 4 per cent of their lands; half of what they turned over to the state consisted of wastes, hills, riverbeds, etc., and was therefore unavailable for cultivation. Less than 3 per cent of the peasantry benefited from redistribution of this acreage. Then, the land reforms of 1972, the first in the Bhutto period, reduced the ceiling of landholding from a maximum of 80,000 PIUs (Production Index Units) to a maximum of 32,000 PIUs. However, by March 1976, only 67,420 peasant households had received 660,000 acres of cultivable land under those reforms, on an average of roughly 10 acres per family.[18] Significantly, both these reform measures of 1959 and of 1972 left the revenue system essentially intact. Then, in November 1975, Pakistan saw its first reform in the revenue structure, whereby owners of up to 12 acres were exempted from all land revenue, and rates were upwardly adjusted for the bigger landlords. Thus, if those measures were fully implemented, 71 per cent of all proprietors would be fully exempted from government dues, 22 per cent would have paid the existing rates, and the top 7 per cent would have had to pay an additional Rs 153 million in revenue.[19]

In this context, the reforms of January 1977 had three significant features. First, the ceiling on landholding was now brought down to 100 acres of irrigated and 200 acres of unirrigated agricultural land; or, in terms of PIUs, the ceiling was now fixed at 8,000. The implementation of this measure, unlikely in any event, would have surely destroyed the basis of semi-feudal ownership in Pakistan; the mere announcement of it, in fact, raised the aspirations of the peasantry, refurbished Bhutto's agrarian electoral base, and provided the militant peasants with a platform for organizing in the future. Second, owners of up to 25 acres were now fully exempted from revenue payments; this measure benefited roughly 91 per cent of all proprietors, who at this stage owned over half of the cultivable area in Pakistan. Third, agricultural income tax was introduced, for the first time in Pakistan, for owners of over 25 acres. This was a necessary correlate of the growing capitalization of agriculture and the rapid growth in real incomes particularly of those landlords who had benefited from the so-called 'Green Revolution'.[20] Moreover, the state needed desperately to expand its tax base. However, this perfectly ordinary reform has been a point of great contention in Pakistan for over two decades, and although various tax exemptions were provided for those landlords who made use of capital inputs on their farms, the big landowners nevertheless saw the very idea of the agricultural income tax as a major encroachment upon their privileges.

These reforms, announced two months before the March elections, were characteristic of the PPP's particular brand of (agrarian) 'socialism'. Basically, they were designed to strengthen the growing capitalization of agriculture, to provide relief for a substantial stratum of petty producers and independent proprietors, and to award the state a larger share, in the shape of taxation, of the surplus extracted by the big landlords. Moreover, lowering the ceilings on the landholdings of the top stratum obviously held out the promise of more land becoming available for distribution among the landless. These, then – namely the middle, poor, and landless peasantries – came to constitute the electoral bloc for Bhutto in the elections that followed. By contrast, the agrarian commercial bourgeoisie, which was already alienated from the regime owing to the earlier nationalization of the agro-based factory units and the establishment of a state monopoly in rice exports, now made a common front with that ultra-conservative fraction of the landlord class which saw the threat of the agricultural income tax but not the benefits of capitalist agriculture. Together, these powerful segments of the agrarian power structure – segments which often overlapped and commanded considerable power not only in villages but also in small and regional towns – became an integral part of the subsequent destabilization campaign. In this dynamic, Bhutto of course commanded the numerical majority, despite manifest repression against the most advanced elements of the peasantry. Besides, the power bloc of the commercial bourgeoisie and the ultra-conservative landlords could have been easily neutralized, for purposes of the elections, by the media blitz and the political machine of the PPP. Thus, reforms of this type, in conjunction with other factors, seem to have already assured an electoral victory for Bhutto. The bureaucratic manipulations which nevertheless occurred – so very gross in some areas, and so highly publicized in the exaggerated accounts which appeared in Western media – made a difference, in our opinion, not to Bhutto's victory in the elections, but to the margins of that victory. In other words, Bhutto could have won the elections in any case, but it was the pursuit of total political power which led to outrageous bureaucratic manipulation of the election results.

In the event, an electoral majority proved to be of no consequence whatever. The destabilization campaign which was launched two days after the elections displayed from the outset such resourcefulness, such a sense of timing, such perfection in the execution of each step, that no one could possibly believe it was not carefully prepared well in advance, with startling expertise. Moreover, the campaign clearly had the blessing of the armed forces, funding from the urban and rural bourgeoisies, and a substantial ideological base among the petty bourgeoisie and the lumpen populations of big cities and medium-sized towns. We should note also that considerable sections of the urban middle strata had seen living conditions deteriorate sharply owing to the current economic crisis in Pakistan, and the ultra-Right was able to make significant inroads among these strata, thus preparing the social base for the destabilization campaign, by isolating Bhutto as the ('socialist') man chiefly responsible for the crisis. Economic deterioration, especially for the urban middle and lower strata, was thus the crucial element in making it possible for leaders of the campaign to present the politics of the ultra-Right as a mass uprising in Pakistan. It is therefore necessary briefly to analyse the structure and scope of this economic crisis which has enveloped Pakistan since the separation of Bangladesh.

The Economic Crisis in the 1970s[21]

Industrial growth in Pakistan, based primarily on import substitution, had already begun to stagnate by the end of the Second Plan period (1960–65), and the agricultural sector had at no stage seemed to overcome the pattern of low productivities based upon a structure of agrarian property which combined the dominant large-scale holdings with fragmented small-scale proprietorship. Then the war with India in 1965 and the prolonged political crisis of 1968–69 further aggravated the structural crisis. The bottom fell out of the economy altogether with the onset of the Bangladesh crisis which raged throughout 1971. Upon taking power immediately thereafter, the Bhutto regime had only to pick up the pieces.

The separation of Bangladesh had led to several crises of foreign exchange, commodity markets, money supply generally, and disruption of production and trade. In the past, jute and tea had earned most of the foreign exchange; now alternative export commodities had to be developed. Similarly, East Pakistan (now Bangladesh) had previously absorbed 40 per cent of (West) Pakistan's manufactures; now alternative markets had to be found. These manufactures could not be exported because of their inherently uncompetitive character; by 1965, for example, 84 per cent of Pakistani manufacturing relied heavily on protection and, on average, Pakistani products were sold in the domestic market at prices 150 per cent higher than the prevailing world market prices. Nor could the manufactures which had previously gone to East Pakistan be absorbed at home because the centralization of wealth combined with mass poverty had severely curtailed the development of the home market. Thus, manufacturing had to decline absolutely. Moreover, this failure to develop an export industry meant necessarily that Pakistan, heavily dependent upon Western currencies and manufactures, would continue to export primary agricultural goods; the development of export agriculture during the Bhutto period needs to be seen in this perspective.

It is estimated that the Pakistan government spent roughly $2 billion on the counter-insurgency operations in Bangladesh, the war with India and the subsequent reorganization of the armed forces. Losses incurred because of the year-long disruption of production and trade are additional. Then, after Independence, Bangladesh promptly nationalized the capital assets of West Pakistanis. This constituted a severe setback not only for the top commercial bourgeoisie but, just as significantly, for such monopoly houses as Adamjee, Dawood, and Isphahani, whose investments were located there.

These enormous losses required a complete restructuring of the economy, which the class position of the regime obviously made impossible. Instead, the Bhutto regime undertook a series of measures premised on familiar bourgeois wisdom, leading to further crises.

First, currency was devalued 130 per cent, and import restrictions were abolished for over 300 commodity items, under brutal IMF pressure. Next came the so-called nationalizations. Significantly, no foreign capital was nationalized, and in 1976 the National Assembly passed a law, the first such in Pakistan's history, specifically exempting foreign capital from future nationalizations. Equally significant is the liberal compensation paid to the 'expropriated' capitalists; the Habibs, the leading monopoly house in Pakistani banking, for example, received Rs 36.31 for each share originally valued at Rs 5. In the manufacturing sector, the key purpose of these so-called nationalizations was to absorb the losses of the private sector in units and branches which were uneconomical. The *Pakistan Economic Survey, 1975–76*, published by the Finance Division of the government, puts it quite succinctly:

It had become necessary as some of these units had come into being on the basis of dubious economic presumptions, and special built-in protections like multiple exchange rates. Due to mismanagement, a number of companies had become bankrupt as their accumulated losses exceeded their paid up capital. With a view to salvaging them, the Economic Reform Order was issued in January 1972.[22]

The impact of these nationalizations on the pattern of capital formation in the industrial sector was none the less significant, especially after 1973–74. Thus, while gross fixed capital in large-scale private industry only rose from Rs 697.3 million in 1973–74 to Rs 1,188.9 million in 1977–78, in the public sector, such capital rose from a paltry Rs 382.3 million in 1973–74 to Rs 5,463.9 million.

Much more significant was the subsequent nationalization (1974) of commercial banks and insurance companies (with the exception of foreign banks and companies, of course, which control just over 12 per cent of the credit in Pakistan but in the key monopoly sector). This measure gave the government significant control over investment priorities, creation and disbursement of credit, and money in circulation, as well as a key resource with which to reward political allies and to shift the locus of capitalism in Pakistan from industry to agriculture, as we shall see presently. Before 1971, 84 per cent of the investment in industry was owed to bank credit. Now the state could, if it so desired, divert all this credit to other sectors and let the crisis-ridden industry simply languish for want of money capital. Similarly, the state was now freer to use the commercial banks for its own deficit financing. Thus, in the five years between 1972–73 and 1976–77, government borrowings from the banking system totalled Rs 14 billion, and notes in circulation increased from Rs 23,000 million in 1971–72 to Rs 57,000 million in 1976–77; in 1975–76 alone, the government borrowed $287 million from these commercial (and nationalized) banks, while the notes in circulation increased in the same year by $200 million, or by 20 per cent. We shall see that this rate of credit formation, heavily tied to borrowings by the state, led Pakistan into an untenable monetary situation so that, as of 1977, only 15 per cent of Pakistani currency was covered with foreign exchange or other real assets.

In addition to this accelerated credit formation, the nationalization of commercial banks was used also for the expansion of banking generally, focusing this expansion primarily on the rural areas and thereby benefiting the upper stratum of the agrarian propertied classes. Thus, between January 1974 and 31 March 1976, the number of bank branches increased by 54 per cent, deposits by 80 per cent, loans by 65 per cent, and bank employees by 35 per cent; 1,080 of the 1,744 bank branches were by then located in rural areas. In 1975–76 alone, $165 million were spread in small and medium-sized loans among landlords, kulaks, and the small bourgeoisie of the semi-rural townships. This rapid rate of expansion in rural credit can be seen in the following table which summarizes the loan grants from the Agricultural Development Bank.

ADB Loans (in millions of Rs)

Item	1971–72	1972–73	1973–74	1974–75
Tractors	370.41	430.65	1800.30	1390.54
Tubewells	180.41	260.42	510.33	860.67
Other farm needs	130.53	470.25	1230.46	930.38

In the same period, loans from other banks for tractors and tubewells quadrupled, while credit for other farm needs rose 600 per cent. Government subsidies for chemical fertilizers also rose from $2.5 million in 1971 to $60 million in 1975–76. It is quite true that much of this credit was squandered on items quite different from the ones shown in bank logs; however, at the very least, this expansion of credit does show tremendous growth in the monetization of the rural economy. Moreover, gains *were* registered in increased utilization of farm machinery, better regulation of water supply, increased aggregate outputs, and higher productivity of land. In the decade 1967–77, per acre productivity rose roughly 50 per cent for rice, wheat, and corn – the main staples. Similarly, while all of Pakistan, inclusive of East Pakistan, had a total of 16,500 tractors in 1968, West Pakistan alone imported 7,000 tractors in 1974–75, 15,000 in 1975–76, and close to 17,000 in 1976–77. The *structural* crisis of the Pakistan economy is of such an order, however, that even this 'development' leads only to further polarization and social conflict.

Some 70 per cent of Pakistani people live in 45,000 villages. Yet agriculture generates only 34 per cent of GNP, and its share is falling, despite the stagnation of industry. In this social context, monetization of the rural economy and capitalization of agriculture have surely expanded the home market by increasing the purchasing power of the big landlords and the kulaks, but they have contributed to their social and political power as well. Meanwhile, food exports have also expanded – from an export of 88,000 tons of grain in 1969–70 to 596,000 tons in 1973–74 – not to speak of huge exports of fruits, vegetables, meat, poultry, eggs, etc. Rice, which hardly figured in Pakistan's commodity exports before 1971, now accounts for 19 per cent of these exports. Conversely, however, domestic stocks of grain declined in this period of higher productivity and output, from 1,099,000 million tons in

1969–70 to 96,000 tons in 1973–74. Worse still, both quality and availability of food on the home market deteriorated sharply, thanks to this export boom, and prices for the three staples – rice, wheat, and corn – which had showed the largest gain in per acre productivity, rose by close to 200 per cent in less than five years. These new incomes have not only increased the socio-economic power of the big landlords and rich peasants; a brand new agro-based commercial bourgeoisie has also risen to great prominence, market relations are rapidly dissolving the primordial social ties in the countryside, and this new money has created a rush upon urban real estate, pushing up the ground rent, land prices, construction materials, buildings, etc.

These new incomes are concentrated, furthermore, not only in relatively restricted social strata but also within those specific regions which are most suited for capitalist inputs in agriculture, which primarily means Central Punjab, the new barrage lands in Sindh (owned for the most part by non-Sindhis), and those districts in Sarhad where the water supply is plentiful and the land is hospitable to farm machinery. For the rest, this new prosperity for some classes in some regions has meant greatly increased regional inequality; and, lacking rising incomes but subject to the same market, the poverty of the poorer regions has in fact increased. Thus, the lopsided 'development' in the agrarian sector has in reality intensified the contradictions of class and region.

And, although the landlords still need the rich knowledge and agricultural skills of the peasantry, increased utilization of farm machinery has undoubtedly aggravated the crisis of rural unemployment. With productive employment declining in the cities as well, and with high wage but slave-style labour markets opening up in the oil-rich Gulf kingdoms, Pakistan has generated an exodus of workers, artisans, and bankrupt farmers to these labour markets, taking with them the whole infrastructure of skills; some estimates suggest that perhaps as many as 8,000 of these wage-slaves were leaving Pakistan every week by mid-1977. Labour power has thus become Pakistan's chief export commodity, earning for Pakistan $575 million in 1976–77 as compared with total receipts of $1,129 million from all other commodity exports. In 1977–78, foreign exchange earnings from remittances were estimated to have doubled again, to $1,149 million, while the merchandise account registered a record deficit of $1,503 million.

This domestic crisis of lopsided development stands in dialectical relation to the crisis in Pakistan's international exchanges, each crisis feeding upon the other. As of 1974–75, exports covered less than half of the imports, while imports equalled 24 per cent of the GNP. The deficit in the balance of current accounts which stood at $130 million in 1972–73 grew almost tenfold in two years, to $1,224 million in 1974–75. This deficit stood at $826 million in 1975–76 and then rose again to over a billion dollars in 1976–77. These deficits have naturally led to a corresponding expansion in net multilateral borrowing disbursements, from $356 million in 1972–73 to $1,070 million in 1974–75; direct borrowings from the oil kingdoms and from private banks were additional. In 1976–77, total loan disbursements stood at $1,443.1 billion and accounted for 49.3 per cent of gross investment in the country. Pakistan's external debt, calculated at $10 billion in 1975–76, is roughly equal to its GNP of 1973–74 and, were it not for the debt relief and rescheduling arrangements, debt service would account for close to 45 per cent of the new inflow of loans; these debt service requirements have tripled in six years, from $122 million in 1971–72 to $369 million in 1976–77.

Directions of trade also tell a significant story. In 1974–75, the Middle Eastern countries supplied less than 20 per cent of Pakistan's total imports, despite Pakistan's near total reliance on imported oil. On the other hand, Pakistan's exports to the Middle East were greater than its combined exports to its other six major trading partners, viz. the United States, Japan, Britain, West Germany, the Soviet Union, and China, in that order. In fact, the Middle East was the only trading partner from which Pakistan earned a surplus. In trade with the four advanced capitalist countries, on the other hand, Pakistan suffered a four-to-one deficit, a pattern that has been constant for two decades. Thus, Pakistan's trade deficit stems from its exchanges with the imperialist metropole, which none the less account for well over half of its trade; the deficit in trade with the United States is predictably the largest, with exports accounting for only 12 per cent of imports. Significantly, the statistics also show that the Soviet Union and China together account for less than 5 per cent of Pakistan's trade and debts, the two sharing this small margin equally, with Soviet aid being greater than that from China. So much for the much publicized 'special relationship' between China and Pakistan.

The composition of imports again shows a marked deterioration in this period. In 1970–71, imports of consumer goods had amounted to $383.7 million, whereas machinery, transport equipment, and raw materials for capital goods stood at $378.1 million, the two categories of imports thus being roughly equal. In 1974–75, however, the relevant figures were $1,284.3 million and $356 million respectively; the consumer items thus accounted for almost four times the expenditures on the other goods. This is remarkable indeed for a country which has no steel mill and produces less than 15 per cent of the machine tools it needs.

The precise reverse of this is to be noted in the case of escalating military expenditures. These have always been high but were sharply increased in the process of reconstructing the repressive apparatuses of the state. Thus, over a twenty-two-year period, 1949–50 to 1971–72, military spending accounted, on average, for 44.4 per cent of revenue receipts, while its share as a percentage of GNP rose steadily from 3 per cent in 1949–50 to 7.6 per cent in 1971–72. In the period under consideration, however, the aggregate allocations for military and internal security (the paramilitary, spy agencies, police) more than doubled in four years, rising from $404.9 million in 1971–72 to $841.7 million in 1974–75. Thus, military spending came to account for 55 per cent of the budget allocation, and the combined expenditures on health and education stood at $190.3 million, a quarter of the expenditure on the repressive apparatus of the state. This parasitic expansion of this apparatus is the key factor in the enormous growth of the servicing sector as a whole, which now accounts for just over 50 per cent of the GNP. The *Annual Report* of the State Bank of Pakistan for 1976–77 notes this general trend, in the following – rather bland – terms:

The growth in GNP over the past five years has been due more to the expansion of the servicing than the commodity producing sectors. The increase in value added in agriculture has averaged only 2.1 per cent per annum while the growth in value added in manufacturing has averaged 3 per cent. In consequence, the share of commodity producing sectors in gross domestic product has gone down from 52.4 per cent in 1972–73 to 49.7 per cent in 1976–77.

The writers of the State Bank *Report*, as well as some other commentators who have noted this phenomenon, have failed, however, to distinguish within the servicing sectors between those social services and infrastructural constructions which create value, on the one hand, and those parasitic elements which create no value at all, on the other. In our view, the real parasitic character of the servicing sector resides in the staggering elaboration of the repressive apparatuses of the state.

All these factors have led to enormous inflationary pressures and a very great monetary crisis. Between July 1976 and March 1977, for example, gold and foreign exchange reserves declined by $203 million, or by roughly 35 per cent, down to $404 million only. Meanwhile, currency issued against foreign currency reserves increased from Rs 7.21 billion in December 1971 to Rs 16.23 billion in April 1977, while the ratio of gold and foreign reserves to the notes in circulation has gone down from 23.6:100 in 1971–72 to 13:100 in 1977. This expanded money supply did not lead, however, to greater productive investment, especially in the industrial sector where the rate of investment as well as production registered significant decline. Calculated in constant prices, industrial investment stood at $135.9 million in 1964–65, then declined to $99.5 million in 1970–71, to $83.7 million in 1971–72, and to $70.8

million in 1973–74. This decline in industrial investment was paralleled by a decline in production in a broad range of industries of an import-substitution type, such as cotton textiles, sugar, rayon fabric, sewing machines, paints and varnishes, etc.; this decline had much to do with new, IMF-sponsored import policies as well as the uncompetitive character of Pakistani manufactures.[23] In the words of the *Pakistan Economic Survey, 1977–78*, 'The share of this [i.e. manufacturing] sector in GNP has been continually declining since 1971–72 and was recorded at 13.4 per cent in 1977–78.'

These grave contradictions in Pakistan's productive system – the crisis of agrarian capitalism, the parasitic proliferation of agencies of repression, the stagnation of industry, imperialist exploitation and intervention – were reflected naturally in the escalating living costs for the masses of people whose relative poverty grew throughout the period. Thus, for example, the wholesale price index, using 1959–60 as the base year, which had risen to 150.3 by 1971–72, or by less than 5 per cent annually throughout the decade of the 1960s, now rose to a staggering 288.8 by 1974–75, or at a rate of 46.1 per cent annually, with the sharpest increases being recorded in the prices of the main staples. For the great majority of the people, it was a period of declining living standards and heightened social insecurity.

Summation of the Social Crises

The current crisis of state power in Pakistan must be seen in the perspective of this economic crisis. In other words, the crisis is structural, not institutional (though it is that as well) and the obvious crisis of the superstructure (i.e. the repressive political and ideological apparatuses of the state) at once reproduces and deepens the crisis of the economic base. Moreover, an understanding of the structural crisis helps us clarify three further points.

First, the specific features of this crisis show how very limited Bhutto's reformism was and could not but be, and how much this reformism was a *response* to a preexisting crisis of the propertied classes; how much the Bhutto regime relied *in practice* on imperialism, and on the elaboration of the repressive apparatus at the expense of the labouring classes. Second, this analysis shows why those sections of the masses who were opposed to the 'Islamization' of the ultra-Right could not have been mobilized against it to defend Bhutto while he was still in power and therefore wholly identified with the repressive state and its economic policies. Third, we can see now the objective basis, beyond the many alienations in the realm of the purely ideological, on which a sizeable stratum of the urban petty bourgeoisie and the lumpen sectors

– especially the lumpen, who had seen their ranks swollen but their options markedly narrowed – might be mobilized by exhortations of the ultra-Right into a movement of apparent mass opposition against the Bhutto regime, in the name of Islam, yes, but propelled by the daily misery of their material existence.

As of now, the struggle among political fractions within the dominant classes has been settled, provisionally, in favour of the monopolistic bourgeoisie,[24] the ultra-conservative stratum of the landlord class,[25] and those fractions of the petty bourgeoisie who are allied with these class forces.[26] Conversely, we can see a major, though perhaps only temporary, setback for the power bloc of the reformist landlords, kulaks, that segment of the petty bourgeoisie which was politically organized in the PPP, and their allies among the administrative elite and the bureaucratic bourgeoisie.[27] Meanwhile, the 'socialism' of the reformist power bloc has been replaced by the 'Islamism' of the ultra-Right – a metaphysical concept of state power which implicity recognizes that the crisis of society and its state power cannot be resolved within the predicates of the existing material relations, and which therefore attempts to shift the terrain of class struggle from the political to the moral and from the economic to the millenarian. To understand this shift in the terrain of ideological class struggle, we must demystify the 'Islamism' of the present regime and its material function in Pakistan.

First, the concept of an 'Islamic nation' is the main ideological weapon in the hands of the regionally based dominant class in their struggle to deny the rights, even the separate existence, of the oppressed nationalities; this is a particularly significant function of a *centralizing ideology* in a country where the national question in the minority provinces has been posed very sharply. Second, fundamentalism is indispensable for reconstructing the ideological basis of the state; now that Pakistan is no more the 'national homeland' for all, or even most, Muslims of the subcontinent, its *raison d'être* must be that it is the home of the *good* Muslims, the last and much beleaguered fortress of piety, fundamentalism, and the like. Third, in explaining the crisis of the state, this 'Islamism' shifts the focus from material relations and claims that Pakistan got dismembered in 1971 not because of internal contradictions but because of an external 'international conspiracy' against Islam. Fourth, 'Islamism' posits a similar explanation for the economic crisis itself, and hence the poverty of the masses, which is now said to be a consequence neither of neocolonialist imperialism nor of indigenous systems of ownership and appropriation, but a divine punishment for 'un-Islamic ways of life', namely corruption, conspicuous consumption, alcohol, lack of prayers, and the propensity of women to leave their kitchens sometimes. Fifth, 'Islamism' provides the ideological justification for the lawlessness of the state, making it possible for the regime to speak of 'partyless democracy', to institutionalize mass repression in the name of collective purification, to justify physical torture (such as public floggings) on the basis of Quranic injunctions, in short to violate each and every social contract in the name of divine sanctions. Finally, an ideology of religious alienation is an ideology of the last resort, after the failures of the 'developmentalist' ideology of the Ayub era (1958–69) and the reformist 'social democratic ideology of the Bhutto period (1972–77). If Bhutto's 'socialism' was the ideology of a period when the state could still afford to implement some reforms, the 'Islamism' of the present regime signifies the ideology of a later phase when the state needs ever more, but canot make any further, accommodations. In the midst of these shifts, what interests us most, however, is the necessary *conjunction* of factors: (1) the return to economic power of the monopolistic bourgeoisie and its allies; (2) the rise of 'Islamism' in the terrain of ideological struggle; and (3) the restoration of the dictatorial state under the hegemony of the military elite. This conjuction defines a specific structure, so that ideology appears not as an opaque, ahistorical, 'cultural' phenomenon, but as a material coordinate of the changes in the nature of economic and state power.

Let us now summarize the main features of this crisis. First and foremost is the economic crisis. On the level of the economic class struggle, the July 1977 coup signifies a decision to strengthen immeasurably the repressive aspects of the Bhutto regime while dismantling its reformist aspects. The reformist aspect had simply meant that the economic and ideological struggles between the possessing and the dispossessed classes were being mediated constantly by a certain stratum of the radical petty bourgeoisie which sought to reconcile the contradictory interests of the antagonistic classes. When that buffer is abandoned, as it now is, class struggles become more acute while the installation of the military dictatorship strengthens the coercive power of the dominant classes. This is the first consequence of the coup. Second, when the repressive apparatus of the state also becomes its political apparatus and when mediation is sought not through the radical petty bourgeoisie who command a certain legitimacy in the social structure, but through political forces, such as the Jama'at with its strident rightwing ideology, which constitute the objective basis for fascism in the country and which are none too popular either, the social base of the regime is much narrowed. Third, a state dominated by the repressive apparatus is always a *centralized* state; the extreme centralization of the politico-repressive authority intensifies the centrifugal tendencies very sharply, especially in Pakistan where the officer corps is based mainly in Punjab[28] and where the struggle for national self-determination in the minority provinces is a very considerable part of the social and economic struggles on the whole. Then, prolonged military rule has also eroded the equilibrium between the various institutions within the machinery of governance (the armed forces, the civil bureaucracy, the judiciary, the political parties, etc.), thereby creating an institutional crisis of state authority. 'Islamism', meanwhile, corresponds to the ideology of very restricted social strata[29] and points once more to the failure of ideological legitimation of the state, thus reducing even further the capacity of the state to expand its social base. This identification of repression with 'Islam', and of democracy therefore with secularism, is the fifth major consequence of the coup, specifically in the ideological domain. All these crises of state power – the economic, the institutional, the ideological, etc. – have exacerbated the crisis of the legitimacy of the state itself, so that the perennial unspoken question of Pakistani politics – whether the state of Pakistan is itself worth having or not – is being asked more openly and rather frequently. Finally, all the consequences of the coup have had the effect of creating a very great, and potentially revolutionary contradiction between the democratic movement (movements, one should say, in the plural) and the socially isolated armed forces (i.e. the repressive apparatus of the state which is currently also its political apparatus).

It seems fairly clear that the democratic struggle is now developing its own dynamic and it cannot be merely a struggle to restore the *status quo ante*; for that reason, it would be best if the basically mass character of the movement is not overshadowed by its links with Bhutto's personality cult. Relative to the present dictatorship, the Bhutto period surely had distinct progressive aspects; he is at present a victim of arbitrary state action precisely because of these aspects, and his very courageous defiance of the military authorities since the July coup has been a crucial element in the emergence of the democratic movement. For all these reasons, Bhutto rightfully belongs within this movement. Moreover, if he returns to power, he will be forced, even for his own security, to liquidate the political apparatus of the Jama'at and its allied strata, and to purge those sections of the officer corps which are today most clearly identified with the regime; that alone would constitute a very great gain for the democratic movement. But the other aspect is less agreeable, for in the event that Bhutto returns to power, this even partial restoration of the *status quo ante* is likely to create as many problems as it solves. His blind pursuit of complete dominance for his own apparatus, his intransigence on the national question (exercised most bloodily in Baluchistan), his reckless anti-communism, and so on, are not mere character flaws which could be corrected through lonely reflections in a prison cell – they are predicates of a concrete class position. Bhutto is no Allende, nor a Sihanouk, nor even a Sukarno; he has admired all three of them but partially, and even demagogically; in the actual practice of his politics, he is rather more akin to Indira

Gandhi, in a country that has no entrenched bulwark of democratic institutions to restrain his authoritarian impulses. This intractable reality is likely to prove disastrous for the democratic forces, especially the national-democratic forces in Baluchistan, if he were to return to power at the head of a Perónist-style movement.

The Repressive Apparatus and the Jama'at

We cannot undertake here to predict the future with any great precision. Bhutto's life may still be spared, even through imperialist pressure, which destabilized him so recently and which now needs, nevertheless, a regime in Pakistan which has popular support in Punjab and Sindh. Since Bhutto can assure conditions of reasonable tranquillity in Sindh and Punjab, and since Zia cannot, Bhutto's bargaining power is not yet fully eroded. Alternatively, it is also wholly possible that the Generals, whose lives will be very much endangered in the event that Bhutto returns to power, will proceed with the hanging anyway, disregarding long-term repercussions, at home or in the region as a whole; this outcome is all the more possible because the coup of 5 July represents not merely a narrow feud of personalities, which could be settled among individuals, but a far-reaching schism within the ruling apparatuses whereby semi-secret, proto-fascist organizations, such as the Jama'at, are fully mobilized, alongside the armed forces and police, to alter fundamentally the social and ideological parameters of the constituted state.

Be that as it may. What interests us here, beyond Bhutto's personal fortunes, is the manner in which the politics of the coup have been elaborated, and the balance of forces as it now stands.

It is now beyond doubt that the purpose of the destabilization campaign (March–July 1977) and the subsequent coup was to hand over power to political parties of the ultra-Right which could not possibly have come to power through the electoral process. The so-called 'civilian government', appointed by General Zia, consists predictably of the Jama'at, ML, and JUI, namely parties which had together gained less than 15 per cent of the vote in 1970, the only time reasonably fair elections were held in Pakistan. Thus, the recent coup is *structurally* different from the two previous ones in 1958 and 1969: not only has the repressive apparatus arrogated to itself the tasks of the political apparatus, it has also undertaken to transform the state in such a manner that the ultra-Right will now be propelled into a dominant position in all the basic structures of authority without any electoral mandate. Here, it is vital to recognize the significance of the emergence of the Jama'at as the spiritual guide of the leaders of the coup and as the senior partner in the coalition of the ultra-Right parties, and hence as the dominant force in the process of restructuring the state, because it is in the Jama'at, more than in any other political force in the country, that the social base for a dictatorship of the fascist type has been organized into a political party of the fascist type with all its various covert cells, departments, organizations, and ideological superstructure. It is therefore necessary to comment briefly on the Jama'at.

The Jama'at is a peculiar construct, and the method in its madness is indeed extraordinary. Prior to 1947, it had opposed all anti-colonial movements: the Communists because they were communist, the Indian National Congress because it was predominantly Hindu, and the Muslim League (which led the movement for the creation of Pakistan) because of its non-theocratic programme; objectively, the Jama'at was at that time a tool, though a rather blunt and ineffective tool, of the British. Since the creation of Pakistan, it has been the chief vehicle of anti-communist propaganda, and its American connections are well known. In Bangladesh, it organized goon squads, in cooperation with the Pakistan army, to conduct assassination campaigns which took the lives of scores of Bengali intellectuals and political workers; similar, and bigger, squads are now operating in Pakistan.

The Jama'at has always been a semi-secret, conspiratorial organization of trained and highly disciplined cadres, giving priority to organizational efficiency and loyalty over numerical strength. In its political work, it has always concentrated on urban centres rather than the countryside, which it considers largely irrelevant for its political strategy of urban agitations, selective terror against the urban Left, recruitment from among the urban petty bourgeoisie, and infiltration of existing apparatuses (the army, bureaucracy, etc.) and ideological structures (educational institutions, the media, the mosques). In its ideological stance, it has stood for a certain version of fundamentalist Islam, pro-Americanism, defence of private property, and a unitary Pakistan with a strong centre, simply denying the separate existences of the various nationalities – a set of ideological precepts, that is, which define common ground between the bulk of the urban petty bourgeoisie, on the one hand, and the ruling classes of the dominant nationalities as well as the military-bureaucratic elite, on the other. For a social base, the Jama'at has relied mostly on the lumpen and petty bourgeois sectors, especially merchants, contractors, service employees, and the lower stratum of the bureaucracy. Meanwhile, it has always attached special significance to the ideological apparatuses, especially the press and the educational institutions. And, like any fascist party worth the name, it has covert special cells for targeting the revolutionary Left and for the training of infiltrators, *agents provocateurs*, professional agitators, goons, and assassins. All in all, we can say that whereas the Jama'at, like any other political formation of its type, is subject to a number of class determinations, it is above all an instrument of self-realization for those sections of the petty bourgeoisie who have seen their marginal class privilege considerably enlarged in the type of peripheral capitalist development Pakistan has experienced in recent years (expansion of commerce, contracting, and servicing; proliferation of bureaucracy, etc.); who have a great stake in fighting against the radicalization of politics in Pakistan; who have seen some of their margins being eroded by the recent economic crisis; and who blame Bhutto's so-called 'socialism' for the general atrophy of economic life in the country. These strata are not *merely* agents of imperialism, monopoly capital, and feudalism; rather, they have a distinct class position which is articulated in a specific conjuncture with that of the other dominant classes and which indicates the strategic position of the petty bourgeoisie in modern class society as a whole, especially in the Third World.

Moreover, the bulk of the urban petty bourgeoisie of the dominant nationalities has turned to the Jama'at and its associates in the ultra-Right at a specific political juncture which has at least three significant aspects. First, the government of the PPP, and the radical stratum of the petty bourgeoisie acting from inside that government, clearly failed to protect the interests of the petty bourgeoisie as a whole, especially of its salaried segment, nor has this stratum organized itself into an alternative political formation that could contend for political power; in a characteristically vacillating fashion, the bulk of this class has thus swung to the extreme Right. Second, the manifest failure of the bourgeoisie to organize a stable political party, which would in turn have representational ties with the petty bourgeoisie, has created a crisis for the latter which has become, in this vacuum, particularly susceptible to the fascist parties. (Parenthetically, we should note that the Tehrik-e-Istiqlal represented the only recent attempt on the part of the Pakistani bourgeoisie to create a political party predominantly its own, and even up to the time of the coup imperialist media had focused on Asghar Khan, the leader of Tehrik, as 'fit material to be Prime Minister', as *The Times* of London put it; the army itself had appeared until then to be neutral between the Jama'at and Tehrik. It was the emergence of a pro-Jama'at faction to a position of dominance within the armed forces which forced Tehrik into the background.) Third, the struggle on the national question is now so far advanced, especially in Baluchistan, that the petty bourgeoisie of the dominant nationalities is turning increasingly to the repressive apparatuses, and to ideologies forged specifically for the political dominance of these apparatuses, to ensure the continued existence of a highly centralized state in Pakistan.

The Jama'at had given up hope of coming to power through the electoral process soon after the electoral humiliation of 1970, when it received less than 5 per cent of the vote. Instead, it started concentrating on preparing a coup and on initiating a social process, particularly in the ideological domain, whereby the coup could be legitimized after the fact. First, it greatly expanded its proselytizing campaign among the armed forces where it found fertile ground for a variety of reasons. The generational shift in the high command from the British-trained, secularist officers to the less literate, more traditionalist officers, drawn largely from among either the migrants from east Punjab (for example, leaders of the July coup) or the unirrigated Potohar region, has given rise to a group of generals who are socially conservative, inbred, and highly susceptible to a puritanical ideology of the type the Jama'at professes. Similarly, patterns of recruitment have also changed whereby not only the rank-and-file but even junior officers tend to come increasingly not from among the relatively more prosperous peasantry of central Punjab but from among the bankrupt farmers of the northern districts, representing a more backward social formation and a fundamentalist religious ethos. Third, the generalized demoralization among the armed forces in the wake of the defeat in Bangladesh (1971) had opened the way for the permeation of a millenarian ideology, in the absence of a rational one – that is, given the failure of the Marxist Left to grasp the need for ideological work among the ranks, the average soldier turned to Islamism, as preached to him systematically by the Jama'at, for an explanation of his failure as well as his future purpose. Fourth, it is also clear that closer integration of the Pakistani armed forces with their counterparts in the reactionary oil kingdoms, particularly Saudi Arabia and the UAE, has had consequences in the ideological domain as well. Most important, however, is perhaps the fact that Jama'at propaganda among vast numbers of troops was officially sanctioned by commanding officers at the battalion level and above. Generals like Zia himself, a close relation of Mian Tufail, the present chief of the Jama'at, provided ample protection for secret cells of the Jama'at inside the armed forces; it was the only political organization which had such opportunities.

Since the elections of 1970, we have witnessed a similar process in the Jama'at's (successful) bid to infiltrate every other civic institution and social structure as well. In addition to the army and bureaucracy, which are of course critical in conspiratorial takeovers, the Jama'at has attached special significance to educational institutions and the vernacular press, partly in pursuit of long-term ideological hegemony over the petty bourgeoisie but more urgently because students and newspapers play a decisive role in the mass-scale urban agitation which is in turn necessary to create the type of social crisis that can be used to legitimize political intervention by the armed forces: for instance the urban agitations of March–July 1977 which provided the justification for the coup that followed. Jami'at, the student front of the Jama'at, is now the largest and most disciplined youth organization in the country; this dominance has been obtained through years of perseverance, painstaking development of elite cadres, monetary benefits for its members, enormous amounts of available funds, and organized terror campaigns against opponents among students and faculty alike. Similarly, the vernacular press is dominated by the Jami'at: *The Urdu Digest* among periodicals, *Zindagi* among the weeklies, and *Nawa-e-Waqt* among the dailies, in addition to a host of other publications. The student front and the press, not to speak of the myriad mosques, help the Jama'at not only in recruitment of members and sympathizers but also in projecting itself as a party of far greater weight than it actually commands; this projection is in turn used to legitimize the dominant position of the Jama'at in the new 'government' without any reference to the actual social and/or electoral base it may or may not have in the event of general elections.

General elections are doubly impossible in Pakistan today. First, because Bhutto's PPP is still the largest party in the country, regardless of – one might say, because of – the regime's campaigns of annihilation against it. Second, because the Jama'at, the real mentor of the ruling junta, is not the largest even among the anti-Bhutto parties; Tehrik and NDP are unquestionably larger parties. So, no matter how much the future elections are rigged, the Jama'at simply cannot win a dominant position in an elected legislature, not to speak of other apparatuses of the state; consequently, it must seek to establish its dominance over the state through the increasingly elaborate and transparent activity of the repressive apparatus. Besides, the Jama'at represents a minority grouping even among fundamentalist Muslims; it needs to exercise naked repression in order to impose its own version of Islam over other such groupings. In order to appoint a 'civilian government' composed of the Jama'at and its allies, the Zia regime has had not only to suppress the PPP but also to undermine and actually break the PNA as well; only after the departure of Tehrik and NDP from the PNA did the Jama'at begin to look like a big political party.

We cannot say how long this regime of a minority-within-a-minority will last; in the foreseeable future, it will all depend on the will of the commanding officers. Nor can we say whether or not Pakistan itself, as a state, will outlive this dictatorship. Meanwhile, the immediate objective of the ultra-Right, led by the Jama'at, is to dismantle the PPP, the major democratic opposition. The repression unleashed in the service of this objective is vast. Six divisions of the army are said to be deployed in Sindh and Punjab, to control the explosive situation in these provinces. Sindh alone is said to have 30,000–40,000 political prisoners. According to one estimate, 10,000 members of the PPP are currently imprisoned; this number obviously includes the leadership. And yet, the PPP has shown remarkable resilience; it never was much of a party, but now, in the hands of its left wing, it has surely become a broad-based movement. Recently, for example, roughly 3,000 persons were apprehended in Lahore alone on the night of 14 October, merely to prevent the PPP from observing a 'Protest Day' which was scheduled for the day after. At least ten persons have attempted to immolate themselves; at least four are known to have died of burns. Meanwhile, the flogging of political prisoners has become a routine affair, even for raising slogans in a public place. And all this is before the actual hanging of the deposed Prime Minister. No one can dare predict what will happen if he really is hanged. Perhaps not very much on the next day; not many people know how to fight an army. But the iron will have gone deeper into the soul.

The second objective of the ultra-Right is to capture a hegemonic position in apparatuses of authority. Since the repressive apparatus is said to have been secured already, attention is now focused on the administrative and ideological apparatuses. So, a flurry of purges, transfers, and fresh appointments is already under way, though on a limited scale so far. Over the years, the Jama'at has maintained covert cells in all walks of life, especially in government service, educational institutions, and the media. These voluminous dossiers are now at the disposal of the regime, the covert cells are functioning as the regime's eyes and ears, and the paramilitary squads of the Jama'at are being reinforced; the Muslim League, the second political party in Zia's so-called civilian government, is fast developing similar covert cells; the goons of the Jama'at have openly terrorized students across the country in order to capture leadership of the students' unions, and, along with their counterparts in the ML, they are on the offensive against PPP processions in all major cities. There is, however, no general onslaught against the Marxist Left in Punjab and Sindh yet, precisely because the immediate crucial preconditions – annihilation of the PPP, and a hegemonic position in all constituted apparatuses of authority – have not been obtained, and the ultra-Right, so patient and methodical over the years, so poised now for the big kill, does not plan to overreach itself.

Postscript: June 1980

The preceding text was completed in October 1978, before the sentencing and execution of Prime Minister Bhutto. The concluding sections in particular were drafted rather hurriedly. Both these elements – the extraordinary uncertainty of that conjuncture, as well as the haste in formulating these conclusions – have introduced some elements into the text which now need scrutiny. So much more has happened in the past months that one is tempted to update the entire narrative, so as to clarify the altogether new conjuncture that has arisen partly as a result of domestic upheavals, but in considerable measure also because of events on the regional scale, principally in Iran and Afghanistan. Rewriting of that magnitude, however, is clearly beyond the scope of a postscript. I will, therefore, restrict myself to clearing up certain ambiguities and rectifying some errors of the original text, and conclude by summarizing those later developments which have had a bearing on the trends that were anticipated in the original text.

1. The earlier sections of this text explicitly define the limits of Bhutto's reformism and the perimeters of bourgeois politics within which he organized his exercise of power. His 'anti-imperialism' had very obvious limits. What needs to be added today, however, is that his propensity to capitulate to militarism and imperialism also had its limits. More than that. In the thirty-odd years of Pakistan's history, Bhutto was the only bourgeois politician who had a fundamental and passionate sense of the limits beyond which he could not be coerced; there was quite a lot that the Generals and the imperialists could take *with* his consent, but in order to take more they had to walk over his dead body. He was not a revolutionary, nor even a consistent nationalist; but in that mire of degradation which is the history of Pakistan's ruling class, he was the only one who had a sense that certain stakes are worth the price of one's life, and that in the Third World in times of ultimate danger one turns not to imperialism but to the masses. Even this sense was neither consistent nor highly developed in him, but he did have it. In his class, he was the only one.

2. There was in our original text too glib an identification between the present regime and the return of the big bourgeoisie. Military dictatorship in Pakistan is in no functional sense an instrument of the big bourgeoisie. If the return of the big bourgeoisie is found to be impossible *in practice*, the military apparatus, whose primary interest is the pursuit of its own dominance, is quite willing to make a different set of alliances and utilize the expanded public sector to reward those allies and to place its top officers at the commanding heights of the economy. Political instability of the regime is undoubtedly one of the primary constraints hampering long-term investment decisions. Originally, the military regime was keen to revert to the politics of the Ayub era. It was quite determined to denationalize industry, banking, and the educational apparatus; and it was anxious to offer all sorts of concessions and tax holidays to foreign and domestic capitalists. However, objective constraints have been too many, and no significant denationalizations, or large-scale private investment in industry or banking have taken place thus far.

3. Nationalizations, as a form of state capitalism, occur on the capitalist periphery as part of the increasing interventionist role of the state in peripheral economies. The mode and extent of these nationali-

zations are determined not by the ideology of rulers, but mainly by the modalities of capitalist development in specific formations. As such, once implemented and integrated into the structure of economic production as a whole, nationalizations are extremely difficult to reverse, especially in the industrial sector, as is shown by the experience of Sadat's otherwise very stable regime in Egypt. In Pakistan, the nationalized banks have become so important a source for the state's own deficit planning; the stratum of the bureaucracy that administers the nationalized sector has developed such a vested interest in the continued existence and even expansion of that sector; the workers in the nationalized industries who have made considerable economic gains as a result of nationalizations are so hostile to the return of the big bourgeoisie; the teachers in the nationalized institutions have gained security of tenure and salary, while the students have obtained expanded facilities, thus uniting in so vehement an opposition to the return of the business sharks who used to run educational institutions purely for private profit that the regime is forced, under multiple pressures, to reverse its earlier commitment to denationalization.

4. The genesis of industrial and finance capital in Pakistan was always tied to the merchants' capital, and the big bourgeoisie never wholly completed its transition from merchant to industrialist. Over the past decade, as its crisis deepened, this bourgeoisie became very reluctant to undertake the long-range risks of industrial accumulation. Some, perhaps many, have departed for more lucrative openings in the Gulf and even to the metropolitan centres of Europe and America. Others have rediscovered their vocation in wholesale trade, import/export trade, contracting, hoarding and speculation, smuggling, labour exports, and so forth.

A lot of quick money is still being made in these activities, thanks to the accelerated pace at which money and commodities are circulating in the country, owing mainly to the expanding influx of remittances into the domestic market, the rising incomes in the export sector of agriculture, the elaborate expenditures by the state, and the growth of real estate as the main field of investment for savings. A lot of money is being made, perhaps more than ever before, but this is hardly what one would describe as the return of the monopolistic bourgeoisie.

5. As regards agriculture, the regime has of course forced the country to forget about the last set of land reforms, which Bhutto had announced in January 1977. For the rest, the structure as well as the directions of its transformation remain the same. Export orientation, capitalization of the instruments of agricultural production, expansion of rural credit, and so forth – i.e. the hallmarks of Bhutto's agricultural policy – are in the interest of all owners of agricultural property. These continue apace. Certain strata of the agrarian bourgeoisie had been hard hit by Bhutto's

initial nationalization of certain agro-based factory units; these, however, he himself had been forced to denationalize in the course of the political confrontation which paved the way for the July coup; the Zia regime has merely implemented that particular denationalization. In other words, there has not been a shift of power from one sort of landed property to another, as our rather opaque distinction between 'reformist' and 'conservative' landlords might have suggested. There has been, however, a marked shift in the relationship between the direct producers and the landlords, whereby the latter have regained, under direct encouragement from the dictatorship, many of the political and social – and hence economic – initiatives which they had lost during the Bhutto era; the accelerated pace of eviction of tenants, sharecroppers, and squatters is indicative of this shift in the balance of class power.

6. The military regime has indeed been unable to obtain full cooperation of large segments of the civilian bureaucracy, but the reasons for this are rather more complex than our earlier writing suggests. It is not the case that the Zia regime has curtailed the power of that segment of the bureaucracy which directly administers the nationalized sector of the economy; that, in any case, would have been a rather simple matter for Zia to handle. The reasons for the alienation of much of the civilian bureaucracy from the military regime must be understood in rather different terms. Of these, three processes are especially worthy of note. The first is that the period since 1968 has been one of growing politicization in Pakistan, and the bureaucracy itself has been drawn into not only administering the formation but also participating in its political currents. During the Bhutto era, a large section of this bureaucracy swung towards the PPP, but there were other segments which, resenting the power of the political machine of the PPP, become avid supporters of other political parties; allegiances to the Jama'at grew especially rapidly among the lower ranks. As the military dictatorship stabilized itself at the expense of all the political parties, the various segments of the bureaucracy, allied as they are with the different political parties, are all becoming alienated from the dictatorship, to a lesser or greater extent. Second, in so far as in countries like Pakistan the state is the largest employer, countless individuals find jobs in its apparatuses while still holding strong reservations regarding the role and ideology of those apparatuses; as the democratic movement gradually encompasses all varieties of political tendencies and social strata, resentment towards the military dictatorship is also likely to grow within the civilian apparatuses. Finally, the elaborate influx of the military personnel in commanding positions throughout the body of the state (e.g. the military courts functioning parallel to and now above the High Courts; military officers taking key posts in police and administrative

services; the takeover of ministries, policy-making institutions, even institutions of everyday repression, etc.) leads to general resentment in the civilian bureaucracy as a whole, for its relegation to a subordinate position, and for the nexus of corruption moving more and more towards the military officers.

7. A similar error was made in summing up the relationship between the military apparatus and the political parties of the ultra-Right. The following statement, for example, is indicative of this imprecision:

> It is now beyond doubt that the purpose of the destabilization campaign (March–July 1977) and the subsequent coup was to hand over power to political parties of the ultra-Right which could not possibly have come to power through the electoral process.

Not quite! The coup has certainly helped the parties of the ultra-Right enormously. However, the armed forces obviously had a different 'purpose', namely that of using the destabilization campaign for imposing their own dictatorship, at the expense not only of Bhutto's electoral majority but also over and above the minority parties which had created the requisite conditions for the coup. The empirical facts elaborated in our text were correct, but the text did not wholly specify the unequal nature of the relationship of forces, i.e. that the coup makers were indeed allied with the ultra-Right but that they, and not the political parties, were the dominant partner. We predicted correctly, on the basis of our analysis, that the Generals would under no circumstances call for general elections, but we also asserted, wrongly as the facts prove now, that the Jama'at would be the permanent titular guardian of whatever government the junta would ultimately devise. What assumptions led to that prediction? And, why did the Jama'at fail to attain that status?

The assumptions were several. One, that the army would in the long run not rule under its own name and would insist, as it has done since the first coup in 1958, on rapidly devising a civilian facade. Second, since the Jama'at was politically and ideologically closest to the orientation of the leaders of the coup, the junta would naturally choose it to be the favoured political party in the fig-leaf civilian government. Third, pro-Jama'at elements within the officer corps, including Zia, were expected to play a crucial role in devising this configuration. Fourth, although the Jama'at is a small political party, composed of elite units and covert cells, it could become a sizeable force, thanks to the technical efficiency of its political machine, the support it gets from the regime, the control it has over the media and the students' organizations, and the ideological mobilization that it could effect among the petty bourgeoisie and the lumpen mass of the dominant Punjabi and

Urdu-speaking nationalities. These assumptions were indeed substantial, but contrary facts were even more so, and subsequent events have clarified what could have been perceived even then.

(a) Given the scale of repression that has been necessary in order to keep the dictatorship in place, the Generals, despite their textbooks, could not possibly devise the benign facade of a civilian government for themselves; they have had to accelerate, rather than decrease, the direct role of the armed forces in the processes of governance, administration, and repression.

(b) The Jama'at is so very small that its presence in government in no way makes the government seem representative or democratic, and a political party that does not help legitimize military rule is useless for the Generals; repression, even Islamic repression, they can conduct themselves.

(c) The Jama'at is, indeed, the most disciplined political organization in the country, and its potential for fascist terror under the aegis of the military is truly frightening; but the zeal and discipline of its cadres, drawn as they are from among the urban petty bourgeoisie, cannot sufficiently offset the abysmally low level of its leadership and its lack of a popular base.

(d) The dilemma for the Jama'at, therefore, is this: it cannot become a powerful organization without extensive patronage from the repressive apparatus of the state, but any close identification with the Zia regime, given its universal lack of popularity, is, for any political party, tantamount to a kiss of death. Hence its prominent participation in the 'civilian government' appointed by Zia at an earlier stage, as well as its hasty withdrawal from that government on the eve of Bhutto's execution. Hence also, the paradox that the Jama'at relies on the army for weapons, training, and protection of its goons and assassins, but it must also occasionally mount demonstrations against the military dictatorship in order to disavow its covert connections.

(e) The civilian government composed of certain ultra-rightist parties, which Zia had devised before Bhutto's execution and which was in place at the time of writing, proved to be a short-lived affair because it served no one's purpose. Because the parties were much too small to give the dictatorship an air of legitimacy it saw no lasting value in them. Conversely, the parties which had participated in government found that the military regime was unwilling to concede even a small share of real power to them, while the identification with the dictatorship was eroding what little constituency they had in the general populace. The dictatorship has no choice but to rule in its own name.

8. The execution of Bhutto produced, as we had predicted, no grand upheaval on the day after. The iron has gone deeper into the soul, but why was the news of the execution greeted, *en masse*, with suppressed

rage, even sullen petulance? Why did the rebellion not materialize in or before April 1979, as Bhutto had so ardently – so wishfully, so mistakenly – expected? Some of the answers are obvious enough.

Clearly, the regime's tactics had had considerable effect. By dragging out the process over approximately fifteen months, it achieved two things. One, the general populace had begun to live with the idea that Bhutto probably *would* be executed; and the failure of the smaller actions organized by the middle-ranking cadres of the PPP, combined with the steadfast inertia of its landlord leadership, had bred a general demoralization on the one hand and cynicism on the other. Two, selective terror throughout those long months had effectively neutralized thousands of militants, thus pre-empting spontaneous aggregation of open dissent; everyone knew that he/she was being watched, and thousands carried the emblems of torture on their bodies.

Equally clearly, the masses, especially in Punjab and Sindh where the democratic movement at that point was most vociferous, were shocked into silence by their sudden awareness that, in fact, they did not know how to fight an army. And everyone knew that it was a time like none other in (West) Pakistan's history: that there would be tanks on the streets of Lahore and Karachi. Memories of Dacca!

The decisive element, however, was neither the regime's cunning nor the fear that stalked the streets. There was also the legacy of the Bhutto period. He, in his time, had already done a superb job of disorganizing precisely those institutions of popular initiative which might have otherwise organized the sort of rebellion he now wished for. The Peoples Party itself, the majority party in the country, came to look less and less like a political organization and more like a feudal entourage. Within the party there were no elections, system of planning or accountability, no professional or technical division of work, no venues for initiative or autonomy; everything had revolved around the whims and outlooks of the patriarch. Once the patriarch had been overthrown, imprisoned, and besieged, the party developed two poles of attraction: one around the landlordist segment of the leadership, and another around the wife and daughter of the departed leader. The two intentions, of charismatic defiance and of easy capitulation, obviously could not overlap; the party, which by then had become the symbol of a mass dissent, began to divide against itself. The landlordist group was despicable but consistent: it wanted accommodation with the dictatorship – no two ways about it. The Bhutto ladies, on the other hand, were enormously courageous but, sad to say, not very consistent; they wished for a mass uprising, but strictly according to those bourgeois ways which were characteristic of their class and for two decades had been the hallmark of their family's mode of politics; the anger of the masses was for them a bargaining counter and a trump card against the military dictatorship. Nusrat Bhutto's oft-repeated slogan was thus hollow, but also symptomatic: either the regime holds elections, or *we* shall make the revolution. In the event, neither party was serious about its promises; Mrs Bhutto was about as prepared for revolution as Zia was for elections. Caught between brutality and hyperbole, the country learned to live with the expectation, and then the fact, of Bhutto's execution. And those who had seen their own flesh torn under the military's Islamic whip began to wonder whether they had made a mistake.

9. The Zia regime is socially more isolated today than any Pakistan has had in the past. What, then, accounts for its ability to endure? Four factors are at present of paramount importance: fragmentation of the opposition, the shared need within the military apparatus to close ranks behind the dictatorship, an ambiguous economic situation, and the the commitment on the part of China and the American–Saudi axis to work closely with the existing configuration of power in Pakistan. The question of the opposition – its variegated interests and tactics, its fragmentation and underdevelopment, etc. – is too complex for exposition in a postscript; the homogeneity of interest among the military officers, on the other hand, is obvious enough, for present purposes. We shall therefore comment, of necessity briefly, on the latter two factors only, namely the economic situation and the nature of the imperialist interest in the emerging conjuncture.

10. We had argued in our original text that declining standards of living, especially for the urban middle and lower strata, had opened the possibility for the ultra-Right to organize a mass movement of opposition to the Bhutto regime in the key urban centres. It is doubtful that the military regime's performance is any better, and in reality it is perhaps much worse. Whether we look at inflationary trends or at trade deficits, whether at the monetary crisis at home or at foreign exchange reserves abroad, the situation is alarming indeed. In the first six months of the dictatorship, July–December 1977, figures had begun to indicate a sharp decline. The inflation rate had risen to an annual average of 30 per cent, fully comparable to the *worst* period of Bhutto's rule, i.e. 1972 and 1973, when the economy was faced with vast dislocations caused by the Bangladesh crisis. In the two weeks between 24 October and 7 November 1977, currency notes in circulation had risen by 69.64 crores, a record increase unparalleled since the birth of the country. Similarly, the National Bank's *Economic Newsletter* for November 1977 had noted: 'A *decrease* of Rs 60.61 crores, or 14.54 per cent, was recorded on 13 October 1977, in Pakistan's approved foreign exchange reserves and balances held abroad ... The trade deficit during the first quarter of 1977–78 (July–October 1977) amounted to Rs 102.51 crores.' And so on. These trends have continued, and in some respects intensified.

How has the regime managed, then, to stay afloat? First, the cyclical improvements in crop yields. While Bhutto's last two years in office were marked by the worst floods in Pakistan's history, and hence by much depleted crops, the dictatorship's first three years have been marked by excellent weather and hence bumper crops. This may be God's own gift to a devout dictator but even God's mercy is limited, especially in matters of agriculture. There are indications already that the stress is mounting: state subsidies to agriculture have already been cut back, and retail prices after the budget of 1979–80 rose by 35 per cent. What will happen to these prices when the weather becomes unkind to crops, bringing floods or drought, cyclically, as it tends to do?

Second, remittances from Pakistanis working abroad now truly constitute the only spine the economy has. In 1978, when we pointed out that labour power had already become Pakistan's chief export commodity, remittances constituted two-thirds of all such earnings, rising from $228 million five years ago to an expected $2 billion dollars for 1980. One million Pakistanis now work in the Gulf and the Middle East, half of them in Saudi Arabia. The quadrangular character of this relationship with the oil kingdoms is remarkable: Pakistan imports oil from the Middle East worth a billion dollars, exports commodities worth $343 million (in 1979–80), and receives remittances worth about $2 billion dollars; and the investments by the Gulf states and Saudi Arabia in Pakistan are now approximately $1 billion, with another $500 million already on the way. This spectacular rise in funds flowing from the oil kingdoms, principally in the form of remittances, has, until recently, been the main element salvaging the foreign exchange situation, even as the domestic structure of the economy has become increasingly hollow and directionless.

Now, however, there is a third element. On 12 June 1980 the Aid-to-Pakistan Consortium, meeting under the aegis of the World Bank and the policy direction set by the United States, approved $980 million for 1980–81 – up from a previous high of about $700 million in the past. More significant than that is the willingness to reschedule the debt payments, under explicit US prodding. Pakistan's total debt now stands at $10.3 billion, half of which is owed to the Consortium. If aid were held at previous levels without rescheduling, the entire amount would have gone for servicing the debt; with the new arrangements, however, Pakistan gets a reprieve worth $700 million and a fresh injection of almost a billion dollars. Not bad for a brutal dictatorship in the era of 'human rights'! In the long run, moreover, the substantial economic significance of this decision may be overshadowed by the political significance of the fact that the explicit espousal of this policy by the United States, reversing the earlier policy set by the US Congress not to

approve rescheduling, indicates the expanding imperialist interest in
Pakistan.

11. Even though it has neither very important raw-material resources
nor a developed enough industrial infrastructure to attract much metropolitan capital, Pakistan has always enjoyed a significant position in
imperial designs in Asia and the Middle East because of its strategic
location (a) on the borders of the world's three largest states, namely
the Soviet Union, China, and India, and (b) in such close proximity to
the oil-producing Gulf region. This importance of Pakistan in US
calculations in relation to the region had somewhat declined from the
mid-1960s onwards, thanks to the growing volatility of Pakistan's
internal politics and, even more importantly, because Iran, with its
monarchical stability and petrodollar wealth, had by then emerged as
the main base of American military power in the region, serving the
same function in relation to the Soviet Union and occupying a far more
strategic place within the Gulf region itself. This equation became even
stronger in recent years as Bhutto was seen as at least unpredictable if
not altogether hostile, while the power of the Shah loomed larger on the
horizon and even the Daud regime in Afghanistan accepted status for
itself as an Irani client.

All this changed dramatically with the two recent revolutions in the
region, in Iran and in Afghanistan, one Islamic-nationalist and the other
Communist. Whatever the retrogressive aspects of Islamism in the
internal politics of Iran may be, the departure of the Shah and his
monarcho-bourgeoisie has also brought about the dismantling of the
entire structure of American power and presence in Iran; the emerging
Irani regime is, in its international aspect, radical-nationalist, similar in
some ways to the Nasserist regime in Egypt or the original regime of
the FLN after Algerian independence. This alone propelled Pakistan to
a central place in American military calculations in the region. But with
the coming of the Khalq regime in Afghanistan, the strategic importance
of Pakistan has been enhanced to an unprecedented degree, for, in US
calculations, Pakistan is now the most forward of all the frontline states
– in fact, the strategic centre – in the twin wars *against* communism and
for Gulf oil.

In our original text we had emphasized the depth of the economic
crisis, the social isolation of the regime, an insurgent mood in large
sections of the politically active population. Since then, the economic
crisis has deepened and the other two factors have persisted, though to
a lesser degree. The key change, however, is in the regional military role
of Pakistan. It is quite possible, therefore, that as Pakistan comes to
occupy the position in US policy that Iran used to have in the past and
as it becomes the chief proxy in the US war in Afghanistan, while it
continues to play the military role that it has been playing for some

years in the Arab sheikhdoms of the Gulf, imperialism may develop a serious stake in the continuation of a military regime, and funds flowing for a war of that kind may even resolve the economic crisis for the next decade or so. It is of course also possible that the Afghanistan revolution on the one hand, and the radical-nationalist current in the Irani revolution on the other, will serve to radicalize the mass movements within Pakistan.

Azad's Careers:
Roads Taken and Not Taken

Maulana Abul Kalam Azad was undoubtedly one of the seminal figures in the Indian National Movement, and he came to occupy, after Ansari's death in 1936, an unassailable position among the nationalist Muslims as they were represented in the Indian National Congress.[1] His Presidential Address at the Ramgarh Session of the Congress in March 1940, just before Jinnah was to unveil the historic Resolution at the Lahore Session of the Muslim League, demanding separate political entities for Indian Muslims, is one of the noblest statements of Indian secular nationalism and a definitive refutation of Jinnah's 'two-nation theory'.[2] Similarly, his attempt at reinterpreting Islamic theology itself in such a way as to make it compatible with the religiously composite, politically secular trajectory of India, which found its most extended statement in the unfinished *Tarjuman-al-Quran* in the 1930s, represents a distinctive contribution to Indian Islamic thought. If we take as axiomatic the assertion of the late Fazlur Rahman, the eminent Pakistani scholar of Islam, that post-medieval Islam has had neither an *Ilm-al-Kalam* ('Theology' in the Christian sense) nor a *Fiqh* (Jurisprudence),[3] we might say that *Tarjuman* is indeed one of the more notable efforts on the part of Indian theologians to fill that vacuum, at least on the level of general principles. And, surely, *Ghubar-e-Khatir* (1946) is one of the enduring books of Urdu literary prose. Azad himself seems to have become bitter in his later life for not being allowed to remain President of the Congress after 1946, hence missing the opportunity to play a pivotal role in the politics immediately preceding Partition, or to become the first Prime Minister of independent India. Whether or not that was a realistic possibility is questionable, but he had by then doubtless come to command within the Congress, and in the National Movement generally, that kind of stature.

Azad's achievements are myriad. I have highlighted the particular ones in the above paragraph for three reasons. First, it is with his *writings* that I am here most concerned. Second, I specify three areas of his work I want to discuss here, separately but also in tandem with each other, because it is in the *overlap* of these areas that the breadth of his engagements truly lies: his political trajectory as it is reflected in his writings, his way of connecting Islam with politics, and his status as a writer of Urdu prose. Third, as even a glance at the above paragraph would indicate, I believe that Azad's essential achievements as writer and scholar came only in the latter part of his life and they came only after he had either abandoned or greatly modified the positions that had governed his thought and actions up to and into the Khilafat Movement. In this last emphasis, my views seem to run counter to the main trends of Azad scholarship as it has developed since his death in 1958, both in India and in Pakistan.

Contrary to general impressions in India, where it is presumed that Azad would be neglected in Pakistan because of his commitment to secular Indian nationalism, he is in fact an extremely popular author there and collections of his writings are promoted a great deal, mainly by the conservative, fundamentalist groupings which concentrate on what I would call the *Al-Hilal* decade of Azad's life[4] and many of which take Azad to have been – before his 'Gandhian error' – the precursor of the kind of Islamic politics which came to be represented in Pakistan by men like Abul A'ala Maudoodi and organizations like the Jama'at-e-Islami.[5] More enlightened Pakistani scholars, such as Qazi Javed,[6] counter this predominant tendency by essentially eliding the question of his later anti-Pakistan politics, and emphasizing his anti-colonial activities during that same *Al-Hilal* decade; this alternative narrative basically ends with affirmative descriptions of the concept of *umma-wahida*,[7] which Azad resurrected in 1920. The uncanny convergence between these contrasting strands of Pakistani representations of Azad resides in the fact that both emphasize that same decade as the period of his true achievement and both tend to ignore his later life, except for cursory reference to *Tarjuman* and his epistolary work.[8]

In mainstream scholarship in India, there is of course no inhibition about recognizing the seminal importance of Azad's later career, of the kind that exists in most Pakistani scholarship, and the precociousness of Azad's early growth, bordering on genius, is also justifiably and readily recognized. But then what happens is that the insights gained in maturity are read back into the youth, so that one has the impression of a seamless growth, unproblematic and always fully enlightened and secular, from the start.[9] The procedure, from which only a few depart,[10] is to see Azad as a man not only of exceptional talent and intelligence but also always in full possession of himself: commanding great reservoirs of knowledge since childhood; a mature writer by the age of fifteen (when he establishes the journal *Lisan al-Sidq*, in 1903); already in possession of a religiously pluralistic anti-colonial ideology by the age of twenty-four (when he starts publishing *Al-Hilal*, in 1912); launched already, as he came out of Ranchi prison in 1919, on the trajectory that would take him inevitably to the apex of the National Movement; always teaching others, but himself a perfect autodidact, in literature as well as politics, right into his thirties and beyond. It is this image of perfect, linear growth which I want to examine.

I

As one tries to think of the *whole* of Azad's career – or, rather, his many careers – one has the sense not of a continuity, nor even of a contrast between the young and the mature man, but of unceasing shifts, of a heart riven by contrary desires and a mind tempted by irreconcilable convictions; not only of a life constantly remaking itself after every few years but also of a *voice*, in his writings, which constantly changes its own timbre and texture, while also continually shifting facts and emphases in the process of recounting what the life has been in the past, always superimposing upon that past a continuity it never had.

These shifts begin early. Azad was fond of recounting in later life how he was born in Mecca and how Arabic was his mother tongue. By 1899, when he was presumably eleven years old, he was publishing his own Urdu *ghazals* which were characteristic of what was then in vogue, at the turn of the century, following the manner of Dagh and Ameer Minai, profane and romantic and somewhat decadent in image and sentiment, but in tone and vocabulary remarkably fluent for someone who is said – by Malik Ram among others – to have not known the language only a couple of years earlier. By 1903, when he established his first full-scale journal, *Lisan al-Sidq*, he was writing a prose somewhat like Hali in its Islamic revivalist nostalgia, somewhat like Syed Ahmed Khan in its modernizing and reformist aspiration, but, like Hali and Sir Syed, he too was then modelling the written sentence on educated daily speech. Over the next three years he grew personally close to Shibli and his prose took on tonalities indistinguishable from those of the master of Nadva. By 1910 he had written his first masterpiece, entirely free of those successive influences, finding his own distinctive voice for the first time, closer to the spirit of his early *ghazals* but infinitely superior in the truth of its passions on the one hand, and revealing, on the other, his increasing penchant for a style at once oracular and digressive: the essay 'Hyat-e-Sarmad Shaheed', on the life of the Sufi who was a companion of Dara Shikoh and was similarly beheaded by Aurangzeb. What the essay celebrates, in a prose passionately eloquent despite its repeated rhetorical departures from the spoken vernacular, are the transgressions of forbidden sexual desire, the heretic grandeur of sufic ecstasy, and the courage to defy powers at once puritanical and monarchic.[11]

But that first masterpiece also heralded the end of a phase, and Azad was never to permit himself to write anything resembling that essay, or let the public gaze fall on that aspect of his sensibility, for the next thirty-five years – until the appearance of that last magnificent epistle in *Ghubar-e-Khatir*, on his love of classical Indian music, which too he included not in the first two editions but only in the third, issued in February 1947. Instead, we have, starting in 1912, the *Al-Hilal* phase which espoused, in its emphases on piety and *fiqh*, views that were diametrically the opposite of those he had upheld less than two years earlier. By 1915, he was announcing the imminent publication of a magisterial, multi-volume work of Quranic translation, exegesis and commentary, claiming confidently that he would take this scholarship beyond the point where Shah Waliullah had left it in the eighteenth century, because, as the announcement in *Al-Balagh* put it, 'God had reserved this task for the editor of *Al-Hilal*'.[12] In reality, of course, no such work ever appeared. But *Tazkira*, which Azad drafted in 1916 and was published in 1919, had the predominant purpose of associating Azad's entire family over many generations, hence by implication Azad himself, with precisely that tradition of pietistic *sharia*, descended from Sheikh Ahmed Sirhindi, to which Sarmad had been opposed and which had therefore taken his life.[13] By the time the Khilafat Movement reached its highest climax, Azad had identified himself with the move to have him appointed, by formal consent of the Indian *ulema*, as *Imam-al-Hind* – a Chief Theologian for India, an institution Indian Islam had strictly never had – so as to supervise, among other things, a network of *sharia* courts throughout the country.[14] This hope was finally dashed by the time Jami'at-e-Ulema-e-Hind met in its session of November 1921, eleven years after the publication of the 'Sarmad' essay, bringing to a close what we have called the '*Al-Hilal* decade' of Azad's life. He was arrested the next month and soon thereafter delivered his famous prison oration, *Qaul-e-Faisal*, which launched him firmly on the path of Congress nationalism, as was indicated by his election as President of Congress for the Special Session that was held soon after he came out of prison, in 1923.

One might think that there would be a direct line of development to trace after that date. But there isn't. Azad tried to return to journalism and undertook several ventures in that direction,[15] including the attempt to revive *Al-Hilal*, so that twenty-five issues of the revived journal were in fact published between June and December 1927. He remained active in Congress politics but it was a time of relative ebb in national politics, despite the communal frenzy of the late 1920s, the commotion surrounding the Nehru Report, and Gandhi's two major attempts at satyagraha in the early 1930s; Azad was in any case overshadowed by Ansari who was less flamboyant but senior and more sagacious. The two extant volumes of the *Tarjuman* were also prepared and published in this period, in 1930 and 1936 respectively. During these years, then, one might say, Azad was yet again trying to assert his status as a key Islamic theologian and was still pursuing, in whatever contradictory and half-hearted fashion, the goal he had set for himself in the 1910s: that of becoming a new *mujaddid* ('renovator') for the world of Islam. What was remarkable about this renewed attempt was the alacrity with which it was given up when the opportunity arose, especially after Ansari withdrew from politics in 1935 and then died the following year, for Azad to return to centre stage in national politics, as election campaigns were launched in the aftermath of the 1935 Act. Over the next twenty-two years, and even when he had plenty of leisure during his imprisonment in Ahmednagar Fort in the early 1940s, he neither returned to the *Tarjuman* nor wrote anything else of that kind.[16] The Ramgarh Address of 1940 then defined the new creed, which was notable thereafter for lack of Islamic juristic reference. The prose of *Ghubar-e-Khatir* – a prose of profane pleasure and secular civility, one might say – stands in sharp contrast not only to the apocalyptic prose of the *Al-Hilal* decade but to *Tarjuman*'s own theological preoccupation as well. By the time he came to dictate the notes from which Humayun Kabir then carved *India Wins Freedom*, he could say things diametrically opposed to what he had written in his *Al-Hilal* days while claiming all the while that he had held the same beliefs since 1912. On the last page of the main narrative, for example, we find the following:

> It is one of the greatest frauds on the people to suggest that religious affinity can unite areas which are geographically, economically, linguistically and culturally different. It is true that Islam sought to establish a society which transcends racial, linguistic, economic and political frontiers. History has however proved that after the first few decades or at most after the first century, Islam was not able to unite all the Muslim countries on the basis of Islam alone.[17]

History, in other words, had superseded the original Islamic design, and one had to accept history's verdict: nations had their basis in profane facts, not in religious belief. The truth of the statement is of course undeniable, but it is also indicative of the road Azad had travelled since the days when he used to declare that Constantinople was the 'political centre' (*siyassi markaz*) of 'Islam's global nationhood' (*Alamgir Islami qawmiat*)!

One might also note here that it was *after* he had abandoned the *Tarjuman* – he didn't say so, but he had in effect abandoned it after

1936 – that he adopted a secular politics. The mode of thought that runs from the Ramgarh Address to *India Wins Freedom* is radically opposed to not only the Pan-Islamism of the *Al-Hilal* period but also to the mode of the philosophical thought of the *Tarjuman* itself, in the sense that the search for a religious form of legitimation is now, after 1940, abandoned altogether and political principle is derived exclusively from the specificity of India's own distinctive social history and from the requirements of secular nationhood, making it compatible with socialistic redistribution of wealth, non-*shariatic* civil law, and universal adult franchise. The Ramgarh Address in fact describes the thousand-year history of India up to the twentieth century as a *symbiosis* whereby Hindus and Muslims have become more *alike*; the practitioners of both religions, he says, now resemble each other much more than they resemble the Hindus and Muslims of centuries past. In a remarkable aside, he says that the principle of conservation is necessary for religious and moral values, suicidal for social and political processes. In the light of all this, then, he pointedly says that Muslims of India need what everyone else needs: secular democracy, progressive economy, decentralized administration, and a genuinely federalist Constitution. Except for its emphasis on decentralization, this position is indistinguishable from the Nehruvian positions.[18]

II

There are, thus, constant shifts throughout Azad's career. Nor are these shifts reducible to the familiar demarcations between early and late writings, or between youthful and mature patterns of thought. What one encounters, in fact, are two quite different kinds of dynamic. One is the evident precociousness of his early life, which indicates a certain kind of early maturation. It *is* true that the *ghazals* he wrote at the age of eleven and twelve were as well-polished as anyone else would write, with luck, at thirty, so that his claim that he and his brother were already being treated in the Calcutta *mushairas* of that time as *senior* poets is credible. Sarojini Naidu's famous quip – that Maulana Azad was fifty years old at birth – referred mainly to the gravity of manner which Azad had assumed at an early age and which amused her and Jawaharlal a great deal, but it also referred to that same precociousness. The other dynamic we find is not one of growth, in the sense of refining or deepening existing patterns and insights, but of outright repudiation. Of these many repudiations Azad himself underscored only two, and both from early life: his move out of his family's orthodoxy, and his later repudiation of the so-called 'Aligarh tendency'. For the rest, he claimed a straight line of belief and action from the founding of *Al-Hilal* to the political premises of *India Wins Freedom*. Both these claims would bear some examination. Given his highly pietistic positions during the *Al-Hilal* phase, especially in *Al-Balagh*, and given also the enormous pride with which he narrates the history of his family's orthodox traditions in *Tazkira*, his own assertion that he had irrevocably broken away from those traditions by the age of fifteen, appears questionable.[19] One might say, rather, that the decade signifies his return, precisely, to those very traditions and that what he now wanted was to become not merely a *pir* of a limited and scattered community of *murids*, as his father had been, but an *imam* for all of India: a grand *pir*, so to speak. And, of course, the line between 1912 and 1958 was anything but straight, as we shall see in more detail presently.

We cannot, however, simply say that Azad changed his position every few years and leave it at that. A broader periodization of his life is indeed possible, and the task really is to identify stresses and turns within each broad period. In this more flexible perspective, it is possible to say, though only schematically and for analytic purposes alone, that the essential trajectory of Azad's life alternated constantly between a scripturalist Islam and a liberalizing, quasi-secular Islam. Unable to reconcile these contrary attractions and impulses, his allegiances seemed to swing dramatically, even violently, from one extreme to the other. This tendency we could illustrate by citing the transition he made during the Khilafat movement which is bracketed, on the one hand, by his crucial decision to throw in his lot decisively with Gandhi and, on the other, by the equally decisive failure of his attempt to be accepted by the Indian *ulema* as *Imam-al-Hind*; the document of this transition, if one need be identified, is his brilliant oration in prison, at the time of his sentencing in February 1922, entitled *Qaul-e-Faisal*. Up until 1920 Azad had projected himself as a leader of Muslims almost exclusively, and it was in that capacity that he participated in the larger National Movement. It was the convergence of Khilafat with Non-Cooperation at the grassroots, mass level – combined with his failure to obtain an unchallengeable theological preeminence among the Islamic *ulema*, his personal convergence with Gandhi, and his rapid promotion to the very apex of the Congress – which brought about a sea-change in Azad, who continued to *represent* Muslims in Congress but who now became a leader of the National Movement as such. There is nothing natural about this entirely new direction in his career after 1922–23, nor can it possibly be read back from *Al-Hilal*. In reality, this monumental shift changed everything, including his theology and his prose style. Much from his earlier life, including some of its insecurities and self-preoccupations, he took into the second phase – which begins firmly with his election as President of the Special Session of the Congress in 1923 and the crisis of his Pan-Islamicist intellectual formation that he had to face fully with the Kemalist abolition of the Osmanli Caliphate in March 1924 – but he also discarded a very great deal.

'Style', Whitehead once said, 'is the morality of one's mind.' The contrast between the two phases of Azad's life is obvious in the great shift that takes place in his prose. *Tazkira* (1919), the crowning classic of the earlier phase, which purports to be a biographical account of his ancestors and includes an uninformative appendix on his own youth that sits uncomfortably with the rest, is written in a style so digressive and forbidding, so full of circumlocution and turgid Arabisms and plain pretence, that no one could possibly want to read it, except, as in my case, for research interest. *Ghubar-e-Khatir*, the epistolary masterpiece of the latter phase, is written, by contrast, in a prose so well inflected and nuanced that few literate readers of Urdu would find it possible to put it down; in its own way, despite its dogged fictionality and extensive artifice, this is probably the one thing we have in the language that reminds one of Ghalib's letters – which is high praise, indeed. Schematically speaking, we might say that changes in Azad's prose style mirror, at every stage, his shifting relationships with that complex tradition which we associate with the figure of Sir Syed Ahmed Khan. The complexity of that tradition and Azad's relationship with it will be examined in a later section of this text. Suffice it to say here that Sir Syed had drawn upon the three traditions of Urdu prose represented, respectively, by the vernacularization of secular prose by the writers and scribes of Fort William College, the simplification of religious prose by Shah Abdul Aziz, and the modernization of tone and cadence that we find in Ghalib's epistolary prose. Combining these influences with what he learned from the English traditions of the 'essay', as he found them in such writers as Addison, Steele, and Lamb, Sir Syed gave to Urdu its first major *oeuvre* of a rationalist prose designed for printed communication among large sections of the literate population. Azad's own prose before the *Al-Hilal* decade was modelled precisely on this tradition, which he then repudiated during his Pan-Islamist phase and to which he gradually returned as his commitment to secular nationalism became stronger, expressed fully in public documents such as the Ramgarh Address and the superb literary prose of *Ghubar-e-Khatir*.

The same contrast is there in the structure of Azad's religious sentiment in the two phases. His Islam of the 1910s is for the most part furious, apocalyptic, unforgiving, and in the strict sense fundamentalist.[20] The promise that God's wrath is soon to wipe off the reign of the *kuffar* is a major theme of Azad's essays in *Al-Balagh*, the short-lived but equally legendary journal which he founded after the banning of *Al-Hilal*. It is symptomatic that Azad insistently uses the word *kuffar* for Europeans in these essays. Plural of the word *kafir*, the epithet carries such intensities of pietistic indignation that mere 'non-Muslim' cannot

convey the meaning; 'infidels' or 'heathens' as used for Hindus and
Muslims in Christian missionary hysterics would be closer. I am thus
using the word 'fundamentalist' here in a more or less technical sense. It
connotes, first, the exclusive emphasis on the canonical text and the
assertion that the text is *all* you need for the structuring of life,
individually and collectively. 'The Quran is the source of all knowledge',
is Azad's constant theme in this whole phase and is reiterated in a great
many variations. Second, there is, in the fundamentalist, an uncompromising emphasis on one's own religion as the source of all politics. Azad
develops this theme copiously throughout this phase so that it is not
uncharacteristic of him to say that '[a]ll governments of the world,
except *mazhabi* [religious, theocratic] governments, are oppressive in
their fundamental makeup'.[21] Third, the fundamentalist asserts the primacy of the most meagre kinds of religious textuality over secular and
profane knowledges. Azad's following statement, about the Baghdad of
the Abbasid period, is also characteristic in this regard:

> Muslims take great pride in the civilization, knowledges, and the arts
> of Baghdad. But those were mere decorations for the pleasure of the
> rulers. We deem them worthy of no pride. Rather, a single *hadith*
> [saying] of the Prophet, which Imam Bukhari has collected by travel-
> ling a hundred miles, is a thousand times more precious than all those
> knowledges.[22]

That Abbasid Baghdad would come in for such contempt also fits. It
was there, and in that period, that Neo-Platonism, which had entered
Islamic thought initially through scholars of northern Syria, was fully
developed into schools of theology, such as that of the Mautazila.
Debunking that magnificent Renaissance, which combined the Greek
strands of thought with the Islamic, is a patent theme of subsequent
fundamentalisms.

It should be said in favour of Azad, though, that his essay 'Iraq aur
Laila-e-Iraq', in the very next issue of *Al-Balagh*, had the merit of
starting with the ecstatic and profane love poetry of Qais-e-Aamri (the
famous 'majnoon') addressed to Laila; in a short but significant paragraph of that essay Azad celebrates those same 'arts and knowledges'
which he had debunked the previous month. However, his ability to
enunciate such contradictory ideas in successive issues of the same
journal points again to his enduring inability to make his choice between
the ecstatic tradition of figures like Sarmad and the *shariatic* tradition
descended from Ibn Tamiyya.

The Pan-Islamist anti-colonialism of the *Al-Hilal* decade was in any
case inconsistent on many counts. The characterization of all Muslims
of the world as a single *qawm* (nation) with a political centre (*siyasi*

markaz) located in Istanbul (Constantinople), with a Caliph of Islam who was also the Sultan, specifically, of Turkey, left the Indian Muslims in a highly ambiguous situation, which was resolved only rhetorically, in the language of metaphor, but never in terms of rational, analytic discourse. How many *nations* could one belong to, simultaneously, with how many *political centres*? If the *sharia* enjoined that one always be the *subject* of the Caliph/Sultan of Turkey, what status would one have if India were independent and there were to be a war between the two countries or, in the less dire case, if the Sultan simply forbade one to obey Indian laws? What happens, in that case, to the concentric circles which appeared on the Khilafat stationery, to dissolve in a metaphor the difficulty of belonging to two nations simultaneously, one territorial and Indian, the other religious and transcontinental? It is also indicative that Azad always spoke emphatically of the *exclusive* rights of Muslims in *Jazirat-al-Arab* – in which he specifically included Palestine, Syria, and Lebanon in addition to Peninsular Arabia – while routinely ignoring the *indigenous* non-Muslim populations of those regions. Did *they* have no rights? What rights *could* they have, considering that Azad had explicitly said that theocratic government was the only just form of government? How does one reconcile minority rights – or even majority rights, for that matter – with theocracy? It is doubtless the case, furthermore, that his articles in *Al-Hilal* and *Al-Balagh* focused on mobilizing Indian Muslims against colonial authority. It is also the case, however, that these same articles have little to say *to* – or even *about* – the non-Muslim population inside India. There was doubtless some vague sense that there should be anti-British cooperation; but there are also statements to the effect that Muslims need to learn nothing, and certainly accept no leadership, from Hindus. So, what happens to this Muslim–Hindu cooperation if the British do actually leave, considering that one stands already for a theocratic form of government? Even the idea of *umma-Wahida* started surfacing in his writings only in 1920 and only as an *oppositional* unity *against* the British. What was to be the *positive* form of this unity if the British did actually leave, and how were the Muslims – with their belief in theocratic government and their loyalty to the Turkish Caliph – to live in an independent polity where non-Muslims were in the majority? Even the basis of this idea of *umma-Wahida* was problematic. The theological justification which was found in the precedent of the Hudaybiyya Treaty of AD 628, whereby the Prophet of Islam had made his peace with Jews, was certainly useful in inducting the pietistic, Pan-Islamicist cadres into a countrywide agitation which spread more or less seamlessly from the mosques to the *kisan sabhas* (peasant associations) and from Gandhian Non-Cooperation to medical aid for Turkey. With the help of this precedent from early Islamic history Azad 'asserted', as Mushirul Hasan puts it, 'that uniting with one category of non-Muslims, the Hindus, against another category of non-Muslims, the British, was obligatory'.[23] So, a provisional 'unity' was forged, so long as the 'treaty' was in effect. But what happens to this 'treaty' if the common enemy, the British, disappears, considering that Muslims were a minority in India and could not possibly have an *Islamic* theocracy? Azad was to resolve these political problems only much later, around 1940, when he abandoned the search for a pietistic justification for Hindu–Muslim unity and accepted the secular premise.

For the latter period of his religious thought we have, meanwhile, the ecumenism of *Tarjuman-al-Quran*. In the light of his revisions of some conventional perspectives in this text, it has often been asserted that this reformulation of theological positions in ecumenical directions itself provides the basis for secular politics. That is doubtful, and I think the task of taking the measure of his achievement here requires of us that we not overstate the case. Azad's project in the *Tarjuman* is strictly that of a modern-day theologian at his limited best, temperate and traditionalist and generous all at once, who seeks a certain kind of modernization and reformation within the terms of his belief, with the objective that was once stated most succinctly by Sheikh Mohammed Abduh, the Grand Mufti of Egypt under Cromer: 'not to subject Islam to science, but to bring back into Islam those who believe in science'. Had this kind of reformation been undertaken in the sixteenth century, soon after Luther nailed his theses to the chapel door in Wittenberg, or even in the eighteenth, in direct conflict with Mohammed Abdul Wahhab's pietistic and strident narrowings of the *sharia*, the work would have been truly revolutionary. In the 1930s, one hundred and fifty years after Voltaire and Montesquieu, over a hundred years after the Jannissar Force (Jannissaries in English) was dispersed to open up the way for *Tanzimat* in Turkey, fifty years after the Egyptian *Nahda*, and generally in the wake of the first wave of Muslim modernism that had enveloped vast regions from Central Asia to North Africa,[24] Azad's work in the *Tarjuman* turned out to be surely erudite but at best rather tame. It had none of the apocalyptic ferocity of the *Al-Balagh* essays; its engagements were broad and generous; but it was still self-divided between its ecumenism and sufic possibility on the one hand, and, on the other its final appeal, again and again, to Ibn Taymiyyah, the conservative medieval *faqih* of the Hanbalite School of Sunni Islam. What the *Tarjuman* preached, in political terms then, was not secularism but a combination of personal piety and generous tolerance.

The main contribution of the *Tarjuman* was its concept of *Wahdat-e-Adyan* ('Unity of Faiths') which was perfectly compatible with many strands of sufic thought, including the concept of *Wahdat-al-Vajud*, which was first expounded by Ibn Arabi but was then greatly extended and popularized in India by several of the sufic orders. At a later stage, in the epistles of *Ghubar-e-Khatir*, Azad himself was to comment that the sufic principle of *Wahdat-al-Vajud* was the same as (in his words) 'Upanishadic pantheism'. From this of course one could derive a straightforward non-denominational, composite culture as well as an ethics of very broad tolerance and even highly syncretic religious practices. Had Azad remained steadfast on this syncretic principle, and had he found a popular idiom both for this religious innovation and for political style, he might have become for Indian Islam what Gandhi substantially became for the Hindu reform movement. Unfortunately, the concept of *Wahdat-e-Adyan* remained at best an abstract, more or less cerebral concept, and when Azad was challenged by other Islamic theologians he basically retreated into affirmation of the more traditional, pietistic positions based not on sufic transgressions but on normative *fiqh*. Asked whether *namaz* (the ritual prayer binding on all Muslims) was both necessary and distinctive for a Muslim, as distinguished from non-Muslims, and whether the Quran offered the same salvation for those who accepted the Islamic *kalima* (the liturgical affirmation of the primacy of Allah over other gods, and of the Prophethood of Mohammad) and those who didn't, Azad was forced to give only evasive replies, speaking copiously of *raboobiyat* ('nurture'?) as Allah's main attribute which applied to all created beings, but never answering the direct question. The concept of *raboobiyat* we shall discuss below, but the larger difficulty was in the text of the *Tarjuman* itself, which had simultaneously invoked the esoteric sufic traditions as well as the literalist and canonical textuality of the *fiqh* tradition – and, further back, in Azad's desire to inhabit equally the ecstatic world of Sarmad (as in the 1910 essay) and the punitive, puritanical world of Sirhindi (as in *Tazkira* of 1919). It must be said, though, that the main thrust of the *Tarjuman* was in the direction of tolerance, magnanimity, ecumenism, and the treatment of religion not as a mandatory and exclusivist ritual but as essentially an inward, aesthetic experience. This was not at all a bad sign in an illiberal political climate; the intensified communal conflicts of the latter 1920s were the immediate backdrop for the composition of the *Tarjuman*, and the subsequent communal frenzy was to rip the country apart, quite literally. But the age when a liberalist reinterpretation of a religion could transform the lives of nations had passed, and Azad, at once a leader in a mass movement but also an erudite theologian, could not fully acknowledge that progressive transformations of society now presumed not a *better* interpretation of religion but a firm secularity, a *separation* between religion and politics. In the event, *Tarjuman* became, for all its eloquence and magnanimities, a matter of debate only among theologians and some limited sections of the modern Muslim intelligentsia, with no impact on general political life. Despite the limited impact, however, it is also the case that the essentially humanistic and ecumenical thrust of the *Tarjuman* stands in sharp contrast to the stridencies of the *Al-Hilal* decade.

One thinks in this context, oddly, of Gandhi. After all, Gandhi too, for reasons of deeply felt personal predilections but also because he considered it the most opportune way to stem the tide of Hindu communalism, had opted to be not a secularist, in the Nehruvian sense, but a *Hindu* reformer. Operating within the predicates of caste society, he had upheld the concept of the four *varnas* and yet declared the lowest castes 'the children of god' (*harijan*); it has been argued, by Ambedkar among scores of others, that it was a middle-caste solution for the conciliation of the upper and the lower castes, and that the victims of the caste system needed the abolition of that system, not the verbal consolation that they were the offspring of the brahminical deity. Deeply wounded by the communal conflicts between groups of Hindus and Muslims, he preached tolerance, ecumenism, *ahimsa*, magnanimity, bridling of greed and competitiveness if not exactly universal *brahma-charya*; this society of tolerable living conditions for all and of mutual respect among former adversaries, he called, within the traditionalist lexicon available to him inside Hindu reformism, *ram rajya* (the rule of Ram). The burden of Azad's social thought in the *Tarjuman*, when shorn of all theological finesse, is that a civilizational compact of mutuality between Muslims and Hindus of India, and among the various religious denominations generally, is the paramount need both of the nation-state and of a religious life lived in political liberty. For a contemporary secular scholar who has no particular preference for the lexicon either of Islam or of Hinduism, there appear to be uncanny similarities between Gandhi's idea of *ram rajya* and Azad's sense, encapsulated in the twin notions of *raboobiyat* and *Wahdat-e-Adyan*, of possible compatibility between Islamic humanism and non-sectarian existence, especially as both espouse an ecumenical reformation in their respective religions so as to make those religions compatible with modern needs. The objective in both cases is at once the refurbishing of piety and the creation of a harmonious multireligious polity which is justifiable in the terms of the religion that each espoused; what joins the two views is the common ground that both wish to occupy, but not to the exclusion or diminution of the other. There appears to be, in other words, a kind of *ahimsa* between Gandhi's *ahimsa* and Azad's *Wahdat-e-Adyan*.

Tensions and differences, though, are also obvious enough. One, clearly, is that the existence of adjacent but distinct world-views, however tolerant of each other, does not constitute a secularism, so long as the two world-views are expressed in specific – and different – religious lexicons. The lexicons of Islamic theology and of Hindu piety are, after all, constitutively different, and the deployment of these lexicons – not as in Kabir, overlappingly, but as in Azad and Gandhi, who speak culturally and religiously differentiated languages – does create differential effects and sensibilities, despite their shared universalist messages, so that the two religious groups thus addressed become, by virtue of that very lexicon, intensely aware of their differential and mutually exclusive cultural locations. And, if one is seeking for *ram rajya*, what, after all, is there to prevent Mr Advani from claiming that his *rath yatra* too was in search of the same?[25]

Another way of encapsulating this same difficulty might be this: the fact that both Gandhi and Azad spoke in the religious idiom created difficulties enough for an emerging secular society, but that they spoke in *two* religious idioms, considered by most as mutually incompatible, had the effect of each cancelling out the other, as so much *talk*, hardly relevant to the way life among followers of the two religions was to be lived in the aftermath of the Partition. The difficulty, in Azad's case, was compounded by the fact of his immense and always present erudition in Islamic traditions, and by the level of his language. In this particular respect, the difficulty was not simply that his was the thought growing out of Islam, the religion of a minority, nor only that he spoke and wrote in Urdu, the language of relatively few Indians. That was in fact a minor matter, in the sense that Urdu could always be translated and that certain kinds of 'Islam' – the syncretic kinds, which he affirmed very sparingly and lived not at all – were by no means unfamiliar to a great many who were not Muslims themselves. The difficulty, much less so than at earlier stages of his life but still formidable until the end, was that it was the culture of the Muslim *elite*, and of the *traditional* elite at that, which Azad actually abided by in his personal life and public persona, so that it was hardly accessible to the mass of Muslims and certainly not available to the non-elite bulk of the non-Muslim population. Gandhi's language was so much the language of the mass culture that much of it even the Muslim peasant, often rooted in syncretic cultural overlaps, could fully comprehend; Azad's, on the other hand, was so rooted in the elite traditions that many, Muslims and Hindus alike, could admire him, but few – none below the propertied middle class – could actually *identify* with him.

It is doubtless the case that in some rare moments after the Ramgarh transition Azad did gain a new kind of ability to speak publicly and sympathetically about his love of the transgressive, ecumenical, artistic, even hedonistic traditions in certain kinds of Islam and in the life of Muslims generally – an ability which he had done so much to conceal for some thirty years after the publication of his famous essay on Sarmad in 1910. Some reference to Gandhi here may again be revealing. For Gandhi had tried to reconcile in his life the Bhagavad-Gita with Gita-Govinda, Mahabharata with Meerabai, and all these with a rhythm of daily life embedded in popular ritual, vernacular existence, and threadbare frugality of consumption. Azad was different on most of these counts. (The last place Azad could imagine for himself would be a village, less still an *ashram*.) His own allegiances, at least in public life, had always been divided between *fiqh* and *tasawwuf, shariat* and *tariqat*.[26] In the days of *Al-Hilal*, he had wilfully presented himself as a dogged partisan of *shariat* and of the high textuality of Quranic commentaries in the traditions of Kalam. By contrast, his magnificent last letter in *Ghubar-e-Khatir* – on his lifelong secret passion for classical music, mainly Indian but also Arabic – entirely overturns the pietistic self-image he had projected in that earlier phase and testifies to his longing for profane pleasures. It is significant, though, that it remained a lonely passion, never lived publicly; he concealed it from the world in adult life, as he had concealed it from his father when he was a boy. By the time he came to write *Ghubar-e-Khatir* he had changed sufficiently – and it was, in the terms of Azad's life, an enormous change – to speak of such things in print, at least once or twice; but beyond that he could never go. The difficulty, again, was that the gap between his private love of sufic doctrine and profane music, and the public persona of theologian and jurist, had been too great; Azad could not bridge that gap in later life, even if he wanted to, without ruining his own political career – and perhaps even inner balance. Syncretic traditions of the common Muslim were there for him to contemplate, in some secret ways even to envy, as is obvious from his loving account of the way Hindu devotional music had enveloped the lives of countless Muslims, but the public persona never made room for unconventional, transgressive conduct, because there was always that dominant aspect of the self which remembered with pride, or at least imagined with much passion, that it was descended from a lineage of theologians which had once upheld the pietistic traditions in the halls of Emperor Jehangir's hedonistic court. Gandhi, of course, had no such claims and inhibitions.

It may be useful here to press a bit further the question of Azad's religious ecumenism – its directions and its limits – especially with reference to the twin concepts of *raboobiyat* and *Wahdat-e-Adyan* to which he came to subscribe in later years. The concept of *raboobiyat*, which has a central place in the *Tarjuman* as Allah's main atttribute, Azad had borrowed from Ibn al-Arabi, for whom the term had connotations of lordship from the point of the slave, with unmistakable suggestions of obedience and devotion, indeed loss of the self in the will of the lord. True to his eclectic methods, Azad gives an erudite account of Arabic etymologies but shifts the meaning radically, in ways that are not easy to grasp conceptually. The Christian concepts of 'love' or 'mercy' or 'beneficence' do not come even close, but reference to the

Hindu trinity of Creator–Preserver–Destroyer might help. Simply put, traditional Islamic theology has as a rule emphasized the attributes of Allah as 'Creator', whereas Azad shifts the emphasis towards 'preserver', the provider and protector of the conditions of life for the created order, hence the predominant meaning of *nurture* in the concept. In terms of Hindu cosmology, in other words, the shift is in the Vaishnavite direction. This shift becomes all the more interesting when we see that in some of his rhetorical flourishes in the latter part of his life, Azad did attempt a Kabir-like dissolution of differential Hindu and Muslim categories. I have referred already to his assertion in one of his epistles that the sufic doctrine of *Wahdat-al-Vajud* was the same as 'Upanishadic pantheism'. In that same epistle, he also says that of all the religions of the world Hinduism had achieved the most refined concept of monotheism, before the casteist degeneration; a statement of that kind becomes plausible if one is thinking of *advaita*. So, it is not surprising that in his speech at Viśva Bharati, in Śantiniketan, on 22 September 1951, Azad also declared that the term *advaita* 'translated into Arabic ... would read as *Wahdahu la shareek*'. The central doctrine of Kabir-*bhakti* is thus made identical with the central doctrine of Islamic piety. Eclectic but sweeping statements of this kind indicate a desire to effect a philosophical reconciliation between Islam and Hinduism. Four aspects of this attempt are, however, notable. One, the reconciliation is attempted not on the level of popular syncretic traditions but on the level of high textuality and philosophical abstraction – between the Upanishad and *Ilm-al-Kalam*, so to speak. Second, it is Hinduism that is selectively incorporated within Islam through the process of establishing complementarity and even identity between some discrete concepts of the two, while the whole surrounding edifice remains Islamic. Third, no *praxis* or community follows from the conceptual revision: no *panth*, no *tariqa*, no *matth*, no *zawiya*, no *ashram* – only the aesthetic beauty of reconciliation-in-contemplation. Fourth, there is never any direct statement of the intent; it is only from a collection of discrete statements that the intent may be inferred. Formally, Azad remains a strict *Islamic* theologian – though unsatisfactory to most of the theological elite, whom he primarily addresses, precisely because of his ecumenism. The whole project remains peculiarly disembodied, precariously dislocated. No wonder that it was abandoned.

III

I have suggested already that, regardless of all the fame that came to him early in life, the most substantial part of Azad's achievement occurred only in his maturer years. It is useful to summarize, however, what

Azad had to leave behind before he gained the certainties of later life, for it is only by grasping the magnitude of what he discarded that we can fully grasp the quality of later achievement.

Uncertainty appears to be the hallmark both of Azad's own personality in the early years of his life and of the documentary evidence pertaining to those years. A large part of the difficulty is that we simply do not have any independent accounts; such as we have always refer back to what Azad himself said or is claimed to have said. One of the few independent accounts came from Azad's older sister, Fatima Begum, in an interview that was broadcast from All-India Radio, Delhi, on 22 February 1959, and then printed in the Urdu journal, *Aaj Kal*, in the September issue of the same year. The document is invaluable, both because it is so rare to get an account of Azad's early life from any source other than himself, and – even more significantly – because of the insight it provides into the self-image he seems to have created for himself as a child and cultivated carefully all his life. The following extract from that text, for example, speaks volumes:

> As a child Azad was never fond of the games children usually indulge in. Even at the age of eight, his games were unique. Sometimes, he would line up trunks and boxes and pronounce them to be a train. Then he would tie one of father's turbans round his head and taking his seat on one of the boxes, he would ask us, his sisters, to shout and cry 'Give way, give way, the Maulana from Delhi is on his way.' When we said, 'Brother, there is no crowd here, whom should we push aside or ask to get out of the way', he would remonstrate, 'Can't you follow this simple make-believe? Can't you visualize that a large crowd has come to receive me?' Then he would get down from the box and walk off slowly and deliberately, like an elderly person. Sometimes he would climb a raised platform and ask his sisters to surround him and applaud him, imagining that he was speaking amidst thousands of persons who were cheering and applauding his speech.

Several features of this memory are striking. There are, first, the two images of desire: a great theologian, and a great orator. In both cases, moreover, there is the image of a man in the crowd, but a man apart: deliberate, grave, superior, admired. There is, finally, no role for anyone else; others may cheer, or control the cheering crowds, but they are anonymous parts of the spectacle, never *sharing* in the spectacle, which is centred on the theologian–orator. It is a great pity that we have so few accounts of Azad's childhood from anyone other than himself; we might have learned more about the person who was always so well concealed behind the deliberate gravity.

Compounding the difficulty of assessing Azad's life until after he had become famous as the editor of *Al-Hilal* are the problematic status and the inner contradictions of the accounts that are attributable to Azad. Of the two that are known to have been written by Azad, *Tazkira* is no autobiography at all. Most of it refers to his early ancestors, and the little that Azad says about himself is so shrouded in insinuation and rhetorical flourish that nothing resembling a fact emerges. We shall return to the significance of this particular arrangement later. Meanwhile, it is useful first to specify the actual status of *Ghubar-e-Khatir*, the other direct source of biographical information. It purports to be a collection of private letters addressed to an actual friend, Nawab Habibur Rehman Khan Sherwani, but they were never mailed and were published in a book well before the purported addressee saw them; the first three letters in the collection bear dates after his release from prison, the third one tells elaborately how private letters have come to be published instead of being mailed, and the key last letter was added only in the third edition of the book. The whole design is full of artifice, and Malik Ram's suggestion that Azad had probably seen the Arabic translation of Voltaire's *Persian Letters* and had borrowed the form from that book, is astute. The so-called letters have, in other words, the formal status of *epistles*, i.e. a literary genre, meant for public circulation but written in the form of a private communication. Even here, the only epistle which gives us truly illuminating information about any period of his life is the magnificent last one; numbers 10 and 11 elaborate only on the first fourteen years, in ways both careful and misleading, and adding little to what we already know from the impressionistic account in *Tazkira*; for the crucial ten years of Azad's early life, between the ages of fourteen and twenty-four, these two epistles tell us nothing factual and are even more brief and elliptical than the evocations in *Tazkira*. To this too we shall return later.

It is useful also to clarify the status of the two lengthy 'autobiographical' accounts which are said to come from Azad but have been prepared by others. *India Wins Freedom* was published posthumously, based on Azad's dictation in Urdu and Humayun Kabir's condensation and rearrangement of those materials in English. In his Preface, Kabir recapitulates the process, emphasizing that each chapter had been revised under Azad's guidance, and that Azad had approved the final draft of each chapter separately as well as the final manuscript as a whole. We have no reason to question Kabir's integrity otherwise, and it is in any case very unlikely that Kabir would be interested in misrepresenting Azad's *early* life; it is worth remarking, however, that no authenticated final copy of the text exists to prove Azad's approval. The book says little about the period prior to 1935 in any case, and what little we do get in the 'Prospectus' which precedes the main text is highly problematic, as we shall see. Then we have the peculiar text of *Azad ki Kahani Khud Azad ki Zubani*, also published posthumously in 1959, by Abdurrazzaq Malihabadi, Azad's close confidant of long standing. The title is misleading, since it suggests that the text is from Azad himself; critics have challenged the authenticity of the text on the ground that the prose itself shows it to be not Azad's work. The point about the quality and cadence of the prose is correct, but it is somewhat misplaced. The title page of the first edition itself reveals that Malihabadi never claimed it to be Azad's own language; it clearly says '*ba-rivayat* Abdurrazzaq Malihabadi', i.e. 'as told by' Malihabadi. The problems are of a different kind.

Malihabadi says that Azad told him the story in 1921 in prison; in fact, Azad was incarcerated from 10 December 1921 to 1 January 1923. Malihabadi's error in remembering the correct year seems to suggest that he wrote it down much later, when the memory of precise dates had receded; if he could forget such a large fact about the origin of the book, it is legitimate to question the accuracy of facts recounted within the text. Furthermore, the contrast with Humayun Kabir's book are striking. For Kabir, Azad gave the dictation during the last two years of his life and it is perfectly credible that the book appeared posthumously because of Azad's unexpected death. According to Malihabadi himself, thirty-eight years elapsed between dictation and publication, which raises the question of Azad's approval. Kabir says explicitly that Azad approved drafts of each chapter; the difficulty of course is that we have only Kabir's word for it and no independent means of corroborating it. Malihabadi makes no such claim of making public an approved text, says explicitly that he had no intention of ever showing it to Azad (on the ground that Azad would have forbidden publication and confiscated the manuscript), and that he managed to retain the script all these years because Azad had simply 'forgotten' about it – with the inescapable implication that Malihabadi was waiting for Azad to die so that he could publish the story! That Azad would have forbidden publication is most likely, but it is inconceivable that a man of Azad's prodigious memory would forget a whole book that he had dictated.

Matters are complicated further by the fact that Malihabadi's text covers exactly the ground that is said to have been covered by Azad – whether by writing or by dictating is unclear – during the Ranchi internment, after the composition of what we know as *Tazkira*. Fazluddin Ahmed, who occupied the same position in Azad's confidence then that Malihabadi was to occupy later, and who was responsible both for prodding Azad to write the book and for having it printed, says explicitly in his Preface to *Tazkira* that it is only the first of a projected two-volume work. That second volume never appeared but the general description of its contents which Fazluddin specifies there makes it sound remarkably like the contents of the Malihabadi volume. Is it that Azad dictated the materials not to Malihabadi in 1922 but to Fazluddin some five years earlier, who then disappeared after falling out with Azad but somehow left the manuscript – otherwise presumed lost – in such a way that Malihabadi, who subsequently took charge of all Azad's journalistic and publishing affairs, found the manuscript and silently kept it? In that case, there would be no question of Azad having 'forgotten' anything; whatever Fazluddin had was presumed lost. This would also address the curious fact that no *original* manuscript (i.e. plausibly taken down thirty years prior to publication) of the Mali-habadi text, even in Malihabadi's own hand, has ever been found; perhaps the original was in someone else's handwriting, and Malihabadi had good reason not to preserve it! The alternative is to believe that Azad never dictated anything, that upon his death Malihabadi simply pieced together a memoir based upon what he had heard from Azad over the years, and then, using an artifice worthy of Azad himself, wrote it up *as if* Azad had actually dictated it. In either case, it would be unfair to hold Azad directly responsible for any mis-statement of fact in that volume. Such, however, is not the case for the 'Prospectus' in *India Wins Freedom* where Humayun Kabir had no interest in distorting Azad's version of things and which he describes in his Preface as a 'synopsis' of a projected volume expressly approved by Azad.

Textual authenticity is a major issue in Azad studies because the facts of his early life are far from clear, because the various accounts are mutually conflicting, and because our understanding of his later career depends in part on the determination of those early facts. We can agree that he was born in Mecca, and 1888 is very likely the year of his birth; we also know that his father, Maulana Khairuddin, had given him the historical name 'Feroz Bakht'. Beyond that, facts become ambiguous. In the first known letter, addressed to Abdul Razzaq Kanpuri, he gave his name as 'Ghulam Muhiyuddin Azad'; the same name appears with the publication of his *ghazal* in that same year in a journal from Lucknow, *Khadang-e-Nazar*. 'Muhiyuddin' does rhyme with his father's name, so it is probable that it too was the real family name. 'Ahmed' was then inserted two years later. But the whole construction was then dropped, and the name as we now know it – Abul Kalam Azad – appeared for the first time in 1903, when he established his first journal, *Lisan-al-Sidq*; but then he also added 'Dehlavi', which seems curious considering that he had never visited Delhi until then and none of the other members of his family had ever used that kind of identification.[27] By 1912, when Azad was twenty-four and started *Al-Hilal*, the name became appropri-ately more Arabized: 'Ahmed al-Makani Babi al-Kalam Azad Dehlavi'. Even the origins of the name 'Azad' are unclear. In the 'Prospectus' Azad asserts that he adopted this name to indicate his rebellion against his family's orthodoxy.[28] It seems equally likely that he adopted it at the time his first *ghazal* was to be published, with an eye to the fact that the journal in question published the poets in alphabetical order and he who had his name beginning with the sound 'ā' (an *alif* and a *mud'*, in Urdu) would be the first.[29]

The question of when his family returned to India is equally unclear, and needs to be determined because that would clarify the nature of Azad's linguistic formation in the early years of his life. He is said to have not known much Urdu as a child because his mother was Arab and knew none. This is curious, considering that there is reason to believe that her parents had actually migrated to Mecca from the northwestern province of pre-Partition India, and it would be surprising for the *daughter* of an Indian *Alim* to know only Arabic and no Urdu, or any other Indian language.[30] In his Introduction to *Ghubar-e-Khatir*, Malik Ram writes that 'when his father came to India from Hejaz for the last time along with his family in 1898, Maulana Azad, who was then roughly ten years old, knew very little Urdu' (p. 19). This is exactly what Azad says through Malihabadi in *Azad ki Kahani*, and he often implied something of this kind elsewhere as well, without giving precise dates. Malik Ram in fact goes on to suggest here and in the Introduction to *Tazkira* that Azad later wrote such Arabic-laden prose because of his early upbringing in Arabic and his consequent uncertainty in Urdu. All of this seems very doubtful. That Azad would at times, in earlier stages of his life and in moments of weakness, want us to believe something like this makes a certain kind of sense; one's stature as a theologian is all the more secure if Arabic can be shown to have been one's mother tongue and the language of one's formative years. But that a scholar of Malik Ram's acumen and devotion to verification of facts would say such a thing is surprising. In *India Wins Freedom* Azad himself says categorically, 'In 1890, my father came to Calcutta with the whole family ... A year after we came to Calcutta, my mother died and was buried there.' This is contrary to Azad's earlier suggestions, but we do have this categorical statement from his very last book. If *this* is true, then Azad was two years old when he arrived in Calcutta, into an Urdu-speaking milieu, and three at the time of his mother's death. That there was knowledge of Arabic in the family is beyond doubt; but this other dating would suggest that Arabic was the language mainly of scholarship and piety, while Urdu was indeed the language of the family and the social milieu. Furthermore, there is the evidence of his Urdu *ghazals* of 1899 and 1900, which are fluent and well-inflected in that particular style, as in the following two couplets:

> Nashtar-ba-dil hai Aah kisi sakht jan ki
> Nikli sada to fasd khulaigi zuban ki

and

Kyun aseer-e-gaisu-e-khumdar-e-qatil ho gya
Hai, kya baithe bithai tujh ko ai dil ho gya

No boy who has freshly returned to India with scant knowledge of Urdu and with Arabic as his mother tongue could possibly write *ghazals* of this kind, with their evident combination of *spoken* Urdu tonality and Farsi linguistic construction, of the type that was characteristic of the traditional Urdu *ghazal*. We might add that his prose of the next decade, up to 1910, demonstrates a similar fluency of style but an even simpler diction, in the manner of Hali and Sir Syed, with no suggestion that the author is in any way steeped in Arabic or deficient in Urdu. The Arabic-laden style of the *Al-Hilal* decade which Azad thereafter cultivated was thus a repudiation of that earlier mastery of fluent Urdu and amounted to a willed Arabization designed to convey the author's great absorption in Islamic canonical texts, for writings which were addressed precisely to the *ulema* whose recognition Azad needed in order to become the 'Renovator' he had dreamed of becoming.

The existence of these published *ghazals* and of the prose he wrote even before he began editing *Lisan-al-Sidq* raises some questions also about the portrait he has given us of his early education under the rigidly orthodox and harshly restrictive regime of his father and the teachers who were handpicked by his father. In epistles 10 and 11 of *Ghubar-e-Khatir*, he gives a very vivid picture of this regime. 'The part of my life which may be called my student days did not last longer than up to the age of fourteen or fifteen', and 'He [the father] adopted the method of teaching me either himself or by getting teachers who would live with us and teach me, so that I had no opportunity to put my foot out of the family compound' (p. 97). He also says that a sense of full-scale rebellion set in at the age of fifteen but he had experienced no sense of conflict or dissatisfaction with the values of his family until then because he simply did not know that there were other ways of thinking and believing in the world. The picture we get in *India Wins Freedom* is less detailed and oppressive, but he does say, 'I was able to complete the course by the time I was sixteen ... It was soon after this that I first came across the writings of Syed Ahmed Khan' (p. 3). The difficulty with all of this is that Azad was by his own account fourteen in 1902, sixteen in 1904, but he had published in 1899 *ghazals* which had not even a shadow of that sort of training and his essays of 1902 already reveal the extensive influence of Syed Ahmed Khan. Nor can *ghazals* of that kind be written all of a sudden; a person has to be steeped in that culture for a while before even the phrases could come. Moreover, Azad was reciting his *ghazals* in open *mushairas*, along with his brother, and both are said to have gained a literary reputation very quickly. We know very little about their sisters, but it seems that they too were composing *ghazals*. All this profane literary activity seems not to correspond to an orthodox regime of such harshness that the boy is not allowed even to set foot outside the family compound. It is worth recalling here that the mother had died, perhaps in 1891, and that all the children, boys and girls, were brought up under Khairuddin's direct supervision. The father, in other words, was not detached from the children's upbringing even to the degree that was normal in traditional homes of that era; that they, even the girls, could indulge their literary tastes and write profane *ghazals* inside that household says something about the atmosphere which prevailed there. Yet we get variations on the same story of extreme restrictiveness and complete lack of contact with anything but purest orthodoxy until the age of fifteen, in all the four accounts that can be attributed to Azad, directly or indirectly. It appears probable that he greatly exaggerated the extent of the punitive orthodoxy within the household in order to make all the more dramatic the break he made when he refused to follow his father's desire that he succeed him as a *pir*.[31]

Since Azad published a great deal of work between 1899 and 1907, while also editing several journals and newspapers during the last five of these years, it is relatively easy to follow his career even without – and sometimes against the grain of – his own accounts. We face great difficulties for the next five years, until July 1912 when he begins to edit *Al-Hilal*. Some accounts, including Azad's own in the 'Prospectus', would have us believe that he was quite substantially involved in the revolutionary underground in Bengal at this time, and also that he travelled extensively in West Asia and France, perhaps in 1900. Azad's own impressionistic account in *Tazkira* of his period of love, drunkenness, and sexual excess, as well as his accounts in epistles 11 and 24 of *Ghubar-e-Khatir* of not only these 'sins' but also his love of music, which he says he pursued extensively in all kinds of places, from the Taj in Agra to the Opera House of Cairo, mention hardly any precise dates but it is possible to surmise from internal evidence that this was also the period of all that hectic hedonism. The precise chronology is very hard to determine, but the matter of his trip to West Asia, Egypt, and Turkey in particular, should delay us considerably, for that is directly connected with three key issues: the process whereby he came to reject the thought of Syed Ahmed Khan in such wholesale fashion; his understanding of the distinct intellectual formations of Abduh, Rashid Rida, and the man, Jamaladdin, who went under the name, alternatively, of Afghani and/or Asadabadi; and his understanding, also, of the politics of West Asian countries generally, and of Turkey in particular, at the time when he plunged into the polemics of *Al-Hilal* on the issue, first, of the Balkan War and, second, of the Khilafat itself.

IV

In the last, magnificent letter of *Ghubar-e-Khatir* Azad writes about the two Arab singers, Ahmed Sallama and Taira, whom he heard and came to know personally when he visited Cairo.[32] Unfortunately, we have not even a sentence, either in his own writings or in the subsequent biographies which make so much of his visit to West Asia, about the actual political figures – Arab nationalists, Young Turks, members of Mustafa Kamil's National Party – whom he is said to have met there.[33] This is a matter of some importance, since Azad himself cites this trip – with subsequent biographers simply taking him at his word – as evidence of his direct knowledge of the politics of that region and as an occasion when he fully understood the need for a united struggle of Muslims and Hindus against colonialism. There is in reality scant evidence, in all of Azad's copious writings of the crucial decade between the founding of *Al-Hilal* and the demise of the Khilafat Movement, to show that Azad understood even the primary political facts concerning that region. In *India Wins Freedom*, Azad suggests that during his trip of 1908 his ideological affiliation was mainly with the reformist aspects of Sheikh Abduh (misnamed in the book as 'Abdullah', on p. 7) and the modernist secularism of Mustafa Kamil; his writings of the *Al-Hilal* period, by contrast, would appear to be inspired by the more extreme sections in the circle that arose around Rashid Rida, in direct opposition to Abduh's reform and Kamil's relatively irreligious modernism. On a cognate theme, Azad simply states: 'When I went to Turkey I became friends with some of the leaders of the Young Turk movement. I kept up my correspondence with them for many years after my return to India.' It is regrettable that we do not know the names of the 'leaders' whom Azad befriended or what they told him, about Khilafat among other things, either at the time or in the course of their correspondence over the 'many years' subsequently. For the ideas that Azad expounded in the *Al-Hilal* period were diametrically opposed to the ones the so-called 'Young Turks' themselves held, with little evidence to suggest that Azad actually knew what those ideas *were*. At the very least, one can say that if Azad's intellectual affiliations at that time had been really with the thought of Abduh, Mustafa Kamil, and the 'Young Turks', he would have found it impossible to dispense with the thought of Syed Ahmed Khan so easily, as we shall presently clarify.

When and where did Azad go, whom did he meet, what did he learn?

Azad's own references to this visit in *India Wins Freedom* put the visit in early 1908, before his father's death, and mention Iraq, Egypt, Syria, Turkey, and France as the countries he visited; in Egypt, he says, he 'spent a long time'. The difficulty with this account is that his work on the two journals, *Vakeel* and *Dar al-Saltanat*, shows him as being in India until the beginning of 1908, while his father died on 15 August that year; we *know* that Azad was in Calcutta at this later date, and Azad himself says that he was already in Paris when he heard of his father's illness. Given the difficulties of travel in those days, it appears unlikely that one could visit five countries, spend a 'long time' in Egypt, strike up 'friendships' with 'leaders' of the Young Turks in Turkey, go all the way to France and be back in Calcutta, so very quickly. Since the claim seems somewhat far-fetched, and because we know so little of the roughly two years that elapsed between his father's death and the founding of *Al-Hilal*, the temptation is to move the trip to this latter period. Thus, V.N. Datta gives no particular dates but says flatly, 'After his father's death in 1908 Azad visited the West Asian countries and also France. This increased his knowledge of men and he became a man of the world.'[34] We shall come later to what a 'man of the world' should have known. It is significant nevertheless that Datta adds in the very next sentence that 'we get scant information about him in the interlude between the death of his father and his launching of *Al-Hilal*'. But two pieces of firm information he does offer. First, 'On the first death anniversary of his father, quite a large number of people including Khairuddin's disciples tried to persuade Azad to assume the office of *pir* but he declined' (p. 23); this appears to place Azad well inside India in August 1909. Further corroboration comes then, in a peculiar way, with the second piece of information: 'Azad's love episode took place in Bombay around 1909' (p. 25). Datta offers no evidence for fixing a date for this 'love episode', but it is possible to infer this from *Tazkira*. Azad's own handling of the 'episode' in that text is so full of poetic ballast that it is impossible to extract from it what one may reasonably call a 'fact', but he does say that he gave up his life of *rindi-o-havasnaki* (drunkenness and sexual greed) at the age of *ikkees-baees* (twenty-one/twenty-two), which does seem to place the 'episode' in 1909–10, provided that we accept 1888 as the year of Azad's birth.[35] None of this can be asserted with any degree of certainty, but it seems fair to assume that Azad was inside India in 1909 as well.

In *India Wins Freedom*, meanwhile, he twice mentions the year of 1908 as the time of his travel and says explicitly that he was in Paris when he was informed of his father's illness and had to cut short his journey. It is possible that he forgot the actual year of his travels, but it seems highly unlikely that he would forget where he was when he heard of his father's last illness, especially if he was so far from home. So, the most we can say is that he was in India in the early months of 1908, and the brief spell between that and August of that year was the only time when he might have journeyed abroad; if he visited five countries he could not possibly have stayed anywhere for 'a long time'. That he had travelled to Baghdad with his brother in 1906, got ill, and was promptly sent back to Calcutta, is much clearer; the famous Urdu writer, Sajjad Hayder Yildrim, was serving in the British-Indian Consulate there, and we have his testimony for the event.

Be that as it may. The issue of his actual travel is far less significant than the issue of what he knew, then and later during the *Al-Hilal* decade, and how his knowledge has come to be seen subsequently. In all probability, Azad's knowledge of those parts of the world was derived mainly from his understanding of the *Salafiyya* Movement of Rashid Rida, a Syrian Islamic scholar who had made his home in Egypt, and that, too, primarily through such journals as Rida's own *Al-Manar*. One can also assume that he was familiar with the writings of Jamaladdin, either directly or – what is more likely – in some derivative form. Beyond that, nothing is very clear. Azad was of course magnificently well read in the traditional knowledges available in Urdu and Arabic, but it is much to be regretted that we are not informed as to what else he might have known. He seems not to have known until after the *Al-Hilal* days enough English to read anything serious in it; everything he wrote about European history or culture during that decade is, at best, embarrassing.[36] Meanwhile, the knowledge he gained at the time about the complexities of modern history and international affairs was likely to remain very sketchy and highly tendentious, because his main sources were drawn overwhelmingly from the publications of very conservative *ulema* who tended greatly to exaggerate their own role and both to belittle and misrepresent the ideas and actions of other, far more important and powerful forces. It is generally recognized that key leaders of the Khilafat Movement, such as the Ali Brothers and Azad, were utterly dumbfounded by the fact that the Turks could themselves abolish the Osmanli Caliphate and dynastic rule,[37] and the movement, entirely unprepared for this denouement, petered out in confusion. One wonders why they were so unprepared for the emergence of a *Europeanized* republic in the event of any part of Turkey regaining sovereignty after the First World War. Why, in other words, had they staked the passions of Indian Muslims on the fate of a moribund institution, namely the Osmanli Caliphate, which had been exceedingly unpopular with the great majority of its Turkish and Arab subjects since its revival by Hamidian despotism in the 1870s? Since the question of Azad's actual understanding of the politics and predominant political currents in Egypt and West Asia is directly connected with the broader, more crucial question of both the ideological foundations as well as the nature of the collapse of the Khilafat Movement, it might be useful to introduce two substantial digressions to address this question and, in the process, to address also the extremely complex matter of the shifting relations between Azad's thought and that of Sir Syed.

V

The main reality of Turkey that was overlooked in the Khilafat Movement was that, well before the Meiji Revolution in Japan though much less thoroughly than in Japan, Turkey had had, of all the Asian countries, the most far-reaching movement of bourgeois reform of state and economy, collectively known as *Tanzimat*, starting with the abolition of *timars* (military fief, and the material basis of Osmanli feudalism) in 1831, and going through first a radical phase under Mahmoud II until 1839 and then a less radical one which also lasted until after 1861, when Sultan Abdel Majid died.[38] Given that the bulk of the Balkan subjects of the empire were non-Muslim, as was the mercantile bourgeoisie of Armenian Christians and Turkish Jews which dominated the modern sector, the essential thrust of this reform movement was towards secular governance; this thrust was made all the sharper by the cultural Europeanization of the leading figures of the movement. Thus, for example, the separation between the *sharia* courts, with very limited jurisdiction, and the general civil and criminal courts, with paramount jurisdiction, had been affected in the Osmanli realms in the very first decade after the break-up of the Jan-nissar Force, greatly diminishing the special powers of the *mevleviat* (the religious orders), in 1826. The Caliphate, which was revived after the retreat of *Tanzimat* and was then enshrined in the Osmanli Constitution of 1876 ('His Majesty the Sultan is, in his capacity of Supreme Caliph, the protector of the Muslim religion'), and which was to become such a large issue in Indian Islam half a century later, had actually signalled a defeat of the reform movement by Sultan Abdel Hamid who started by abolishing the Parliament. This unpopular Sultan had raised the slogan of 'Islamic Caliphate', in other words, to gain support in more traditional circles, mainly in the provinces of the Osmanli Empire which had already been lost to Tsarist Russia. Inside Turkey, it was largely an unpopular slogan both because it was raised by an unpopular autocrat and because the idea of a theocratic institution ran counter to the main trajectory of the *Tanzimat*, which had taken deep roots over a span of roughly forty years, among military officers as much as civil servants, the aristocracy, and the vast majority of the urban Third Estate, even though some intellectuals like Jevdet Pasha kept advocating a mildly Islamic caste to the legal structure in order to keep a link between the old and the new.

Meanwhile, there were two other kinds of nationalism which were far more popular than the royalist Pan-Islamic nationalism. There was, first, 'Osmanli nationalism', which referred not to the dynasty but to the territory of the empire as a whole, was secular in its outlook, and sought to include all the subjects of the Osmanli Empire as it was then constituted, irrespective of religion or linguistic background. This was espoused by a great many intellectuals as well as by the main political formation arising out of the defeat of the *Tanzimat* in the 1860s, namely the Committee for Union and Progress (CUP) among whose members the so-called 'Young Turks' were a tendency. (The phrase 'Young Turks' was of French coinage, taken over by the British, and used pejoratively by them just as the word 'Wahhabi' was used to designate all kinds of Muslim anti-colonialism.) The other was 'Turkic national-ism', which envisaged a state of Turkish-speaking people and was expounded by such personages as the sociologist Ziya Gokalap and the military leader Enver Pasha; this too was stridently secular, but it was willing to give up the non-Turkic Balkan subjects if it could regain the Turkish-speaking provinces annexed by Tsarist Russia. It was, in other words, willing to cut a deal with the Franco-British axis against Russia to let go of the Balkan provinces if it could reclaim the Tsarist annexations; pressed from both sides, though, it found itself allied with Germany. Mustafa Kemal, who eventually took power in 1919 and established the secular Republic in 1923, was a close associate of Enver Pasha and belonged to this tendency; hence the name he then took in the 1930s, Ataturk, Father of the Turks.

Meanwhile, there were burgeoning movements of Arab self-determi-nation against the Osmanli imperium, which were doubtless exploited by European colonialism but had histories of their own. Both Syria (which included Palestine and Lebanon at the time, and was part of the Osmanli realms) and Egypt (which was no longer in those realms, except in name only) had had their own reform movements. The most advanced expression of those ideological developments had come in the shape of the Egyptian *Nahda* (Resurgence) of the 1880s, sweeping the Third Estate, especially the new professional petty bourgeoisie, even more than the bazaar, though not the traditional *ulema*, who all had their social roots in the only serious effort at industrialization under-taken anywhere in Asia and Africa during the early years of the nineteenth century, in Mohammed Ali's Egypt which had seen itself as a rival of the Osmanli dynasty and as both a reforming force and a natural leader in the whole of the Arab region. Thanks to realities of this kind, there was little enthusiasm for the Osmanli religious claims in the Arab world as well. Even Rashid Rida,[39] from whom Azad took so many of his ideas, was secretly in sympathetic touch with the British-sponsored Sherif of Mecca against the Osmanlis.[40]

Azad says that he met some 'Young Turks' in Egypt in 1908 and then made friends with some of their 'leaders' when he visited Turkey later that year; he says he corresponded with those 'leaders' for some years subsequently. Now, 1908 was the year of CUP's decisive coup against Abdel Hamid, the monarch who had made the largest claims for 'Caliphate' in the past and who was now deposed and exiled to Salonika; it was this coup which first brought the term 'Young Turks' into wide currency, referring to their swift use of military force. There was an attempted Islamicist uprising against the CUP, very large and very brutal in the provincial town of Iderne, but not so effective elsewhere. Mustafa Kemal, who was to abolish the Caliphate in 1924, was, in 1908, the Chief of Staff in Shafqat Pasha's army, second only to Enver Pasha, when it marched into Istanbul and suppressed the pro-Hamidian agitation. Was Azad still in Egypt or was he already in Turkey, perhaps in the Istanbul of Kemal's troops and gunfire? His bland statements in *India Wins Freedom* refer to nothing that was actually happening in Turkey. His father died in August, and Azad says that he had already visited Turkey and had arrived in Paris when he heard of his father's illness; he returned to Calcutta before his father died. Was he in Turkey in, say, April? That was when Kemal had opened fire on the Islamicist opposition! Had Azad been anywhere near Turkey at the time he would have known that the Caliphate was finished, that the new rulers were modern and Europeanized, holding the new monarch a prisoner in his palace. The subsequent Balkan War, which launched Azad on his Khilafatist career, led to the iron rule of the troika of Generals – Enver, Talat, and Jemal Pashas, none of them notably religious – which guaranteed CUP dominance through all the war years, until the final defeat in 1918; Kemal rose from strength to strength, thanks to his victories first against the British at Gallipoli and then in resistance against the combined invasion. By the time a campaign for the restoration of the Caliphate was fully launched in India, with Azad declaring it as an act of *sharia* and divine injunction, the fate of the institution inside Turkey had been sealed by the defeat itself as well as by the deliberations of the military officers who used the Sultan's name only because his writ still ran in the mosques and because the defeat in the war had made it impossible properly to install a successor. Throughout the *Al-Hilal* decade, Azad never penned an analysis of CUP, the burgeoning Kemalism, the power structure that actually obtained in Turkey; instead, he offered a highly embellished picture of a beleaguered Turkey, fervent in its religious faith, united behind its Caliph, waging war against the infidels on behalf of the whole Islamic world.

Why such a gap between the facts as they actually were in Turkey and the representation of those facts by Azad over roughly a decade? Was it ignorance of facts, or studied suppression of facts? One possible explanation of course is that Azad *knew* the facts, kept hoping that the small Islamicist tendency inside Turkey would prevail against the predominant structure of power, methodically avoided writing the truth about the overwhelmingly Europeanist thrust of the Turkish establishment, and presented it in a religious light instead, in order to mobilize the Indian Muslims on the issue of religion and unite them under the leadership of the *ulema* headed by himself as *Imam-al-Hind*, not so much to help change things in West Asia as to combat the secularist tendencies in Muslim Indian politics, which he associated with the 'Aligarh' tendency and with men like Jinnah certainly, but also with far more powerful figures like Mohammed Ali, editor of the competing journals, *Comrade* and *Hamdard*, who had not been until the Allied invasion of Turkey particularly religious. It is likely that something of this kind was going on in Azad's mind at the time, though not in so stark and Machiavellian a way, since any one-sided emphasis on such a scheme presumes, at the very least, that Azad did really understand the facts correctly and that his own Pan-Islamicist passions and rhetorical turn of mind did not fundamentally distort his understanding of the facts. It is equally likely that his knowledge of the facts of West Asian and Egyptian affairs was in reality very sketchy and that he was prone to misinterpret even what little he knew because of his prior disposition to see everything in Pan-Islamicist terms and in accordance with the highly tendentious materials which he had been receiving in the mail from such groupings in the Arab world, mainly Cairo.

Certain kinds of Pan-Islamicist thinking took a hold on sections of the Muslim intelligentsia in the first quarter of this century. Throughout the *Al-Hilal* decade Azad had preached a Pan-Islamicist anti-colonialism as an antidote to the pro-colonial royalism of Syed Ahmed Khan and the 'Aligarh tendency' generally. This attack on Sir Syed from a Pan-Islamicist, pro-Khilafatist position had first surfaced at the time of Jamaladdin's initial impact in India, and subsequent accounts of the period have usually reduced the terms of that multifaceted confrontation to the single issue of 'loyalism', hence setting up the debate in such a way that Pan-Islamism is shown to be both anti-colonial and anti-communalist while the whole complex issue of what Sir Syed actually represented is dissolved into the charge of capitulationism.[41] This simplification is what we should like to examine in relation to Azad whose career in *Lisan-al-Sidq* started as a disciple of Sir Syed, who then repudiated and virulently attacked his erstwhile intellectual mentor during the *Al-Hilal* decade when he adopted a Pan-Islamism of the Jamaladdin kind, only more obscurantist, and whose positions after the *Tarjuman* came to resemble very many of Sir Syed's positions, as we shall argue below. In view of this extremely complex triangular relation between Jamaladdin, Sir Syed, and Azad, it is best to clarify the exact nature of the many differences between Jamaladdin and Syed Ahmed and the way they came to be played out in Azad's own life at different junctures.

VI

Like Azad himself, Jamaladdin was also a man about whose origins and early development we know little, because, in each case, the protagonist has either remained silent or provided contradictory information. It is by now fairly assumed in the relevant scholarship that his claim of being by birth an Afghani was false. He probably assumed this identity to pass himself off as a Sunni among Sunnis, given the fact that he spent most of his time among the Sunnis of India, Egypt, Turkey. Inside Iran where he had some unfortunate encounters with the Crown, his presumed Sunni and Afghani identity protected him from being treated as a subject of that Crown. He is now presumed to have been born in Asadabad, an Irani provincial town, in a Shia family. There are also strong suggestions that in his youth he secretly joined the Babi tendency, which eventually flowered into the Bahais, first treated as a dissident sect within Islam and then as non-Muslims, something like the Ahmedis in Pakistan. Like Azad, he too was accused, in his day and for decades thereafter, of having adopted the traditional Islamic personality as a 'pose'. That is doubtful, in both cases, and the most that can be said about Jamaladdin on this score is that he was surely a maverick and was given to radically altering his stance from one situation to another, confusing his orthodox critics, precisely because he believed not in an inflexibly orthodox version of Islam but in an instrumental use of religion in the cause of national defence. As he altered his personality from one place to another, so he also altered his versions of Islam from one context to another. This he regarded not as opportunism or lack of scruple but as a necessary subterfuge in furthering his cause, indeed as a higher duty in promoting Pan-Islamism. That there was a core of religious belief, however flexibly articulated, thus seems beyond doubt. The other charge against him is more grave and somewhat less easily refutable, namely that he was *always* an agent of the Turkish Sultan, the conservative Abdel Hamid, who had revived the forgotten claims of the Caliphate in order, precisely, to win support of the Muslim masses in the British domains and to use that support as a pressure on Britain to obtain concessions in the European theatres of war and trade. It is said that Jamaladdin was despatched by the Sultan to the various countries either ruled by Britain or with substantial British interests (India, Egypt, Iran, Afghanistan) to incite the Muslim populations against the British and to propagate the idea of the Osmanli Caliphate among people who

had not taken the idea very seriously for some generations. The suggestion was first made by British intelligence, which renders it suspect; but
Jamaladdin did attach himself openly and permanently to the Sultan's
court in the last years of his life, and the evident fact that this man, with
no visible source of funds, would so regularly appear in greatly divergent
places at critical junctures, always pressing the issue of religious loyalty
to the Turkish Sultan, does seem curious.

When Jamaladdin came to India, he attacked Syed Ahmed Khan not
on two issues but five: the latter's subservience to the British; the issue
of multi-religious unity against the British; Syed Ahmed's departures
from orthodox *sharia*; the issue of materialist philosophy; and the issue
of modern education. Contemporary historiography, submitting itself
to Pan-Islamicist positions, recalls only the first two issues but elides
the last three, in which the real complexity of Sir Syed lies and on which
Jamaladdin's thought was at best vacuous and often obscurantist.

On the issue of Syed Ahmed's pro-British stance, this historiography
is absolutely right, although we need to keep two other factors in mind
as well. The first is that Jamaladdin's own penchant for the most
retrograde Muslim rulers *because* they were Muslim after all, also
deserves some scrutiny. Second, the question of 'loyalism' is itself
complex, in the sense that, without in any way defending Sir Syed's
mendicancy with respect to the British, it is worth remarking that
such mendicancy was fairly characteristic of most nineteenth-century
reform movements, including much of the so-called Bengal Renaissance
– not to speak of Gandhi himself who had a long career of such
'loyalism' until many years after Sir Syed's death. Thus, summing up his
own attitude on the eve of the Boer War, Gandhi had declared: 'My
loyalty to the British rule drove me to participation with the British in
that war. I felt that, if I demanded rights as a British citizen, it was also
my duty, as such, to participate in the defence of the British Empire.'[42]
Even as late as the First World War, Gandhi was not only recruiting
soldiers for the British army but also writing to the Viceroy: 'I love the
English nation, and I wish to evoke in every Indian the loyalty of
Englishmen.'[43]

In context, then, the issue of Sir Syed's 'loyalism' is somewhat
complex. In brief, the loyalism and wholesale abjection in the face of
the colonialist forms of British thought which we find in Sir Syed, who
represented the most advanced sectors of the Muslim zamindars of Uttar
Pradesh in the latter half of the nineteenth century, was neither greater
nor structurally different from identical attitudes on the part of analogous representatives of the Bengal Hindu zamindars and Company
gumashtas at a comparable level of class development in the first half of
the century. Sir Syed's loyalism stands out sharply because (1) it came
after 1857; (2) we tend to compare it with the different kinds of

development among the professional and commercial strata in those other parts of the country which had had longer periods of gestation within colonial society; and (3) this modernist loyalism was contradicted, among sections of UP Muslims, by the anti-British activities of the segment of the *ulema* tracing their ideological lineage from Syed Ahmed Barelvi, a group of whom had founded the Dar-al-Ulum at Deoband in 1876, barely a year before Sir Syed founded his Muhammedan Anglo-Oriental College at Aligarh. The paradox of this last comparison of course is that while Sir Syed's political position on the colonial question was doubtless retrograde in comparison with that of the Deoband *ulema*, it is equally beyond doubt that his social and educational philosophy, and even his theological position, was comparatively far more advanced. On the issue of law, for example, Syed Ahmed's ideas were identically those of the Turkish *Tanzimat* and the Central Asian *Jadidya* of Shihabaddin Marjani, all of which he had studied fairly closely: a vastly narrowed *sharia* for strictly religious affairs, and a much wider and more powerful domain of *qanoon* (civil and criminal law), both secular in inspiration and dynamic in development, for the governance of society as such.

Sir Syed shared with Ghalib – and before Ghalib, Rammohun and others – a certain fascination with positivist rationalism, utilitarian social thought, and technological scientificity, which he associated, like them, with 'Western civilization'. Like Rammohun, he took this positivist and utilitarian world-view into a revisionist rereading of religious ideology and tried to combine this, exactly as Rammohun had done some fifty years earlier, with what he knew of Arab–Islamic premodern rationalism on the one hand, Christian Unitarianism on the other. Rammohun knew much more about Unitarianism and commanded the additional ingredient of Vedantic philosophies as well; Sir Syed's knowledge of medieval Muslim rationalism was far more extensive and he was not willing to go nearly as far as Rammohun, but some of the basic elements in the blend were the same. Nothing remotely resembling Brahmo Sarmaj came out of Sir Syed's revisionist project, which remained within the traditions first established by the Mautazila, but he did establish a new trend in Islamic exegetical learning which has given to it an ecumenism and a modernist liberality in sharp contrast to the pietistic tradition of Shah Waliullah, which Sir Syed partly accepted but largely overturned. The breadth of this ecumenism can be gauged from the following, for example:

> God sent his prophets for their moral improvements. It is absurd to believe that the prophets appeared only in Arabia and Palestine to reform a handful of Arabs and Jews, and that God condemned the peoples of Africa, America, and Asia to ignorance . . . it was immaterial

whether the prophet was from China, America, Mongolia, Africa, India, or Iran, or if he preached God's message to the savage or the civilized.[44]

There is nothing in the tradition of Shah Waliullah which would authorize a statement of this kind, nor does Azad's later and overly famous doctrine of *Wahdat-e-Adyan* go notably beyond this formulation, which specifically denies the primacy of Islam or Christianity over other religious traditions. We might add that it was this kind of heterodoxy, combined with Sir Syed's burgeoning affinity with modern secular thought, which drew Jamaladdin's special ire, so that the diatribe he penned against Sir Syed, *Refutation of the Materialists*, which is in the Arab world the most widely known of all Jamaladdin's writings, is focused not on the issue of 'loyalism' but on the issue of heterodoxy, secularism, and modern rationality, namely issues on which Jamaladdin expounds with breathtaking obscurantism. Even on the issue of 'loyalism', in fact, Jamaladdin's denunciations are related not only to the specific issue of British colonialism but to the much larger issue of Sir Syed's modernist assertion that Muslims could live very well under the rule of non-Muslims provided that freedom of worship and rights of property were guaranteed. Part of Sir Syed's hostility towards the Osmanli Khilafat, which Jamaladdin unreservedly supported, was caused by his loyalism towards the British; but part of it was rooted in Sir Syed's own ideas about the religiously composite territorial nation in India, as we shall see below, as well as his hostility towards Hamidian despotism in Turkey as an autocracy. In this latter emphasis, Sir Syed was much closer to the bourgeois liberalism of the *Tanzimat*, which Hamidian despotism had overturned, as well as to the spirit of the later 'Young Turks' – from CUP to Kemalism – with which Azad was to claim affiliation but which he seems to have misunderstood.

Azad's own relationship with (1) Sir Syed's *thought* and (2) with the Aligarh tradition as such, needs to be periodized as well as disaggregated. As a young boy, launched on his own career with *Lisan-al-Sidq*, Azad had modelled himself on the traditions and thoughts of Sir Syed as he found them in the *writings* of the latter. His views seem to have started to change when he came closer to Maulana Shibli. It is well to remember that Shibli had himself been associated with Aligarh, but, driven by a view of Islam much narrower than that of Sir Syed, he had left Aligarh in protest not just against its colonialist moorings but also its predominant emphasis on modern education, because what Shibli truly wanted was not a university, in the modern sense, but a *Dar-al-Ulum*, in the seminarian sense, where some rudimentary training in modern subjects may be undertaken but where the emphasis would remain on the training of a religious intelligentsia, which is more or less what he subsequently tried at Nadva. A far more strident version of this very attitude appears in Azad's writings of the *Al-Hilal* decade, after he had imbibed the most conservative aspects of Jamaladdin's ideas through the writings of Rashid Rida who had produced a far more systematic knowledge of Islamic *sharia* than anything that Jamaladdin had ever been capable of; and had pitched himself directly in opposition to the Sir Syed-like reforms of Mohammed Abduh. Alongside his justified denunciation of Aligarh for its loyalism, there also runs, in Azad's writings of this period, an exaggerated invective stream which portrays the university at Aligarh as a hotbed of *Ilhad* (atheism).[45] In reality, the general balance of the social milieu in Aligarh at the time was character-ized, rather, by a peculiar blend of a very colonial kind of limited Anglicism, on the one hand, and on the other, extreme social conserva-tism characteristic of the more provincial sections of the Muslim landed gentry and the emergent professional petty bourgeoisie, while the grand *taluqdars* hardly ever sent their sons there. Few, if any, actually *lost* their religion at Aligarh, and Sir Syed himself had been so much on the defensive on the question of Islamic conservatism that his own theology had not been taught during his own lifetime in the very college that he had founded, with religious instruction remaining firmly in the hands of very conservative *ulema*. By the time Azad came to write about Aligarh, that situation had changed substantially but not fundamentally. That is why there had not been, in the history of Aligarh College up to that time, any analogue even for the kind of minoritarian but in its own way highly influential role that, for example, the Derozians and 'Young Bengal' generally had played in the history of the Hindu College in Calcutta at a comparable stage of institutional development. That Azad would so often castigate Aligarh for *Ilhad* throughout the *Al-Hilal* period tells us less about Aligarh, and more about his own cast of mind at that time.

The other issue, namely that of Hindu–Muslim unity, is even more complex. Sir Syed undoubtedly is much to be faulted, but the modern casting of him as a pure Muslim communalist is something on which Pakistani historiography and the Hindu communalist historiography in India are much too readily agreed, producing as evidence Sir Syed's conspicuously strident opposition to Muslim participation in the Con-gress, especially after 1887. What is said about his stridency is doubtless true, but it too needs to be seen in perspective. There is considerable evidence to suggest that in large areas of his social work and in his educational activities, in Ghaziabad for example, he made little distinc-tion between Hindu and Muslim; a large number of Hindus, in turn, made contributions to the construction fund of the Muhammedan Anglo-Oriental College at Aligarh. He had in fact held between 1857 and 1884 a view of Indian nationhood very much like the one that

Azad was to uphold in his maturer years. Thus in 1884, on the eve of the establishment of the Congress, he was to say in his famous reply to the Address presented to him by the Indian Association of Lahore:

By the word *qawm*, I mean both Hindus and Muslims. That is the way I define the word nation (*qawm*). In my opinion, it matters not whatever be their religious belief, because we cannot see anything of it, but what we can see is that all of us, whether Hindus or Muslims, live on the same soil ... I designate both the nationalities that inhabit India by the term 'Hindu' – that is, the nation (*qawm*) which lives in India.

There are numerous such statements scattered through Sir Syed's writing, so that it is very difficult to think of him as a communalist, in the contemporary sense. Two other things, though, can be said with fair certainty. One is that as a representative of the Muslim propertied classes, it was the sectoral interest of those classes that he was the most obsessed with; in this too he was not very different from most nineteenth-century reformers, who were as a rule concerned mainly with the interests of the class and community to which they belonged. 'Communalism' in that sense was a widespread phenomenon, among Hindus and Muslims alike. Second, he was certainly blindly opposed to the Congress, silently for the first three years after its inception in 1885, more and more stridently thereafter. Reasons for that are complex too, and we need not go into them here, but it is worth remarking that in the two decades prior to the founding of the Congress, Hindu nationalist and revivalist tendencies had grown in many circles, especially among the Bengali *bhadralok* and including groupings which were to be active in the Congress.[46]

Specifically, the *combination* of empathizing with British colonial rule as a desirable civilizational project, on the one hand and, on the other, the casting of the Muslim as the true oppressor of the Hindu 'nation' was more common in late nineteenth-century Bengal than is generally conceded. In a sense, then, the combination of pro-British loyalism and devotion to Muslim particularity that we find in Sir Syed was a mirror image of a number of positions that were both fashionable and powerful in a great many 'Hindu' formations – and not only 'Hindu' either; as Sumit Sarkar points out, even groupings within Brahmo held similar views. These coordinates of the historical situation do not excuse Sir Syed's own role, but they do help us understand why the man who wanted to use the word 'Hindu' for the whole of the Indian nation, and one who had refused to grant, on the issue of the Osmanli Khilafat, that Indian Muslims owed any extra-territorial loyalty to anyone outside

India, could himself start taking outright sectarian positions. It is also worth remarking that the question whether the Congress was truly secular and whether, therefore, it could really represent the 'Muslims' – i.e. the Muslim gentry who had a stranglehold on much of the Muslim population – was to remain the perennial question of the National Movement throughout its history, culminating in the tensions that erupted when the Congress first formed ministries in the Muslim minority provinces during 1936–37 and in the subsequent political crises leading up to the Partition. Sir Syed's irreconcilably hostile attitude after 1887 was certainly unjustified, but the question he was raising was a real one.

In Egypt, where Jamaladdin had the widest influence, his followers were split in two camps. After some years of close association with him on all issues, Mohammed Abduh, Jamaladdin's closest associate, renounced his Pan-Islamicist radicalism, adopted a pro-British stance analogous to Sir Syed's loyalism, got himself appointed the Grand Mufti under Cromer, launched various 'reforms' within the colonial predicates, most notably at Al-Azhar, preparing the ground for far-reaching revisions in the existing patterns of Islamic juridical discourse and legal practice, along the lines already made familiar in Turkey through reforms of the *Tanzimat* and not unlike the Civil and Penal Codes that the British were instituting in India. Rashid Rida, who had not known Afghani but had been initially very close to Abduh, repudiated the trajectory, distanced himself from his erstwhile guide, and while Abduh concentrated on modernizing institutional reforms at Al-Azhar and in the legal codes and judicial procedures of governmental courts, Rida took over the journal *Al-Manar* ('The Minarate' or even 'The Light-house'), which had until then been a magazine of liberal opinion, and gave it an increasingly conservative, even revivalist orientation. Similarly, he captured leadership of the movement that Abduh had initiated, known as Al-Salaffiya (after the Arabic term, *Aslaf*, meaning 'ancestors' but in this context referring specifically to the Companions of Prophet Muhammed as the true 'ancestors'), and gave to it an equally revivalist tone. In the process, he drew much closer to the more conservative of Jamaladdin's ideas but, unlike the master who had produced very fragmentary and mostly polemical writings, Rida settled down to produce a vast body of writings for systematic exposition of these revivalist, and at times Pan-Islamicist, ideas. Between the dissemination of the journal, the organizational structure of the Al-Salaffiya, and the authoritative religious writings addressed to the scholars and the more literate among the Faithful, Rida came to have an influence qualitatively very different but in scope at least equal to that of Abduh. Out of his revivalist circle arose Hasan al-Banna, the founder of the Ikhwan-ul

Muslimun (Muslim Brotherhood) which then spawned a whole host of fundamentalist movements in the Arab world over the greater part of this century. In India, it was principally through Azad's writings of the *Al-Hilal* period that Rida was to exercise an indirect influence. By the 1970s, the Ikhwan were to exercise much more direct influence over the Jama'at-e-Islami, doubtless more in Pakistan than in India. What is remarkable about Azad's writings of the *Al-Hilal* period is that he seems greatly to exaggerate the importance of the Pan-Islamicist Movement in the very countries, in West Asia and Egypt, with which he was then the most concerned. Rida represented in his time a relatively small tendency. In the Egyptian Revolution of 1919, which erupted as Azad was coming out of Ranchi internment and about which he had nothing knowledgeable to say, Rida's group, not even organized as a political force, played no part; the revolution was led by the entirely secular Wafd and made by the urban masses under the leadership of the secular elements in the Third Estate. Under the circumstances, Egypt could no more have a Khilafat Movement than did the Turkey of CUP and Mustafa Kemal. It is unfortunate that Azad did not at the time understand that. Had he and other leaders of the Khilafat Movement in India understood the full complexity of the situation as it in fact prevailed in Egypt and West Asia, they might have been able to channel more productively the enormous passions they had aroused, and they might also have salvaged out of the collapse of the movement somewhat more than they actually did.

In context, then, we may justifiably dislike Sir Syed's colonialist loyalism but we cannot so easily dismiss his warnings regarding the Osmanli Caliphate, that Indian Muslims should not be asked to have extra-territorial loyalties towards an Islamic imperium located elsewhere (Azad's famous 'political centre' of the Islamic world in Constantinople). Likewise, we may equally justifiably castigate Jinnah, at a later point in history, for his constitutionalist distance from the Non-Cooperation Movement, but we cannot so easily dismiss his emphatic warning that the Caliphate was an 'exploded bogey' and that a mass movement which aroused such passions on so ambiguous an issue would inevitably disintegrate into mass disaffection and directionless despondency. For the paradox of the Khilafat Movement turned out to be that while it was the first time that large masses of Indian Muslims were mobilized into the anti-colonial movement, it eventually petered out in such disarray that little could be retrieved out of that wreckage to stem the tide of Hindu–Muslim communal conflagrations which came close on the heels of the Hindu–Muslim unity of the Non-Cooperation/Khilafat days. The decade of the 1920s began in euphoria but ended in chaos – worse than chaos, because communal strife at the mass base was matched by an impasse in elite politics so profound that by 1928, when the Nehru Report failed to resolve the differences, Jinnah reportedly wept and declared, prophetically as it turned out, that the failure marked the final 'parting of the ways'.[47]

VII

Azad is a difficult person to write about. Unlike Gandhi, for example, who had an obsessive penchant for constant public confession, much of Azad's life, especially up to the late 1920s, is shrouded in large silences, even mystery and misdirection. One has the impression of a life formidable in historical stature and social consequence but also one that remained very largely sketchy and unformed. The difficulty, perhaps, is that Azad did undertake a very great deal but most of what he undertook he had the habit of leaving unfinished.

There are four texts that could reasonably give us an autobiography, but we are not sure about even the authorship of large parts of this work and, together, they give us no consistent or reliable portrait for any phase of his life except roughly the last decade before the Partition. The imminent publication of a great work of theology was announced in 1915 but the project remained unrealized for the next forty years or more, and the *Tarjuman*, which was published, covers only half of the Quran, with the *Tafseer*, incorporated into the translation, remaining at best fragmentary. It is said that he joined the revolutionary underground in Bengal, but the evidence is so indirect and sketchy that it is reasonable to doubt the extent of his actual involvement; his scheme for a *Dar-al-Irshad*, a centre where volunteers could be trained simultaneously in Islamic piety and anti-colonial militancy, remained, like so many of Azad's plans, mostly a dream. In a great many circles his reputation rests upon the writings of the *Al-Hilal* decade, but roughly the last two decades of his own life are, in effect, a repudiation of the theological premise, the Pan-Islamicist political thrust, even the prose style of that famous decade. He spent that decade defending the cause of Turkey and mobilizing immense resources of Indian energies in the service of that cause, but his own writings would be the last place that one would go to if one wanted to know something about the Turkey of that time. The fame of his literary genius is enormous, but as we look for the achievement we have only *Ghubar-e-Khatir* and, much less, *Karavan-e-Khyal*, two collections of epistles; *Tazkira* is not only largely unreadable but its doggedly medievalist method stands also in direct opposition to the tradition of modern Urdu prose, from Ghalib to Premchand and far beyond, which has sought to give to the spoken vernacular the status of true literature. Azad was India's first Education Minister and held that post for over a decade, but he has left behind neither a personal influence on the actual system of education in India nor any work on educational philosophy; we know what Nehru's foreign or economic policies were, but we know nothing very clearly about Azad's education policy, beyond of course some superbly written Addresses which provide us with general statements of decent desire. He was a famous scholar of Islam, a powerful political leader, doubtless deeply concerned about Indian Muslims, but he never built an institution, a school of thought, a political movement, or a group of scholars that would carry on his kind of work in that arena. His great erudition is of course unquestionable, but the evidence of his writing does not suggest that this erudition included, in even vaguely systematic way, anything other than the very traditional knowledges that were available in Arabic, Farsi, Urdu. About the world beyond India and the Islamic Middle East, his knowledge was sketchy, and even in his preferred domains of theology and poetry – especially in poetry – he paid scant attention to twentieth-century achievements.

We have written at length about Azad's swift turns through much of his life up to the Ramgarh Address as well as of his shifting relationship with Sir Syed's ideas. This matter might bear some concluding remarks. For Sir Syed died in 1898 and Azad published his first *ghazal* in a major journal the next year. One career ended, in other words, as the other was poised to begin. It is unclear from Azad's own accounts just when he started reading Sir Syed's work; the Malihabadi text says that he came across it while the older man was still alive, but *India Wins Freedom* gives a considerably later date. We know, in any case, that Azad knew that work exceedingly well by the time he established *Lisan-al-Sidq*, which was modelled in some ways on Sir Syed's famous journal, *Tahzeeb-al-Akhlaq*. We also know that he began to depart from those positions very soon thereafter and the founding of *Al-Hilal*, in 1912, involved a full repudiation of all of Sir Syed's positions. We have suggested also that the doctrine of *Wahdat-e-Adyan* which Azad expounded in the 1930s was in some ways a return to the kind of ecumenism we find in some of Sir Syed's revisionist theology; also that the fully secular basis for Indian nationhood which Azad finally adopted in the Ramgarh Address in 1940, implicitly repudiating the search for a religious definition, was not much more advanced than the positions that Sir Syed had often held up to 1884. And, we have also suggested that the marked change in prose style that we find from *Tazkira*, the purported masterpiece of the *Al-Hilal* decade, to the post-Ramgarh collection of *Ghubar-e-Khatir*, amounts, in sum, to a return to the main tradition of Urdu prose as it had been fashioned in the nineteenth century principally by Ghalib and Sir Syed. What we find, in other words, is an intellectual career which, in its formation, begins where Sir Syed had already arrived by 1880 or so, and which returns in its mature years, after a very long detour of thirty years or more, to positions that Sir Syed had already occupied; it was only on the issue of 'loyalism' that Azad's intellectual career was, in relation to Sir Syed, from beginning to end a real advance.

But that breakthrough Azad had achieved already by 1906, thanks to the shifts that had taken place in the political climate of the country. Had he combined that breakthrough with a commitment to modern and secular ideas, he might have been able to make the break into popular idioms of resistance that Sir Syed never could, because of the colonialist allegiance and elite location. Instead, Azad started following the chimeras of Pan-Islamism and orthodox theological eminence, devising for himself in the process a personality that was remote from mass struggles and a cultural idiom which was not even intelligible to common people. It is indeed the case that the colonialist modernization which was led by men like Sir Syed in India and Mohammed Abduh in Egypt was far from adequate, but the Pan-Islamism that arose in opposition to that project proved to be even narrower and more disorientating. If Abduh ended as Cromer's Grand Mufti, Jamaladdin ended up as a courtier of Sultan Abdel Hamid. If the 'Aligarh tendency' gave rise eventually to an intelligentsia which became one of the backbones of Muslim separatism, Jamaladdin's brand of Pan-Islamism became narrowly revivalist under Rashid Rida, giving rise to the retrograde fundamentalisms of the Muslim Brotherhood in a dozen countries.

It is much to be regretted that when Azad recognized, as a young man, the limitations of Sir Syed's kind of modernization, he could find no means of transcending it in the direction of a better secularism, a genuinely popular and enlightened anti-colonialism, a programmatic mobilization of the poverty-stricken Muslim masses against the landed gentry and the commercial interests which eventually organized the politics of the Partition. Instead, he descended into hyperboles of revivalist fundamentalism and the dream of leading the Muslims of India as an *Imam-al-Hind*. From all that he was eventually rescued by the rise of Kemalism in Turkey itself and his increasing assimilation into the Indian National Movement. In the latter phase, we find him affiliated with the secularist position and uncompromising nationalism. But unlike Gandhi who mobilized scores of millions by combining anti-colonial nationalism with social and religious reform, and unlike Nehru who represented programmatic positions on a whole range of issues from diplomacy to land reform, Azad always remained a man of orations and conferences, unable to transcend elite forms of politics or to frame a mobilizing programme of social and religious reform among Muslims that might have detached them from separatist politics by linking anti-colonial sentiment and secularist political vision with demands of social and economic justice. Men like Abdul Ghaffar Khan who were able to do precisely that remained regional leaders, finally ineffectual in saving the Congress from communal politics on the all-India scale.

The sharpest contrast in any case is with Jinnah. Their social origins could not have been more different: Azad traced his lineage back to the master theologians of Delhi in the days of the Mughal court and to Mecca in more recent times; Jinnah was the son of a trading petty bourgeois, from the Gujarati-speaking Khoja minority among Muslims, and from the then-provincial town of Karachi. Jinnah's entire legitimacy as an intellectual came from Lincoln's Inn, Azad's from traditions of learning in Arabic, Farsi, Urdu. Azad knew little English, Jinnah knew little besides English. Law had been the vocation of each: English law for Jinnah, Islamic *fiqh* for Azad. When in the 1910s Azad was speaking of a universal Islamic nation (*qawm*) with its '*political* centre' in Constantinople, Jinnah was being called 'the ambassador of Hindu–Muslim unity'. When Azad was arousing passions on behalf of the Osmanli dynasty of Turkey as the last remaining bastion of Islam, Jinnah referred to that same Caliphate contemptuously, as 'an exploded bogey'. And, if Azad thought of the Khilafat Movement as a grand political awakening of the Indian Muslim masses, Jinnah thought of it as a wave of hysteria brought about by the dying social stratum of the Muslim theological elite and utilized by Gandhi – very cynically, Jinnah thought – to establish himself as the unchallengeable leader of India generally and in the Muslim constituency especially. They, Azad and Jinnah, had never seen eye to eye; that much was clear enough. But, as the 1920s progressed, their respective roles began reversing, in ways not at all predictable from their respective careers up to that point. As Azad shot to power and prominence in the central leadership of the Congress first in the Khilafat years and then again after 1936, he surely came to represent the Congress Muslims, first in the company of men like Ansari and then uniquely all by himself, as their unquestionable sole leader; but he was also a key leader of the National Movement as such, along with Patel and Nehru, behind Gandhi. Jinnah had never been in the centre of things to the same extent, nor did he recover his national stature after Khilafat; instead, he sulked on the sidelines for some years, in his London retreat for some more years, and then remodelled himself into the leader of the Muslim sectional interest.

He who never tired of referring to his birth in Mecca came to represent the non-denominational, composite, secular nationhood of all India; he who had cut his professional teeth in the law firms of Bombay and whose own cut of clothes matched those of Mountbatten came to declare, in a peculiar blend of communal sectarianism and European theories of cultural and linguistic nationalisms, that the religious difference between Hindus and Muslims constituted a *national* difference. It is one of the great paradoxes of modern Indian history that traditions of

Islamic piety, from Azad to the Deoband *ulema*, eventually found their way into a composite cultural and political nationalism; theories of modernization, as taught in British and proto-British institutions, from Lincoln's Inn to Aligarh, begat, on the other hand, communal separatism. This paradox deserves separate scrutiny. Suffice it to say here that what Jinnah understood was something crucial about what colonial capitalism had wrought in the Indian polity: that he could bypass the entire trajectory of bourgeois nationalism on the one hand, the Communist movement on the other, by appealing directly to the structurally weak Muslim segment of the Indian bourgeoisie and to the professional interests of the more ambitious sectors of the Muslim petty bourgeoisie, in tandem with British partisanship and patronage. If they could obtain a brand new state, that weak segment could become the new ruling class, and the educated middle class could staff the new civilian and military bureaucracies, becoming what Engels once called the 'governing caste'. This Jinnah's 'two-nation theory' promised them and eventually delivered to them in the shape of a Partition and the making of Pakistan. The vision of religious ecumenism and of a culturally composite India which Azad evolved in his maturer years had room neither for such class opportunism, nor for such a fundamental division of common ethos and common civilizational patrimony, nor for such collusion with British design. For that essential decency, despite his defeat, Azad shall be in posterity chiefly remembered.

In the Mirror of Urdu: Recompositions of Nation and Community, 1947–65

Independence and Partition were doubtless key watersheds in the chequered history of the Urdu language and its literature, in the sense that the thematics of this literature as well as the reading and writing communities were fragmented and recomposed drastically, in diverse ways.[1] But *when* did this, the 'First Decade', end? It is an integral part of the argument in this essay that the divisive forces unleashed in 1947 matured fully only by the early 1960s and that the next decisive event occurred in 1965, when the Indo-Pakistan War stabilized a different kind of literary map. The 'First Decade', therefore, will be extended to eighteen years. I shall be concerned mainly with India, but in so far as literary maps and linguistic communities are more flexibly structured than the rigid territorialities of nation-states, Pakistan must also be included.

I

The year 1957 was by no means insignificant. It witnessed the publication of N.M. Rashid's collection of poems *Iran mein Ajnabi* ('A Stranger in Iran'), and the last *ghazal* in *Zindan Nama* ('Prison Chronicle') of Faiz Ahmed Faiz was composed in March of that year. Since the founding of the Progressive Writers Association (PWA) in 1936, Urdu literature had been dominated by the Left, but it was opposed ideologically by the tendency that came to be known simply as 'modernity' (*jadidyat*).[2] Faiz and Rashid were, all would agree, the most important poets in these respective tendencies, and the two books are arguably their most representative works, respectively. The hegemonic power of the Progressive Movement had by then begun to decline quite perceptibly, and 'modernity' was already on the ascendant. This shift in ideological anchorage by 1957 was much clearer in Pakistan, where the state had played a direct role in suppressing the Left intelligentsia and had used the Rawalpindi Conspiracy Case to build an anti-communist consensus. The new wave of repressions that came after the *coup d'état* of 1958 then broke the Left entirely for some years to come. In India, the shift was more prolonged and the role of the state was far more ambiguous. Here too, however, the breakup of the writing community, in consequence of the Partition, was soon followed by the onset of the Cold War and the injection of American money in the field of literature, through such agencies as the Congress for Cultural Freedom, the United States Information Service, the Fulbright Exchange Program, etc. The new crop of Urdu 'modernists' during the 1950s took up the anti-communist vocation much more actively than had been the case previously. Thus, what became unmistakable after 1965 had actually begun even in India some ten years earlier.

Considering the First Decade after Independence, then, one may fruitfully examine these ideological tendencies. To leave it at that, however, is to leave unexamined the principal shaping force: the consequences of the Partition itself, which were certainly reflected in these shifts, but which far exceeded the boundaries of the progressive–modernity debate. One could think of other events. The death in Pakistan of Maulana Zafar Ali Khan (1965) and in India of Maulana Abul Kalam Azad (1958) signalled another sort of ending. Since the founding of *Zamindar* (Lahore) in 1910 and of *Al-Hilal* (Calcutta) in 1912 had brought to Urdu entirely new kinds of journalism, the passing away of their founders, and that of Hasrat Mohani, the maverick Maulana, in 1952, seemed the ending of an age. Urdu journalism was now to be dominated by allegiances of far narrower and vapid kinds.

The deaths of the older men, in quick succession, symbolized the passing away of a much older generation. But Saadat Hasan Manto, who died in 1955, was, at forty-two, a young man. Through the enormous range of Urdu fiction about the Partition, he was one of the most vivid chroniclers of the homicidal brutalities that accompanied the event. His stark naturalism, which he had learned less from Chekhov, more from Zola and Maupassant, but which he had then combined with a secular humanism, puts him squarely in the Left-Nehruvian ideological current, which then goes some way in explaining his ambivalences about both the 'progressives' and the 'modernists'. It is at least arguable that the Partition broke Manto's sturdy heart, and the ensuing sufferings then drove him first to drunkenness, then to death.

Having grown up in Amritsar, Manto had lived some of his youth in Lahore, but it was in Bombay that he had spent the happiest years of his life and found his intellectual community. After the Partition, family circumstances forced him to move back to Lahore, where he continued to think of himself as a refugee. The city of Lahore he loved and he might have adjusted well enough to it, but the Partition and all that went with it, including the new society it begat, Manto hated whole-heartedly, and portrayed it in his fiction with irrepressible anger. A number of his stories – 'Toba Tek Singh' and 'Khol Do', among others – are memorable documents of that anguish; and the book of his Partition sketches, *Siyah Hashye* ('Black Margins'), expresses that same combination of anger and liberal spirit, despite its propensity on occasion to become simply maudlin and sensationalist.[3] In his hatred of the Partition and of the self-satisfied triumphalism that was rampant in the new power structure in Pakistan he was by no means alone, but most such people had found a home in the culture of the Left. Manto, a Bohemian *par excellence*, had estranged himself from that culture through venomous polemic, and he had been paid back in like coin. On the Right, meanwhile, he was reviled for being 'pornographic' and 'anti-Pakistan', often by the very people who made a lot of money from publishing his work. This loneliness was inseparable from the circumstances of his death.

Aside from Bengal, the Partition had shown its most murderous face precisely in the regions where the great majority of the Urdu-writing intelligentsia lived: Punjab, United Provinces or Uttar Pradesh (UP), Bihar, Madhya Pradesh, Kashmir, Andhra, Delhi. Some of this intelligentsia had migrated to Bombay before Partition, and many were to move to Karachi in the aftermath. The immediate outcome was that the narrative literature (novels and short stories) which came immediately after Partition, was predominantly that of naturalistic documentation of the kind we find in Khushwant Singh's English-language novel *Train to Pakistan*. A reflective summation of what it all meant, in the form of metaphor and image, came earlier in lyric poetry. It took a more explicitly political form in the verse of poets associated with the Progressive Movement, as for example in the justly celebrated poem 'Subh-e-Aazadi' ('The Dawn of Freedom') by Faiz Ahmed Faiz, but even the textures of bereavement and nostalgia which pervaded the verse of younger poets like Nasir Kazmi was doubtless connected with that same sense of loss and dislocation. In fiction, however, there was an immense preoccupation with documenting the detail, as if what had disappeared needed now to be retrieved by transcription, and as if the act of writing itself may perhaps exorcize the ghostly memories of what had been seen far too vividly, suffered much too viscerally. Among the more successful of such writings were the two novels, Krishan Chander's *Ghaddar* ('Traitor') and Ramanand Sagar's *Aur Insan Mar Gaya* ('And the Human Perished'), both depicting the mass killings and gang rapes as well as the camps and the caravans of the refugees in and around Lahore in the summer of 1947. Rajinder Singh Bedi's magnificent short story, 'Lajvanti', may be cited here as perhaps

the most subtle but also the most heartbreaking tale of that remem-
brance, exorcism, expiation, the re-living of an irretrievable loss. Lajo,
the abducted and defiled woman, is returned to her husband, and the
two, without guilt or blame, only with love and sadness and grit and
mercy, try to rebuild their shattered lives, but they cannot, because
what has settled between them, irretrievably, is a silence, a mutual
inability to find a language in which the right questions may be asked,
the pain expressed and overcome. What breaks them in the aftermath
of what has happened is not any lack of sympathy for each other but
the plain finitude of human capacity in the face of a suffering that is
strictly incommunicable.

By the time Manto died in 1955, his kind of naturalistic documentation was beginning to ebb anyway. There had emerged two other major
themes more or less simultaneously, and these were to find increasingly
wider and more complex elaboration. The sense of exile and dislocation
which had accompanied Partition meant, inevitably, that the memory of
what had been left behind was itself to emerge as a major preoccupation
of the new narrative; not just the moment of rupture, but in far greater
detail the structure of that which had been ruptured. This new kind of
fiction that sought to narrate the pre-Partition society of north India,
characteristically in the realist mould but often with romantic overtones,
was preoccupied with a sense of *location* in particular communities and
of historical time before the *dislocation* and the attendant ethical collapse. But as the years passed and the new post-Independence society
began to take definite shape, the kind of society that had arisen out of
decolonization and Partition became a major theme. The short story
remained the principal genre of Urdu prose fiction, but this broadening
of the time frame – the larger processes of pre- and post-Partition social
configurations – led inevitably to certain generic shifts towards novels
and novellas. If Hayatullah Ansari's five-volume novel, *Lahoo ke Phool*
('Blood Blossoms'), tells of the Freedom Movement itself, along with
the decay of the old *jagirdari* system of land allotment, in the Indian
perspective, Shaukat Siddiqui's *Khuda ki Basti*[4] tells of slum-life and
profiteering in post-Partition Karachi. There were scores of such tales,
some good, many not so good. One must be mentioned, since it came
at the very end of that first decade and was not only hugely influential
but was also symptomatic of the general ambience in Urdu fictional
narratives at the time.

The central literary document of this decade in Urdu was undoubtedly Qurratul 'Ain Hayder's *Aag ka Darya* ('River of Fire'), completed
in December 1957 and published the next year in Pakistan, and the year
after that in India. As a novel, it does not quite hold together and is
good only in patches. Even if we were to overlook the overwrought
sentimentalities of the prose, the borrowings from a number of Orien-

talist texts, such as Basham's *The Wonder that was India* and Herman Hesse's *Siddhartha*, are much too obvious and undigested. It could also be shown fairly easily that the whole novel is, from start to finish, a very upper-class affair, at times insufferably so; her own novellas that followed soon thereafter – the superb *Sita Haran*, as well as *Housing Society* and *Chai ke Bagh* ('Tea Estates') – are undoubtedly superior. *Aag ka Darya* is a central document, nevertheless, both as a personal account of the author's sentiments, and in the larger ideological ensemble of Urdu literature as it existed between the Partition of 1947 and the Indo-Pakistani War of 1965.

Daughter of the famous nationalist intellectual and writer, Sajjad Hayder Yildrim,[5] Qurratul 'Ain had made a precocious debut in Urdu letters with short stories that were published in major literary journals while she was still an undergraduate. A collection, *Sitaron se Aage* ('Beyond the Stars'), appeared in 1947, the year she finished her M.A. in English. Her first novel, *Mere Bhi Sanam-Khane*, came two years later, with its nostalgic portrait of the milieu in which she had spent her student days in Lucknow. That milieu had been distinctly upper-class, and its ideas of a 'composite' Indian culture were derived largely from that world of *taluqdars* (the landholding aristocracy of eastern UP) and the upper echelons of the Indian Civil Service which Hindus and Muslims of that class relished with remarkable lack of mutual friction. In its politics, however, the setting was secular, cosmopolitan, left-of-centre, Nehruvian. Then, after a sojourn in England she found herself in Pakistan where *Aag ka Darya* was initially published, in the year of Ayub Khan's coup.

We may not in retrospect think of it as a very good novel but it was surely a *tour de force*. For it plots the stories of three main characters – Champa, Gautam Neelambar, Hari Shankar – from Buddhist times up to the novel's own present, in the 1950s. Other major characters are introduced with the passage of time: Kemal in various incarnations since the Sultanate period, Cyril with the East India Company, and so on. Chronology in the earliest pages is opaque, but Gautam does begin as a brahmin youth, an artist, and a scholar of *Natyashastra* on the eve of Chandragupta's expansionist expeditions, and his many incarnations include that of a Company *gumashta* (agent) in Lucknow during the nineteenth century; by the end of the novel, he has become an ambitious member of the post-Independence Indian Foreign Service, attached to Krishna Menon. Champa, or Champak, who begins as a kshatriya princess during that same early period, passes through even more transformations, ending up in the second half of the novel as Champa Ahmad, daughter of a petty-bourgeois Muslim family from Moradabad. Inclined towards the Muslim League, her father would have liked to send her to Aligarh. She ends up at Isabella Thoburn College in

Lucknow, however, because her mother, herself hailing from Benaras, is more ambitious for the daughter. The novel is divided into four parts: roughly from the advent of the Mauryas up to 1940; the seven years leading up to the Partition; the post-Partition years which are spent mostly in England, in the student and immigrant communities; and a brief last section in which both Champa and Kemal return to India. Then Kemal decides to go to Pakistan. The last two sections are preoccupied, aside from personal involvements of a different kind, with the question of return – where, and how, does one return to a country so irrevocably divided? This clearly was the central question of Qurratul 'Ain's own life at the time, considering that she had returned by then to Pakistan but was to return, some years later, to India. At the end of the novel, Gautam returns to India as a senior member of the diplomatic service – secure, successful, and self-centred, as he has been in all previous incarnations. Champa, meanwhile, returns to Moradabad, reconciled with her petty-bourgeois and provincial Muslim origins in a post-Partition India full of hopes and ideals. Kemal, originally from the Lucknow upper class, and from the family around whose house the tale of the 1940–47 period unfolds, returns to Lucknow and Dehra Dun, where the palatial family homes have been declared evacuee property and allotted to new inhabitants, and where he finds that candidates with lesser qualifications but of Hindu origin are preferred to him. He passes through Moradabad, aimless and with 'divided loyalties', envious of Champa's sense of belonging in a solidly grounded milieu, but himself moving ambivalently but inexorably towards Pakistan. He has in fact nowhere to go.

What is significant about the plotting of the novel, indeed its narrative structure, is that although the whole of it is a sustained exposition of the cultural meaning of the Partition, the event itself is simply absent, doggedly held back. We have the period before the Partition and the period after, but for the event itself we get barely a page, and that, too, not in Manto's manner of naturalistic documentation but in the form of a straightforward rendition of that famous passage, familiar to every reader, where an ambivalent Arjuna, son of Kunti, begs Lord Krishna to be released from the duty to kill his kin. In rejecting the possibility of naturalistic depiction, the novel thus reenacts the same narrative impasse that Lajvanti, the female sufferer in Bedi's story, had found so very daunting: the absence of a language adequate to the scale and intensity of the horrid tale.

What matters, for our present purposes, is the sociology of the novel's composition and reception. For at one level, the novel offers the classic nationalist narrative of the continuity, oneness, and endurance of India's cultural ethos. In the novel, as in the typical nationalist narrative, this India is in fact simply the Gangetic valley, the urbane classes, a social whole with no notable internal conflict. Within this India the site of narration may move from Magadh and Pataliputra to Jaunpur; from the Calcutta of the Company to the Lucknow of Ghaziuddin Hayder; back to the Calcutta of nationalist agitation and the Bengal Famine, back again to the Lucknow of the Empire's twilight, and on to London – but the structure of thought, sentiment, aspiration retains a recognizable continuity, in which the Hindu female centre of the novel effortlessly becomes a secular Muslim self, with the vernacular commonality of the name of the flower, Champa. This sense of modulations within a structure of fundamental stability is repeated, then, in a lexicon which is replete with ancient place-names and even some Sanskrit vocabulary in the opening 140 pages, but then begins to accommodate more and more words of first Farsi and then English origins, giving to the second half of the novel a broad tonal texture drawn as much from modern Hindi as from modern Urdu, both modulated by a distinctly English college education. Thus, quite aside from asserting the whole range of nationalist ideological formulations in the form of specific statements, the novel in fact re-enacts this ideology in its narrative and lexical arrangements. In the process, it also subverts the genre of the historical novel as it has been usually practised in Urdu.

The modern and hybrid history of this genre in Urdu begins with Ratan Nath Sarshar's *Fasana-e-Azad*, which is on the whole a work in the picaresque mould but which then, in its later section, translates the protagonist into a crusading, chivalric character and sends him off into warfare in defence of a Muslim imperium (Turkey, in this case). The latter practitioners of the genre, for example, Abdul Halim Sharar, retained this basic plot device of making the hero a crusader for Islam but only in the medieval past and only against Europe – in North Africa, Turkey, Spain – not in India, where an Islamic heroic crusader might have had to collide with Hindus, which the practitioners of the genre did not want. *Aag ka Darya* is preoccupied with history but it departs from the established traditions of the quasi-historical novel in Urdu on at least three major counts. First, it remains within India and initially within a Hindu past; the so-called Muslim interregnum is represented here not by the Mughal Empire but by the provincial locales of Jaunpur and Lucknow. Second, the novel is pitched ideologically *against* the Muslim imperium. Third, in plotting the quasi-historical novel around a female protagonist, the novel subverts the genre that casts the protagonist in the chivalric, crusading mould. The 'heroism' of the female protagonist, Champa, appears only fleetingly and precariously, at the very end, to return to a community at once restrictive and rooted; for most part, such 'heroic' quality as she possesses is that of ordinary life itself. Qurratul 'Ain again makes a narrative choice of the nationalist and even romantic kind, which we may generically designate as 'Nehruvian'. Within this ideological structure, then, Kemal's choice – to go to Pakistan – can only be seen as a betrayal.

Now, with India's own social ambience becoming incomparably more communalized, and with the character of the dominant intelligentsia in Pakistan itself having shifted decisively since the war of 1965, it is perhaps difficult to recall that in the Pakistan of 1958, when the novel first appeared, more or less simultaneously with Pakistan's first military regime, it was immediately received as a modern classic. No Urdu novel in the present century has commanded such immediate recognition from such wide strata, excluding only the small, rabid rightist fringe. Its artistic achievement was, if anything, vastly overrated, precisely because of the general ideological empathy which most of the readership felt. Virtually everyone in the Urdu-speaking literary intelligentsia identified emotionally with Kemal's crisis of loyalty, and with Champa's return. Nor did Qurratul 'Ain's migration back to India, which came soon thereafter, make any substantial difference to her popularity in Pakistan. Certain circles, of course, attacked her viciously, as they had also attacked Manto earlier for portraying the devastations of the Partition, but Manto is also the only writer of Urdu fiction who can rival Qurratul 'Ain in general public approbation and popularity. There is simply no Urdu writer, with the possible exception of Maulana Azad, whose work appears so regularly in pirated editions throughout Pakistan. That these writers, Azad, Manto, Qurratul 'Ain, so very diverse in their social location and intellectual preoccupation, would be popular in India is, so far as ideological constructions are concerned, obvious enough; secularity and belief in composite Indian nationalism, combined with a stridently anti-Partitionist stance, are after all pervasive positions which are, in addition, approved by the state. But why Pakistan?

This question is related directly to the main thesis of this essay, namely that the bulk of the writers of Urdu at the time of the Partition constituted, regardless of religious or regional origin, an identifiable social group, a community with a dense and shared feeling. This lasted far beyond the Partition itself, despite the massive demographic disloca- tions in the ensuing years; a secularist belief in the composite culture of Hindus and Muslims in India was the predominant ideological position in this community. Decisive shifts came later. Despite the scale of human suffering at the time of the Partition, the factors leading up to it did not decisively break up the emotional structure of this community. It was, rather, the accumulating processes of the succeeding years, in the postcolonial phase, culminating in war and its repercussions, that stabi- lized those divisions in ways that have subsequently appeared to be irrevocable.

II

Although the publication in 1957 of the two representative works of Faiz and Rashid, which we cited in the beginning of the previous section, may give the illusion that the First Decade constitutes some kind of unity, the mapping of Urdu language and literature requires a longer time frame, 1947–65. For this cultural history exists within the boundaries established by the decisive events of political history. In the political arena, the Partition of 1947 did indeed break up the writing community by redistributing its members into two separate territorial nations. This redistribution had at least three notable aspects. First, communal violence and large-scale migration meant the departure of the Urdu writers of Sikh and Hindu origin from Pakistan and their resettlement in India, and the similar departure of very many Urdu writers of Muslim origin from India to Pakistan. Second, the communal claim that Urdu was specifically a language of Muslims, which had remained quite marginal before the Partition, was gradually accepted over the years by wide sections of the liberal intelligentsia on both sides of the newly obtained national borders,[6] with the upshot that while Urdu became a state-imposed 'national language' in (West) Pakistan, it lost its previous importance in systems of education and administration in India and came to be seen as a matter of 'minority right' and 'Muslim interest'. Third, the key political decision by the Indian Parliament to abandon a common lingua franca of Hindustani and to adopt Hindi as the preferred 'national language' eroded the official status of Hindustani altogether, so that it disappeared even as a census category and certainly as a living link between Urdu and Hindi which now became more and more distant from each other, especially in their written forms. Radical reorganization of the nation occurred in consequence of a singular event, in August 1947; the consequences of this traumatizing surgery for the reorganization of the writing community were no less stark but were more cumulative, becoming wholly apparent only over a generation. In the long run, the writing community was as radically reorganized in the cultural domain as the nation had been in the political domain. Thus it is that the two terms, *nation* and *community*, at once political and cultural, are the framing realities for this particular 'mirror', which we call Urdu. For it is in the texture of these terms that relations between state ideologies and literary ideologies, between their durability and their mutation, are inscribed.

By 'nation' is meant here what is generally understood by the term 'nation-state'. Since what is involved is the re-circulation of a language and a literature in what became two nation-states, it is best to think of India and Pakistan more or less simultaneously, for the particular tension of my present argument is derived from the idea that for almost a whole generation the community tried to remain one while the nation-states became two. I shall also offer some statistics to indicate the magnitude, the arbitrariness, the fantastic manner in which statistics are produced and inserted into official and communal ideologies, which then determine perceptions of linguistic communities.

It is the agreed position of Hindu and Muslim communalisms that Urdu is the language of Muslims and that there is a direct link between Islam, Urdu, and Pakistan. One of the clearest expressions of this belief came from none other than Liaqat Ali Khan himself, the first Prime Minister of Pakistan, in 1948, in response to a Hindu member of Pakistan's Constituent Assembly who had suggested that Bengali be permitted in the Assembly:

> Pakistan is a Muslim state, and it must have its lingua franca, a language of the Muslim nation. The mover should realize that Pakistan has been created because of the demand of a hundred million Muslims in this sub-continent, and the language of a hundred million Muslims is Urdu. It is necessary for a nation to have one language and that language can only be Urdu and no other language.[7]

This was at best peculiar. Only three years later, in 1951, the Census Report of that same government which had been headed by Liaqat Ali revealed that only 7.2 per cent of the Pakistani population thought of themselves as Urdu-speakers.[8] In that same year, 1951, the Indian Census also revealed that only 38 per cent of Indian Muslims considered themselves speakers of Urdu. Even in UP, only 48 per cent of Muslims returned Urdu as their language. The overwhelming majority of Indian Muslims – 62 per cent – spoke some other language. In Pakistan, the proportion of Muslims who did not think of themselves as Urdu-speakers was of course much higher, at roughly 93 per cent. The irony here is that the percentage of Muslims who thought of Urdu as their language was much higher, five times higher, in India than in Pakistan. The absolute number of Urdu-speakers in India was also roughly four times as great as in Pakistan.

It is worth remarking that if 62 per cent of Indian Muslims and 93 per cent of Pakistani ones showed no particular attachment to Urdu barely four years after the Partition, the idea that there is some imma-nent link between the language itself and some purported Muslim consciousness appears at least far-fetched. Most communal arguments ignore this kind of data, and they posit further that the Muslim communal consciousness resides in the language itself since it is said to derive from Arabic and Farsi. This too is odd. Urdu is doubtless written in a modified form of the Persian script, but so were several other languages of northern India including Sindhi and Brahui. No one has yet suggested that Sindhi, with its much higher proportion of Arabic words, or Brahui, a patently Dravidian language, is a special vehicle of this so-called Islamic consciousness. Nor does anyone doubt that the phonetics, the morphology, and the entire syntax of Urdu are derived strictly from a Prakritic base. What remains, then, is the issue of vocabulary, the favourite *bête noire* of Hindu communalism.

On this there are far more reliable statistics than those on population. *Farhang-e-Asafiya* is by general agreement the most reliable Urdu dictionary. It was compiled in the late nineteenth century by an Indian scholar little exposed to British or Orientalist scholarship. The lexicographer in question, Syed Ahmed Dehlavi, had no desire to sunder Urdu's relationship with Farsi, as is evident even from the title of his dictionary. He estimates that roughly 75 per cent of the total stock of 55,000 Urdu words that he compiled in his dictionary are derived from Sanskrit and Prakrit, and that the entire stock of the base words of the language, without exception, are derived from these sources. What distinguishes Urdu from a great many other Indian languages and makes it rather similar to Kashmiri, Punjabi, Sindhi, and Balochi is that it draws almost a quarter of its vocabulary from language communities to the west of India, such as Farsi, Turkish, and Tajik. Most of the little it takes from Arabic has come not directly but through Farsi. Two things here need to be noted. One is that any examination of the dictionary itself shows that the lexicographer, coming from the elite of Delhi, was prone to include a great many words of Farsi origin and ignore a great many of indigenous origin. In the hands of a different lexicographer, the proportion of the Prakritic words is likely to have been much higher. Second, there is also the issue of the level of discourse. Most words of West Asian origin are words of specialized vocabulary, technical or highly literary. Very few such words surface in the language of daily life, speech, and thought, except for the highly educated. If, that is, 75 per cent of the word-stock of *Farhang-e-Asafiya* is derived from Sanskrit and Prakrit, one can imagine how overwhelmingly Prakritic the language would be in the mouth of the common speaker.

To speak of the morphology, the syntactical structure, the lexical base of a language is to speak of the traditions of sense and sensibility, indeed of the inherited metaphysic and the forms of cognition that the speaker of the language apprehends directly from these repositories of linguistic form. Most speakers of a language do not encounter these forms of their language in the shape of the classics of high literature, or as theological treatise; they are apprehended much more directly, in relations that are social, sensual, and dialogic. Nor do words come to us emptied of meaning, for us to fill them with whatever connotations we like. Words come to us dense and laden with prior use, and the meaning of words is nothing other than what has been given to them, what inheres in them already, before an individual speaker takes hold of them. Changing the meaning of individual words is hard enough; to change the meaning of a whole vocabulary is virtually impossible. What all this implies for our present argument is that if it can be shown that through an evolution of five hundred years or more Urdu has remained overwhelmingly tied to its Prakritic structure, primarily through its relationship with Khari Boli, then the question arises whether Urdu has taken all this linguistic structure, all the grammatical forms, all the stock of words, simply as inert objects, to be moved around at will, or has this evolution given to Urdu a basic metaphysic and a cognitive mould indistinguishable from those adjacent linguistic forms that have evolved in the same, shared social space?

This issue of trying to distinguish between one linguistic structure and another is posed by the Census Reports in ways at once poignant and paradoxical, since demographers always try to observe distinctions which speakers of the languages themselves often fail to make. The statistics of 1951 are, of course, hard to interpret since we lack any comparable data for the quarter century immediately preceding the Partition; a comparable linguistic breakdown is not available for 1941, and the 1931 Census had the category only of Hindustani, not Urdu and Hindi. Prior to that, half a million people had returned Urdu as their language in 1911, a million and a half in 1921. We have no reliable way of interpreting why the Urdu-speaking population suddenly increased threefold during those ten years. We do know that the linguistic consciousness among educated Indians had begun to shift drastically in the first quarter of this century as volumes of Grierson's magisterial *Linguistic Survey of India* began appearing, from 1902 to 1916. For, while Risley, the Director of the 1901 Census, had subscribed to the fantastic notion that each language was an expression of a set of *racial* characteristics, and this notion could be dismissed more easily, Grierson's lasting and devastating contribution to Indian demography was the pseudo-scientific presupposition that each individual is born with one, and only one, 'mother tongue', and that speakers of each 'mother tongue' resided in a specific locale or region.[9] Variants of such ideas had been in the air since Gilchrist and Fort William, but it was left to Grierson to present them with the full splendour of positivist belief. By 1911, Census Reports were being prepared on the basis of this so-called science.

We do not know how to account for a threefold increase in the number of Urdu-speakers between 1911 and 1921. Something similar happened between 1951 and 1961, for the number of Urdu-speakers during these ten years jumped by 60 per cent, from 13.5 million to 22.8 million, so that Urdu-speakers now accounted for 5.2 per cent of the Indian population as compared to 3.8 per cent ten years earlier.

What precisely had happened? Were the Urdu-speakers breeding faster than the rest? The oddity was all the greater because indeterminate numbers of Urdu-speakers, certainly in the hundreds of thousands, possibly more, had migrated from India to Pakistan in the early 1950s, but rather fewer had come in from there after 1950. The communalist answer is that more and more Muslims who did not know Urdu were returning Urdu as their language anyway. If that is true, it only shows that a communalist perception of Urdu was greater fourteen years after Independence than in the immediate aftermath of the Partition. But another sort of clue is found in the extraordinary statistics that were returned from UP.

The nationalist position in the years preceding Independence, as upheld by Gandhi and Nehru, was that the proper way to bypass the deeply divisive Hindi–Urdu controversy, and to have a 'link' language for the nation based not upon elite linguistic formations but on the spoken vernacular, was to adopt Hindustani. Nehru had advocated the Roman script for this 'link' language but was persuaded to join Gandhi in proposing that Hindustani could be written in either the Devanagari or the modified Persian script. This position had been eroded by 1946 and was then formally abandoned by the Indian government and by Nehru himself. However, the memory of that nationalist position seems to have remained vivid in UP, especially in the rural areas, immediately after Independence. As time passed, the communalist positions hardened, and Hindustani was seen to have lost ground. The mass of people in UP reconciled themselves to the new realities.

In 1951, over 6 million of the rural population of UP had returned Hindustani, but only 2.1 million had returned Urdu, as their mother tongue. In 1961, the figure for Hindustani in rural UP plummeted to a mere 100,530; for Urdu, it rose in those same areas by 152 per cent, to 5.34 million. The distancing from Hindustani in the urban areas was very dramatic by 1951; only three-quarters of a million returned Hindustani as their mother tongue. By 1961, however, this number had declined to zero. The number of Urdu-speakers in the urban areas remained more or less constant, increasing by less than 10 per cent in ten years, which seems reasonable. It was in the rural areas that the sea-change had occurred. The only way one can explain the stupendous increase in the number of rural Urdu-speakers is to surmise that two to three million among those who had previously returned Hindustani as their mother tongue now shifted to Urdu, while roughly an equal number shifted to Hindi. In the process, Hindustani, which had had some 50 per cent more speakers than Urdu in 1951 (and three times as many in the rural areas) basically disappeared from the official statistics by 1961. Urdu not only registered a net gain of some 80 per cent but also became, in UP, an overwhelmingly rural language. The rural and urban segments of Urdu-speakers had been almost exactly equal in 1951, but two out of three among all Urdu-speakers in UP resided in the rural areas by 1961 – or so the Census would have us believe. This, too, is odd. The same Census tells us that Urdu is the most 'urban' of all languages in India, with 40 per cent of all Urdu-speakers residing in urban areas; only in UP, it now transpires, were almost 70 per cent rural.[10]

We are dealing, then, with two kinds of movements, each affecting millions of lives: movements of people across territorial boundaries of newly constituted nation-states as a result of the partition, and the later movements of millions of people within a nation-state, namely India, from one language category to another. For the mass of people in UP in the first decade of Independence, the three language categories, Hindi, Hindustani, Urdu, were at least very fluid, perhaps also quite meaningless; for countless people, they constituted a single structure of mutual intelligibility, and they returned one or the other for Census records purely in response to external demand and pressure. These identities were fixed, in other words, by a privileged personnel involved in administration, education, the professions, including the profession of politics. They imposed a bourgeois order (in this case, a viciously communal bourgeois order) upon a predominantly agrarian society, and demanded of them that they have only *one* language.

What happens, one wonders, to someone – culturally, emotionally, ontologically – when he decides that what was his 'mother tongue' ten years ago is no longer so? What happens to a nation which tells millions of its citizens that a language actually exists and is theirs, but then tells them some years later that it probably does not exist and is useless anyway? What coercions, cultural, communal, religious, official coercions, are involved when a person is made to make a practical choice between Hindustani and Hindi, Hindustani and Urdu, in an atmosphere already intensified by the virtually unbearable pressure which presents the choice between Hindi and Urdu as a choice between Hinduism and Islam, nationalism and foreignness? The coercive demand that each person must have only one language was hard enough to reconcile with the fundamental trajectories of India's linguistic past. As Mohan Singh Diwana eloquently puts it, even though he too uses the terms – mother tongue, provincial language, common Hindustani language – made fashionable by Gilchrist and Grierson:

> ... there was hardly any poet from Gorakh of the tenth century to Ghulam Farid in the early half of the nineteenth century belonging to Maharashtra, Gujrat, Bengal, Agra, Oudh, Bihar, Delhi, Punjab or Sind, who had not written in three languages – the mother tongue, the provincial language and the common Hindustani language, Hindui,

besides Persian or Sanskrit, such as he could command. Even Zafar and Sauda wrote in Punjabi; even Guru Gobind Singh wrote in Persian, in Braj, in Rekhta and in Khayal; even Guru Nanak Dev wrote in Persian, in Sanskrit, in Kafi, in Lahndi; even Namdev, Kabir, Raidas and Dadu wrote in Punjabi and Hindui. In Bengal the writers of Brajboli thrived. Mira wrote in Rajasthani, in Gujrati and in Hindui.[11]

The peculiar pressures from politicians and demographers in the twentieth century have required, of course, that these multiplicities of enunciative capacity must now be abandoned and be replaced by a mere 'mother tongue'. But what happens if one ceases to know what the boundaries of that tongue really are? Where does Hindi end and Urdu begin, especially when the connecting bridge of Hindustani has been made to collapse?

The 'nation' was not, so far as Urdu is concerned, reorganized once and for all at the moment of Partition. There were also rather drastic internal reorganizations in succeeding years. If for the majority of what turned out to be Urdu-speakers in 1961, Urdu and Hindustani had been in 1951 simply interchangeable, then Urdu carried at the time no identification with being a Muslim, for either the Hindu- or the Muslim-speaker. This interchangeability of Urdu and Hindustani – perceived more correctly and viscerally by the speaker, and misperceived and misrepresented by the communal ideologue – has been a central element in giving to the Urdu literary community of that period its predominantly secular, progressive, and humanist stance.

III

The word 'community' in this particular context means something more complex and tenuous, less tangible than the concept of the 'nation-state'. The predominant meaning of this word 'community' in today's India refers to religion. Hindus are called the majority community, Muslims, Sikhs, Christians, and so on, minority communities. The consequences of that sense of 'community' in past and present histories have been by and large catastrophic. The term 'community', as I use it here, is very different, more complex, certainly not co-terminal with religion, much less bounded by empirical quantification, and yet not something merely *imagined*. This word signifies, first, a very considerable degree of historical sedimentation; second, something that human beings actually *choose* to become, thus in its own way not just a determined entity but a *praxis*. Communities not only endure, they are frequently recomposed, and in certain sorts of crises they simply fall apart. In the broadest sense at least one meaning of the word 'community' converges with that very complex thing that Raymond Williams calls a 'structure of feeling', even though at times Williams tends to associate that phrase, 'structure of feeling', with what a generation within a given culture might come to share, perhaps imperceptibly, at a given time.

Out of the thousands of poems, short stories, and even novels written in the Urdu language between, say, the Pakistan Resolution of March 1940 and the Indo-Pakistani War of October 1965, there is not even *one* which has, by any critical standards whatever, any sort of literary merit and that *celebrates* the idea of Pakistan. The first Urdu poem that is distinctly pro-Pakistani[12] in sentiment and that does have considerable literary merit in the formal sense – politically jingoistic, hence objectionable, but written with great literary flair – is Safdar Meer's poem on the clash of Indian and Pakistani military arms near Sialkot in 1965.[13] 'Literary merit' in this context, refers to *agreed* positions as they are reflected in literary journals, annuals, anthologies, collections of verse or fiction issued by the established publishing houses. What is excluded from this consideration, of course, is the kind of propagandist doggerel that is made to order and is recognized as such by the whole of the literary intelligentsia, Left and Right. When we consider this very broad spectrum of literary productions, on both sides of the border, the sheer absence of a literary text which is pro-Pakistani in sentiment seems most remarkable and indicative of a certain consensus of perspective. Furthermore, in all the voluminous literature in Urdu that came out of the events of 1947, there is a complete, and very curious, absence of any sense of spontaneous or enduring celebration of decolonization and Independence. That sense of achievement is submerged entirely in the aggregations of grief surrounding the Partition.

The point is not any lack of anti-colonial sentiment. The history of that sentiment in Urdu literature is very old indeed, as old as colonialism itself. And, the period between 1937 and 1947, namely the period of the hegemony of the Progressive Writers Association in Urdu letters, witnessed the accumulation of a vast body of anti-colonial literary texts, composed most often from the perspectives of the Left but sometimes also from the perspectives of maintream nationalism – that is to say, Nehruvian nationalism and (in some rare cases) Gandhian nationalism.[14] And, there were a great many texts in the aftermath of 1947 that sought to recapture, even perhaps preserve and reconstitute, that earlier ambience. So, anti-colonialism is not at issue. But the moment of decolonization itself is experienced in the whole range of Urdu literature of the period not in the celebratory mode but as a defeat, a disorientation, a diaspora. In this context we have already cited the work of Manto, Bedi, Faiz, Hayatullah Ansari, Krishan Chander, Shaukat Siddiqui, Ramanand Sagar, and Qurratul 'Ain Hayder. The archive of such works is in fact much too vast even for citation. Two deserve special mention, however: Khadeeja Mastoor's *Aangan* ('Courtyard'), and Abdullah Hussein's *Udas Naslain* ('Generations of Grief'),[15] both appearing in Pakistan in the early 1960s, and generally regarded, along with *Aag ka Darya*, as the more significant novels of the period.

The two are composed on contrasting scales. *Udas Naslain* begins in the days of Tilak, in Delhi and in a village that would be in present-day Haryana, and it ends in Lahore immediately after Partition. The peasantry it portrays is Muslim, Hindu, and Sikh. The village is owned by descendants of a *jagirdar* who obtained this status as a reward from the British in 1857. These descendants have acquired all the trappings of old Awadh *taluqdars*. The only character who comes out unscathed and prosperous at the end is the direct heir of the family, who moves to Pakistan, takes up a high post in the civil service, and acquires a vast property left behind by a Hindu family. Naim, the chief protagonist and son of a rich peasant from the same village, moves between the village, Delhi, and Calcutta. As a forced recruit in the First World War, he serves in southern Europe, then returns, joins the Congress, begins moving towards the Congress Socialists, but then falls in love and marries the daughter of the illustrious and loyalist *jagirdar*. He thus begins a tortuous life of ambivalence between his political preferences and his newly cemented class alliance through marriage. Broken eventually by this ambivalence, by advancing age, by the sweep of communal killings, he finds himself in 1947 on the trek to Pakistan in the midst of millions among whom he is ultimately lost.

Abdullah Hussein's composition is in very many places rather weak. He tries to represent Naim as so many different types of person that characterization becomes simply incoherent. Still, *Udas Naslain* is on all counts a remarkable novel from a relatively young Punjabi Muslim civil engineer in the Lahore of the early 1960s. In Urdu, certainly, it is the most nuanced portrait of a marriage that goes wrong and the individual selves that get eroded, inexorably, because of incompatibility of class and politics, regardless of all efforts to adjust. But the author also has a remarkable inwardness about the rhythms of daily life among the Sikh peasantry, quite worthy of Balwant Singh or even Rajinder Singh Bedi. Equally remarkable is the sense of that same kind of inwardness, a vivid feel, for Congress politics, from the days of Tilak and Gokhale onwards; for the actuality of Jallianwala Bagh; for the gradually accumulating sense of defeat as the country moves towards decolonization and the sea of refugees moves towards the newly fixed borders. And the fact that it is Naim himself who gets lost on the way, without a trace, is a good novelistic device to signify a situation in which a nostalgia for the lost world is inextricably tied to a literal loss of direction and connection on part of the 'hero'.

Aangan, with its story starting in the early 1930s in UP and ending twenty years later in Pakistan, is largely confined to domestic space. It is told from the perspective of its main protagonist, Alya, the daughter of a declining and fairly traditional landowning family. She experiences the three great political forces of the time, the Congress, the Muslim League, the Communist Party, largely from within the courtyard. In its constrictive scale, therefore, the contrast with *Udas Naslain* but also with *Aag ka Darya* could not be sharper. The tone of the novel is poised between a sense of personal confinement, the sheer multiplicity of relations available within that courtyard, and an external world large in itself but knowable only through its immediate impingements as they get refracted through familial relations. The family is actually caught in the decayed mores of a moribund class on the one hand, and in the whirlwind variants of nationalist politics, on the other. The various male protagonists choose politics through patriotic idealism, communal opportunism, or a bitterness born of deprivation, but always only half comprehending the consequences of their own choices, and the deepening social crisis of the family as a whole. The mutually inseparable processes of decolonization and Partition, amounting to the loss of whatever was good in her world, leave Alya also without any supports. In the end, a refugee in Pakistan, she learns to provide for herself and those she can still support. It is a very narrow and painful kind of freedom that comes her way. But it *is* a freedom, of sorts.

The striking thing about this ideologically unified body of literary texts from Manto and Bedi to Khadija Mastoor, is that such texts are produced on both sides of the border by writers, male and female, whose origins can be traced to diverse regions and religions and whose political positions were by no means uniform. Because of this diversity among the Urdu writers of the period, the tendency in their writing community was to see themselves as something of a microcosm of subcontinental society as such, as it was before Partition and as it became thereafter. This was the cultural consequence of the fact that Urdu was not a language of any particular region or of any identifiable religious group. To the extent that writers of the language constituted a community, their unity was the language itself and the cultural institutions built around it. The Partition of the country had partitioned other languages as well: Bengali, Sindhi, and Punjabi in particular. In the singular case of Punjab, of course, the linguistic partition was double-edged, in the sense that the bulk of the Punjab's literary intelligentsia, and the literate segments of the Punjabi urban population generally, had been essentially bilingual, using Urdu at least as frequently as Punjabi in the composition of its literary utterances. Hindu was for most of them remote and marginal.

Adjustment to what India became after the Partition has required enormous and entirely *willed* losses of memory. Few historians, literary historians included, care to remember that since Urdu had become the language of cultural literacy for large numbers of Punjabi intellectuals, for whom Lahore was the main centre, the Partition of the country meant that large numbers of Urdu writers moved not only from India to Pakistan but also from Pakistan to India. As one surveys the Urdu literary periodicals of the first post-Independence decade, one comes across dozens of writers of Urdu from the Punjab who sought to reorganize themselves into a cultural community in postcolonial India. Here their children had neither public facility nor need to learn Urdu, but they themselves were trapped in the cultural ethos they had inherited. The greatly talented are now part of the contemporary history and modern archive of the language. But there were others, of minor talent but equally great cultural loneliness, who wrote perhaps a few poems, perhaps a few short stories, and then faded out of history and archive. There were others, thousands, perhaps hundreds of thousands, who were Hindus and Sikhs, for whom Punjabi was the spoken language, but Urdu the language of reading and writing, and who then reconciled themselves to the new realities in all sorts of painful and impoverishing ways. Not even the rudiments of any study exist that might tell us what happened to such people. One picks up Urdu periodicals and one notices names characteristic of the middling Hindu castes, fewer than before but still there; but one also notices that Sikh names are now at the point of vanishing. One has friends who feel a certain emotional partiality towards Urdu, the language of their parents; but it is no longer theirs.

IV

What accounts for the structure of feeling that was still dominant and pervasive in the years immediately after the Partition? The strongest and proximate shaping force was, of course, the Progressive Writers Association that became the hegemonic ideological force, with electrifying speed after its inception in 1936, to such an extent that it defined the broad social agenda and cultural consensus among the generality of Urdu writers for a whole generation. This also included a great many of those who were neither members of the Association nor in overt sympathy with it. Those who did not subscribe to the broad consensus were relegated to the fringes of the writing community. In regions such as the Punjab, Uttar Pradesh, and Andhra, where the most influential clusters of Urdu writers were assembled, the movement was given further authority by affiliation with people like Premchand, Maulvi Abdul Haq, Jawaharlal Nehru, Sarojini Naidu, Qazi Abdul Ghaffar, and by a sense, crucial to the sustenance of a 'national' subjectivity in the Urdu writing community, that to belong to this consensus within the community was to belong to a multi-lingual, all-India reality that far exceeded the bounds of Urdu itself. This hegemony survived well into the 1950s and was to be eroded only over a decade or more. The defeat of the revolutionary movement of the peasantry in Telangana, the stabilization of the Partition and its consequences, the further communalization and deepening of the Hindi–Urdu divide, the emergence of new clusters of rightwing literati on both sides of the border, the retreat of the Communist movement in Pakistan as well as the Gangetic heartlands of India, not to mention the great industrial cities of Bombay and Kanpur, two of the historic homes of progressive thought in modern Urdu, were among the contributing factors.

The hegemony which the progressive writers of Urdu were able to establish for a generation or more did not materialize out of thin air. It was part of the National Movement, and the explicitly left-of-centre ambience of Urdu writings declined precisely to the extent that the radicalizing compacts of the National Movement itself were eroded and gradually abandoned. This erosion was faster and more dramatic in Pakistan, for obvious reasons. In India, the process was more gradual, more ambiguous. For the Urdu writing community, nevertheless, the inability of Gandhi and Nehru to hold the line on the issue of Hindustani, the swift abandonment of Gandhian politics, the regionalization and domestication of the Communist movement, and the defeat of the Nehruvian theoretical position in practice proved in the long run decisive.

Those were the immediate shaping forces: the PWA and the National Movement. But none of it would have worked if the writers who mediated the relation between these shaping forces and the actual processes of literary production had not been able to draw upon huge reservoirs of prior tradition. Memories, after all, are the very stuff of which futures are built. What facilitated the creation of this new kind of hegemony were certain features of the historical evolution of the language itself, the traditional structure of the language community, and the socially composite nature of the writing community in modern times. Hence the ideological structures and even the metaphysic that were embedded in these linguistic and social formations.

Taking the Census of 1961 as a rough guide, we might say that there were three modern trends. Urdu was, according to these figures and even after the sudden insertion of millions of rural people of Uttar Pradesh into its fold, the most *urban* of all Indian languages. Forty per cent of all Urdu-speakers lived, according to that Census, in urban areas. Second, it was the most *widespread* language of India, having a substantial presence in more states of the Union than did any other language, including Hindi. Third, the incidence of bi-linguality was reported to be much higher among Urdu-speakers than speakers of any other language; 22.1 per cent of all Urdu-speakers claimed to be bi-lingual as compared to roughly 14 per cent for Punjabi, Kannada, and Marathi, which all came roughly second to Urdu; Hindi-speakers, at 5.1 per cent, displayed the lowest incident of bi-linguality, according to these statistics.

Such statistics and percentages should not be accepted at face value. Rather, these are indicators of trends and beliefs, and what they indicate is sometimes quite different from what they are supposed to signify. That such a large number of the so-called Urdu-speakers but such a small number of the so-called Hindi-speakers would declare themselves bi-lingual has much more of a social and political import than a linguistic one. On the level of speech, after all, the distinction between Hindi and Urdu is not so great. That the speakers of Hindi and/or Urdu would *not* normally consider themselves bi-lingual itself reflects a remarkable level of belief in the kind of linguistic boundaries that Census officials, communalists, and officialdom in general have been advocating now for a century.

The three elements – high incidence of urban location, a certain spread through the country, and fluidity of linguistic boundaries – are neverthe-less punctual features of Urdu, even though these features are largely unquantifiable and are reflected in Census figures in an arbitrary fashion. It could not be otherwise, because Urdu has never been, at any stage of its evolution, the language of any particular religious or regional group, and it has always been the language of urban and peri-urban social exchange. It is the favourite theme of the modern communalist that Urdu is the language of Muslims and that the Hindus who speak it and write in it have simply imbibed something called 'Muslim culture'. The matter is more complex. The point to stress here is that the Hindus who have been part of the Urdu writing community have certainly not been passive recipients of anyone else's culture; they have *created* a culture of their own by shaping and modifying the culture of the literary com-munity as a whole. Evolved variations of that culture, in which an equal scholarship in Sanskrit and Farsi was common among the literati, were already well in place by the nineteenth century, in northern India as well as the Deccan.

If the literary community in modern Urdu is in very large sections still not a communalized Muslim community, one of the sizeable reasons is the central position which persons and clusters of Hindu origin have played in the very formation of this literary sensibility. The tallest shadow on the tradition of Urdu fiction is that of Pandit Ratan Nath Sarshar; the second tallest, that of Premchand; Bedi, Krishan Chander, Manto, Qurratul 'Ain come from inside this older tradition. The largest archive of printed Urdu books in the earlier part of this century was created by the publishing house of Munshi Naval Kishore; Maktaba-e-Jadeed came much later, when much else had already happened. The early history of Urdu journalism is equally indicative. With the exception of the very short-lived *Fauji Akhbar*, which Tipu Sultan established in 1799 exclusively for his soldiery, the first Urdu newspaper was *Jam-e-Jahan Numa*, which came out in Calcutta under the joint editorship of Lala Sada Sukh and W.E. Pearce. The first regular monthlies, *Mah-boob-e-Hind* and *Favaid-e-Nazirin*, came out in Delhi in the 1850s, under the editorship of Professor Ram Chandra of the Delhi College. In Punjab, Urdu journalism began in January 1850, with the weekly *Koh-i-Noor*, under the supervision of Munshi Harsukh Rai. The second weekly in Lahore – *Akhbar-e-Aam* – appeared in 1870 under the editorship of Mukand Lal, a Kashmiri pundit. The *Avadh Akhbar*, the first weekly to appear in Lucknow, was established in 1859 but circulation remained meagre until Sarshar took it over. Indeed, every estimate of the denominational profile of the Urdu literary community that has been assembled from the time of Garcin de Tassey up to the Partition suggests that about two-thirds of the writers have been Muslim and about one-third non-Muslim. In other words, Muslims have had a larger relationship with Urdu but by no means an exclusive one.

The Progressive Movement had self-consciously built upon these multiple traditions. The fact that persons of various religious and regional origins actually wrote in the same journals, coexisting side by side through the same networks of personal and public lives, made it possible to consign to the fringes those who sought a communal identification for the language and its literature. That social cohesion was greatly damaged by the Partition as well as by the ideological fragmentations leading up to it and arising from it, but the immediate reaction of the fragmented community was to reconstitute itself through new networks. Right up to the 1965 war, for example, Urdu journals on both sides of the border published writers from all parts of the subcontinent and presumed the existence of reading communities in the same old places, with only names and numbers shifting from place to place, even though the underlying ideological matrix had kept shifting imperceptibly. How much the ground had shifted became fully obvious only in 1965. For, the reaction of the Pakistani segment of the Urdu literary intelligentsia to that war was the exact opposite of the reaction, in the earlier phase, to the Partition itself. As has been argued, in the entire body of Urdu literature up to 1965, there is not a single document of any great literary merit which *celebrates* the creation of Pakistan. In 1965, by contrast, virtually all the well-known Urdu writers in Pakistan, many of them previously associated with the Left, took public positions indistinguishable from that of the Ayub regime, and even Faiz wrote a rather ambiguous *Sipahi ka Geet* ('Soldier's Song'). Only Habib Jalib and Farigh Bukhari wrote openly against the war, while others opposed to the war, almost all of whom were connected directly with the outlawed Communist movement, were driven to silence. Jalib himself was periodically interned and tortured. It was in the crucible of that war, in other words, that one could recognize the irrefutable fact that in some sections of the Pakistani segment of the Urdu writing community the previously hegemonic position of the Progressive Movement had been overthrown entirely; those who still clung to the previously hegemonic position were now a beleaguered minority within their own community. In India, meanwhile, the progressive hegemony was lost but not to the same extent. The secular-nationalist consensus, nevertheless, remained within the community, even though the broad political centre in the country kept moving closer to the communalist position of identifying Urdu with the Muslim sectional interest.

V

The title of this essay uses the metaphor of mirroring. It is an old and rich metaphor, familiar enough to literary theorists, especially of the Marxist kind, but it is also a central metaphor in Urdu poetry, and Ghalib has used it with nuances virtually infinite. For the outstanding feature of mirrors is that they are fragile things capable of rendering truth as well as illusion, but inordinately prone to blurring and breakage. They are humanly made, and they can reflect and render what appears in front of them, for the duration of time that is usually determined by actual persons. Mirrors are instruments of reflection, but also of erasure. A slight movement, and the image is altered, even erased. It is in the human act, mirrored in the mirror, that the act of reflection is done – or undone.

PART II
Politics of the Far Right

Fascism and National Culture: Reading Gramsci in the Days of *Hindutva*

I am deeply honoured by your invitation to me to deliver the Amal Bhattacharji Memorial Lecture of 1992.[1] I regret that I never had the privilege of knowing Professor Bhattacharji, but I am told that one of the guiding principles of his scholarship and teaching was the insight that a sense of *reciprocity* between Asia and Europe had to take the place of the conventional, colonial idea of Europe as the source of knowledge and the image of Asia as the object of knowledge. He would have also agreed, I am sure, that the history of Europe has not been a forward march of liberty and democracy, rationality and liberality, as bourgeois historiography claims. This history has also produced enormous machineries of mass irrationality and extreme, systemic violences, directed not only at non-European peoples, in the form of colonialism and imperialism, but at large sections of the European populations as well, in great many forms, including the fascist form. There is much to be learned from the study of European societies, and one of the things we might think about is the phenomenon of Fascism, which has been a considerable part of their modern past and which now appears to be a possible future for us here in India as well. Gramsci, who entered a Fascist prison at the age of thirty-five and spent all the rest of the ten years of his life in those prisons, except the last three months, when he was a broken man, may be a good person to listen to, at the point where we have now arrived.

When I first received your invitation some six months ago, I had assumed that I would speak exclusively of Gramsci's thought. Since Fascism's open and massive assault on the Indian Constitution on 6 December, however, it is obviously not possible for any of us to think of a European communist purely in the European context. I have adjusted the topic of the lecture accordingly, and even though I have tried to write about Gramsci, you are going to hear a somewhat *composite* text, neither about Gramsci nor about our present, but about the space that conjoins, howsoever tentatively, his world with ours. I have the time neither to speak of his life, nor to undertake any *evaluation* of his historical judgements, nor perhaps to maintain a cogent line of argument. Here, I am concerned only with reconstructing a certain line of Gramsci's own argument about the historical origins of Italian Fascism – more narrowly, with those unresolved trajectories of the past that to him seemed to contribute to a certain fascistic tendency in the Italian culture of his time. This concern on my part arises obviously from our present situation, even though I do not at all believe that reflections and formulations that arise in one national situation may be straightforwardly applicable in another. What you will find in my reflections, rather, is analogue and resonance, some signs of recognition, some ways of thinking about others that may help us think about ourselves.

I

There is, first, the matter of history itself: those uncanny resemblances and resonances between the respective pasts of Italy and India which Marx had once cryptically underscored, so that Gramsci's reflections upon Italian history offer us rich analogues for reflecting upon our own. For Italy is different from other countries of Europe in that it was home, in its antiquity, both to a classical civilization and to a fully structured empire of continental proportions; Latin, the language of this classicism and empire, became also the language of a hierarchical and institutionalized religious order, standing above and in opposition to all vulgates and vernaculars, and acquiring over the centuries a paradoxical status wherein it was at once the language of rule, the language of ecclesiastical privilege, the mark of difference from the cultures of the common people, but also the very ground upon which the new modern language was to grow. Italian was eventually to establish itself as much in opposition *to* as it was a consequence *of* Latin, but then, in a further paradox, Italian was to become – in the wake of the Risorgimento and national unification – a 'national' language and an obvious sign of privilege in a social situation where only a very small cross-section of Italians actually spoke the language.

A diffuse sort of parallel – not linguistic, but a historical and social parallel – with Sanskrit is here obvious enough, for Indian history of what we now call our classical and early medieval periods. For Sanskrit too has been the language both of classicism and of brahminism, of imperial rule and of 'high' culture, opposing and opposed by the vernaculars of India for centuries, and yet coming to modulate the very crucible out of which so much of the subsequent linguistic formations of at least northern India were to be shaped. Brahminism of course never could constitute itself as a centralized Church and a Universal Religion, nor did it ever come directly to command as much property as did the Catholic Church, but it is really quite beyond doubt that High Brahminism did in fact seek that kind of homogenization of populations in belief systems and social practice; it assigned to itself that same sort of cultural supremacy, that special relation with the language of belief and command, and that agential role as the ideological guardian of the Indian systems of tributary exploitation of the peasantry. The upper layers of this priestly order were interwoven into the structures of rule itself, and the special relation of this priestcraft with Sanskrit, hence with Shastric knowledge, has had no mean historical consequence.

The vernaculars had to wage many of their cultural struggles against Sanskrit and against that brahminical classicism which is so large a part of the national heritage associated with Sanskrit. That language of classicism of course receded with the passage of time, reduced as it eventually was to a purely scholastic function, but at least two broad developments for the later centuries are of some significance here. First, India never did develop any indigenous vernacular language to replace Sanskrit as a language of *rule*. Kingdoms that gave any central role to the vernacular in state formations remained, for the most part, local and transitional; in the successive imperial and cosmopolitan centres of the north, by contrast, Sanskrit was succeeded first by Farsi and then by English – and a fluency in the latter continues to be a mark of privilege in present-day India, much as fluency in Tuscan might have been for Gramsci's own generation of Sards. And, second, the Fascist intellectual appears among us today in the garb of the traditional intellectual, invoking and appropriating the classical text, refashioning the old brahminical world into a new kind of marketable Hinduism, which is then asserted against our own modern traditions of secularity, socialism, rationality, religious tolerance, and plurality.

The paradox of Italian history of course is that, for all the antiquity of its civilization, and despite the early stability of the imperial institution as well as the ecclesiastical order and Latinate culture, what we today know as Italy never did become, after the collapse of the Roman Empire and until late in the nineteenth century, a unified political entity. The country's cultural fragmentation, despite its newly gained political unification, was still there as Gramsci, the semi-rustic youth from Sardinia, became, towards the end of the First World War, a leader of Turin's Factory Council Movement and then of Italian communism as such. This paradox of great civilizational depth combined with endemic national fragmentation was a result, according to Gramsci, of a re-doubled failure, first of the Renaissance to unify Italy culturally or politically by effecting a reformation, and then of the Risorgimento

which did achieve political unification but failed nevertheless to institute
a secular culture free of the Vatican or to set in motion an irreversible
national-popular dynamic even of a capitalist kind, by incorporating the
peasant interest in the bourgeois national project. Gramsci was to write
of both these failures copiously, though often very cryptically; the
failure of the Renaissance he was to trace directly to the position of
the religious institution and the persistence of Latin which had given to
Italian intellectuals not a 'national' temper and function but a cosmopolitan temperament and a continental function. There was, in Gramsci's
opinion, a certain relation between the failure to obtain a religious/
intellectual reformation and the failure to create a modern nation-state
despite great civilizational depth.

But Gramsci knew also that the failure was not only of a cultural
kind, and that it was not a matter merely of 'national' unity either. For
it was the cumulative effect of a whole host of blockages – the
undisturbed supremacy of the High Church over the rest of society; the
absence of an indigenous bourgeois revolution, even of the Puritan type;
the lack of a consolidated secular authority; the consequent fragmentation of the country into regional structures of power; the early accumulation but continued fragmentation of the merchants' capital; the lack of
an agrarian revolution; the inability of the literary Renaissance to anchor
itself in a revolutionary dynamic, even of a bourgeois kind – that Italy
was henceforth to remain the object of internecine warfare between
regional powers, and hence an easy prey to external armies and maraud-
ers, which only increased its social fragmentation and postponed for
centuries even the beginnings of an industrial society. When political
unification came in the nineteenth century, with the corresponding
political ideologies and intellectual currents of the Risorgimento, it had
a centuries-old legacy of economic backwardness, religious reaction, and
social fragmentation in its background; the bourgeoisie was as a class
internally too weak, with the result that its political intellectuals possessed
hardly any concrete project of revolutionary social transformation, as
the Jacobins had had in France. The 'nationalists' of the Risorgimento
tended to romanticize narrow indigenist localisms; its 'cosmopolitans'
simply tried to replicate the dominant currents of France and Germany,
merely on the level of *ideas*, with no social basis for those ideas to take
material form, while both the 'nationalists' and the 'cosmopolitans'
shared in a certain kind of vacuous arrogance and complacency bequeathed by the traditions of classicism and empire, and by the role of
the Vatican as the magnificent spiritual centre of a materially backward
country.

It would be dangerous to seek real parallels or merely to *apply* ideas
which arose in a different context of formulation and application. There
are resonances, nevertheless, of a ghostly kind. One thinks, inevitably,

of an old and intensely felt civilizational compact, the Indian one, which failed nevertheless to give rise to a linguistic idiom, no matter how broad or hierarchically structured, that could be basically *shared*, at least *understood*, by all, the ruler and the ruled, from one region to the next. One thinks also of that whole history of internecine warfare and waves of conquest, throughout India's medieval centuries and right up to the modern times, which built kingdoms and empires but never a unified polity, and which in fact served to accentuate regional difference and social antagonism. One remembers, too, that neither merchants' capital nor the whole history of popular religious movements nor the rise of popular literatures could, in our own history, quite break the twin powers of tributary landholdings and High Brahminism, nor prevent the consolidation of foreign conquest.

The accumulation of the merchants' capital had been, after all, fabulous in many regions through every phase of our history, so one recalls all the more vividly those shifting alliances of the mercantile and the warrior castes, in myriad regional configurations, through the whole expanse of Indian medievality, in the pursuit of agrarian surplus, which nevertheless failed, again and again, to define our own paths into the modern world. One thinks of the Farsi language, which served for centuries and in large parts of the subcontinent as a language of rule, but of little else. One remembers also that India too was rocked, again and again, for a millennium, roughly from the eighth century to the eighteenth, by a whole host of powerful religious movements of a popular kind, and by something of a literary renaissance that was rooted in the common vulgates of the peasantry and the artisanal classes, and was often opposed as much to caste society as to the 'high' Shastric textuality. Why did it all fail, one wonders, to give rise to a unified social agency or a revolutionary project, even in an embryonic form, as Bhakti arose, in region after region, century after century, to challenge the monarcho-landlordist, Sanskritic, brahminical orders, and then subsided, in region after region – some of it assimilated back into the body of high textuality – without reshaping the structure of material productions in any appreciable degree and without shaping even an ideological counter-hegemony of a 'national' scope, beyond the regions? And, as one comes closer to one's own times, one thinks also of the many trajectories of nineteenth-century reformism, a Risorgimento of sorts, parts of which even got called 'the Bengal Renaissance', whose main battles were fought not over the issue of revolutionizing material productions but between the twin attractions of indigenist, often obscurantist, revivalisms on the one hand, and the empty 'cosmopolitanism' of the Anglicizers on the other – often ending with some uneasy, schizophrenic accommodation between the two. Cases of individuals like Bankim Chattopadhyaya of course illustrate quite powerfully how very palpable these self-divisions between indigenism and cosmopolitanism could be.

What are the consequences for nationalism as much as for the communist revolution itself, Gramsci was to ask, of the kind of imperial and classical pasts which Italy had inherited; of the centrality of the religious institution in the life of Italians, right up to his own past, so that religion, rather than language or 'nation', had long been the main unifying cement; of the blockage of the bourgeois revolution; and of the contemporary fragmentation, in *his* time, of the 'nation' into regional economic units as well as regionally differentiated idioms of culture and language? What are the means and forms of bourgeois hegemony in a 'nation' so fragmented and not even entirely bourgeois? For the Italian south had surely come under the sway of northern capital but was hardly capitalist in its own economic organization. The demise of feudalism without proper capitalist construction there had given rise to a new, post-feudal system of vassalage wherein the peasant was trapped by the local latifundia in a system of primordial loyalties and was bound, further, both to the latifundia and the national bourgeoisie in a coerced tributary relation, so that the intensified exploitation of the agrarian region had itself become a condition for the further development of the industrial zones, with no social or cultural bonds existing between the northern proletariat and the southern peasantry, and with the differentials of wealth between region and region, centre and periphery, the city and the country, assuming colonial proportions.

What kind of emancipatory project, what type of political organization and programme, what mode of cultural articulation, would be required, Gramsci was to ask himself even in the catastrophic loneliness of a Fascist prison, to create a 'national' bond between the subaltern classes so alienated from each other, between regions that were bound together in so stark an exploitation of the one by the other, and among a people who did not even speak the same language? Indeed, the alienating divide between north and south in Italy was not merely economic; it was cultural and linguistic as well, and it was often felt, on both sides, as a *racial* difference. What would be the means and forms proper to the task of constructing the counter-hegemony of the emergent revolutionary state, if one were to arise, within this set of alienations? In whose idiom, then, does one speak, and how many different idioms does one require? And if there is no nationally shared medium even of common speech, how does one make the revolution on the national scale? How does one prevent the revolutionary organization, that is to say, from developing either a purely regional character or becoming, on the other hand, a plaything of the urban strata, away from the most impoverished sections in the countryside? And, what does one do with an institutionalized religion whose sediments and encrustations in society have the glue of two thousand years attached to them, gathering to themselves peculiar blends of sophistication and backwardness, and which therefore serves as the reactionary 'common sense' for the populace at large while also bestowing upon its most urbane intellectuals the veneer of cosmopolitanism and imperial arrogance? The complex of ideas which Gramsci was to hold together, howsoever fragmentarily or tentatively, under the terminological heading of the 'national-popular', had such strategic dilemmas of the communist movement in their backdrop.

II

The first thing to be said about Antonio Gramsci is that he was a communist militant and a leader of the largest proletarian uprising that occurred in Europe in the aftermath of the First World War and the Bolshevik Revolution. He was not an Italian version of Mahatma Gandhi, as Bipan Chandra largely suggests; nor was he a cultural critic, on the model of Matthew Arnold, Julien Benda, Michel Foucault, Jacques Derrida – as poststructuralist appropriations of his thought pretend. Not a single piece of his writings between 1918 and 1936 – whether as editor of *L'Ordine Nuovo* or as leader of the Turin Factory Council Movement or as a key founder of the Italian Communist Party (PCI) or as prisoner of Fascism – makes any sense if we do not remember that his entire project had the single purpose of reconstituting a Leninism that would be appropriate to the conditions of a backward, largely peasant, indifferently industrialized society – in the face of Fascism. Even as we negotiate our way through the familiar Gramscian concepts of 'hegemony', 'war of position', 'national-popular', 'passive revolution', and so on, it is best to recall that Gramsci wrote of these matters with the acute awareness of the isolation and defeat of the Turin working class and the subsequent Fascist victory. He knew very well that Bordiga's sectarian leadership of the Italian Communist Party had been a major target of Lenin's criticisms in *Left-Wing Communism – An Infantile Disorder*. 'Revolutions are *prepared*,' Lenin had shouted at the Italian delegation during the Second Congress of the International, 'you want to reap what you have not sown.' Thus it is that Gramsci in his *Prison Notebooks* repeatedly credits Lenin with the theory of 'hegemony' because the concept itself had come to him from Russian debates, notably from Plekhanov, Axelrod, and of course Lenin himself; the term 'war of position', in the military sense and in its political implication, he had taken from Trotsky. Gramsci credits himself only with the attempt to *elaborate* that theory in specific Italian conditions.

The three terms – hegemony, national-popular, war of position –

designate in Gramsci's thought three aspects of a single problematic, namely the relation between consent and domination. The theoretical problematic was embedded, however, in concrete experience. Although the largest uprising in Europe at the time, the Factory Council Movement in Turin had been not only defeated by the state but had also signally failed to obtain much support among the Italian workers outside Turin, let alone from the bulk of the party or the peasantry; most advanced in conception and militancy, it had nevertheless failed to *lead* because, as Lenin put it, 'revolutions are *prepared*' and you cannot reap what you have not sewn. Hence Gramsci's subsequent and virtually obsessive emphasis in the *Notebooks* that no politics can actually *lead* unless it has already become the common sense of the people in the form of a national-popular consciousness so that an eventual seizure of power may be *prepared*, in the Leninist sense, through a war of position.

But there had also been, during those same years, the victory of Fascism, which had progressed with tantalizing speed from its few enclaves in 1918 to domination of the state by 1923 and nationally hegemonic power by 1926. Both terms of this dialectic – the defeat of the working class in Turin, and the victory of Fascism in the whole of Italy – are there in the theoretical problematic of consent and domination, domination and consent. For what is also striking in Gramsci's thought is that he thinks of Fascism neither in terms of Mussolini's specially charismatic personality, nor as simply a retrograde conspiracy of the ruling class, nor, as had been common among key communist thinkers, as the last desperate orgy of violence on the part of an inevitably declining finance capital. For him, Fascism was a specific resolution of the structural crisis of Italian capitalism able to mobilize diverse strata of Italian society in favour of that resolution; and he emphasized those historical features of Italian social formation which contributed to the mobilizing power of Fascism as a popular movement. In his *structural* analysis, Gramsci was so audacious as to compare the Fascist state in Italy with the New Deal in the United States and even the central planning mechanisms in the Soviet Union as three contemporaneous instances of the 'passive revolution' whereby a state sets out to resolve existing crises of the economic structure; so severely materialist is Gramsci that in *this* part of his *structural* analysis, he is not much concerned with the revolutionary character of the Bolshevik state, the progressive power bloc of the American New Deal or the retrograde violences of Italian Fascism. When he returns from this structural analysis of the Fascist resolution to the *political* superstructure of Fascism, hence to its cultural-ideological specificity, Gramsci sees in this superstructure a culmination of tendencies in Italian social formation dating back to the Roman Empire and the early Latinate Church. The history which eventually culminated in Fascist hegemony included, for Gramsci, the elitist tendencies in Italian Humanism; the reactionary character of the Italian Renaissance; the failure of the Risorgimento to found a new type of national-popular state; the failure of northern capital to create a uniform industrial society; the reactionary role of the southern intellectuals with their roots in agrarian backwardness and their predominant place in apparatuses of the Italian state; the absence of a confident liberal state in its confrontation with working-class militancy; and the ability of Fascism to draw on these and many other such factors in building a national bloc to take hold of the state and obtain consent from large sectors of society – especially the capitalist class, the state functionaries, the petty-bourgeois intelligentsia – which were not originally Fascist in outlook. The victory of Fascism is forged, in other words, in the overlap between social history and economic structure; the *culture* of Fascism is the condensation of that structure in its historical aspect.

In the early 1920s, when Parliament still commanded some degree of autonomy and the liberal centre had not fully caved in, when both the Communist and the Socialist Parties were still functioning and the Turin working class had not been fully defeated, there had been many moments when Gramsci himself had thought of Fascism as a superficial, superstructural phenomenon, bound to be defeated in the short run – in much the same way as many of us think of *Hindutva* these days. And, of course, that kind of complacency about the fascist threat in India today is all the more possible because, after all, the Left Front still rules Bengal and because we do have many Communist MPs in Parliament, and we know that there are very many secular, non-fascist elements in the centrist parties. So we feel free to carry on with our sectarian habits.

By the time Gramsci entered prison in November 1926, that kind of optimism had turned out to be illusory and the recognition grew that the true power of Fascism lies in the many pathologies of national life which are the products of particular historical realities and which are then condensed in the Fascist movement. The realization also that Fascism is not merely a factional pathology that occupies its own discrete space while the bulk of the nation marches on towards greater liberality, secularity, and prosperity preordained by the march of nationalist history; that the Fascist movement is in fact able to forge a national project for diverse social strata by endowing them with power, purpose, and institutional location. The recognition, in other words, that far from being a mere superstructural phenomenon, Fascism in fact draws its personnel from the very strata thrown up by the economic structure and by the rot of an anachronistic history. As culture, Fascism is not merely opposed to and by nationalism; it is a kind of nationalism, drawing upon, and interpreting in a fascist way, that same national tradition which other – secular and democratic – nationalisms also invoke.

III

The more mature writings of Gramsci have had a peculiar fate. Unlike Marx or Lenin or Mao, whose political writings were composed and published for immediate debate, there was a gap of several decades between the moment of Gramsci's actual writing and the moment of its mass dissemination. The bulk of his prison writings were undertaken between 1929 and 1934, but their publication even in Italian started only in the 1950s and, so far as English is concerned, which has regulated *our* access to his work, I might point out that except for a very small selection which was already available by 1958, the publication of even any considerable cross-section of this work is a matter, really, of the 1970s and beyond. Some dates may be useful in framing this problem. Thus, Quintin Hoare's *Selections from the Prison Notebooks* appeared in 1971; Lynne Lawner's edition of *Letters from Prison* in 1973; the two volumes of *Selections from Political Writings* in 1977 and 1978 respectively; *Selections from Cultural Writings* in 1985; a systematic edition of the bulk of the *Prison Notebooks* is now, for the first time, in progress. Alongside these, Fiori's influential biography became available in English in 1970; Alastair Davidson's even more illuminating biography came in 1977; Paolo Spriano's cautious little book which opened up new perspectives on the prison years came in 1979. Among the interpretations that set the terms in England and the United States, the key books edited by Chantal Mouffe and Anne Showstack Sassoon came in 1979 and 1982 respectively, Buci-Glucksmann's *Gramsci and the State* in 1980, and Perry Anderson's seminal essay, 'The Antinomies of Antonio Gramsci', in 1977. In India, the first substantive reference that I know of came in Sumit Sarkar's book on Swadeshi in 1973; but the two more extended – and I might say, alarming – uses came in Bipan Chandra's Presidential Address on the Indian National Congress at the Indian History Congress in 1985, and in Partha Chatterjee's book on nationalist thought in 1986; and all of us are doubtless aware of the highly problematic and eclectic ways in which Gramsci is invoked in the subaltern project in general.

This lag between formulation and publication represents not merely a span of time but also a sea-change in context and perspectives. At the time when Gramsci actually wrote those notes, Fascism was already in command not only in Italy but also in what was the most formidable industrial power in Europe, namely Germany; the decisive battles in

Spain were being fought as he was composing those notes. By contrast, this work went into *print* in the postwar years, well after the Italian Communist Party had itself played domestically the key role in anti-Fascist resistance and in the subsequent establishment of the parliamentary republic; by the late 1960s the Italian Party had grown as wistful about the parliamentary road to socialism as the German Party had been in, let us say, 1905. By the time Gramsci's writings appeared in France and the Anglo-Saxon countries, Eurocommunism had become the predominant tendency in Left politics, and the campus rebellions of 1968–69 had given way to a radical theory, across several academic disciplines, which was cultural*ist* in the precise sense that it posited the realm of culture as both autonomous and primary. It is best to recognize, I think, that the Gramsci that has come to us has been filtered already through Eurocommunist and culturalist readings. The consequences of these readings are too many to elaborate here, but one I may mention.

Quite aside from the fact that Gramsci is supposed to have argued that socialist revolutions are *prepared* through cultural criticism and philosophical debate, primarily by academic intellectuals, which is mostly what one hears from literary theorists these days, there is also, in the field of *political* theory, a remarkably wide consensus, from Buci-Glucksmann to Chantal Mouffe to even Perry Anderson, that Gramsci's uniqueness in the *oeuvre* of classical Marxism was that, unlike Marx or Lenin or Mao, he was preoccupied with the question of building socialism in conditions of liberal democracy, which are said to be the presumed and permanent conditions prevailing in the 'West', of which Italy was a part, as against the 'East', which includes everything from Russia to China and beyond. Let us be quite clear as to what the *difference* of Gramsci *is*, according to this consensus.

Marx's *political* vision, according to this thesis, is bound, *on the one hand*, by the revolutionary wave of 1848, when he devised the formula of a 'permanent revolution' whereby the bourgeois revolution leads uninterruptedly to proletarian revolution, in something of a prolonged civil war; and bound, *on the other hand*, by the experience of the Paris Commune, which gave to Marx the model of the workers' insurrection and the embryonic socialist forms of self-governance. *This* model Marx could follow, it is said, because he was writing before parliamentary democracy became the essential feature of the bourgeois state, hence before the emergence of stable forms of consent to bourgeois rule; conversely, then, insurrectionary communism is rendered anachronistic in the 'West' by the time of Marx's death, more or less. Lenin, meanwhile, never had to face the problems of building socialism in conditions of parliamentary democracy thanks to Tsarist autocracy; the '48-ist formula and the Commune model served for him as well, though

he too had to be sensitive to the *different conditions* prevailing in the
'West', as we see in such texts as the documents of 1921 which Trotsky
drafted on the issue of the United Front and which Lenin had fully
endorsed. Mao's uniqueness is of course said to reside in his having
devised a strategy proper for a backward, overwhelmingly peasant
society. Or so the argument runs!

It is *against* this legacy that the figure of Gramsci is posited, as one
who had to confront, uniquely, the issue of a socialist strategy in a zone
of the capitalist world, the *West*, where parliamentary democracy had
become the basic, universal form. In a subsidiary but very persistent
register, it is also posited that next to the procedures of parliamentary
democracy itself, bourgeois hegemony is also constructed in the key
area of *culture*. The implication is that capitalist culture is capable of
generating spontaneous consent from the working classes as no other
culture has ever been, so that the twin areas of socialist struggle are
parliamentary democracy and 'culture'. I might add that the word
'culture' in the culturalist readings of Gramsci is used in the conventional sense of *ideas* – philosophical and literary and social-scientist
ideas – with a remarkable degree of privileging for the aesthetic zone.

It is this settled view of Gramsci which I should like to question,
since both the polarities of this interpretation appear to me to be largely
overstated. It is certainly true that Gramsci said many trenchant things
about parliamentary democracy and 'the West'; also that his interest in
historical linguistics, in theatre and folklore and popular literature, and
in culturally hegemonic figures like Machiavelli or Dante or Croce, was
indeed extensive. But the crux of the work lies, I believe, elsewhere –
and it lies precisely in that thing which is always acknowledged as the
condition of his imprisonment but always sidelined as the linchpin of
his reflections – namely, *Fascism*.

In the three European countries where the workers' movement had
been the strongest in Gramsci's youth – Italy, Germany, and Spain –
that movement had not been defeated by parliamentary democracy but
violently suppressed by Fascist squads and Fascist states; the Vatican
had been, in all three cases and in the case of even largely Protestant
Germany, an ally of Fascists and Nazis. Many of the communist
policies, some fashioned by national parties and others by the International, had certainly been suicidal and there had been periods when
their hard line against social democracy had been at least highly indefen-
sible. Some of Gramsci's prison writings were surely designed as self-
criticism and as criticism of some general policies. But it is simply not
true that the defeat was owed primarily to suicidal policies or to mere
intransigence towards liberal parliamentarians and social democrats.
Social democracy was, in that period and subsequently, at least as hostile
towards communism as communism was towards it.

Be all that as it may. The immediate horizon against which Gramsci wrote was not parliamentary democracy but Fascism, for Italy in particular but also Europe in general; even when he spoke of *consent*, he wrote more often of processes which account for mass consent for a *Fascist* project than he did about parliamentary democracy as such. He wrote sparingly about any country where the parliamentary form had become truly sturdy, and when he did so he scarcely wrote about parliaments as such. Let me illustrate this with two examples. In the singular case of the United States, no reading of the remarkable text, *Americanism and Fordism*, is possible without noting that the *consent* he is writing about is not to parliamentary rule but to the capitalist mode of production as such. Even more crucially, the specificity of America for him, as distinct from Europe, is that the hegemony of the capitalist class there is produced not in the realm of so-called 'culture', by the humanist intelligentsia, but at the point of production itself, by the techno-managerial intelligentsia. The European bourgeoisie needs the philosophizing of the philosophers, lay popes like Croce, he argues, because European capitalism is ridden with too many anachronisms and its grandeur has to be proved philosophically; capitalist production is so brisk in America, he says, the processes of production are revolutionized so constantly, that it needs no philosophical justification and the prosperity it produces justifies itself, through the effort of technicians, managers, scientists. The lack of a powerful humanist culture is overcome, in other words, through the sheer productivity of industry itself. This contrast was certainly more true of the inter-war years, the interlude of the Depression notwithstanding, and one may have some reservations about Gramsci's prognosis even for that period. The key point remains, however, that in the American case industrial productivity impressed him far more than did representative democracy.

My other example refers to France, which interests Gramsci essentially on three counts. First, he suggests that although the Counter-Reformation prevailed in France, the energies which the Reformation had mobilized erupted later in a far more secular form, during the Enlightenment, among the Encyclopaedists, and eventually in the Revolution of 1789; in Italy, by contrast, the victory of Counter-Reformation was so complete that when the Risorgimento and national unification came, any revolutionary energies were remarkably absent from them. Second, it is in relation to France that Gramsci first offers a *historical* definition of what he elsewhere calls the 'national-popular' and which surfaces here under the guise of the term 'Jacobinism', by which he simply means a radical refashioning of the 'nation' by a dynamic urban force that establishes its leadership over the countryside by incorporating the peasant interest into its own project through a programme of radical agrarian transformation (the Chinese Party in the period of the War of Liberation and 'New Democracy' may be cited as what Gramsci might have meant by a communist kind of 'Jacobinism'). The *lack* of such a force in Italy accounts, in his analysis, both for the conventionality of the Risorgimento and the Fascist resolution of the crisis in the 1920s, not to speak of the communist failure itself. To this too we shall return. But the third thing that interests him about France is that he divides the whole of its modern history, borrowing somewhat from Kautsky, into two periods: the first from 1789 up to 1870, which he describes as a period when the French bourgeoisie fought a war of movement against the successive revolutionary tides; and the second starting from the decisive defeat of the Commune, after which the French bourgeoisie was able to establish a stable hegemonic rule, in the form of a war of position, thanks considerably to the new imperialist economy based on wars of conquest in Africa and Asia. It is only with the defeat of the Commune, he says, that the dynamic unleashed by 1789 is fully exhausted, and only with the rise of the new imperialist economy that the bourgeoisie gains the ability to fight a war of position. Defeat of the working class, the growth of an imperialist economy, and, for an earlier period, a dynamic alliance between town and country: these are the terms in which Gramsci essentially thinks of the French bourgeoisie's hegemony, not primarily in terms of its parliaments and philosophers.

Let me say, in summary, that the astonishing thing about all the major points Gramsci makes about France, the country that served for him as the very model of the bourgeois revolution, is his virtually complete lack of interest in the parliamentary form as such. What interested him, rather, was the historical physiognomy. This is even more true of his reflections on Italy itself, where he had first been a leader of the Turin insurrection and was then, after 1926, a prisoner of Fascism, but where he had also been, in the interval, a deputy in Parliament. The Parliament to which he had been elected was dominated already by the Fascists and was rendered even more powerless by the combination of Mussolini's decrees and the open Fascist terror; nor could he have forgotten, in later years, that he himself had been arrested despite the immunity he was supposed to enjoy as an elected deputy.

In our own context, the appropriation of Gramsci's revolutionary thought takes the form essentially of first ignoring that he was a Communist militant; second, of presenting him essentially as a *thinker*, a maker of *concepts*, whose concepts, then, can be quite detached from the political project which gave rise to the concept to start with; and, third, of detaching particular concepts from the overall architecture of that conceptual apparatus as such. Thus it is that Bipan Chandra can detach the concept of 'war of position' from Gramsci's Communist purpose and invoke it in celebration of Gandhi. The concept of 'passive revolution' can likewise be detached and used as explanatory model for individual nationalist careers such as those of Bankim or Gandhi or Nehru, as is done by Partha Chatterjee. Gramsci's individual formulations on the role of Catholicism in structuring the peasant world-view in southern Italy can be similarly and effortlessly applied to caste consciousness among sundry subalterns in India. More generally, he is represented as the theoretician of cultural superstructures with such extremity that any idea of *structure* as the condition of possibility and the limiting horizon of that superstructure simply disappears; left-wingish culturalism can then be posited as an autonomous realm with no necessary relation with class politics. In at least one highly influential school of historiography, the all-purpose term of 'subalternity' is used *conceptually* as an alternative to classical Marxist categories of class structure, and *politically* as a weapon to attack the organized Left; in its various deployments, the term 'subalternity' becomes so mobile and indeterminate that virtually everyone becomes, in one situation or another, a subaltern. In this same school of historiography, invocations of Gramsci are routinely combined with the most extreme denunciations of the Enlightenment, rationalism, and historicism – the very positions which Gramsci upheld as the enabling conditions of his own thought.

This is not the time or the place to engage fully with these many ways of domesticating Gramsci's revolutionary thought. As regards the contemporary emphasis on the purported centrality of the democratic state in Gramsci's thought, it is indeed true that the problem of building a socialist movement in conditions of political democracy does surface in his reflections but only in a secondary register. The key question in much of his prison writings is a radically different one, namely: what are the chief characteristics of the Italian historical legacy that may account for the fact that the intellectual movement that accompanied national unification and independence was so conservative, elitist, and 'passive' that it paved the way, some sixty years later, for not a progressive but a Fascist resolution? In other words, he traces the widespread consent for Fascism in his own time back to the inadequacies of Risorgimento nationalism, and the inadequacies of this nationalism back to lineages of conservative political culture that this nationalism had inherited and done little to break up. Thus, the need to reflect upon the whole of Italian history arises for him in the crucible of a failed nationalism and a triumphant Fascism. Some fifty years elapsed in Italy between the triumph of nationalism and the rise of Fascism to national power. We too are now approaching the fiftieth anniversary of our national Independence, and it is quite unclear as to where the Republic, with its great civilizational resources and its cruel class structure, is now headed.

IV

The starting point in Gramsci's reflections on Italian history is that being the inheritors of a great classical civilization and powerful imperial consolidations in the past is not only a mark of achievement and a source of pride, as 'traditional' intellectuals and upper-class nationalists claim, but also a terrible burden, since the sediments, traces, outlooks, and social relations that those great traditions leave behind in the form of 'national heritage' frequently make it very difficult to create a modern, secular, egalitarian society in the present. In other words, it was the *combination* of the class positions of the nationalist leaders on the one hand, and the accumulated anachronisms of Italian history and its ancient civilization on the other which ensured that the Risorgimento, accompanying the nationalist movements and the eventual unification and independence of Italy in the 1860s, would fail to lay the foundations for a democratic, secular, progressive society – and it was the nature of the nationalist failure that fed into the emergence of a fully fledged Fascist resolution some sixty years later.

Before anyone is tempted too strongly to slot Gramsci as a modernizer, plain and simple, let me quote a passage where he warns against overly hasty judgements against what is generally called 'tradition':

A truth that is forgotten is that what exists has had its justification, it has been useful, rational and has 'facilitated' historical development and life. It is true that at a certain point this stops being the case, that certain forms of life change from being means of progress into a stumbling block, an obstacle ... Hence it is necessary to study the history of each way of life, its original 'rationality' ... what one tends to ignore is that these ways of life appear to the people who live them as absolute, as something 'natural', as they put it, and to indicate their 'historicity' is of itself a formidable step, to show that they are justified so long as certain conditions exist, but when these conditions change they are no longer justified and become 'irrational' ... it is wrong to suppose that just because a way of living, acting or thinking has become 'irrational' in a given environment it has thereby become irrational everywhere and for everyone. (SCW, pp. 126–7)[2]

One can see that this is a strongly historicist passage, with its respect for a certain rationality of the past *in* the past; the sense that 'rationality' as much as 'irrationality' of particular human practices is always a matter of specific historical contexts; the assertion that a great many survivals of the past may indeed serve 'irrational' purposes in the present; the belief that every present has the right and even the duty to discard much of its own past. The context of the passage, in any case, is Gramsci's reflection on and even a degree of defence of certain social mores which persist in peasant life, but one can see quite readily that he is not opposed to all traditions, nor to 'tradition' as such, but to those particular ones which have become 'irrational' and yet survive either as signs of stasis in popular life or as oppressive encrustations in the social make-up of the upper classes, and hence in the state formation and ideological superstructures as such. This would apply in our case, for example, to the matter of 'caste' which has had, as it were, its own 'rationality' in the ancient division of labour but has also been a principal source of prejudice and violence in our society, for centuries. And it would apply equally to a number of patriarchal, racialistic, and religiously sanctioned beliefs which seem so 'natural' and 'absolute' to their own practitioners that any discussion of their 'historicity' becomes difficult, and which perfectly modern power-brokers may then invoke in the name of 'tradition' in order to construct particular kinds of national consensus in favour of particular kinds of irrationalist politics.

One of the most powerful ideological positions which arises out of that upper-class sense of 'tradition' is of course the ahistorical myth of the 'nation' itself, or, as Gramsci puts it,

> the rhetorical prejudice (originating in literature) according to which the Italian nation has always existed, from ancient Rome to the present day. This and other totems and intellectual conceits, although politically 'useful' in the period of national struggle as a means of stirring up and concentrating energies, are critically inept and become, ultimately, a weakness. (SCW, p. 201)

These words should have, I believe, a special resonance for us. For, we too have inherited an anti-colonial past in which the sense of an enduring Indian 'nation', from Vedic times to the modern, had been, as Gramsci puts it, 'useful' in 'concentrating energies' against British dominion. But the power of this 'intellectual conceit' has been such that far too many of us have come to believe in the very myth that we ourselves made and which was in its own time essentially of a functional nature. Too many of us are now unwilling to recall that the 'nation' is a modern construct, something that arose in the course of the anti-colonial movement itself; that the 'nation' is not a *thing* which, once made, simply endures; that 'nation', like class, is a *process*, which is made and remade, a thousand times over, and, more than process, 'nation' is a *terrain of struggle* which condenses all social struggles, so that every organized force in society attempts to endow it with specific meanings and attributes. It is also striking that Gramsci would use the phrase 'intellectual conceit' for that whole mysticism which claims that the nation has always existed, from times immemorial, and that he would trace the origins of this mysticism to literature. What he seems to be stressing here is (1) a certain revivalist tendency inherent in this mystical definition of the 'nation', (2) the specific role that traditional intellectuals play in propagating this mysticism which then envelops the discourse of the modernizing nationalists as well, and (3) the preponderant use of literary sources of the past in fashioning this mysticism. In general, he seems to be pointing towards a class complicity, as some other passages from Gramsci will soon make clear. The intellectual strata that are unwilling to undertake the tasks of a revolutionary restructuring of society and polity, and thus *make* a modern nation, would necessarily overvalorize the monuments of the past; if mythic literature can be said to be history itself, and if the founding myths of the nation are already there in the Ramayana, then the utter destitution of a third of the Indian population can be made to sink into insignificance and the rebuilding of the Ram *Mandir* can be posited as the crux of national salvation. This much is clear, in our own situation, about the Sangh *parivar*. What is far less than clear is the extent to which our nationalist overestimation of our purported spirituality, and our shared uncritical celebrations of our great 'tradition', have contributed to the making of this outcome.

Elsewhere, Gramsci speaks of 'a purely decorative, external, and rhetorical motif' that resides in the 'rhetorical cultural tradition that sees in monuments a stimulus for exalting national glories'. The "nation" is not the people, nor the past that continues in the "people", but 'the set of material things that recall the past' (SCW, pp. 250–51). Or, again:

> In Italy the term 'national' has an ideologically very restricted meaning, and does not in any case coincide with 'popular' because in Italy the intellectuals are distant from the people, i.e. from the nation. They are tied instead to a caste tradition that has never been broken by a strong popular or national political movement from below. This tradition is abstract and 'bookish'. (SCW, p. 208)

In his discussion of the Risorgimento, Gramsci speaks of 'an intellectualistic nationalism' characteristic of 'the traditional intellectual, swollen with rhetoric and literary memories of the past' (SCW, p. 246) and 'linked to the "claim" of finding a national unity, at least de facto, over the whole period from Rome to the present' (SCW, p. 246). He goes on to wonder, then:

> How did this claim originate, how was it maintained and why does it survive even today? Is it a sign of strength or of weakness? ... Or is it instead the reflection of a sinister 'will to believe', an ideological

fanaticism (and fanaticization) whose purpose is precisely to 'patch up' structural weaknesses and prevent a feared collapse? (SCW, p. 245)

He then goes on immediately to say: 'the latter seems to me the correct interpretation, together with the fact of the excessive importance (in relation to the economic formations) of the intellectuals, i.e. of the petty bourgeoisie, in comparison with the economically backward and politically powerless classes' (SCW, p. 245).

Two of these ideas are especially worth noting. First, the suggestion that this mythic idea of an eternal and strong nation, rooted in imperial past and the religious institution, is a pathological response in the face of a 'feared collapse', with the hope that the 'ideological fanaticism' would '"patch up" structural weaknesses'. This pathology then leads, in our own case certainly, to a masculinist mobilization, in the name of a unitary Hinduism, to hold together through violence and 'ideological fanaticism' a national unity in regions where consent to it has been eroded by prior corruptions and violences of the state. We may recall here how the failure of the state to come to terms with a dozen insurgencies, from Punjab to Kashmir to Jharkhand and beyond, has fed into the longings for a strong, centralized, militarized state, invoking a heroic Hindu past and announcing its contemporary readiness to club any and all into abject submission. The second key idea here is that this particular kind of pathological nationalism arises all the more readily where the working classes and the peasantry are passive, while political initiative rests with a caste-like intellectual stratum alienated from those classes. Elsewhere, Gramsci would underscore the fact that in the Italy of his time a full 10 per cent of the population drew its income from the state, in one form or another. Such percentages are higher, I might add, not only in present-day India but in a whole host of postcolonial societies, which then contributes to a certain fetishization of the state, inordinate power in the hands of the state-associated strata, and, in some cases, to an outright fascistic tendency. The rapid penetration of state agencies by the communal organizations in our own time is eloquent testimony of the potential for this fascistic tendency in *any* state that is overdeveloped in relation to the civil society it is designed to serve and administer.

Beyond these conjunctural hypotheses, Gramsci also traces this 'cul-turalist' idea of a supra-historical nation as a particular ideological construct that arises out of the conjunction of (1) a long history of classical and imperial civilization, (2) the contemporary failure of the state to implement any radical change in the lives of the popular classes, and (3) a certain dissociation of the intellectual strata from those classes. It is in this context that a nostalgic kind of cultural chauvinism becomes a substitute for a progressive project. Again, as he himself put it: 'culture, for many centuries, was the only Italian "national" manifestation; ... this "Italian" culture is the continuation of the medieval cosmopolitanism linked to the tradition of the Empire and the Church' (SPN, p. 117). I shall again ignore the vast differences in the two historical situations and will speak directly of the kinds of things in our past that such passages bring to mind. For, 'culture' – and a religiously defined sense of 'community' and 'culture' – has been a rather fatal ingredient in the hundred-odd years of our communal history. Thus it is that the whole history of Muslim communalism, starting from its founding moment in the so-called reform movements of the nineteenth century which produced litterateurs like Syed Ahmed Khan, poets like Altaf Hussein Hali, and novelists like Abdul Halim Sharar, has always been based on a certain nostalgia for the Mughal imperium, the princely state and the specialness of the Persianized culture of upper-class Muslims. But the idea that 'culture' – indeed, spirituality – is the special 'national' vocation of the Indian has led an even more powerful life in the history of Hindu communalism. Already by the middle of the nineteenth century, well before Bankim or Aurobindo or Vivekanada bestowed the idea with such hallowed respectability, so numerous were its purveyors that Madhusudan Dutt was constrained to denounce openly a certain cluster of them, in a felicitous phrase, as 'Ram and his rabble'. The empires that Hindu communalist nostalgia so fondly recalled as its own past – and, by extension, as the real roots of 'national culture' – were not only the real, historical empires of the period prior to the Turko-Afghan invasions, nor just the Rajput or Maratha kingdoms of the early and late Mughal periods, but also the powerfully imagined and religiously believed empires of the mythic past. This pathological will to recoup a certain kind of virility by obliterating lines of demarcation between history and mythology is already dense by the time of Bankim, whom our subalternist theorizers recall, preposterously enough, for positivism and as an agent of European Enlightenment, but not as one of the founding fathers of the more hysterical kinds of communalist imaginings, in literature but also far beyond literature. Bajrang Dal is, after all, in some ways, a reenactment and a logical denouement of that same *Anandamath* and the *Bande Mataram* tradition against which Tagore was to warn some seventy years ago.[3]

In a very different historical context, Gramsci was to perceive the obvious fact that in circumstances where cultural invocation replaces the projects of radical economic change, nationalism becomes more literary, rhetorical, spiritualistic, so that invented memories of the past not only compensate for present weakness but also continue to fuel an imperial imagination long after the old empires have disappeared.

[F]rom the sixteenth century onwards Italy contributed to world history especially because it was the seat of papacy and ... Italian Catholicism was felt not only as a surrogate for the spirit of the nation and the state but also as a worldwide hegemonic institution, as an imperialistic spirit. (SCW, pp. 220–21)

Gramsci is writing here, of course, of the numerous intellectuals of Italian origin who continued to play a directive function in the Latinate culture as a whole, as this culture survived to a considerable degree in various parts of Europe well after the Italian Renaissance. I must confess, though, that passages of this kind have a peculiar resonance for me. For I cannot help recalling Vivekananda setting out with his message of syndicated Hinduism, on his way to Chicago, hoping that the message would radiate from there to the rest of the world so that a colonized, economically backward country may indeed conquer the world spiritually. Since that fateful trip we have sent a host of *sadhus* and *mahants* to convert the world, without much success of course. But it is precisely this combination of spiritual arrogance and a craving for world-historical spiritual missions that gradually becomes a fantasy of world empire, making it possible for the proponents of *Hindutva*, Malkani for example, to aspire to a fascistic reorganization of the polity at home while also clamouring to fabricate nuclear weapons, so as to strut on the global stage as a 'great power', the poverty and illiteracy of our masses notwithstanding. I seem sometimes to think that nostalgia for past empires and cravings for an imperial regeneration are in some ways worse than the actual possession of an empire, in the sense that a truly imperialist state may at length produce for the home country constitutional government and a welfare state, but when a backward bourgeoisie and bellicose petty-bourgeois strata begin to nurse such hallucinatory nostalgias and cravings, an imperial fantasy necessarily becomes a fascist project.

V

But what were the elements of national culture that account for the nostalgias and cravings which led, in the case of Italy, towards Fascism? On the most general level, Gramsci's summation of Italian history runs as follows:

The reason for the failure of the successive attempts to create a national-popular collective will is to be sought in the existence of certain specific social groups which were formed at the dissolution of the Communal bourgeoisie; in the particular character of other groups which reflect the international function of Italy as seat of the Church and depository of the Holy Roman Empire ... An effective *Jacobin* force was always missing, and could not be constituted; and it was precisely such a Jacobin force which in other nations awakened and organized the national-popular collective will, and founded the modern States ... Italy's particular characteristic is a special '*rural bourgeoisie*', a legacy of parasitism bequeathed to modern times by the disintegration as a class of the Communal bourgeoisie ... Any formation of a national-popular collective will is impossible, unless the great mass of peasant farmers bursts *simultaneously* into political life ... That Machiavelli understood it reveals a precocious Jacobinism. (SPN, pp. 131–2)

The striking feature of this summation is Gramsci's emphasis on those specific characteristics of the Italian intelligentsia which distinguished it from analogous strata elsewhere in the main European formations. The Lutheran Reformation in Germany had had the effect of defeating the authority of the Latinate Church and stabilizing a vernacular intelligentsia; in Italy, by contrast, the Counter-Reformation succeeded so thoroughly that the hegemony of the conservative religious institution remained intact and the priestly class of Italian origin continued to occupy key positions throughout Catholic Europe, thereby escaping the need to reform itself. In Spain, England, and France, absolutist monarchy accomplished at least the task of national unity; in Italy, unification had to wait until the 1860s, and even then lacked a national language as well as a uniform national economy, while the continued power of the Vatican assured the social and intellectual supremacy of the caste of traditional intelligentsia; the lack of an industrial revolution meanwhile assured the preponderance, in the cultural life of the nation as much as in state institutions, of intellectuals and functionaries drawn from agrarian reaction. In France, where too the Counter-Reformation had prevailed, the combined effects of the Enlightenment and the Jacobin element in the Revolution transformed social and cultural life far beyond what the Reformation had accomplished in Germany, which never had a revolution of the Jacobin type; Italy, of course, experienced no such transformation and its intelligentsia remained rooted so much in the traditions of High Church and the imperial past that it had no capacity to align itself with either the peasantry as a class or a popular-democratic project for the nation as a whole. The formation of what he calls the 'national-popular collective will' Gramsci associates with a social revolution that incorporated the peasant interest as the focal point of national interest, in opposition to the 'high' traditions of religion and empire.

In the wake of this general summation, Gramsci then establishes a certain periodization of Italian history, from Roman times to his own present:

> It is necessary to start with the Roman Empire, which produced the first concentration of 'cosmopolitan' – that is to say, 'imperial' – intellectuals, then move on to the Christian times, when the organization of clergy under the Popes gave to the heredity of imperial intellectual cosmopolitanism the form of a European caste system. Only in this way can one explain how only after the eighteenth century – that is, after the first jurisdictional struggles between State and Church began – can one speak of Italian intellectuals as 'national'. (LP, pp. 200–1)

By 'intellectuals' Gramsci of course means all those individuals and strata whose function in the social division of labour is to organize various kinds of productions and institutions. In this sense, priests are as much the 'intellectuals' of the ecclesiastical institution as state functionaries were of the Roman Empire, or the techno-managerial strata may be the 'intellectuals' of the modern capitalist enterprises. By 'cosmopolitan', meanwhile, Gramsci means that conduct and outlook of the intellectuals which separates them from the life and aspirations of the common people. A key indicator of this 'cosmopolitanism' for Gramsci is the separation between the language of intellectual function and the language of daily life, that is to say, the fact that Latin remained the predominant language of all intellectual function while no consolidation took place for Italian, and the masses of people continued to function in their regional languages and dialects. This extreme linguistic fragmentation is well indicated by the fact that when Italy was unified in the 1860s as an independent state, only a small fraction of the population was able to speak the Italian language, so that when Gramsci himself went to his rustic school forty years after independence, in the first decade of the present century, the Tuscan variant of Italian which he heard from his teachers was as foreign to him as English was for me when I first went to a small-town, vernacular school in Uttar Pradesh some forty years ago – or, indeed, as what passes for 'Hindi' these days might be for most children in UP or Bihar or Madhya Pradesh who enter school with their own vernaculars and are then taught this 'pure' Hindi as their 'mother tongue'. The philological analysis of Gramsci's prose that Pasolini, for example, has offered suggests that as late as 1918, after Gramsci had had five years of university education and had already emerged as not only a key leader of the Turin working class but had also been the founder-editor of the legendary *L'Ordine Nuovo*, he still wrote what Pasolini ironically calls 'ugly Italian'.[4] Gramsci entered the Fascist prison some eight years later, in 1926, and in the ensuing

ten years, he was to think often of what that 'cosmopolitanism' –
that distance between the language of intellectuals and the language of
the common people – might have contributed to the failure of the
intellectuals even of the Left to construct what Gramsci was to call a
'national-popular' culture. But, then, his repeated denunciation of the
'cosmopolitanism' of the 'traditional' intellectuals is also quite frequently a veiled criticism of the tendency among Communist intellectuals to treat the hackneyed Soviet textbooks as sacred texts and to
neglect the national specificity in favour of global abstractions, as well
as the tendency of the International to interfere constantly in the tactical
work of the national parties. The tendency towards intellectual arrogance bequeathed by the imperial tradition and towards orthodoxy as a
result of centuries-old Catholic education had had profound consequences, he argues, for the cultural and psychological outlook of the
Italian intelligentsia as a whole, as much on the Left as on the Right.

As regards the long-range trajectory of Italian history, Gramsci traces
this retarded development of the Italian intelligentsia all the way back
to the failure of the communes, in the twelfth and thirteenth centuries,
which became free of feudal domination but failed to go beyond the
political form of the city-state; that bourgeoisie remained local, mercantile, and devoted to its own corporate interests, lacking any national
project whatever. This combination of intellectual cosmopolitanism
inherited from traditions of church and empire, and the non-revolutionary character of the communal bourgeoisie accounts, for Gramsci, then,
for the reactionary character of both Humanism and the Renaissance in
Italy, as follows:

> Humanism, with its cult of Latinity and Romanity, was much more
> orthodox than the erudite vernacular literature of the thirteenth and
> fourteenth centuries. (This claim can be accepted if one distinguishes
> within the movement of the Renaissance the break which occurred
> between Humanism and the national life which had gradually formed
> after the year 1000, if one considers Humanism as a progressive
> process for the educated 'cosmopolitan' classes but regressive from the
> point of view of Italian history.) (SCW, p. 220)

A decisive moment, in other words, was the victory of Latinate
Humanism over the popular movements that had arisen in the vernaculars but which were defeated and subordinated by a persisting classicism,
even though these vernacular literatures admittedly left many marks on
popular culture. The Indian historical experience of course has no real
analogue for this development in Italian history, but the point Gramsci
makes should provoke us to think about ourselves, for we too have
experienced, generally speaking, some arresting reversals. It is well

enough known that the devotional theisms which arose in medieval India and which had more or less exhausted their energies by the end of the eighteenth century did much to vernacularize culture as a whole, pushing its centre of gravity towards the artisanate, the peasantry, the low caste, and the women, as never before. But two reversals are striking: (1) that certain strands of Bhakti chose to fold themselves back into religious and social conservatism; and (2) that the re-Sanskritizing movements of more recent times are in fact in direct conflict with that massive vernacularization, with inevitable consequences for caste and class hegemonies. The career of the Hindi language is significant in this regard. For the project of the re-Sanskritization of Hindi has been so spectacularly successful at the institutional level that we already tend to forget how recent it is, how much it has been a matter not only of communal politics but of caste and class hegemonies, how much it is invested in defining a revisionary kind of Hinduism, and the many insidious ways in which it has been implicated in the decline of progressive trends among the intelligentsia of the Gangetic regions and the rise, instead, of what is essentially an intolerant intellectual temper, a caste arrogance, and an authoritarian personality whose spontaneous tendency is towards fascistic forms of domination.

VI

It has been a staple of certain kinds of hidebound Marxism, especially as it came to us in Soviet textbooks, that the bourgeoisie and the landed aristocracy are antagonistic classes and that the rise of the one necessarily involves the demise of the other. This binary representation of the principal propertied classes has made it difficult to understand the characteristics of the anti-colonial movements of the bourgeoisie as well as the class structure of postcolonial societies as they have emerged in the post-Independence era under the dominance of the bourgeoisie. Part of the problem arises, of course, from the historiographic error of treating the French Revolution as the prototype of all bourgeois revolutions, instead of seeing it as a very notable exception, which is what it was. In both Britain and Germany, the emergence of industrial capitalism involved not the destruction of the landed classes but compromises between the bourgeoisie, on the one hand, and aristocrats and junkers on the other, with growing embourgeoisement of the latter; the growth of commercial capital had helped in both cases in transforming the aristocracy into a bourgeoisie of the ground rent. Indeed, one might go so far as to suggest that British capitalism was agrarian before it became industrial-bourgeois.

Gramsci offers fresh insights on this score, which have far-reaching implications for analyses of nationalist movements and postcolonial societies. For the early nineteenth century, he emphasizes two factors: the growing conservatism of all European bourgeoisies, including the Italian bourgeoisie, after the French Revolution, and the failure of Italian literary Romanticism to become linked to any popular movement for social change, of the type that Jacobinism signified in the case of French Romanticism. Here, his essential argument is that the radical alliance of the bourgeoisie and the peasantry, as represented by the Jacobins, had so inspired the French working class that their insurgent radicalism began to threaten the power of the bourgeoisie itself, and although the Terror managed to contain the French working class, national bourgeoisies everywhere else learned the lesson that they could not afford to break with the landowning aristocracy entirely, lest they themselves be attacked in a revolution that runs out of their control; the national revolutions that came *after* the French Revolution took the form, in other words, of a bourgeois–aristocrat alliance in order to pre-empt the possibility of a combined worker–peasant insurgency in the dynamic of a 'permanent revolution'. He thus speaks of the 'birth of the modern European states by successive small waves of reform rather than by revolutionary explosions like the original French one', and then goes on to say:

> The 'successive waves' were made up of a combination of social struggles, interventions from above of the enlightened monarchy type, and national wars – with the latter two phenomena predominating. The period of the 'Restoration' is the richest in developments of this kind; restoration becomes the first policy whereby social struggles find sufficiently elastic frameworks to allow the bourgeoisie to gain power without dramatic upheavals, without the French machinery of terror. The old feudal classes are demoted from their dominant position to a 'governing' one, but are not eliminated . . . instead of a class they become a 'caste' with specific cultural and psychological characteristics, but no longer with predominant economic functions. (SPN, p. 115)

The distinction between 'ruling class' and 'governing caste' of course goes back to Engels, as for example in his comments on Britain. It is in those comments, and especially in his reflections on the division of government departments between the bourgeoisie and the aristocracy, that one begins to gain the insight, not much developed by Engels himself, that the parliamentary form of governance in a predominantly agrarian society necessarily gives a very prominent role to those owners of landed property, and those clusters of commercial capital which are associated with agriculture, who have special preserves in rural constituencies and vote banks. The main point, however, is that Gramsci detects a growing conservatism already in the European nationalist movements of the nineteenth century, which come to rely on a bourgeois–landlordist alliance against the potential threats of the peasantry and the working classes, well before the Bolshevik Revolution or even the Paris Commune. It is in this moment of the fear of what Gramsci calls Jacobinism that the national bourgeoisie of the emergent states, such as Italy and Germany, begin to renounce their revolutionary function and align themselves with monarchies and landowners, while landowners themselves play a brisk role in building capitalism, as in Germany and Japan. In this crucible of national revolutions that are, in class terms, indistinguishable from restoration itself, a new political passivity sets in among the literary intelligentsia as well, and Romanticism itself becomes merely a literary style:

> Certainly many definitions have been given to the term [Romanticism], but we are concerned with only one of them, and with the narrowly 'Literary' aspect of the problem. Among its other meanings romanticism has assumed that of a special relationship or bond between intellectuals and the people, the nation. In other words, it is a particular reflection of 'democracy' (in the broad sense) in literature (in the broad sense) . . . In this sense, romanticism precedes, accompanies, sanctions and develops that entire European movement which took its name from the French Revolution . . . in this specific sense romanticism has never existed in Italy. Its manifestations have been at best minimal, very sporadic and in any case of a purely literary nature. (SCW, p. 205)

As regards the economic structure as such, this non-revolutionary path of national unification and independence produced only a fragmented and frightened bourgeoisie, which in turn produced retarded industrialization, a conservative alliance between northern capital and southern latifundist landowners, non-industrial and lopsided urbanization, a preponderance of state functionaries in society at large, and of 'southern intellectuals', especially, in organs of state. We shall return to the issue of 'southern intellectuals', but I want first to cite two passages – on the kind of urbanization which retarded industrialization entails; and on the pernicious role that some intellectuals play in propagating what Gramsci calls a 'fetishized conception of unity' – which will have some bearing on our present predicament. Thus, he notes:

> An 'industrial' city is always more progressive than the countryside which depends organically upon it. But not all Italy's cities are 'industrial' . . . Urbanism in Italy is not purely, nor 'especially' a phenomenon of capitalist development or of that of big industry.

Naples, which for a long time was the biggest Italian city and which continues to be one of the biggest, is not an industrial city; neither is Rome – at present the largest Italian city. Yet in these medieval-type cities too, there exist strong nuclei of populations of a modern urban type; but what is their relative position? They are submerged, oppressed, crushed by the other part, which is not of a modern type, and constitutes the great majority. (SPN, p. 91)

This passage doubtless displays too great a belief in the progressive role of the modern-industrial, the reactionary nature of the rural/ premodern. To this we shall return shortly. Significant in any case is Gramsci's emphasis on the *semi-industrialized* nature of Italy as late as the 1930s; unlike London or Amsterdam or New York, megacities where the texture of life had by then come to be marked deeply by capitalist enterprise and finance, Rome and Naples were not yet 'especially' marked by such development. And, even though Gramsci's characterization of them simply as 'medieval-type cities' underestimates the extent to which a distorted form of capitalist modernization had been grafted on top of the inherited medieval structure, the essential character of the problem he is trying to clarify for himself becomes altogether apparent if we recognize that under the phrase 'population of a modern urban type' he is trying to think mainly of the proletariat. In other words, he is quite accurate in his observation that in urbanization of this type the proletariat remains a relatively small segment of the urban population and is 'submerged, oppressed, crushed' by the numerically far greater number of those who have no roots in a modern, industrial culture. This is accurate about the Italy of his own times and opens up useful ways of thinking about the great cities of our own region and time, even though what Gramsci does not sufficiently clarify is that it is not so much the 'medieval-type' city but particular patterns of capitalist urbanization – based as they are so largely on the exodus of the peasantry from the country-side and on networks of consumption and services, while most industrial production is carried on elsewhere – which give to such cities their largely non-industrial character and accumulates in them vast numbers of individuals who are proletarianized without becoming a stable proletariat, while being stripped of their traditional moorings, hence of traditional moral economies. In the great Indian cities of our own time, these urban crowds are forced to live in social and economic circumstances that are simply barbaric, so that entire communities and neighbourhoods become shifting but fertile grounds for crime gangs and fascist mobilizations, making the formation of proletarian moralities very difficult. The social degeneration of Bombay in fact illustrates the moral and political decay of a city which once was and is no more 'industrial', even though it never was of a 'medieval type'. And it is quite beyond doubt that it was the enormous influx of the rural population into Teheran in the wake of the spiralling oil wealth during the 1960s and after, which accounts for the decline of the communist/liberal political culture among that city's insurgent population during this period, providing, instead, the ready-made social basis for mass mobilization in the Khomeniite, millenarian, clerico-fascist takeover.

Elsewhere, Gramsci also speaks of a 'hysterical unitarianism' despite – perhaps, because of – a virtually semi-colonial relationship between town and country and even between large regions of the territorial nation-state. Some formulations here should give us pause. I therefore quote a longish passage:

> During the Risorgimento, moreover, there already appeared, embryonically, the historical relationship between North and South, similar to that between a great city and a great urban area. As this relationship was, in fact, not the normal organic one between a province and an industrial capital, but emerged between two vast territories of very different civil and cultural tradition, the features and the elements of a conflict of nationalities were accentuated ... The Mezzogiorno was reduced to the status of a semi-colonial market, a source of savings and taxes, and was kept 'disciplined' by measures of two kinds. First, police measures: pitiless repression of every mass movement, with periodic massacres of peasants. Second, political-police measures: personal favours to the 'intellectual' stratum – in the form of jobs in the public administration; of licence to pillage the local administration with impunity ... i.e., incorporation of the most active Southern elements 'individually' into the leading personnel of the State ... Thus the social stratum which could have organized the endemic Southern discontent instead became an instrument of Northern policy ... men like Croce and Fortunato abetted this form of corruption, even if passively and indirectly, by means of their fetishistic conception of unity ... This form or hysterical unitarianism was especially prevalent among the Sicilian intellectuals. (SPN, pp. 92–5)

As we negotiate the terms laid out in passages like these, we might begin by recalling that Gramsci, who accuses formidable intellectuals like Croce and Fortunato of 'hysterical unitarianism', and who refers here so contemptuously to 'fetishistic conceptions of unity', certainly did not want large nations to break down into little units. He himself was a champion of 'national unity' to such an extent that for earlier phases of European history he admires even the absolutist monarchy – even, explicitly, the Roman Empire – for having obtained political and cultural unity for big territorial units and large concentrations of diverse populations. There is in Gramsci no assumption, as has become so common in postmodern identitarian discourses, that large, multi-national states are intrinsically coercive or that there is something fundamentally wrong with projects of national integration which seek to bring together historically different regions – with their cultural differences, differential levels and patterns of economic development, distinctions between town and country, industrial and agricultural zones – into a well-articulated national formation. His concern is, rather, with a particular experience, that of the Italian Risorgimento, where, as contrasted with the French Revolution, he detects a massive failure of bourgeois nationalism to undertake precisely those processes of democ-ratization and dynamic development which alone could have created a fully integrated national unity. Here, as elsewhere, he has in mind what he calls the making of 'the national-popular will' or more cryptically 'Jacobinism', i.e. a bourgeoisie that becomes 'national' not simply by virtue of being indigenously born but by adopting the peasant interest as the crux of the formation of democratic nationhood. Lacking such a dynamic mode of national development, the 'nation' in a predomi-nantly agrarian society would simply come to rest on an authoritarian bourgeois–bureaucrat alliance which will necessarily corrode what insti-tutions of liberal governance might have been created in the first flush of obtaining the nation-state; hence the increasing decay of such insti-tutions in Italy within the first quarter-century after unification and independence. The task of making a nation is for Gramsci historically indispensable but the task, he says, can be accomplished only from below, not from above. Hence his constant concern with 'national unity' *and* his contemptuous dismissal of 'hysterical unitarianism'. In other words, he assumes, for that whole modern period inaugurated by the French Revolution, that (1) revolutionary restructuring of the life of the masses, especially the peasantry, is the only possible premise for national unity, and that (2) 'fetishistic conceptions of unity', even when espoused by liberal intellectuals like Croce, can only lead to the institutionaliza-tion of massive corruptions and escalating violences. We might add that such institutionalization of corruption and violence in the name of 'unity' of the nation can lead only to the thickening of the fascistic temper at large, paving the way for an openly authoritarian state and a widespread consent, among the beneficiaries of 'unitarianism', for per-manence of extra-legal action against dissents, minorities, regions. In context, then, Gramsci's specification of two types of 'discipline' – 'pitiless repression', and 'personal favours to the intellectual stratum' – have a familiar ring.

Gramsci characterizes the Risorgimento as 'the period of restoration-revolution, in which the demands which in France found a Jacobin-Napoleonic expression were satisfied by small doses, legally, in a reformist manner', and then goes on to ask: 'But, in the present conditions, is it not precisely the Fascist movement which in fact corresponds to the movement of moderate and conservative liberalism in the last century?'

The ideological hypothesis could be presented in the following terms: that there is a passive revolution involved in the fact that – through the legislative intervention of the State, and by means of the corporative organization – relatively far-reaching modifications are being introduced into the country's economic structure ... In the concrete framework of Italian social relations, this could be the only solution whereby to develop the productive forces of industry under the direction of the traditional ruling classes ... Whether or not such a schema could be put into practice, and to what extent, is only of relative importance. What is important from the political and ideological point of view is that it is capable of creating – and indeed does create – a period of expectation and hope, especially in certain Italian social groups such as the great mass of urban and rural petty bourgeois. (SPN, pp. 119–20)

Fascism, in other words, has two faces. On the one hand, it engages the whole nation in a massive social upheaval in the ideological-cultural domain out of which arises the machinery of terror; but simultaneously, it also enacts a comprehensive programme of economic restructuring in order to serve those interests of the liberal bourgeoisie which that bourgeoisie has not been able to legislate through machineries of the liberal state; thus it is that the liberal bourgeoisie, or large segments of it, *become* fascist. The precise combination of terror and legislation would of course vary from one country to another, but it is somewhat alarming that while the RSS *parivar* and Shiv Sena boldly utilize their legal and extra-legal machineries for fascist mobilizations and even for terrorizing major cities, and while the Congress busies itself in turning its anti-communal face one day and its communal face the next, there appears to be a wide consensus on those agendas of the bourgeoisie that are quaintly called 'liberalization' and which have doubtless inaugurated, with ample aid from the media, 'a period of expectation and hope' among 'the great mass of urban and rural petty bourgeois', many of whom are otherwise partisans of the RSS and the like. Supposing the Congress variety of 'liberalization' does not succeed, shall we then be ready for an authoritarian resolution? Shall, then, 'the mass of the urban and rural petty bourgeois' demand that the machinery of terror and the machinery of 'liberalization' be one and the same?

VII

At the end of his 'Notes on Italian History', in *Selections from the Prison Notebooks*, we find a somewhat enigmatic passage:

> In the present epoch, the war of movement took place politically from March 1917 to March 1921; this was followed by a war of position whose representative – both practical (for Italy) and ideological (for Europe) – is fascism. (SPN, p. 120)

I am not entirely certain what this formulation actually means, in the sense that what is cryptically described here as a phase of the 'war of movement' could well be referring, equally provocatively but in somewhat different ways, to (1) the Soviet Union, (2) Europe in general, or specifically (3) Italy. Generally speaking, Gramsci seems to be proposing that the bourgeoisie (Italian *and* European) was forced to adopt highly flexible and varied tactical manoeuvres during the short period of the revolutionary upsurge (1917–21) but was then able to adopt Fascism as the *main*, stable form of the strategic response to the defeated but persisting movements of the working class. What is striking, in any case, is that while Gramsci often identifies Fascism as a passive revolution in the economic sphere, he equates it here equally clearly with a war of position in the political sphere. This designation for Fascism needs to be understood in relation certainly to the question of consent in any hegemonic project, which is central for Gramsci in all wars of position. His essential point here is that *all* forces that contend for hegemony, in whatever conditions, have to pass through phases of wars of position as well as movement; once the apparatuses of state have been secured, a *confident* bourgeoisie also wages a war of position in order to enforce the requisite structural changes, with or without representative democracy.

If the passage I have cited above were to be read exclusively in relation to Italy, the phase in which Fascism fought the war of movement would be seen to include the period in which Turin witnessed the largest uprising in all of Europe during that period; by 1922, Fascist squads were of course destroying the very offices from which that uprising had been led. After that, Fascism's war of position could then be waged once it had come to occupy apparatuses of the state, using those apparatuses for disorganizing the opposition, extending social consent for its own dominance, and completing that dominance by 1926. In our own circumstance today, we might say that the forces of *Hindutva* are waging a war of rapid manoeuvre, while constantly extending their social base and their penetration of the state apparatuses. By contrast, the secular forces, which predominate both in civil society and in apparatuses of state, but which are splintered into a great many different political organizations and therefore possess neither a 'collective intellectual', so recognized by all, nor a joint programme of national-popular social transformation, have been forced to wage a highly defensive war of position that rests on an unstable combination of numerical majority and strategic inferiority. We cannot yet predict the outcome of this unstable equilibrium, but the fact that the anti-communal forces are waging their battle from a static position of strategic inferiority is amply demonstrated in the absence of a common programme, the paucity of mass initiatives, the always local and reactive character of the initiatives that are taken, the effects of which are then necessarily diminished for lack of a leading agency and incremental elaboration. But the equilibrium *is* unstable and the strategic drawback for the forces of the far Right appears to be that they must yet rely mainly on their legal and parliamentary machineries, and while their ability to manipulate disinformation through the media grows apace, there is still relatively little and relatively sporadic social consent for unremitting terror.

VIII

Let me end this rather complex argument by briefly recapitulating three of Gramsci's general warnings. First, Gramsci's reformulation in the *Prison Notebooks* of what he had earlier called the 'Southern Question' suggests that a weak link between the communist movement and the peasant masses expresses itself within the anti-Fascist movement in the form of a great preoccupation with the ideological formation of the urban classes, which serves, in turn, to reinforce the 'cosmopolitanism' of the intellectuals and their distance from the bulk of the population. In consequence, the struggle between the Fascist and the anti-Fascist forces becomes a struggle essentially between the various segments – the reactionary and the radical segments – of the petty bourgeoisie, while the working masses are left to the mercy of the 'traditional' intellectuals, especially in the countryside.

Second, Gramsci warns against a positivist kind of economic determinism and posits a more open relationship between structure and superstructure, in the following words:

It may be ruled out that immediate economic crises of themselves produce fundamental historic events; they can simply create a terrain more favourable to the dissemination of certain modes of thought, and certain ways of posing and resolving questions involving the entire subsequent development of national life. (SPN, p. 184)

The Marxist idea of *determination* of the superstructure by the structure does not mean, in other words, a direct reflection or one-to-one correspondence, but simply that the structure serves as the condition of possibility and a limiting horizon for all superstructural development. *How far* this horizon is pressed, and *which* possibilities are eventually realized, depend on organized expressions of the human agency. Hence, the repeated insistence, throughout the *Prison Notebooks*, on the organization of what he simply calls 'the national-popular collective will'. Gramsci's emphasis here is obviously taken from Marx's famous formulation that the fundamental contestations in society do have their roots in the economic structure but they are *fought out* in such superstructures as politics, law, culture, and morality – even religion, 'the sigh of the oppressed'. Any real acceptance of this formulation requires then the organization of a collective human agency which addresses the linkages between moral reform and the transformations of material life – a linkage for which the term in classical Marxism is 'class struggle' as it unfolds in the overlapping domains of economy, politics, and ideology.

Third, Gramsci warns against what he elsewhere calls 'revolutionary fatalism':

When you don't have the initiative in the struggle and the struggle itself comes eventually to be identified with a series of defeats, mechanical determinism becomes a tremendous force of moral resistance, of cohesion and of patient and obstinate perseverance. 'I have been defeated for the moment, but the tide of history is working for me in the long term.' Real will takes on the garments of an act of faith in a certain rationality of history and in a primitive and empirical form of impassioned finalism which appears in the role of a substitute for the Predestination or Providence of confessional religions . . . That the mechanical conception has been a religion of the subaltern is shown by an analysis of the development of the Christian religion. (SPN, p. 337)

History does not, in other words, lead automatically to Reason, Progress, Socialism; it may, and often does, equally well lead to mass irrationality and barbarism. History is no more on the side of the proletariat than it is on the side of the bourgeoisie, and no purposive action is possible without seriously examining the possibility of defeat and the factors that may contribute to defeat. Hence Gramsci's well-known preference for Romain Rolland's dictum: 'pessimism of the intellect; optimism of the will'.

Within this framework, then, Gramsci first calls for analysis and struggle at two levels simultaneously:

> in studying a structure, it is necessary to distinguish organic movements (relatively permanent) from movements which may be termed 'conjunctural' (and which appear as occasional, immediate, almost accidental). Conjunctural phenomena too depend on organic movements to be sure, but ... they give rise to political criticism of a minor, day-to-day character, which has as its subject top political leaders and personalities ... Organic phenomena on the other hand give rise to socio-historical criticism, whose subject is wider social groupings – beyond the public figures and beyond the top leaders. (SPN, pp. 177–8)

The elaboration of BJP's mass politics since the *rath yatra* would be an instance of 'conjunctural' movements, and it is absolutely essential to understand the techniques of mobilization, the power of specific slogans, the role of particular leaders, the differential strategic deployment of the various branches of the Sangh *parivar*, the patterns of recruitment among specific social strata, the differential tactics used in different parts of the country and abroad, BJP's dealings with other political parties, voting patterns, conduct of state governments, and so on, in order to comprehend this 'conjunctural' movement. A comprehension of this conjuncture is of fundamental importance, but to stop at this level is to become a prisoner of such epiphenomena as fluctuations in voting patterns, changeover of leaders, short-lived alliances and manoeuvres, the relative success or failure of particular mobilizing tactics, the mediatic construction, etc. What is of crucial importance, then, is to link the understanding of the 'conjuncture' with a comprehension of the 'organic movement', which brings up such long-wave issues as the revivalist component in nineteenth-century thought, the sanctification of certain religious emphases in nationalist mobilizations during the colonial period, the old and new imperatives of gender politics among the middle classes, the shifting kaleidoscope of caste confrontation and alliance, the modalities of our capitalist development and the miseries of the new petty bourgeoisies in both the urban and rural sectors, the culture of our textbooks, classrooms, films, and videos, and so on. In any political analysis, the dialectic of organic movement and conjuncture has a status quite equal to that of the dialectic between structure and superstructure.

But this struggle to understand needs then to be combined with a positive project of intellectual and moral reform which addresses the most fundamental issues of the structure itself: 'Intellectual and moral reform has to be linked with a programme of economic reform – indeed the programme of economic reform is precisely the concrete form in which every intellectual and moral reform presents itself' (SPN, p. 133). Structural transformation of a national-popular kind is thus at the heart of any anti-fascist struggle. An ideological struggle against *Hindutva* fascism must recoup, as a significant element, those traditions of humanism, ecumenism, agnosticism and anti-casteist world-view which we have inherited from our medieval anti-brahminical movements and which have left such an indelible imprint on the spiritual life of the peasantry and the artisanate throughout this land. Similarly, we have inherited powerful legacies from a national movement which brought twenty million peasant households into the anti-colonial struggle on the triple platform of representative democracy, secular polity, and agrarian reform; that the peasantry in India continues to define its political world in terms of these basic values is undoubtedly one of our main resources against the fascist forces. But it would be illusory to imagine that the struggle can be won on the ideological plane alone, because in order to be credible enough for the popular classes to engage *actively* in the anti-fascist struggle, the ideologies of secularism and democracy must take the concrete shape of radical restructuring of systems of property and governance, so that the people generally have a real, tangible stake in that struggle. Nor is it possible truly to mobilize the peasantry on a secular-nationalist platform without first offering a credible plan for returning the land to those who work it. A very large part of the question of the anti-fascist struggle in India is, like much else, simply a question of what Gramsci once called 'economic reformation'.

This economic programme must then be combined with the formation of what Gramsci elsewhere calls 'the collective intellectual'. For, as he puts it: 'The decisive element in every situation is the permanently organized and long-prepared force which can be put into the field when it is judged that a situation is favourable' (SPN, p. 185). An anti-fascist struggle requires, in other words, that complex thing for which Gramsci often used the cryptic term 'Reformation' – a Reformation, that is to say, not of a religious kind, but of a communist kind. For our own time, this word 'Reformation' can only mean the refounding, in the post-Soviet era, of a new communist movement actually capable of becoming a 'collective intellectual' for the anti-fascist forces in general, and thereby to help initiate a new century of revolutions.

IX

In a highly provocative periodization of the general revolutionary dynamic in modern history, Gramsci remarks that the dynamic that was unleashed by 1789 took many forms in Europe as well as in the Americas but was fully exhausted only with the Paris Commune. The implication clearly is that it simply was not possible to transcend the historical predicates of the bourgeois revolution until after some practical shape of proletarian power had been glimpsed, even though the immediate materialization of it was speedily liquidated. As we know, those simultaneous developments – the exhaustion of the bourgeois-*revolutionary* dynamic and the speedy liquidation of the first rudimentary form of proletarian power in the form of the Paris Commune – were succeeded by almost fifty years of the most intense period of colonial conquest and capitalist hegemony. But we know also that those were precisely the years when the first mass working class parties appeared on the world scene; that it was precisely the issue of the colonial re-division of the world that led to the First World War; that the capitalist world hegemony was then challenged, in the middle of that war, by the first Proletarian Revolution; and that the October Revolution then contributed immeasurably to the emergence and eventual triumph of the anti-colonial movements as well.

It is possible that the particular dynamic unleashed by the October Revolution has now been exhausted, not just because of the continued material power of capital but because of the Stalinist form that managed to contain the revolutionary potential of October wherever class revolutions occurred subsequently, and because the immense energies of the anti-colonial revolutions too have been contained in those alliances of the indigenous propertied classes which made common cause with modern imperialism for fear of their own worker and peasant masses. For, if the October Revolution inspired the colonial peoples into the praxeological belief in mass uprisings against colonial state apparatuses, that same revolution instilled in the propertied classes of our countries the fear that the anti-colonial revolution may indeed proceed uninterruptedly to an anti-capitalist one; the anti-colonial revolution was made and unmade in that same condensed moment for which Gramsci used the term 'revolution-restoration' – in our case, a revolution against foreign rulers but also an immeasurably powerful 'restoration' of the rule of the indigenous propertied classes as well.

That particular dynamic is, as I said, perhaps exhausted. The dissolution of what little socialism there ever was in the Warsaw Pact countries has brought miseries of unspeakable magnitude, to be witnessed not only in Russia where the savings of two generations have been wiped out in a matter of three years but, most starkly, in the former Yugoslavia where fascisms of various sorts already stalk the land. Meanwhile, the simultaneous making and unmaking of our own national revolution has brought us, step by step, ever closer to at least a cultural hegemony of the RSS, which itself had been inconceivable a mere five years ago. This RSS hegemony intends to undo not only our communist tradition – the sins of Bengal and Kerala, so to speak – but also our traditions of Nehruvian social democracy; Gandhian ecumenism and tolerance; the movements for women's emancipation which have intensified in each generation for a hundred years; the more compassionate strands in our reform movements; and those struggles of the menial and peasant castes which have conjoined all our humanist traditions, from the medieval to the modern. It desires, in other words, a complete restructuring of our society based upon complete negation of all that has been progressive in our history. To the extent that the fascist offensive is against the most cherished aspects of our national compact as such, the refounding of the communist movement must include the defence of this compact; and to the extent that Indian communism has had a long and complex history intersecting with that of liberal democracy itself, a *national* anti-fascist front in present-day India is really not possible without the simultaneous refounding of the communist movement and a reconstitution of a nationalism from the Left, of the sort that we once glimpsed in, say, Nehru's 'Red years' around 1933–36 and then fleetingly in the early 1950s.

X

In the *Eighteenth Brumaire*, Marx remarks that the revolutions of the nineteenth century go forward by constantly criticizing themselves. It was in the close analysis and criticism of the preceding revolutions that the dynamic of the Marxist-Leninist revolutions of the twentieth century was eventually arrived at. A criticism of the revolutions of the twentieth century will also have to be an integral part of the struggles against the many fascisms that are growing all around us, so that the revolutions of the coming century may then be superior to the revolutions of the century that has just closed, just as the revolutions of the twentieth century were so much superior to the revolutions of the eighteenth and the nineteenth.

On the Ruins of Ayodhya: Communalist Offensive and Recovery of the Secular

The brief given to me by the organizers of this workshop is that I should attempt to 'synthesize . . . the key issues that the workshop seeks to address'.[1] I doubt that any one paper can offer such a synthesis, but a point of sharp focus is already implicit in the choice of dates for the workshop itself, for these dates impel us to think of the categories of Culture, Community, and Nation not abstractly but with some specific reference to the destruction of Babri Masjid a year ago, on 6 December 1992, and what that destruction has now come to mean in the life of the body politic.

As images of the mass hysteria that accompanied the wanton destruction of that obscure little mosque in Ayodhya were flashed, over and again, in the mass media, I was surely not the only one who saw in it not an event of inter-denominational strife – in other words, a 'communal' act – but a fascist spectacle, in the classic sense.[2] There was, first of all, the audacity of it: a huge mob trained and assembled by the fronts of the RSS, including the Bharatiya Janata Party (BJP), the second largest political party in the country, openly set out to destroy what the highest court of law in the land had sought to protect through all the force at the disposal of the state and central governments, on a piece of land located within the state ruled by the self-same BJP whose key leaders were present to bless the destruction. What was visually the most striking, however, was the immaculately methodical staging of mass hysteria and the orgiastic destruction; the spectacle had been most carefully prepared but then released with the force of a hurricane that left much of the country simply stunned.

As a secular intellectual, I experienced in the destruction of a mosque neither the feeling of a religious hurt nor any sense of a clash or crisis of identities. I did then, and I still do, regard that event as a fascist assault on the Indian Constitution, a matter far more grave than the issue of denominational identities. In a lecture I wrote up soon after that event and which I delivered in Calcutta towards the end of December 1992,[3] I had argued, alongside some reflection on Gramsci, that a potential for fascist resolutions is particularly strong in those semi-industrialized societies such as ours which have inherited powerful traditions of classicism, cultural conservatism, and authoritarian religiosity, and which have failed to undertake revolutionary transformations of cultural life and a radical redistribution of material resources. The present text is in some ways a continuation of that argument, but with far more direct reference to our present predicament. The question with which I should want to begin these reflections is this: was it only in the heat of that macabre moment that one had felt the palpable presence of the spectre of fascism, or is it still legitimate, and in what sense could it be legitimate, to speak of 'fascism', a very loaded word indeed, in this context? In posing this question, moreover, I want to assume that most of the basic facts about the career and composition of the Sangh *parivar* are generally quite well known,[4] so that the argument may proceed mainly on an analytic level.

A great problem in raising such a question is that discussions of fascism tend to get bogged down in the issue of analogies and paradigms. There is a more or less paradigmatic description of fascism that is derived largely from the Nazi experience (even Italy comes up in India very rarely and for secondary consideration only) so that all other movements that seem to belong to this analytic category tend then to be compared with the German paradigm in all sorts of ways, to be judged as to how truly fascist they are; predictably, most are found wanting in one respect or another. This procedure strikes me as being faulty. Every country gets the fascism that it deserves, i.e. the historical *form* of fascism always shifts according to the historical, economic, political, social, even religious and racial physiognomy of a given country, and it is useless always to seek an approximation with the German experience. In its heyday during the years between the two world wars, fascism triumphed in few enough countries but it was a *general* tendency throughout Europe, taking quite different forms and reaching quite distinct ends in different countries; and European fascisms inspired a whole host of related movements around the globe, from Latin America to the Middle East to Japan. In our own time also, fascistic movements are arising across the globe, even though the word 'fascism' has by now fallen in such disrepute that hardly any one of such movements likes to refer to itself by that word; the Italian one continued to use that designation for itself for some decades, then called itself 'post-Fascist' for a while, then abandoned the word altogether, and eventually settled on a more innocuous self-description, as 'National Alliance'. It seems more appropriate, therefore, to begin not with an abstract paradigm to be applied to specific movements but to examine the basic structure, actions, and objectives of a particular movement – in our case, *Hindutva* in general and RSS and/or Shiv Sena in particular – to see whether or not it can be judged as being fascist in the proper sense of the word.

The logical structure of the present text arises out of this very principle. In the opening sections, I offer some analytic comments on the fascistic nature of the actions, organizational principles, ideological formulations, and programmatic objectives of *Hindutva*. This leads to a detailed consideration of the specific political conjuncture in India, arising from the demise of the Congress hegemony by the mid-1970s, for the dramatic rise to prominence on the part of *Hindutva* forces that had been languishing on the margins of the polity since the 1920s. It is in this context that certain comparative remarks are offered, briefly about the classic Fascist experience of Italy and Germany before the Second World War, but then in more detail about the rightwing Islamicist radicalisms of the past two decades with which *Hindutva* can be more fruitfully compared. I close, then, with a longish excursus on the history and trajectory of secularism which, I believe, has been historically at the very origin of the rise of democratic demand and conceptions of equality in the political and economic domain. In India, at least, it has not been possible in the past and shall not be possible in the future to uphold ideas of constitutional democracy or socialist equality without a prior politics of secular civility. The opposition between secularism and fascism, in a country such as ours, is thus not incidental but integral.

I

To start with, then, the question itself needs to be posed correctly. If we were to ask whether or not fascist rule is on the horizon in India, my answer would be: no, not in the immediate future. If we were to ask whether communalism as such is a fascism, I would say: no, not necessarily, not all communalism by any means. But, specifically with reference to the destruction of Babri Masjid and the forces that carried it out, I would say that we would forget at our peril the fundamentally fascist character of that event and those forces. This seems clear with regard to the nature of the event, the modes of mobilization, the very structure of the Sangh *parivar*, and the specific ideological form in which it practises and propagates its communalism – all of which makes it rather similar to Shiv Sena, on not only a much larger scale but also with a much more comprehensive and articulated structure, and *distinguishes* it from many other kinds of communalism. Let me briefly explain.

First, the event. As we know, BJP's legally constituted government of Uttar Pradesh, sworn to uphold the Constitution, gave a binding undertaking to the Supreme Court that it would protect the Ayodhya mosque and immediately proceeded to violate the undertaking, with ample evidence that the giving and the violating of that undertaking had been meticulously and more or less openly planned. Meanwhile, the central government, also sworn to uphold the Constitution, fully aware of the preparations, duly warned by the intelligence agencies that destruction of the mosque in defiance of the Supreme Court order was indeed part of the *Hindutva* plan, but following a 'soft saffron' line, did nothing to prevent that violation of the constitutional obligation. Then, after the event, the government made no move to punish the actual culprits beyond empty gestures, despite overwhelming evidence, including photographic evidence, as to the identity of those culprits, their accomplices, and their leaders.

In its internal structure, meanwhile, the destruction of the Masjid has all the characteristics of a fascist spectacle, coming on top of many preparatory spectacles, carefully calibrated over the years.[5] It displayed the familiar fascistic relationship between the parliamentary party and the extra-parliamentary wings; that same chain running from the semi-clandestine group of actual leaders of the RSS abstaining from incriminating attendance, to the leaders of the various mass fronts actually supervising the destruction, to trained cadres, to the mob – bound together by a carefully choreographed hysteria and exhortations to violence. The exhortations were replete with appeals to masculine virility, national pride, racial redemption, contempt for law and civility – so that the liberal Mr Vajpayee, the patrician Mr Advani, the deliberately shrieking Uma Bharati, and those goons of Bajrang Dal who had come to believe that they were, quite literally, monkeys in the army of Hanuman, the servants of Ram and the eventual protectors of Hindu female chastity, were joined together in a public ritual that was expected to propel the purportedly 'non-political' Sangh, through its parliamentary arm but with the muscle power of its non-parliamentary wings, to unassailable state power.

As if the event itself was not enough, video cassettes not only of the event but of many subsequent acts of violence were then distributed throughout the country, so that they could be re-lived, over and over again, vicariously, by a whole host of men throughout the land, as so many moments of regained Hindu virility, as redefined by the *parivar*. This is, I would contend, fascist masculinism with a vengeance. We might add that the Shiv Sena was fully involved, as a partner of the *parivar*, in the destruction of the mosque; that it subsequently took credit for it openly; that when the Sena went on a rampage of murder in Bombay, the *parivar* is said to have supplied it with lists and addresses of those whose houses and flats were to be set afire; that the big bourgeoisie of Bombay was itself so intimidated that it dared not openly call for either the banning of the Sena or the arrest of its leader and Founding Father, Bal Thackeray; and that so blatant and even self-intoxicated have the fascists become that the assassins of Gandhi are openly celebrated in cities of Maharashtra, with no reprisals.

The issue of Shiv Sena we shall here ignore. But we could go behind the destruction of the mosque and the communal orgies that came before and after it, to the self-organization of the *parivar* itself – and we shall be brief, since all this is familiar enough. The image of the family is crucial here, because of its patriarchal resonance, even though the strictly all-male RSS is referred to by fronts of the *parivar* as *mata* (mother). At the head we have a semi-secret, non-parliamentary organization, the Sangh itself, led by a handful of men, mostly of the brahmin caste bound by no norms of democratic representation even in principle, whose methods of internal organization, promotion, decision-making, lists of actual cadres, etc., remain shrouded in secrecy, despite the agreement under which the ban on the Sangh was lifted in the 1950s and which requires legal accountability on these issues. This is the organization which assembles the fascist structure vertically, from the *shakha* (branch) upward, with its organizational ethic of cadre-building, loyalty, and obedience, and its ideological identification of local community, Hindu culture with Indian nationhood; and, it organizes the structure horizontally, by spawning numerous fronts – perhaps fifty or more, as they claimed after the more recent ban in the wake of the Ayodhya vandalism – for women, childen, workers etc., but also for religious mobilization, training of terror squads, and so on. The Sangh's obvious public face is that of the BJP, supposedly a political party like the rest, but even the formation of municipal government in Delhi has shown that all the power is wielded by the RSS itself – not to speak of the Advanis, the Vajpayees, the Joshis, etc., in the central leadership, all RSS veterans. Alongside that are other semi-public faces: the VHP, the Bajrang Dal, the Dharm Sansad (Parliament of Faith): to assist in parliamentary mobilization but also for non-parliamentary mobilization; for the assertion that matters of faith are not subject to law and Constitution; to concentrate requisite force to drive that message home, especially to the religious minorities but also to the country at large. In the vast space that separates – but also connects – Mr Vajpayee and the Bajrang Dal, are the intellectuals, the media manipulators, the experts in electronic fabulation, who interpret the daily events for us through newspapers; who lay out the visual images in those same newspapers to manipulate our sensory experience of what we read; who flood the mass market with films and videos. Here, too, in this sphere of ideological mobilization and remaking, there are levels and calibrations: the national

network of the in-house publications of the RSS is carefully distinguished from a similarly national network of publications which represents the RSS viewpoint without being formally a part of the authorized
network, which is then balanced against methodical penetration of the
liberal media themselves, extending to the upper reaches of the respectable dailies. Thus, the open terrorization of journalists by the Shiv Sena
in Bombay and the Sangh–Sena combine in Ayodhya is delicately
balanced against the freedom of saffron ideologues to use the editorial
pages of such newspapers as the *Times of India* to propagate their views
and thereby become respectable partners in defining the agenda for
national debate. As if all that wasn't enough, we have a battery of
historians and archaeologists to rewrite the textbooks and fabricate a
fantastic history, with a contempt for the facticity of facts that no
poststructuralist in his right mind could ever hope to match.

In its staging of spectacles, in its techniques of mobilizations, in the
multiplicity of its fronts, in the shadowy traffic between its parliamentary and non-parliamentary organs, in the seamless interplay of form
and content in its ideological interpellations, in the connection it asserts
between a resurgent national tradition and the regaining of masculinist
virility, in its simultaneous claims to legality and extra-legality in its use
of religion as a kind of racialism, in its construction of a mythic history
which authorizes it to be above history, and in its organization of a
Dharm Sansad that authorizes it to be above the civil Parliament
whenever it so chooses, the Sangh *parivar* is a classically fascist force –
with large Indian twists of course, as every fascism must always take a
specifically national form.

Because of features such as these, the Sangh represents not only a
communalism, in the ordinary sense, even though minorities in general
and Muslims in particular are its special victims. The true object of its
desire is not mere Muslim submission but state power and the remaking
of India as a whole – politically, ideologically, historically; and, true to
form, this project of remaking India in its own image involves a great
deal of unmaking, both through selective appropriation as well as
outright rejection of very large parts of our past and present histories.
This process of unmaking and remaking involves the rejection of our
secular-nationalist and communist histories; the re-domestication and
redefinition, in the name of 'Tradition', of what little independence
some women in this country have been able to achieve; to slow down
the upsurge of the dominated castes; to control the pluralities of our
intellectual and cultural productions; to club the regional minorities into
submission to a centralized, authoritarian state; and to bestow upon a
backward bourgeoisie nostalgias of an imperial past, dreams of nuclear
power, hallucinations of regional dominance. Communalism, in other

words, is only a cutting edge, even though this edge is quite capable of causing bloodbaths time and again.

The Sangh foregrounds the issues of what it calls 'pseudo-secularism' and 'the appeasement of minorities' because it finds these issues strategically important in its bid to build a national consensus around a whole series of real and imagined resentments, but the object of this consensus is not merely the minority but, most centrally, that majority which we provisionally call Hindu, hence also the even more powerful project of redefining and reordering Hinduism itself, in a syndicated, monolithic, telegenic, aggressive form – part brahminical, part electronic, part plebeian. In other words, the Sangh claims and has always claimed to be a *nationalism* – at once the *cultural* nationalism of the Hindu community, and, because the *community* is said to be co-terminous with the nation itself, the *political* nationalism of the Indian people as such. The inner originary logic of this claim – part communitarian, part nationalist – is of some interest.

This logic is inherent in Golwalkar's famous distinction, as he phrased it, between his own *cultural* nationalism and the *territorial* nationalism of the Congress as led by Gandhi *et al*. In this formulation, cultural nationalism is the nationalism specifically of *Hindus*, whereas territorial nationalism is by definition secular in the sense that it includes non-Hindus as well and does not demand of them that they adopt what Golwalkar would define as Hindu culture. By this definition, it might appear that he recognizes secular nationalism as having a wider scope and the flexibility to represent all Indians, irrespective of religious affiliation, while he himself aspires to represent only the Hindus; in *this* sense he could be said to be the Hindu counterpart of Jinnah who eventually claimed to represent the Muslims only, leaving the Hindus to the Indian National Congress. What Golwalkar means, however, is the direct opposite: that the *real* Indian nation is comprised of Hindus exclusively; that Hindu cultural nationalism, which seeks to create in India not a secular polity but a Hindu *Rashtra* is the *authentic* form of Indian nationalism; that the secular, multi-denominational nationalism which seeks to include Hindus and non-Hindus alike is not only wrong and misguided but also outright unpatriotic and even anti-national; that the territorial nationhood which appears to be wider and more inclusive is in fact anti-Hindu treachery, since it denies the superiority of the Hindu majoritarian claim to the whole of this territory, where others may live only in so far as they accept the superiority of the Hindu 'race'.

To buttress this position, Golwalkar has recourse to an ideological identification between two discursive categories, *pitribhumi* (fatherland) and *punyabhumi* (spiritual homeland), worthy of German Romanticism itself, invoking the quasi-Hegelian idea of a National Spirit, representing the nation in twin images of patriarchal family and religious community, and asserting that the idea of citizenship be derived from one's active participation in the working of that Spirit. Being born an Indian is thus not enough to qualify for true citizenship because 'India' designates only a territory; the *Spirit* of India resides, generally, in religions that arose within India and, quintessentially, in Hinduism, so that to be a true Indian one had to be a Hindu as well; hence the insistence on the essential identity of territory with religion, and of religion with nation. In other words, Hindus were true citizens of India *prima facie* by having spontaneous recourse to that National Spirit by the very fact of birth in a Hindu household, but non-Hindus could *become* citizens by acquiring – that is to say, submitting to – that Spirit – not as *equal* citizens, since nothing could compensate for the taint of inferior birth, but as a protected minority, or as wards of the state as it were. Golwalkar of course cited Nazi Germany as his model for this racialistic definition of citizenship, but what is also striking about this definition is that the purported distinction between cultural nationalism and territorial nationalism is dissolved as soon as it is made, since the entire population residing in the territory of *Bharat Varsha* is thereby required either to accept the cultural nationalism as defined by *Hindutva* or to get out. Any segment that fails to meet this requirement is invited to leave the territory altogether, on pain of extinction. The cultural nationalist, in any case, would not let go of even an inch of that territory, and would welcome, rather, the departure, even the demise, of the unwanted (because impure) segments of the population. In the more extended versions of this quasi-racialistic extremism, it is said to be the historic mission of militarized Hinduism and the *Hindutva* state that it would set out to recapture the territories that Greater India has lost to other states of the subcontinent, Pakistan in particular but also Bangladesh, possibly Sri Lanka, and some other neighbouring territories as well. Purification of the existing territory, expansion into the adjacent territories of other states is thus part of the design. We might add that this design surfaces rather rarely in the rhetoric of the BJP, the parliamentary front, but surfaces more frequently in *The Organizer*, the tribune of the RSS, and is an open and punctual feature of the public exhortations of the non-parliamentary arms of the 'family' – the Vishva Hindu Parishad (VHP), Bajrang Dal, Durga Vahini, and others – whose muscle power and rhetorics of hate are expected to propel the respectable BJP into governmental power.

II

As regards the making of that particular form of Hinduism which the RSS presents as the cultural nationalism of the Indian people, two parallel processes of syndication are striking. The first is the familiar one for which Romila Thapar initially used the term 'syndication', whereby *diverse* and even conflicting practices are sought to be taken over from very different traditions and incorporated into a single, pan-Indian religiosity – a process that begins with certain strands in orientalism and for which, in the RSS version, Ram is said to be the unique, uniform godhead. This is an *invented* tradition, if there ever was one! But something else, and in its own way perhaps even more alarming, is that the RSS has emerged as the unique successor and a point of intersection for a great many revivalist currents which India has inherited from many quite distinct Hindu reform movements of the nineteenth century and diverse, even conflicting, political movements of the earlier decades of the present century. Vivekananda has been a staple of their invocations now for decades, and VHP's special claim to his legacy is so elaborate and strident that the forces of the liberal Left which think that they can unproblematically claim Vivekananda for a more decent formulation of the Hindu cultural ethos need to consider the consequences of that prior claim very seriously. Meanwhile, such things as the convergence between Golwalkar and Savarkar, and the later cooperation of Shyama Prasad Mukherjee and the RSS in founding the Jan Sangh, have meant that the RSS has simply inherited the legacy of what was once the Hindu Mahasabha.[6] Even the old confrontation between the two reform movements, Arya Samajis and the Sanatan Dharmis, has also largely lapsed into a somewhat syndicated rightwing Hinduism and, therefore, into a more or less singular constituency for the Sangh. Large chunks of Bankim and Aurobindo are simply rehearsed as precursors of modern-day *Hindutva*. Gandhi's tactic of keeping such individuals as Hedgewar and such organizations as the Mahasabha inside the Congress for as long as it remained at all possible, not to speak of the subsequent history of cooperation extended to the RSS by such diverse individuals as Sardar Patel during the Partition violence, and by Vinoba Bhave and Jayaprakash Narayan during the *Bhoodan* campaign to persuade landowners to give land to the landless and the anti-Indira agitation respectively, has made it all the more possible for the RSS to assert anti-colonial, reformist, even anti-authoritarian credentials. One of the notable features of this bid for building an alternative national hegemony is that the RSS lays claim, *in the religious sphere*, to the *whole* of the Hindu tradition, from the highest kind of brahminism to the most plebeian and ecumenical kind of Bhakti, as well as to the more modern

kinds of revisionist Hinduism; and, *in the socio-political sphere*, it lays
claim to the whole range of Hindu reform movements as well as to
virtually every major figure in nationalist history, including Gandhi –
with very few exceptions, notably Nehru and, understandably, the
Muslim component of Indian nationalism. Let me note, parenthetically,
that the ability of the RSS partially to co-opt the rhetoric of Gandhian
socialism, Gandhian Swadeshi, Gandhian *ram rajya*, and their unmiti-
gated hostility towards Nehru should give some pause to that section of
our secular intelligentsia, notably the subalternists, who find it so much
easier to be partial towards Gandhi but would themselves be quite as
hostile towards Nehru as the RSS itself, though on somewhat different
grounds. I do not mean that the priorities should simply be reversed, or
that we should now set up some fundamental preference for Nehru over
Gandhi in our narratives of canonical nationalism; simple reversals in
such matters usually do more harm than good. What I do mean is that
we need a far more careful look at those positions – frequently overlapping positions – that Gandhi and Nehru have represented within that
history, even though the fashion these days, on the Right certainly but
also in some sections of the radical intelligentsia, is to pitch them as
opposites. After all, Gandhi's support of him was perhaps the decisive
element that made Nehru the first Prime Minister of independent India;
otherwise, support for Sardar Patel was probably far greater in the
relevant Congress circles.

Be that as it may. Let me explore a little further my proposition that
the remarkable capacity of the RSS to set its own agenda and to register
a gradual but remarkably consistent expansion over a period of sixty
years or more is certainly a tribute to its own organizational genius,
but this genius has met with such success because of its ability to draw
upon a large number of legacies which have been an enduring feature
of diverse reform movements and nationalist articulations throughout
the history of modern India. The idea of uniform Hindu victimization
over a thousand years is as old as Indian modernity itself, and we can
find it there already in Rammohun, who was otherwise also the author
of *Tuhfat-al-Muwahideen*, a book deeply imbued with concepts of
Islamic rationalism, and a pleader of the Mughal king's case in the
court of the Company. For Rammohun, of course, those were fleeting
assertions, by no means a substantial part of his social or historical
vision. But such ideas begin to get articulated far more systematically
by the last quarter of the nineteenth century, with enough of it getting
played out subsequently during the Swadeshi Movement for Tagore to
warn specifically against the tendency. The pursuit of a revamped,
reformed, but also monolithic and even aggressive Hinduism that presents itself as the *real* tradition; the invention of a past, anti-Muslim
nationalism in the form of the sagas of Maratha and Rajput warriors;

the idea that the kshatriya ideal of manhood is the proper ideal for Hindu manhood in general; the emphasis on physical culture and the building of the male body as a key to Hindu redemption; the figure of the heroic Sadhvi leading Hindu men in acts of redemption of the national honour – all these, and much besides, the RSS has inherited from the fictions, the zealotries, the reform movements of the nineteenth century and the twentieth, from Bengal to Maharashtra to Punjab. Its unique achievement is that ideological elements that had in the past remained discrete and largely subordinate to the requirements of an anti-colonial movement are now integrated into a singular, all-encompassing ideological position of a fascist kind and then linked, most crucially, to unique forms of organization and mobilization. Even the image of the RSS as an all-male club of reformers who know best – and that of the *swamikas* as both objects and agents of that reform, at once released and restrained by the reformer, active, above all, in the proper Hindu household, and then in carefully orchestrated family-to-family, neighbourhood-to-neighbourhood networks, and only very selectively on the national scene, whenever the directive agency of the reformer so desires – all this recalls, on a much grander scale of course, the quintessential relationship between the nineteenth-century reformer and the object of his reform – often the wife, the daughter, the sister-in-law. Needless to add, there is much in our secular-nationalist histories that also took over those same ideas, those same models. The secular-nationalist versions had remained essentially paternalistic and condescending, in the way of much nineteenth-century liberalism, but they have unwittingly contributed to the more aggressively masculinist versions of the RSS type.

In other words, by the time the RSS takes over such ideas, they have gathered to themselves the density of very powerful histories, no less historical for being so thoroughly modern. What I am suggesting, first, is that the difference between the so-called Hindu nationalism of the Sangh *parivar* and the secular nationalism of its bourgeois opponents cannot be conceptualized in the binary terms of Tradition and Modernity; the *parivar* itself draws upon a number of very modern traditions, and it is at least arguable that those who have choreographed its fascist spectacles, from the *rath yatra* onwards, know more about modernity than many of our avantgarde artists and historians. But I am also suggesting, second, that the strategists of the *parivar* know perfectly well that many of their ideas resonate strongly with a certain kind of widespread 'common sense' that has been prepared for them already, by other movements, social practices, intellectual productions, all of which they can now selectively incorporate, by rewriting, into their own history as so many precursors of modern-day *Hindutva*. This is by no means the only common sense available in modern India, and it is much to be doubted that the majority of Indians subscribe to the sum of those ideas or even find them relevant. But the confidence that there is a large enough pool of consent is also visibly there, in numerous RSS practices, as for example in the stipulation that every boy who ever comes to any of the *shakhas* (branches) must come with prior consent and daily knowledge of elders in the family; the presumption is that the consent would already be there or can be both obtained and sustained relatively easily. Consent of course comes all the more easily not only because of prior patterns of socialization but also because the RSS, through the *shakha*, is able to offer facilities (such as organized sports) and particular kinds of feelings (such as pride, group bonding, social ambition) that are scarce for the majority of the children caught in the urban vortex.

But there are other kinds of consents, other kinds of violences as well, that potentially contribute to the making of a fascist project. Notable among these is the normalization of the practice of violence as a way of satisfying acquisitive desire and of imposing the will of the powerful on the powerless. An urban middle class that habitually sets its women afire because the dowry they bring does not satisfy the greed of the men of that class; because the women are not sufficiently submissive; or because they are suspected of sexual infidelity, normalizes the idea of violence as normative in gender relations. The agrarian upper castes that periodically set fire to the households of the menial castes normalize the idea of extreme violence in class and caste relations, as much as does the Indian National Congress when it carries out a pogrom in the entire Sikh community to avenge the assassination of Indira Gandhi by her bodyguard. This routinized violence is now a very considerable feature even of the tensions between those lower and middle castes and caste fractions which are upwardly mobile and those which are not, as has been increasingly evident in Uttar Pradesh. The violence against women, which is common to all these practices of violence, stems from older and wider histories which have connected patriarchal households, caste-divided local communities and the so-called national culture in a great many complex ways. Communalism is by no means the only – and, in quantitative terms, not even the largest – structure of routine violence in our society, and there are times when a communal kind of violence comes so easily to so many men, and is exercised against even peaceful neighbours, precisely because this particular form of violence draws upon so many other kinds of aggressions. In contemporary India communalism is certainly, as I said earlier, the cutting edge for a fascist project as a whole, but those other violences – of caste, class, and gender – are always there to *form* the kind of authoritarian personality upon which the fascist project eventually rests.

III

The potential for a fascist condensation of such structures of violence, and for a fascist resolution for crises of such magnitude, is always there in the very structure of centralized states and coerced territorialities. But the conditions for posing the fascist alternative as a credible resolution arise only in exceptional circumstances. After all, for the first fifty years of its existence RSS could convince hardly anyone that it was worthy of ruling even a single state; and even at the height of the communal holocaust in the wake of the Partition there were few takers for the idea of Hindu *Rashtra* – precisely because a left-of-centre, secularist hegemony was then in place. As we look back on that history, what strikes one is that the RSS has demonstrated an astonishing pattern of calibrated growth since its inception in the late 1920s, but it is really from the 1970s, and specifically with its participation in the anti-Indira agitations spearheaded by Jayaprakash Narayan and its subsequent inclusion in the Janata Cabinet, that we can date the elevation of the Sangh to a respectable position in Indian national politics.[7] It was a propitious moment. The Congress model of capitalist accumulation had exhausted its potential by the mid-1970s; the *Gharibi Hatao* (Remove Poverty) campaign of Indira Gandhi was the last of those populist mobilizations that had evoked the promise of a measure of redistributive justice within the predicates of that model. The well-known leaders who had left the Congress at various points had failed either to articulate an alternative model of development or to put together a stable political organization able to challenge the Congress; the desperation of such leaders is well indicated in the fact that it was the movement led by JP and the Cabinet headed by Morarji Desai, formerly a veteran Congressman of Gandhian personal culture and rightwing political persuasion, that gave to the Sangh its respectability.[8] Meanwhile, the old CPI had been split and the ensuing Communist Parties contained in their regional electoral bases.

That was one side of the story. On the other hand, prior histories of British administration, nationalist politics, the emergence of a sovereign polity based on universal suffrage, the continuing viceregal tradition of a weak federalism under a strong centre in post-Independence India, and, above all, the stupendous growth of a national market for commodities and communications alike, with substantial increase in literacy rates and ownership of radio sets as well as the expansion of television networks, had created an objective situation for the invention of, recasting of – and contentions over – an all-encompassing, pan-Indian identity. Previous histories of the anti-colonial movement could no longer serve as the nationalist cement of society, some thirty years after

Independence, unless an equally powerful anti-imperialist nationalism were to arise organically in the new conditions of a postcolonial, sovereign, developing society. But the organization of such a movement was precluded by the regional sequestration of the Left on the one hand, the demise of Nehruvian social democracy on the other. And yet, the very intensification of market relations, the rapid acceleration of communications and travel facilities, the massive elaboration of the institutional mechanisms of the nation-state, even the intricate and pyramidical workings of the political structures of electoral representations – the mechanisms, in other words, that had brought masses of Indians from diverse regions and social background into direct contact and interdependence, for the first time in the history of this civilization – objectively required a powerful ideological cement in the form of a national ideology. A *national* definition of the polity – in other words, a nationalist ideology – was an objective requirement of the material processes that had been unleashed by the very terms of economic and political modernity. It was in the midst of lost political hegemonies of the Centre-Left forces on the one hand, great intensification of market relations and modernization of communication systems on the other, that the RSS launched itself on its new career, after the fall of the Janata government and as the decade of the 1970s drew to a close, with a brand new parliamentary front – the collapsed Jan Sangh reborn now as the Bharatiya Janata Party – with the key non-parliamentary front, the VHP, which had been leading an obscure existence since the 1960s, waiting to be released into entirely new kinds of aggressive assertions in the 1980s.

Let me put it another way. The liberal-Left hegemony of the first two decades after Independence was based on an identifiable heritage and a solid set of achievements. Few political leaders anywhere in the modern world have commanded such hegemonic power over the social visions and even the spiritual life of so many people, as did Gandhi alone – not to speak of those, chiefly Nehru, who were seen as his associates. This, combined with the political capital associated with the leadership of the anti-colonial movement itself, gave to the Congress a unique authority in the Indian polity for a whole generation, even for those who otherwise had good reason to oppose it. Nowhere in the world, neither anywhere in Europe nor in North America, was a model of constitutional government and representative democracy, based on universal suffrage, ever introduced or stabilized with poverty levels and literacy rates as low as the ones that prevailed in India at the time of Independence. Yet, India did become a democratic society. Nowhere in the West did women gain the vote at the very inception of representative democracy; in India they did. Its sovereignty as a nation-state arose out of the crucible of a communal holocaust, yet it refused to become a

Hindu *Rashtra* and opted, instead, to become a secular polity. This, in sharp contrast to Europe where secularism never triumphed in processes of state formation with such low levels of income and literacy. Within these politico-ideological arrangements, India during the first fifteen years after Independence witnessed the making of a largely independent model of industrial growth, a considerable reduction in the power of large-scale feudal landholdings in much of the country, substantial processes of kulakization in the countryside which benefited the upper levels of the peasantry, significant infrastructural development, expansion of educational facilities and technical personnel, etc. In other words, there was a dynamic model of embourgeoisment which at least held out the promise of some redistributive justice as well as benefits of a rapid rise in incomes for substantial sections of the population, especially at the middling levels of class formation. So long as this promise remained credible, the national bourgeoisie, under the political leadership of the reformist sections of the professional middle classes, was able to ward off challenges from the Left as well as the Right and to command the basic loyalty of the immiserated sections of society.

The dynamism of that model, and hence the belief in that promise, had begun decaying by the end of the 1960s, and victory in the Bangladesh War served to prop up that lost hegemony only provisionally and temporarily, so that when the next major challenge came to the victors, in the shape of the JP movement, they could take recourse only to the authoritarianism of the Emergency. It is indicative of the inner erosion of that earlier hegemony that the authoritarianism of that episode was utilized only to buttress personal power but not to implement a new reform package from above, as the 'progressive' supporters of the Emergency, within the radical section of the bureaucracy and even in a section of the Left, had envisaged. Instead, it was during the Emergency that the bankruptcy of the Congress model came fully into view. This of course coincided with the first major opportunity for RSS to gain political respectability and start building its own kind of hegemony out of the wreckage of the Congress model.

In short, it was the collapse of a Left-liberal kind of nationalism that provided the major opening for a fascist kind of nationalism, which set out, then, both to exploit the weaknesses of that earlier nationalism and to formulate a different national agenda. It is often suggested that an aggressive kind of political Hinduism is rising in India today because it expresses the cultural ethos of the vast majority in the country, as opposed to the secularism of the ruling elite. The experience of the first quarter-century after Independence shows that there is no such correlation. If Hinduism itself were the issue, India should have become a Hindu *Rashtra* in the wake of the Partition when the crisis precipitated by the Communal Award of the Partition was the most acute and when violences of denominational strife reached levels unimagined before or since; instead, the whole of the national leadership, led by Gandhi, opted for a non-denominational, modern constitutionality. That the great strides of political Hinduism began a generation later; that its fortunes have seen much ebbing and flowing in succeeding years; that it is weakest in regions where the Left is still strong but also in regions where the Muslim minorities are the weakest and the field much more open for uninterrupted Hindu cultural assertion – all this needs a more conjunctural explanation than the ahistorical one of a permanent Hindu ethos finally asserting itself.

But I want to base such an explanation on a more theoretical argument as well, namely that (1) in a developing society in which the structures of capitalism are fully in place but where processes of state formation are weakly developed and premised on acute unevennesses of region, community, and class, an ideological cement of a nationalist kind is an objective necessity; and that (2) if the Left fails to provide that cement, and if the liberal Centre begins to collapse, an aggressive kind of rightist nationalism *will* step into that vacuum to resolve a crisis that is produced by the objective processes of state formation and capitalist development – and this rightwing nationalism is bound to take advantage of precisely that misery of the masses and the petty-bourgeois strata which the liberal model promised to alleviate and did not. The renewed bid of the RSS to reformulate the nationalist ethos surely coincided with the erosion of that Congress model of the earlier years. It also coincided, however, with powerful processes at work in India – the processes of universal suffrage; a centralized administration; overlapping networks of regional and national education systems and print media; generalization of television and videos; the creation and constant expansion of one of the world's largest home markets for labour and commodities – that have had paradoxical effects on the formation of identities.

The integrative processes of the national market, the national system of information and communication, and the nation-state itself *require* the creation of a pan-Indian identity and produce the requisite conditions for such an identity formation. The intensification of democratic process and demand has had the effect, meanwhile, of creating identity not only on the singular, universal axis of citizenship but also along the multiple axes of numerous situational differences of region, locality, class, caste, language, denomination, and so on. These difficulties of reconciling the universality of citizenship in the nation-state with the situational particularity of specific identities, which is at the very heart of the democratic explosions of our time, is vastly complicated, however, by the very market mechanisms which integrate the economy of exchange and accumulation but serve to fragment the social base of that economy through the constant accentuation of competitions, inequities, and insecurities of many kinds. Indeed, the very system of administration that recruits its personnel on the national, regional, and local levels for different types of employment; the labour market that takes large masses of humanity far from home, sundering them from familiar networks of mutual dependence and hurling them, instead, into a whirlwind of monetization, with extreme insecurities of employment and income; intensities of cultural pressure that require of market agents that they have competence in languages of intra-regional communication even though they may themselves come out of regionally rooted linguistic communities – these and numerous other contradictions of market-induced integration serve to create a national identity while also propelling individuals to seek shelter from the brutalities of the national market in narrower networks of identitarian solidarities. Religion, for instance, declines absolutely as metaphysic and ethic but resurfaces, with vastly greater power, as a sign system of social recognitions which is nevertheless forever being reorganized as commerce and as denominationally competitive commodification. Community collapses into a thousand antinomies of a money economy but is invoked, with regular hysteria, as nostalgia for a past that never was and must therefore be made afresh with all the resource and ambition of a remorseless upward mobility. Caste-based politics itself becomes the ground for highly differentiated and mutually incompatible practices: struggles for justice in some places, a sanskritizing convergence of the plebeian middle castes and the brahminical personnel in other places, even the incorporation of some upwardly mobile lower and middle castes into projects of *Hindutva* as class fractions are recomposed across the country, under the stresses and opportunities of the market economy and the electoral process. As even a formal commitment to 'socialistic planning' was abandoned in the closing years of Indira Gandhi's government, to be replaced increasingly by a 'liberalization' that redistributes the functions of the nation-state outward to multi-national capital and multilateral agencies, and downward into the market as the ultimate arbiter of the social good, it has become less and less clear whether or not India shall in fact survive, in the long run, as a democratic federal polity comprised of very diverse regions and states-within-the-state.

Since Independence, in other words, Indian polity has experienced much restructuring and dislocation, with contradictory tendencies towards greater integrative pressures of the market and the nation-state on the one hand, greater differentiation and fragmentation of communities and socio-economic transactions on the other. As I said earlier, a national *cement* is an objective necessity arising out of these perplexities. But what kind of cement? Equality, it is safe to say, is the only possible ground on which the facts of social and identitarian difference can be reconciled with the demands of justice and the decencies of a universalist civilization. But equality is precisely what has receded further and further away, not only from the actual organization of society but also as the utopic horizon of aspiration upheld by the nation-state. By itself a national identity does not and need not mitigate the existence of other kinds of identities, formed at other social sites – caste, class, region, ethnicity, etc. Indeed, the proliferation of linguistic, regional, denominational or caste-based identities, combined with the extremities of class polarization in a backward capitalist society, serve only to *accentuate* the objective need for the strengthening of a national identity corresponding to the exigencies of the national market and the nation-state, if that market and that state are to reproduce themselves over an extended period of time. However, a developmentalist dynamic stripped of any programmatic promise of redistributive justice is bound to precipitate the crisis of the hyphen that equates the nation with the state in the term 'nation-state'. If the state no longer represents the interests of the nation in the international system of nation-states but comes to represent the interests of global finance to the nation, and if the majority of the nation cannot see in the state an agency that seeks to reconcile with some degree of fairness the competing interests of the various classes and other social forces within the nation, then the very basis and purpose of the nation-state become questionable, especially in a historical situation where energies released by the anti-colonial movement had so very recently endowed the newly independent state with at least a nominal degree of ethical claim. It is in the midst of such stresses of democratic polity and contradictions of historical conjuncture that the need arises to forge, through drastic redefinition, a new kind of nationalist ideology to replace the old one.

That old ideology whose replacement is now sought was of course built around the rational kernel of anti-colonial nationalism, planned and independent economic development, a balance between market exchange and social regulation, popular sovereignty, universal suffrage, the promise of social justice for the oppressed castes, classes, and other subaltern strata, regional autonomy for linguistic nationalities, and secular equality in a multi-denominational society – all the things that have come to be dismissed now, more or less contemptuously, as 'Nehruvian'. It needs to be stressed that the rational kernel summarized above does not describe the actual society that came into being during the premiership of Jawaharlal Nehru – far from it. However, that kernel does signify the utopic horizon that promised to work towards the creation of the conditions of its own realization. The abandoning of that horizon, at once rational and utopic, in a circumstance which continues to require a nationalist ideology, has meant that nationalism itself must now be remade in an irrationalist, fascistic mode: not the utopia of secular civility and narrowing of inequities but the dystopia of cruelty for oppressed classes and minority communities. *Hindutva* in the ideo-logical domain, 'liberalization' in domains of public policy, are the two names of that dystopia.

IV

It is sometimes said that *Hindutva* fascism and economic liberalization are irreconcilable. The argument seems to be based on an analogy with the Nazi regime of the inter-war years. In relation to current Indian politics, moreover, this argument rests on three further propositions: (1) perpetual communal violence is bad for business confidence and those who perpetrate such violence are unlikely candidates for support from Indian big business, multi-national corporations, and imperialist states; (2) since world capitalism is stagnating but not in great crisis, and since working-class militancy is not very vigorous these days, it does not need fascist methods for fighting the working class; and (3) imperi-alist countries are not likely to view Hindu 'fundamentalism' any more kindly than Muslim 'fundamentalism'. None of these propositions seems quite valid. Imperialism has had much difficulty with Muslim 'funda-mentalism' in Iran where it attacked bases for all kinds of American power in and around that country, but no such difficulty with Muslim 'fundamentalism' in Pakistan when it served American interest or in Afghanistan when it fought against the Soviet Union – and of course never in Saudi Arabia, the model fundamentalist state. Even if we grant that *Hindutva* is 'fundamentalist', which is much to be doubted, its friendliness not only towards 'liberalization' but also towards a whole range of US policies will still win it many friends among Non Resident Indians (NRIs), multi-national corporations, etc. As for violence and business confidence, the Sangh *parivar* seems not to be committed to perpetual violence of a kind that rocks urban centres, let alone capitalist enterprises, for any length of time. For the most part, it practises perpetual but low-intensity violence, strictly against its communal tar-gets, to undermine the self-confidence of the minorities and to establish *Hindutva* supremacy among the Hindus with a use of force so judicious that the bourgeoisie has no reason to feel threatened by it. The Bombay riots of 1992, which erupted in the wake of the Ayodhya demon-strations, were an exception rather than the rule, and the reason why neither the state nor the big bourgeoisie nor the dominant media have been much bothered by this violence is that they know how very safe from it *they* are.[9] Indeed, so far as actual use of violence is concerned, the success of *Hindutva* is that it has succeeded in making communal violence a *normal* part of Indian life by giving to this violence a very precise focus; they have also demonstrated in practice that violence does not become more widespread, more unpredictable, more disruptive in the states – the *largest* states in the Union (Uttar Pradesh, Madhya Pradesh) as well as the nerve centre of Indian capital (Maharashtra) – that they have governed. In the Centre, moreover, they promise a no-nonsense, strong, law-and-order state. As regards the argument that imperialism does not need fascism today because the level of workers' militancy is not very high, the plain fact about the history of the past fifty years is that low levels of working-class militancy have never prevented imperialism from supporting a wide variety of dictatorships and authoritarian regimes of the extreme Right in the majority of Third World countries, not to speak of its support for Zionist racism in Israel and apartheid in South Africa, whatever the level of working-class militancy.

The problem with all such arguments is that they proceed through analogy: since conditions prevailing within India nationally and for capitalism globally in the present decade are structurally different from the ones that prevailed for Germany nationally and in its global environment during the 1930s, it is thereby shown that India cannot repeat the German experience. Which is of course all too true, but such logic still begs the real questions: (1) if the *Hindutva* offensive signifies a 'Hindu nationalism', as is sometimes argued, then we still have to specify what *kind* of nationalism it is, considering that fascism has historically risen on the base of ultra-nationalism; and (2) if it is a fascism – in India, at the close of the century – not in the 1930s, not in Europe – then what are the features that are *specific* to *this* place and *this* historical moment, the German experience notwithstanding? It is in relation to this problem of historical and even conjunctural specificity that one needs to enquire why it is, then, that the ideological work and organizational techniques of RSS and other similar organizations, which remained marginal in the political life of India for some fifty years, from the mid-1920s onward, have suddenly begun succeeding over the past twenty – especially the past ten – years. I have argued that it is the lapsing of the Nehruvian, left-of-centre hegemony, coupled with the failure of the Left to provide a national alternative, which has opened the way for this offensive from the Right. This point can be argued in yet another way, through a comparison not with Nazi Germany in the 1930s but with some other states in Asia and Africa during this same period, and through some comparative comments on the rise of Islamicist extremism in the Middle East and North Africa, and *Hindutva* extremism in India.

India's postwar experience is part and parcel of a global experience, and it is sometimes useful to forgo the idea of Indian exceptionalism and to look at ourselves as a part of the wider world. A couple of aspects of this epochal experience are worthy of note here. To start with, the postwar period of fifty years can be more or less neatly divided into two halves, wherein the first twenty-five years witnessed enormous economic growth globally while the latter twenty-five years, from the mid-1970s onward, have been years of general stagnation (even in the advanced capitalist countries), outright negative growth (as in sub-Saharan Africa), and/or systemic collapse (notably in the erstwhile COMECON countries).[10] These distinct phases of prosperity and decline in the economic domain have had remarkable analogues in domains of ideology and politics as well. Those earlier years of relative prosperity witnessed the triumph of Keynesianism in the advanced capitalist countries in the form of welfarist reformism; expansion of the non-capitalist world to encompass roughly a third of humanity; waves of revolutionary upheavals through much of the backward zones of capital and workers' militancy in parts of southern Europe itself; decolonization across Asia and Africa, articulation of radical nationalism and aspiration for independent development on the part of a number of national bourgeoisies in the Afro-Asian zone: from Indonesia to Ghana, including India and Egypt. By contrast, the next twenty-five years witnessed a general retreat from the welfare state under advanced capitalism; the dismantling of the radical-nationalist state in such countries as Egypt, India, and Algeria;[11] the fall of European communism and restoration of capitalism in the remaining states in Asia (China, Vietnam); a general renunciation of revolutionary and radical hopes in favour of a globalized neo-*laissez-faire* implemented in the advanced zones by conservative and social democratic regimes alike (Reagan in the United States, Mitterrand in France), and through pressures of the multilateral agencies in the rest of the world – now, increasingly, in India as well.

During this latter period, we have witnessed three key developments in the ideological domain, two of which have been extensively recognized across the globe: the retreat of Marxism, and the triumph of the neo-liberalist ideas of Friedmanite–Hayekian pedigree. What needs greater recognition, however, is the drastic redefinition of nationalism itself, especially in the erstwhile radical-nationalist states, in a quasi-religious, politically irrationalist mode. This is as true of Egypt or Algeria as of India itself. It is on the prior basis of the dashed hopes of the period of Nasser and the FLN that Islamicist extremism has arisen in Egypt and Algeria respectively, to occupy that same space of nation-alist aspiration which has been left vacant after the lapsing of the left-of-centre secular nationalisms. In that sense, extremist political Hinduism which arises to prominence in India after the demise of Nehruvian radical nationalism is structurally similar to those Islamicist extremisms of Egypt and Algeria. The *difference* is that those Islamisms retain, as regards the question of imperialism, an organic relation with projects of

the radical nationalist past; most of the Islamicist activists who participated in the assassination of Sadat had been Nasserists in their youth
and now hoped that Islamism would achieve for them the anti-imperialist goals that Nasserism promised and didn't deliver. The Islamicist
radicals of contemporary Algeria, who have launched such a bloody war
against secular society in general, seek nevertheless to recoup the
objectives of the anti-colonial revolution in the mould, now, of an
austere, punitive, masculinist, scripturalist, and authoritarian Islam.[12]
Both of those Islamisms, the Egyptian and the Algerian, are, in the most
accurate sense, movements of the *radical* Right, very much in the image
of 'national socialism'. Hindu extremism in India has grown in similar
circumstances of the demise of the radical-nationalist state but it seeks,
by contrast, not the completion of the anti-colonial project but its
repudiation, and seeks not the defeat of imperialism but reconciliation
with it and subordination to it. It seeks not to complete the anti-
imperialist mission that the Nehruvian state failed to accomplish but to
repudiate that mission itself, while what it takes from the legacies of
'national socialism' is the racist content but not the social radicalism:
that is why it defines its so-called 'nationalism' not in opposition to the
colonial rule of yesterday or the imperialist domination of today but the
Muslim imperium of the medieval past. How limited are the capacities
of Islamicist anti-imperialism we can learn from the experience of the
successful revolution of radical Islam in Iran under Khomeini's austere
and brutal leadership, the limits and contours of which foretell the fate
of Islamism in Algeria if it were to succeed. The masculinisms and
brutalities of Hindu extremism are comparable, but its historic visions
and capacities are even more paltry.

A nationalist ideology that can serve as the cement of society is the
objective requirement of a nation-state such as the Indian, in a historical
moment such as the present. But a culturalist, rightward redefinition of
nationalism, stripped of anti-imperialist content but designed for irrationalist mobilization, is also a requirement of this moment of imperialist
triumph, when the liberationist imagination released by the Bolshevik
Revolution is everywhere in retreat and many kinds of irrationalisms
are stalking all the zones of this earth. In this, too, *Hindutva* fascism is
not very original, in the sense that nostalgic and irrationalist populism
of the extreme Right is a *general* tendency around the globe today, in
Western Europe as much as in the Middle East and South Asia; together,
such movements serve to stabilize the defeat of communism and anti-
imperialist nationalism on the global scale, as well as the triumph of
imperialism in a moment of capitalist stagnation. In other words, if
welfarist reformism was the capitalist solution for the period of prosperity and of offensives from the Left, neo-liberalist economy and irrationalist populism may well be regarded as a general solution for the period

of stagnation; and if, within India, Nehruvian social democracy corresponded to the earlier phase, *Hindutva* is suitable for the latter.

It is in this larger perspective that the ideological construct of *Hindutva* and the public policy of liberalization are not only reconcilable but complementary. Policies of liberalization can succeed only if Indian nationalism can be detached from its historic anti-colonial origins and redefined in culturalist, irrationalist, racist terms, so that national energies are expanded not on resistance against imperialism but on suppression of the supposed enemy within: the denominational minority, the communist Left, the 'pseudo-secularist', any and all oppositions to 'tradition' as defined by *Hindutva* and its accomplices among the indigenist sophists. I might add that in this redefinition of nationalism, 'religion' serves in the Islamicist and Hinduizing ideologies much the same function – of exclusion of the other, purification of the self – that 'race' has historically had in the making of imperialist and fascist ideologies in Europe.

If the above proposition is in any fundamental sense true, two further points may be made. First, in our denunciation of what Romila Thapar quite correctly calls 'syndicated Hinduism', on the ground that it is based on a *false* homogenization of a Hinduism which is by its nature only the sum of diverse, local, mutable traditions, we have not paid enough attention to the fact that the issue of truth and falsity, and our way of posing *true* Hinduism as against false Hinduism of the RSS, addresses only a part and perhaps a secondary part of the problem. The power of this *falsely* homogenized Hinduism perhaps lies elsewhere – in the articulation of the growing integration of the Indian market and communicational grids with the invention of a belief system that can be widely shared, easily packaged, reduced to a linear explanatory narrative, ready to serve more or less as a *secularized* ideology through TV serialization and mass spectacle, to give to the nation a symbolic unity, on the terrain of hysterical religiosity, which compensates for the lack of a progressive national project in the material domain. In other words, it is only a homogenizing Hinduism that can serve as compensation and substitute for secular nationalism as such. In the cultural sphere, the decisive moment within this process of mass syndication perhaps came through the agency of neither the scholar nor the political demagogue but in mass media, through print iconographies and popular cinema where gods and goddesses from diverse devotional practices and textual sources got slotted into a small number of plot outlines, so that multiplicity got reduced to a system of equivalences through the narrative structure itself. Perhaps the real ingenuity of the RSS was that it adopted, at the moment of its own inception and consistently since then, the figure of Ram as the one upon whom all narrative structures converge, so that the later televising of the Ramayana and the Mahab-

harata in quick succession created a sense of their mutual continuity, the
story of Ram overlapping with heroic narratives of the sacred nation,
and when Mr Advani's *rath yatra* got going it was seen as an extension
of those epics; hence Advani's audacity in borrowing elements – e.g. the
image of Ram as warrior-king, the *trishul* of Shiva, the charioteering of
Krishna – from *both* the epics in fabricating the symbology of his
pseudo-pilgrimage. The immediacy of the TV screen and the infinite
repeatability of the celluloid image of course served to compress time
into linearity and simultaneity, so that the fictional reenactment of
mythic time could be made to flow with great ease into the political
exhortation of the present moment. Thus, far from being simply the
false representation of a *true* tradition, this syndicated Hinduism is
remarkably true not to its purported origins in 'Tradition' but to its
fabrication in front of our own eyes, almost literally, in the form of
political spectacles, much aided by technologies of film and television,
for mass consumption by all those who participate in an integrated
national market of commodities and ideologies alike, for purposes of a
consumerist, market-oriented nationalism as opposed to an anti-imperialist one.

   If communalism for the RSS is really only the cutting edge for the
popularization of a fascist national project – which gains its strength
both from selectively incorporating and elaborating elements of anteced-
ent reform movements and nationalist articulations; and which came
about to challenge and displace the Centre–Left power blocs that had
previously contended for hegemony – then it necessarily follows that
the posing of secularism against communalism is necessary but insufficient; that the posing of the more humane and subversive traditions
within the belief systems of the Indian past against the Sangh's masculinist and market-friendly Hinduism is necessary but insufficient; and that
it is not possible in fact to challenge a fully articulated fascist national
project without posing against it a superior national project capable of
organizing what Gramsci once called the 'national-popular will'. To the
extent that it is on the terrain of tradition and culture, community and
nation, that the fascist project sets out to assemble popular consent for
a conservative compact on issues of class and gender, caste and denominational diversity, centralized power and regional autonomy, one cannot
abandon the terrain of nationalism itself, and all that that implies for
issues of culture and community, tradition and modernity; but one
cannot *occupy* that terrain empty-handed, without a political project for
the remaking of the nation and its existing structures of power.

   The aim of all cultural politics is the making of a different political
culture, and before setting out to reorganize the field of Indian culture,
the RSS had set out to establish itself organizationally as an alternative
claimant to state power. It is this condensation of the issue of culture as

the issue of state power – that is to say, the problem of taking hold of national culture through an organized political force – that the Left, in all its dispersals and molecular movements, has eventually to address as a collective entity. And, I do mean 'collective entity'. Aside from the enormous financial resources at its command, which the Left by its very nature can never match, the main strategic strength of the RSS is its organizational capacity *simultaneously* to disperse its personnel into numerous forms of activity in all walks of national life *and*, at strategic moments, to concentrate diverse types of personnel for particular mobilizations and spectacles. The spectacle that they organized around the destruction of the Babri Masjid was a high point following upon some years of this momentum of alternate dispersals and concentrations, virtually military in its precision and siege-like quality – alternating between rapid movement and war of position, as it were. For the Left – all of it, 'organized' and 'unorganized' – there are lessons in the elaboration of that painstaking work, and there is reason to reexamine the very mode of anti-fascist mobilizations during these same years, which have been essentially local and dispersed, even mutually discrete, with none of the advantages of initiative that moments of concentration bring.

V

For some sixty years now, the RSS has followed a two-pronged strategy: (1) the building of a hard core of cadres specializing in different kinds of tasks, and (2) the propagation of its ideas in the culture at large through highly innovative means. Over forty years ago, it added the crucial third prong to its strategy, namely the formation of distinct but overlapping mass fronts, the number of which have increased. To the extent that it chose the mercantile bourgeoisie as its principal collaborator and source of finance, and to the extent that it has always treated the urban petty bourgeoisie as the strategic class in the making of insurgencies in modern societies, it has historically devoted less energy and finance to its class fronts among peasants and workers, especially peasants, and has concentrated on four types of fronts: (1) the front of students and intellectuals, (2) the fronts that help it cement ties with the traditional sectors for religious legitimation, (3) the fronts which connect it with the urban lumpen elements, and (4) the crucial parliamentary front. It is through these fronts, and by grooming college students as the bureaucrats and professionals of tomorrow, that it has gained its influence in the media and the state apparatuses, from top to bottom, without taking power. These, then, have been the main elements of the power bloc: mercantile capital, intellectuals and other professional petty bourgeois, the milling crowds on the margins of the modern sector, the urban lumpens – and, to the extent that our modes of urbanization tend to lumpenize large segments of the working class, the lumpenized workers as well. Almost the most striking feature of the recent expansion of the RSS and some of its fronts into the countryside is their ability to make flexible, caste-specific, region-specific alliance with sections of the upwardly mobile middle caste peasantries and the growing rural bourgeoisie in the agrarian economy. Considering that it set out to challenge the formidable political hegemony of Congress nationalism, in the face of grand figures like Gandhi and Nehru, it has displayed remarkable endurance, almost Gramscian in its will to defend its key positions by digging deep trenches. In the process, it has sought to address, from the position of the extreme Right, some organizational questions regarding techniques of insurrection, of the kind on which so much of the Left movement in Europe, Latin America, and India has historically come to grief: (1) the problem of resolving the dichotomy between cadre party and mass party; (2) the problem of organizing parliamentary and non-parliamentary work simultaneously; (3) the problem of organizing an insurgent movement within the parliamentary Republic of the bourgeoisie by making use of the openness of the democratic system and combining that legal work with cadre-based, extra-legal assaults; (4) the problem of keeping nationwide social networks available within the interstices of democratic society for the cadre party to retreat into if and when the weight of state power comes down heavily, without damaging the work of mass fronts and parties; and (5) the problem of avoiding a frontal confrontation with the repressive apparatus of the democratic state and yet gradually forcing the internal erosion of both the repressive and the chief political apparatuses of the constituted state, until state power is ready, like a ripened fruit, for seizure. Fundamentally, it has had to face a historically unique problem: the organization of a movement inspired by historic forms of fascism but in a society marked *both* by backward capitalism, unlike Germany, and, unlike Italy or Spain, by powerful traditions of electoral democracy based on universal franchise in a context of entrenched civil and military bureaucracies largely subservient to secular political authority.

That the RSS has been truly in command of its fronts, despite their enormous size and resources, is quite evident from the fact that at no point in its history has the RSS depended on its parliamentary front for its own expansion. It did not even have such a front until after it was banned in the aftermath of Gandhi's assassination, even though it is said to have acquired upward of 100,000 cadres and active participants by the beginning of the Second World War and perhaps as many as 700,000 by 1948.[13] At no point was there any correspondence between the electoral fortunes of the Jana Sangh, the first parliamentary front and the precursor of BJP, and the rate of growth of the RSS. The slow pace of its growth between 1948 and 1962 is fully explainable in terms of the widespread perception of its complicity in Gandhi's assassination and the national power of Nehruvianism on the one hand, that of the united CPI on the other. By contrast, the contraction of parliamentary seats from 93 for Jan Sangh in 1977 to merely 2 for BJP in 1984 was accompanied by the *doubling* of RSS *shakhas* during those same years.[14] What I am suggesting is that the electoral arithmetic is subject to so many other factors that there is no necessary correspondence between the fortunes of the parliamentary front and the cultural logic or organizational design pursued by the RSS itself. It is perfectly possible, in an extreme case, that the BJP declines definitively as an electoral force while the RSS goes from strength to strength as much in cadre-building as in the building of a national cultural consensus so that countless individuals who vote for other parties actually come to adopt the whole of the RSS world-view, while electoral encashment of the sea-change in the cultural life of the nation takes place much later.

This does not imply that the electoral process does not fundamentally matter. It matters in all sorts of ways: in terms of specific political parties gaining access to enormous material resources and social authority; as legitimation through what one may call the mass psychology of liberal democracy as to who is authorized to rule; and as the central mechanism in the processes for negotiating and renegotiating the intricacies of the social compact. The more unruly the ruling class becomes, the more one needs the integrity of this process to protect what democratic culture and public civility there is. What I mean is quite else. First, the Left parties on the one hand, the RSS and allied forces on the other, are the only ones that represent specific kinds of political culture, and that to the extent that the Left parties are restricted largely to their regional bases, the culture at large is wide open for imperceptible but cumulative shifts towards the positions of the Sangh, perhaps not on specific issues but in their generality. Second, the political discourse of the Sangh has a ring of familiarity in a culture replete with authoritarian forms of religiosity, and every failure to build the new in ways vigorous enough to allow large masses of people to take the risk of novelty must always push large sections of those people to seek refuge in what seems familiar; conservatism is born not only from privilege and the will to protect that privilege, but also from the experience of pain and the fear of future pain. Third, the political imaginary that the RSS propagates is based squarely on the near-universal misery of the proletarianized mass and the lower petty bourgeoisie in our cities, which makes them prone to millenarian ideologies, fascist mobilizations, and cultures of cruelty, by invoking images of a vast community that purportedly offers the securities of a *parivar* in a world where such solidarities are eroded and collapsing, and by invoking hallucinations of power in the midst of powerlessness, real and vast. Because these injuries and the compensatory hallucinations are the fate of the *majority* of the population, parliamentary democracy itself, with its universal franchise, can be made to serve, to an extent, the fascist purpose.

Such are some of the strengths of the RSS, its fronts, its allied forces. Is their success inevitable? The only possible answer is that we do not yet know; that the future is still wide open; that the outcome of their offensive will depend as much on their own strategic abilities as on (1) the capacity of the centrist forces to stem their own ongoing fragmentation and hold the line on liberal values, and (2) the capacity of the dispersed anti-fascist *forces* to build an anti-fascist *movement*. The virulence of the communalist offensive should not be allowed, in any case, to obscure the fact that the factors and forces that are ranged nagainst *Hindutva* in India today are formidable – commanding, among other things, an absolute numerical majority. It is also eminently arguable that the real gravitational pull in Indian political culture, as regards religion, is still towards a tolerant multi-denominationality and heterogeneity of belief systems, despite the homogenizing thrusts of *Hindutva*, the market economy, and the attendant communication systems. And, we shall shortly comment on some key weaknesses of the *parivar*, notably its lack of populist radicalism in the socio-economic domain. However, one also encounters a rather different argument – and one which I would view with some scepticism – to the effect that the balance, indeed the very structure, of class forces in contemporary India precludes the possibility of a fascist resolution. In this context, we may briefly recall some aspects of Italian Fascism which should be of particular interest to us, considering that unlike Nazi Germany, which was the most industrialized country in Europe at the time, the Italy of Mussolini's day was relatively much less industrialized and predominantly agrarian.[15]

The experience of Italy, the classic home of Fascism, shows that Fascism *can* come to power easily and rule confidently in semi-industrialized countries of backward capital, even though the majority of the population may be agrarian and largely illiterate. In deed, the success of Fascism in key rural regions such as the Po Valley was crucial in its emergence as a national force. It shows also that neither finance capital nor the big bourgeoisie in general actually *created* Fascism but then *acquiesced* in its power, once established, when it became clear that no stable centrist force was available for the management of capitalist accumulation; only towards the end of 1920, well after the spread of Fascist squads in large parts of Italy and less than a year before Mussolini's rise to power, did the big magnates of industry and commerce begin even to finance him, while his initial appointment as

Prime Minister, at the head of a minority government, came with the consent not only of the army but also of the historic liberal bloc. The Italian experience also shows that in a semi-industrialized country the principal class forces of Fascism are comprised of mercantile capital (the Milanese merchants were the first sizeable bloc of the urban rich to go over to Fascism), the professional petty bourgeoisie, the educated unemployed (i.e. the potential professional stratum that feels frustrated by low levels of accumulation, few job opportunities, and eschewed distribution of wealth), the lumpenized mass, those landowners who are directly besieged by the peasantry; big capital, on any substantial scale, is the last to join. The fact that the big bourgeoisie neither created Fascism nor played any significant role in its capture or consolidation of power meant that the Mussolini regime remained relatively autonomous of that bourgeoisie even after it made common cause with it. A significant consequence was that after he had smashed the Communist and Socialist trade unions, as the bourgeoisie had desired, he dictated to the bourgeoisie that his party was to have the sole right to form unions; in turn, Fascist monopoly over the unions, which made it impossible for workers to represent themselves in collective bargaining through other means, meant that considerable sections of the working class began then to cooperate with Fascist rule.

In the ideological domain, four aspects of Italian Fascism are striking. First, Mussolini had been an illustrious member of the Socialist Party and continued to speak, even as a Fascist, in a populist language of promising higher standards of living for the poor through brisk national development; his was a radicalism of the Right but a radicalism nevertheless, which he abandoned to a very large extent but only after taking power. Second, he at once *invoked* that nationalism which had fought for Italian independence some fifty years earlier and *criticized* it for not having accomplished enough for the nation, thus presenting Fascism as a re-invigorated ultra-nationalism necessary to correct the wrongs of the misguided nationalism of the previous liberal regimes. Third, anti-communism was woven into the rhetoric of this ultra-nationalism. And finally, Mussolini constantly invoked the classical and imperial traditions of Rome in holding out the promise that the authoritarian, strong nation-state that he was building was necessary for reviving the nation's tradition and glory. In this invocation of 'Tradition', religion played a paradoxical role. In the initial phase of the Fascist offensive against the organized Left and the labour movement, Fascism collided also with the populist religion and agrarian radicalism of the Catholic peasant leagues which were opposed to both Socialism and Fascism at that stage. However, as Mussolini moved to consolidate his power with the help of the liberals themselves, and especially as he aligned himself with the Catholic Church and received the Pope's blessing, the public anti-

Fascism of the 'good' Catholics collapsed. Thereafter, the *political* power of organized Catholicism became a fundamental component of the Fascist regime without Italy becoming in any way a theocratic state. This is useful to recall in the present Indian context, in the sense that hysterical kinds of irrationalist religiosity – more broadly speaking, religious legitimation as such – does not become any the less important in the fascistic mobilizations of *Hindutva* just because the RSS and its allies do not wish to turn India formally into a theocracy.

So far as the relation between the bourgeoisie and fascist politics is concerned, we might say that the point of unity for the capitalist class is capital itself, and what the whole class always wants is a political authority that would ensure stable conditions for the expanded repro-duction of capital. Otherwise, in its conditions of normal political existence, the class is comprised of competing enterprises, groups, and fractions, clustering around different contenders for state power. What happens typically is that *some* units of capital throw in their support for fascism early on, but it is usually in the *process* of fascism's coming to power that more and more units of capital begin to cluster around it; fascism's rise has to take on the appearance of inevitability before competing units of capital suspend their political squabbles and unite behind the rising power. This corresponds to the Marxist postulate of a certain formal separation, in the capitalist mode of production, between (to use Engels's terminology) the 'governing caste' and the 'ruling class' and the relative (only relative) autonomy of the political from the economic. We might add that because fascism comes to power with the force of a mass movement of the radical Right, with formidable bases among the mercantile and the petty bourgeoisies, its autonomy in relation to the 'coupon-clippers' (Lenin's phrase for finance capital) is, in relative terms, even greater than is normal for parliamentary regimes of the bourgeoisie.

In every country where fascism has come to power or even close to power, the crucial elements have been: the size of the army of the unemployed (including the educated unemployed) and the misery of the working classes; the fear and disaffection of the petty bourgeoisie caught between economic disintegration and inflation rates; an acute sense of real or imagined national injuries in the present, combined with a virtually pathological belief in past glories of race, nation, religious community; the existence of social minorities and political radicals that are portrayed as the real culprits in economic decay and national injury; growth of militancy among the immiserated; a collapsing liberal Centre that contrasts sharply with the aggressive and disciplined character of the fascist party. It is the ripening of this conjuncture which eventually tends to press the big bourgeoisie finally to make up its mind in fascism's favour.

That substantial elements of this conjuncture exist in India accounts for the growth of the fascist tendency here, and even the lack of working-class militancy is partially compensated for by the existence of large Communist Parties, the always local but nationwide activities of the anti-communal forces (which are objectively anti-fascist even where their immediate impulse is simply liberal and humanitarian), and the renewed assertion of *dalits* and Other Backward Castes (OBCs), which is a form of class struggle even though the inability of the Left to provide progressive leadership for them opens up the space for oppor-tunists, demagogues, and even criminal elements to fill the vacuum of organization and leadership.

VI

The principal problem for the RSS, in this regard, is not that it lacks the support of the big bourgeoisie but that (1) it is operating in a society far more heterogenous than any where fascism has succeeded in the past; (2) it lacks that class radicalism of the classic fascist parties which could offer to the immiserated something more substantial than the intoxicants of religious ideology and fascist spectacle; and (3) the centrist forces – from the Congress to the Janata Dal (JD) – are already agreed on the destruction of the progressive aspects of the Indian state and its econ-omic policies so that the RSS is unable to offer to foreign monopolies and Indian corporate capital a substantially more attractive economic package. Hence its concentration on symbolic politics and its flounder-ing on the substantive issues. It posits the Mandir issue against Mandal – i.e. an essentially brahminical project against the upsurge of the dominated castes – but then sets out to co-opt the OBCs when the electoral arithmetic so requires. It has a far-reaching alliance with Shiv Sena in both the parliamentary and non-parliamentary domains but then recoils from Sena's rampaging against *dalits* in order to conceal its own overwhelmingly upper-caste character, and to placate the more populist elements in its own ranks. BJP, the parliamentary front of the RSS, sets out to be the party of saffron yuppies but then other fronts of the RSS start opposing, at least formally, part of the BJP's own neo-liberal agenda so as to appeal to the nascent nationalism of the larger sections of the Indian intelligentsia. The RSS supports the most murderously militarist solutions in Punjab but then turns around to placate the Sikhs in Delhi in the course of its own confrontation with the Congress in the city. It presents itself as the party of Hindu purity and rectitude but spawns a parliamentary front, namely the BJP itself, that becomes increasingly indistinguishable from the Congress as regards corruption, factionalism, and power play of all kinds.

The contradictions of these policies ought not to be seen simply as incoherence, since it is the classic ambition of fascist parties to be all things to all people. Yet it is also the case that the immense heterogeneities of Indian society are such that an onward march of a unified fascist force is very difficult in the light of contrary pulls in all the arenas of caste, region, class, community, and faction. The kind of problem the RSS faces owing to its own lack of class radicalism even of a rightwing kind becomes clear if we compare its trajectory to the one situation where a religio-clerical elite, arising in a society which had as much civilizational depth as India itself, did organize a mass movement – based primarily on religious legitimation, mercantile capital, the urban petty bourgeoisie, the proletarianized mass, even substantial sections of the working class – for an insurrectionary seizure of power. I mean, Khomeini'ite Iran! I do not offer any exact parallels here, because situations are always concrete and drawing false parallels is usually very dangerous, but some discrete contrasts may help us comprehend at least some of our own unique specificity.[16]

Unlike the Khomeini'ite religio-clerical forces, which organized their power bloc against a monarchical system commanding no institutions of popular legitimation and where the essential structure of power was concentrated in the hands of a monarcho-bourgeoisie comprised of not much more than two thousand households, the RSS and its allies face in India institutions of the parliamentary Republic where power is too widely distributed, with a vibrant civil society, comprised, in Gramsci's vivid phrase, of ramparts and trenches so numerous as to be unavailable for quick dismantling through frontal assault or a war of rapid movement. Unlike *Athna-'Ashari* Shi'ism of Iran, which has no parallel in histories of Sunni Islam and which is as hierarchically structured as medieval Catholicism, the RSS seeks religious legitimation from belief systems which have neither institutional homogeneity nor a unified clerisy. When one says that 90 per cent of the Irani population subscribes actively to the *Athna-'Ashari* branch of Shi'ism, one means that, as of 1978, the year of the Irani Revolution, the entire elaborate network of mosques and *medrissas* was run by a grand total of less than half a million individuals directly organized in a strictly hierarchical pyramid controlled, at the top, by no more than about a dozen ayatollahs and *Marajai-e-taqlid*. To say, by contrast, that over 80 per cent of India constitutes a majority community bound by a single religious system called Hinduism is, strictly speaking, nonsensical. Not only are divisions of caste and sect and *matth*, of sense and sensibility and belief itself, in local and regional variations, far too numerous, but what we provisionally call Hinduism also has no institutional analogue for the Irani kind of religious pyramid, not even remotely, no matter how many *mahants* and *sadhavis* RSS collects under its banner, and no matter how many

Shankaracharyas wax eloquent in support of religious obscurantism – nor can that kind of homogenization be produced instantly, through modern means of communication and organization of spectacles, because technological fabrication also has its limits. The *Shankaracharyas* themselves have no institutionalized authority even remotely resembling the authority of the Irani *Marajai-e-taqlid*.

But my next point is the more crucial one, namely that the fundamental weakness of the RSS and its fronts is that they are formations of a *conservative* Right, not of a *radical* Right. Ali Shariati's version of Islam was somewhat more radical than the radical nationalism of Frantz Fanon; the programme of redistributive justice advocated by Ayatollah Taleghani was no less radical than that of the Tudeh, the historic Communist Party of Iran – and Taleghani *was* the Ayatollah of Teheran, with the right to use the radio and television on at least each Friday. Taleghani, I might add, commanded a very substantial following in those sections of the Teherani middle class that supported the Irani Revolution – and, so radical was his vision of postrevolutionary Iran that when Khomeini returned from Paris, Taleghani did not even go forward to greet him, because he knew that Khomeini was a man ultimately of the authoritarian Right, even though Khomeini's hatred of American subjugation of Iran was second to none and even though Khomeini intended to nationalize the properties of the monarcho-bourgeoisie, and indeed did so. That monarcho-bourgeoisie ran from his Iran as rapidly as the Tsarist aristocracy had run from Lenin's Russia. In the process, the Irani Revolution redefined for radical Islam a familiar word: *mustazafin*, which came to be the Farsi equivalent for Frantz Fanon's term 'wretched of the earth'.

I am no admirer of the Irani Revolution. Rather, I have used the term 'clerico-fascist' for the regime that ensued from Khomeini's takeover. That, however, is another story. The point I am making here is that the religious idiom that was deployed to build immense resources of political hegemony in Iran addressed issues not just of religious identity but of the monarchical institution, the expropriation of the big bourgeoisie, freedom from foreign economic and military domination, welfare guarantees for the *mustazafin*, strict controls over the vulgarities of conspicuous consumption, radical revisions of property relations. Its economic programme was remarkably similar to the entirely secular programme of Nasserism in Egypt or the original programme of the Algerian FLN as expounded in the Tripoli Declaration before Independence.

What I am suggesting is that the RSS – along with its fronts and affiliates – has a national project for the unmaking and remaking of India in its own image. They take advantage of the *misery* of the majority of the Indian peoples; they build, simultaneously, on the reservoirs of mass resentment and the fatalistic notion of conservative religiosity that all shall be well if homogenized pieties can be imposed upon our personal, social, political lives; and on the notion, made familiar by the Nazis, that the misery of the body politic can be blamed entirely on the *socio-religious* minority, and that periodic pogroms of that minority and the bellicosities of majoritarian ultra-nationalism can help postpone forever the issue of resolving the material bases of that misery. They raise, in other words, the issue of mass misery only to suppress and wilfully misrecognize the sources of that misery.

VII

The issue of secularism surfaces in discussions of the sources and possible remedies of Indian misery in peculiar ways. From the RSS to our indigenist social scientists, not to speak of many avantgarde historians, all sorts of people are agreed that the kind of *hard* secularism that appeals to no religious tradition and seeks to justify itself in terms of its own logic is not suitable for us because of its Western origin and its supposed incompatibility with our traditions.[17] This, I must confess, is peculiar. After all, the same people do use much that originated initially in Europe: railways, aeroplanes, a whole range of Euro-American ideas from the most mundane and conservative to the most fashionably postmodern.[18] The point, I should have thought, was usefulness, and the secular form of politics should get at least the same hearing as railways or computers, with reference not to origins but purposes. Since European origin is the issue, however, it might be best to recall a particular history, so as to clarify that while certain historical forms have indeed been radically different, the problems of denominational and sectarian strife that the transition from theocracy and religious legitimation to secular governance in histories of early modern Europe sought to address are analogous to the problems we ourselves have had to face in the course of the formation of modern, sovereign, democratic states in South Asia and the Middle East.

The historical process that eventually gave rise to fully fledged secularisms in the recent history of Europe, in the sense of a juridical separation between political life and religious life, actually began much earlier, with those crises of the sixteenth century which then witnessed, on the one hand, the rise of a number of centralized states in monarchical and bureaucratic forms; and, on the other, the catastrophic wars of the Reformation and Counter-Reformation, which had the cumulative effect of dividing Europe along religious lines, Catholic and Protestant, and of endowing each large state with religious minorities and dissenting sects: Protestants in Catholic France, Catholics in Anglican Britain, Jewish minorities in overwhelmingly Christian countries, and so on. The idea of a separation between religion and politics, which is internally essential for the emergence of a modern civil society based on equal citizenship, was posed as a secularist compact, first of all, to obtain the peace between neighbouring states founded on prior histories of religious conflict; second, to obtain a modicum of safety for the religious minorities, dissidents, and smaller sects – as Protestantism itself had given rise to many different churches along lines of doctrinal difference; and, third, to gain for the newly constituted centralized states a modicum of freedom from the Vatican even inside the world of Catholicism. The issue of minorities – all kinds of minorities – was thus central in establishing the link between the idea of secularity and the idea of citizenship (or at least subject status) in territorially defined states. Recent researches suggest that what later flowered into the High Enlightenment, centred in France, perhaps had its intellectual origins in a number of currents that arose initially out of the English Revolution of the mid-seventeenth century, ranging from the more moderate Newtonian Enlightenment to those heterodoxies, dissents, and even pantheisms for which anti-clerical ideas were deeply tied to republican anti-monarchism.[19] The movement for the *separation* of religion and state was irrevocably a part, in other words, of the project for the *democratization* of the latter. Prominent among the exponents of such ideas seem to have been the remarkably mobile mass of religious refugees and dissenters: those who had fled from the Restoration in Britain after Cromwell; those who had organized dissents within their own churches and were therefore persecuted or driven away; and Jews fleeing from Christianity, Protestants from Catholicism, Catholics from Protestantism, Freethinkers from organized religion, etc. Many of them congregated in Amsterdam and more particularly The Hague; many of their ideas then travelled to Paris, where some of the Encyclopaedists adopted some of those ideas, mostly in watered-down versions. Traces of those origins are there in genealogies of British liberalism as well, from Locke to John Stuart Mill, where a moderate discourse that began by attempting to reconcile the democratic demand for popular rights with constitutional monarchy proceeded, over time, to pose the idea of *individual* liberty against the autocracy of the *majority*. Lockean ideas were of course deeply marked by the ideology of natural rights wherein the individual is the sovereign subject of his own fundamental rights since these rights are his by nature and thus, in a sense, prior to society; Mill, a century or so later, is able to think of the dilemmas of democracy in terms of the minority of *one* because the central problem of democracy for him is not majority rule but minority rights, and the attendant problem, therefore, of ensuring both the majority's right to rule and the minority's right not only to protection but also to liberty. Hence, the classic question of liberal individualism: does the minority have equal rights and equal liberty even if it is a minority consisting of only *one* individual?[20]

This type of political liberalism could of course as easily become fully secular and anti-monarchical, in the Constitution of the United States for example, as it could become accommodated to not only the constitutional monarchy in Britain but also to a form in which the monarch is also formally the head of the Church of England. In other words, the British liberalism that arose in the aftermath of regicide and Restoration was democratic enough greatly to restrict the prerogatives of monarchy but also conservative enough to retain a formal tie between church and state. In France, by contrast, where the victory of the Counter-Reformation had been unable wholly to eradicate or even to tame the energies released by forces of the Reformation, anti-clericalism gestated in highly radical forms and when the revolutionary upheaval came towards the end of the eighteenth century it was endowed with a much more sweepingly secular philosophical foundation which transformed the ideas of sovereignty, citizenship, rights, and political subjecthood far more fundamentally.

Absolutism had utilized the idea of the divine right of kingship to make sovereignty an attribute of 'eminence' and to define freedoms as restricted and hierarchically structured in accordance with the ties of dependence and subjection under the highest degree of eminence, namely the monarch as Sovereign. In contrast, the secularizing discourse of the 'Rights of Man and Citizen' inaugurated by 1789 redefines sovereignty as an attribute not of divinely ordained eminence but of collectivity, equality, freedom, and citizenship.[21] In that discourse, sovereignty is of course no longer the (divine or profane) *right* of kings; but sovereignty is also not understood here as the attribute of each of the individuals separately, in such a way that they merely pool together their separate freedoms in order to constitute a collective sovereignty through aggregation of individual wills. In other words, this discourse of course denies that rights are given by either a divinity or by 'nature'; however, contrary to many misunderstandings, it also does *not* constitute the *individual* as the sovereign subject of rights in political society. Rather, sovereignty in this discourse is *from the start* an attribute of *free and equal citizens in their collectivity*. The individual comes to have an inalienable share in the prerogatives of sovereignty not by virtue of a *natural right* but by virtue of belonging already in civil society as a subject of civil law, and in political society (the state) as citizen; to the extent that the distinction between civil society and the state is essentially a methodological one, the relatedness of these two forms of belonging may be summarized in the hyphenated term, Subject–Citizen or Citizen–Subject, depending on which sense of the word 'subject' we wish to foreground. Thus it is that sovereignty in this discourse is fundamentally *indivisible* and can be exercised only collectively, not individually.[22]

It is in fact the thought of Rousseau that haunts the moment of 1789. He was of course banned by the Church, but he also radically denies that the 'state of nature' is a domain of rights.[23] He posits, rather, a prior location within society and a certain distance from the natural state ('denatured' is Rousseau's own word in this context) for one to have rights of citizenship. The point of origin for rights, in other words, is neither God nor nature but society itself, or what Rousseau called 'the social contract'. However, what Rousseau calls 'the social contract' is not something 'real', a product of an *agreement* among humans living in a state of nature and deciding to found a civil society; nor is it a moment within temporal history, with a before and an after; the moment of the 'social contract' is not a historically concrete but a philosophically abstract moment, a point zero, which presumes not a negotiated but a common origin, prior to and beyond the realm of individual wills, a point of entry into history already marked by boundedness of civil obligation and social right; Rousseau's 'social contract', unlike Locke's, designates the idea that there is no humanity before society and that society needs no divine sanction to constitute itself. He was deeply suspicious of founding the discourse of rights in the discourse of individuality, prior to society. In an extraordinary aside, Rousseau asserts that he who has individual and unsocial interests can never be a citizen and can only be a bourgeois.

It is from Rousseau's thought, then, that we can trace the productive tension between the conception of citizenship and subjecthood. Historically, the word 'Subject' had carried the predominant meaning of *being subjected* to the power of the prince, the priest, the patriarch. Princely power implied monarchy; priestly power certainly meant dispensation of souls but it also meant special access to knowledge, through Latin and through a monopoly over schooling, very much as brahminism in India historically implied the debarring of women and *shudras* from Sanskrit language, and hence Vedic knowledge. While patriarchal power certainly meant serfdom of one sort or another in the realm of agrarian production, it also meant the subjection of women in that realm as well as within the household. What got transformed, in the course of the political upheavals of the eighteenth century and in the thought of the Enlightenment, was even the linguistic meaning of the word 'Subject'.

The discourse of 1789 may be credited with the revolutionary revisions of the meaning of subjecthood, whereby the idea of popular and indivisible sovereignty is born as a practical political project, so that the socialized individual is reborn as citizen and becomes a subject not *to* the prince or the priest, but *of* history, exercising the liberty of belief in matters of faith, demanding from the state a system of public and secular education, and instead of obeying the given laws actually participating in the social act of *making* the laws whereby state and society are to function. As we know, this battle was not won once and for all even in France, and it has had to be fought over and over again, in many corners of the globe. For Rousseau, in any case, true citizenship becomes thinkable only as the ability of the citizens, in their collectivity, to give laws unto themselves but also, equally, in their collective consent to abide by the laws they had given to themselves. The citizen, thus, was both a subject *of* and subject *to*: at once the author of laws and the voluntary object of laws, thereby the maker of history but also made by history. It was on the terrain of this doubleness – of being subjected to the laws that one had *made* as the subject of law – that the conflicting demands of individuality and community were to be reconciled; the community was to be not the community of local origin or otherworldly faith, but the community of equal citizenship that was freely chosen by citizens already bounded in society, and to which, then, one surrendered a part of one's self-interest. I believe that *this* is the moment in Rousseau's thought which is also, in the history of political philosophy, the point at which the idea of equality, which had started evolving with the issue of secularity within religious society, begins to transform itself into the idea of democracy in the sense in which one would now wish to use this term.

But the truly revolutionary step that Rousseau takes is the second one, in which he asks whether or not citizens who *make* laws and obey those laws, can in fact be equal subjects of the law, as makers *of* and as made *by* the laws, if the distribution of material goods among them is unequal. In other words: is property reconcilable with democracy?[24] Rousseau's thought on this score is both brilliant and faltering, but what I want to suggest through this brief review is that the seeds of democracy are already there in the idea of secularism, because you cannot have popular sovereignty if the state represents a religious majority at the expense of the rights and liberties of a minority; but the idea of socialism is also already there in the idea of democracy because, as Rousseau puts it, citizens who are unequal in the property relation cannot be equals as subjects *of* and as subjects *to* the law. The Citizen-Subject – that is to say, the democratic individual – cannot be born without the abolition of private property. Rousseau did not quite resolve the problem, even on the level of thought,[25] but in pointing to the incompatibility between property and equality he introduced an irreparable fissure within the body of Enlightenment thought. For, if the conformist strands of the Enlightenment had jubilantly appointed the bourgeois male individual as the rational subject of meaning and experience, strands in the revolutionary politics of the Enlightenment were already pronouncing the impossibility of the birth of the Citizen-Subject in a class-divided society. Hence the watchwords of 1789: 'Liberty, Fraternity, Equality' – which could be translated for our own time, word for word, as 'Democracy, Secularism, Socialism'. It was this particular strand in the politics of the Enlightenment that Marxism picked up, giving to it politically and theoretically a vastly revolutionized meaning, and thereby earning the rebuke of poststructuralists and subalternists alike, to the effect that we are mere children of the Enlightenment. All I can say in response is that, yes, you are damned right, we *are* – but not merely; not of the *whole* of the Enlightenment; and not of the Enlightenment *only*. We are also the spectre that is going to haunt this land for a long, long time.

Let us, then, summarize: the idea of religious liberty and of the peaceful coexistence of religious difference has been central, historically speaking, in the formation of the twin ideas of liberty and equality as such; the idea of democratic dissent was posed initially as the idea of *religious difference*. It gradually became the premise for the liberties of the individual in general, but then, in this same sweep, raised the difficult question as to how individual rights were to be reconciled with the common good. In raising the question of equality and equal rights for all, the idea of secularism became the chief motor behind the subsequent idea of political democracy. Democracy, in other words, *presumes* a secularist compact, and it is not liberal democracy that *produces* the secularist idea; it is the issue of secularism – not just religious *tolerance* but the civil *equality* of denominationally different individuals and communities within a given society – that produces the idea of equality *in general*, and therefore the idea of political democracy.

Democracy, in other words, *presumes* a prior social consensus on the issue of secular sociality and secular governance. But, what is also implicit in my argument is that the idea of one kind of equality leads, necessarily and logically, to other ideas of equality: the idea of secularism *leads* to ideas of political democracy, the idea of political equality *leads* to the idea of economic equality; the idea of socio-economic equality among men *leads* to similar ideas about equality between men and women, between individuals of one caste and another, one race or nation and another. I do not mean that these ideational logics bring about changes in the material world automatically; the relations between ideas and the material world are always modulated by the dialectic of given structures and transforming human agencies. What I do mean is that ideas of equality in one domain lead necessarily to ideas of equality in other domains; that the *logic* of such ideas would take us – and *should* take us – far beyond the conventional confines of democracy or social-ism or secularism; that the *logic* of secularism, the *logic* of democracy would take us, step by step, to communism itself – in other words, to that utopic moment which is the only *realistic* resolution of conflicts once the issue of justice has been posed. Because, as I said earlier, once the question of radical equality has been posed, nothing can escape the utopian ends of that questioning.

PART III
The Current Scene

In the Eye of the Storm:
The Left Chooses

This article is being drafted in an interregnum, in the moment of prolonged dread, between 16 May [1996], when Atal Behari Vajpayee, a man
who joined the RSS more than fifty years ago, has been sworn in as the
Prime Minister of India, thanks to a presidential indiscretion that has been
passed off as constitutional propriety; and 28 May, when this man, who
sacrificed his post as Foreign Minister and led his contingent of MPs out
of the Janata Party on the 'dual membership' issue not so many years
ago,[1] is to prove his majority on the floor of the House. As I make my
last revisions on this text, President Sharma, in another part of the city, is
reading to a joint session of the two Houses of Parliament a speech written
by members of the RSS, despite the Opposition's plea that the President
ought not to announce to the nation policies of a government so retrograde and destined to fall in three days. But this presidential action too is
considered the epitome of constitutional propriety, for, without the
Presidential Address, a fresh Parliament cannot be inaugurated even if the
first order of business for Parliament is to dismiss the government. Such
are the strains under which the Indian Constitution, one of the very best
in the world, is struggling to survive. One can only hope that this
government *will* fall and that the Constitution, choked and having constantly to come up for air, will gain a fresh lease of life. Meanwhile, the
city of Delhi, this capital of a formally secular India where five of the
seven seats of Parliament went to the BJP, has witnessed scenes of de-
lirious joy as members of the RSS walked into the corridors of the highest
power in the land. Today, the city wears a macabre air of normalcy.
Between extremes of fear and hope, one begins to collect one's thoughts.

Saffronization and Liberalization

The Lok Sabha elections of 1996 were the first to be held in the
aftermath of two structurally related watersheds, the most momentous
in the whole life span of the Republic since Independence.

The first of these passes under the euphemisms of 'liberalization', 'globalization' etc., and reverses the trajectory of economic development on which the Indian state was initially based in the formative years of the Republic. That trajectory had been in retreat for a good many years but its full withdrawal was announced only with the advent of the Manmohan/Rao regime.[2] As to when the retreat began, honest observers can disagree. It perhaps began with V.P. Singh's assumption, under Rajiv Gandhi, of the office of Finance Minister, an office that was later to be held by Manmohan and is occupied this week by Jaswant Singh; it is of course obvious that Manmohan and Jaswant are the siamese twins of India's New Economic Policy, but that V.P. Singh, the spiritual mentor of the National Front, could perhaps be credited with the initiation of the Policy signifies how broadly held the consensus is within the ruling class and how thin, therefore, the razor's edge that the Left has to tread when it comes to the choosing of allies and the formation of governments.[3] Others may credibly argue that the retreat of that initial model began earlier, with Indira Gandhi's last term, or with the Janata government, which was notable for its hostility towards the Nehruvian past and for the fact of its own domination by the Jan Sangh, the segment that gave to Janata the largest number of its seats, under Vajpayee's leadership. It is also well to recall that it was from the twin origins of Lohia'ite politics and Jayaprakash Narayan's insurrection that there arose those contemporary strongmen of Bihar and Uttar Pradesh – the Mulayams, the Laloos, the Sharad Yadavs[4] – with whom the Left has had to reach some sort of understanding in order to try to *forge* an alliance of sorts against the emerging consensus of the ruling class on saffronization of Indian politics.[5] Finally, it could also be argued quite plausibly that the retreat began much earlier, when Jawaharlal Nehru, the Prime Minister of India, began taking his tutorials from John Kenneth Galbraith, the urbane Harvard economist who came to India as Ambassador of the United States under Kennedy and took up this tutorial post, after a decent lapse of some years, more or less where Mountbatten had left off.

Be that as it may. The point is that the retreat has been long in coming but was fully and dramatically completed only with the advent of the Manmohan–Rao regime. It was only fitting – in one of those not entirely intended justices of history – that the installation of this regime in India roughly coincided with the dissolution of the Soviet Union and all that it had signified in the triangular struggle between capitalism, socialism, and nationalism since the end of the Second World War.[6] The global environment for such a shift in national policy was thus more favourable than at any previous moment in the short and unhappy life of this Republic; for capitalism generally, it was undoubtedly the most auspicious moment since at least the first decade of this century, if not since that Paris Commune out of which mass parties of the working class had initially arisen and whose logical culmination the Bolshevik Revolution had been. It is quite obviously the case, then, that 'liberalization' in India is part of a global offensive of capital in the moment of its greatest triumph – a triumph whose scope is not much diminished, so far as countries of backward capital are concerned, by the relative internal stagnation of advanced capital of the OECD countries.

We have spoken here of the redirection of policy over perhaps ten, possible twenty, plausibly thirty years. These two elements, the global environment and the shifts in policy, refer to the role of imperialism and the state. But what about the ruling class itself and those accumulation processes which guarantee *its* own extended reproduction and therefore determine *its* policy perspectives and attitudes towards imperialism? The crux of the matter in this regard is that much has changed in the world of capitalism, national and global, since India's Independence, and in the attitudes and demands of the Indian bourgeoisie in response to these changes.

Some of these changes can be summarized, more or less telegraphically. (1) Thanks precisely to those same policies of protectionism, import substitution, planned support of the private sector by the public sector etc., which its ideologues now blame for its inferiority in the world market, the Indian bourgeoisie has achieved levels of accumulation that now enable it to demand from the state that protectionism be abandoned and that it be allowed full integration with advanced capital. (2) Thanks, also, to the policy of cheap and broad-based scientific and technical education first formulated in the Nehru years, we have witnessed the stupendous growth of a widespread techno-scientific personnel in India, which now becomes the basis of certain types of advanced production inside India on which indigenous capital could make great profits by cooperating with advanced metropolitan capital in such areas as computer software and other information goods; in turn, imperialist capital is attracted by the comparative advantage of low infrastructural and labour costs, including the scientific/technical labour itself. (3) This process of the integration of Indian capital with that of the metropolis is accelerated further by the disappearance precisely of that alternate pole of Soviet socialism that had underwritten the ideology of the third path – between socialism and capitalism; in effect, a state capitalist sector – and which had provided the technology supports to make it somewhat practicable. (4) This integration is facilitated further by technologies of flexible production which make it possible to fragment the production process and move much of it around the globe in search of short-term profits and pliable junior partners, while new information technologies, availability of huge money supplies for global investment, tax systems, trade agreements, travel facilities, etc. help facilitate the global unfolding of this flexible production. (5) All this has led to multiple sources for investment funds and technological goods (not just from the United States but also from countries of the EU and the East Asian zones), and unprecedented levels of mutual integration among various national capitals across countries and continents, and across quite different levels of development, advanced and backward. Imperialism is internally more united and globally more dominant today. The strategic shift on the part of the Indian ruling class from protectionism to globalization is a considered response to its own interests and capabilities; to its estimate of the scope of the home market in terms of the size of the consuming middle classes and their consumption patterns and aspirations; as well as to the global realities within which it functions and in which *it* sees *its* historic opportunity.

In these global and national environments, then, there has been a comprehensive retreat from the economic nationalism of the national bourgeoisie that once reflected the class configurations characteristic of the last years of the colonial period and the early years of the Republic when this bourgeoisie indeed sought protection. Instead, the bourgeoisie has now radically transformed its own policies and aspirations, and it has launched an immensely powerful offensive against that earlier national compact which it now dismisses contemptuously as mere 'populism'. The scope of the class offensive of the bourgeoisie as it has been articulated thus far can best be gauged from the fact that 'liberalization' today commands a consensus among the bourgeoisie far more absolute than Nehruvianism or anything else of that kind has ever been able to achieve. The two major parties of this class, Congress and the BJP, are entirely agreed on this consensus, to the last comma and dot and smudge of ink. For the benefit of those who believe that a Jyoti Basu[7] candidacy for the leadership of the Third Force would have paved the way for 'pro-people policies', leaving a lasting imprint on state policies, it might be worth recalling that the entire United Front, excepting the Left Front itself, is an enthusiastic and explicit supporter of the whole structure of liberalization. That is why no sustained discussion of fundamental policy was possible – among, say, Surjeet, V.P. Singh, and Chidambram[8] – before the idea of Jyoti Basu's Prime Ministership got floated with such fanfare. Indeed, it is much to be doubted that everyone in the Left Front itself wants to question the modalities of this 'liberalization'. Would the CPI or the Forward Bloc, or a considerable section of the CPI(M) itself, stand firm if a confrontation with foreign capital developed over the cancellation of a handful of contracts, or with domestic capital over recovery of some of the public properties that have been sold off? Now, even history can't quite answer that question.

We might add that the theories of 'liberalization' that the Indian bourgeoisie, together with foreign capital, is implementing today through the Indian state are not derived from the contemporary liberal theory as it has been amended under the impact of social democracy by such theorists as Rawls, Dworkin, or Charles Taylor, wherein the market is to be *curbed* for communitarian ends and the social good. Our 'liberalization' is derived rather from the pristine, dog-eat-dog, nineteenth-century variety as it has been resurrected for our own time by the likes of Hayek and Friedman. In *this* liberalism, especially as it gets applied to formations of backward capital, the state becomes purely 'a managing committee of the bourgeoisie as a whole' and more or less disappears as the guardian of the social good, while its regulatory functions are redistributed downwards into the market and outward to multinational corporations and the emerging world government of the World Bank, IMF, GATT, various IFIs (International Financial Institutions) and multilateral agencies. In this situation, the vocation of the nation-state undergoes a fundamental mutation: the state no longer represents the interests *of* the nation in the world of international competition; it comes to represent, rather, the interests of 'globalization' *to* the nation.

That, then, is the first watershed: an impregnable ruling-class consensus, the ruling class itself very much on the offensive in pursuit of that consensus, with full support from imperialism, apparatuses of the Indian state, the main political parties, the media, the consuming classes in the major cities, 90 per cent of the Lok Sabha itself.

Then, the second watershed: saffron, the spectre of Ayodhya, the emergence of communalism as the dominant ideology of the country's ruling institutions and dominant sections of the middle classes.[9] It is doubtful that much more of the populace at large has been saffronized since 1991; the BJP's rise from 119 seats in the previous Lok Sabha to 160 in the present one has been achieved with roughly the same proportion of the electorate on its side: about 10 per cent, considering that roughly half of the total electorate did not even bother to vote while the BJP thrives on the commitment of a hardcore that *does* vote. What has changed drastically is the level of support communalism now gets from the dominant structures, in terms of class, caste, capital, and party affiliation.

Ayodhya was a watershed in contemporary Indian history because it signified the emergence of a powerful consensus in favour of *Hindutva*, the hard and the soft versions of it, among large sections of the ruling class. Let us recapitulate the well-known facts which I recall here because this too is vital to my argument. In UP, the Bharatiya Janata Party, the parliamentary face of the RSS, was in charge of state government at the time when various fronts of that organization, together with their allies in Shiv Sena, converged on Ayodhya and demolished Mir Baqi's antique little mosque, in a fascist spectacle of gigantic proportions, justifying this defiance of the Supreme Court as a heroic act of redeeming Hindu honour; the spectacle went on for five hours, in full view of the electronic and print media as well as the security and intelligence apparatuses of the state. The Supreme Court itself did nothing to bring the culprits to book and Kalyan Singh[10] was at length let off with a pretty little slap on the knuckles. Eventually, some judges of the Supreme Court rewarded the criminals of Ayodhya with a judgment that went out of its way to declare that *Hindutva* and Hinduism meant one and the same thing. In the ensuing months, the RSS made full use of its exoneration by the highest judicial authority. The Chief Justice did not convene a full bench to review that judgment.

The liberal/Left intellectuals, among whom I too belong, have been a bit too sanguine about what we took to be the chances of *Hindutva* prevailing. In the Assembly elections after the Ayodhya demolition, the electorate of UP gave to the BJP an additional 2 per cent of the vote, above what it had had before the demolition. The electoral arithmetic was such, however, that the short-lived Mulayam–Mayawati alliance managed to keep the BJP out of government.[11] Most of us ignored the BJP's increased share in the total vote and contrived to believe that its immediate inability to form a government in UP was a popular verdict against the Ayodhya demolition in the key state of the country – indeed, in the very state in which the demolition had taken place. Mayawati's later alliance with the BJP came as a rude shock, but we tended to look at it in terms of the BJP's intrigues and Mayawati's betrayal. The idea was rarely entertained that caste-based politics of the downtrodden, led by the upwardly mobile, may itself frequently produce rightwing populisms of a sort that would be fascistic in their own way; that, in the north at least, many of the *dalit* groupings would find it perfectly possible to align with the *manuwadis* against OBC power;[12] that many of the most bitter contests are likely to be not between the uppermost and the lowest castes but between castes that are adjacent to each other, jostling for the same space, or among fractions of the same caste; and that all this may play right into the hands of the Sangh *parivar* – so that caste-based politics, even of the oppressed castes, had to be practised and/or applauded with much caution and restraint. On the eve of the recent elections, liberal-Left social scientists who are supposed to understand such things contrived to see no great enthusiasm for the BJP in UP; in the actual election results, the BJP maintained its winning streak and, thanks to the SP–BSP split, managed to convert its steadily improving share of the vote into a landslide in terms of Lok Sabha seats. In the wake of the Ayodhya demolition Prabhat Patnaik, the eminent Marxist economist, had argued, quite correctly, that the RSS

was indeed a fascist organization but had also argued, more problemati-
cally, that this *Hindutva* fascism cannot gain governmental authority
because Big Business doesn't want it.[13] As years go by, larger and larger
sections of Business, big and small, have been choosing otherwise; this
week's rumour, partly authenticated by the BBC, has it that a wide
cross-section of Big Business is pouring in truckloads of money for the
BJP to buy up the requisite number of MPs before they have to show a
majority on the floor of Parliament.

But then there is also the question of the Congress. The habits of the
canonical, anti-colonial nationalism have taught us that we must look at
the body politic as essentially healthy, the cancerous growth as being
local and marginal, located in the 'backward' sections of society, revers-
ible through measured doses of the correct ideology, while the nation
marches forward on the path of realizing its civilizational ethos of
ecumenical toleration, unity in diversity, etc. These habits focus
especially on the humane and secular nature of the elites. The constant
invocation of the hallowed names of ancestors – Gandhi, Nehru, Azad,
what have you – has helped us conceal from ourselves the rot among
precisely this elite as it reclothes itself in saffron, either the harder or the
softer version of it as expediency at any moment demands. The illusion
about what has been the primary ruling institution has been particularly
strong, and the illusion tends to recur after each dose of reality;
communalism, we made ourselves believe, was a minority position
within the Congress, which could be isolated, perhaps even more readily
than in the nation at large. Facts have long been otherwise.

We have for long had to choose between the programmatic communalism of the BJP and the pragmatic communalism of the Congress. The
communalization of every arm of the state has proceeded apace under
the benign gaze of the Congress; every time the riots broke out, right
up to the countrywide bloodshed in the wake of Ayodhya, the Congress
routinely saw sections of its own police and paramilitary forces, in little
places like Bhagalpur and in great cities like Bombay, join the main
instigators of the riot, often participating in orgies of rape and looting,
uncaring of any consequential measures against them by the state whose
employees, representatives, and agents of law they were. Their understanding of their own governing party was shrewd. At the highest level
of the party and government, communalism was played like a game of
chess: Bhindranwale here, the 'Hindu card' in Jammu there, the mass
killings of Sikhs in the capital itself, the cynicism of the Shahbano case,
the opportunism of getting the locks at Ayodhya mosque opened, the
studied refusal to bring culprits to book, be they personnel of the state
itself or the marauding preachers of *Hindutva* systematically inciting
violence, year in and year out, in contravention of law and Constitution
alike.[14] Then came Ayodhya. This culmination was logical; and the

reaction of the Congress predictable. It did nothing. The intelligentsia was horrified, but most sections of it learned, in time, to recoup the 'lesser evil' thesis with no holds barred.

Considerable sections of the Muslim electorate in Bombay thought otherwise; helpless and furious, they decided to teach the Congress a lesson by voting for their own mortal enemies, the Sena–BJP combine.[15] At least one vicious circle, on which the Congress had banked so heavily, was broken: the cocky presumption that since the Muslims would never go to the hard saffron, Congress was free to pursue its own soft saffron. One does, at times, have to cut off one's nose to spite one's face – given that the face is already disfigured enough and in an advanced stage of decomposition! Then came the Bombay blasts, in the heart of the financial district, which put the fear of God into the hearts of the big bourgeoisie; even the BJP–Sena combine learned, to the extent of their ability, to behave, at least up to now: growing communalization of Maharashtra's state and society under their government, yes, but a communalization that falls well short of orgies of violence. The bourgeoisie, in any case, shook; never again has *Hindutva* been so violence-prone. And, true to form, the Congress displayed infinitely greater alacrity in its efforts to apprehend the culprits of the blast than it ever showed in apprehending the culprits of Ayodhya, who continued to operate as the government-in-waiting, which, as it turned out, they truly were. Why did the government machinery make such determined efforts to apprehend the perpetrators of the blast? Simple: *they were Muslims*. Yet again, the famous 'Hindu hurt' was to be assuaged. With such friends, who needs enemies? The alacrity of the search for the blast culprits led to absurd ends: two of them, smugglers and *hawala* operators,[16] were traced to the homes and patronage of a Congress minister and a BJP MP who was also a known criminal: between varieties of criminality and varieties of saffron, the circle was closed.

We are speaking here of the two ruling institutions of today's India, and we are speaking of the highest levels of the judicial system, the last refuge of legality and constitutionality in the Republic, parts of which appear contaminated by *Hindutva* and whose main pillars feel undermined and hemmed in by the practical refusal of the executive to carry out its injunctions.

At the other end of the political spectrum stands the Left. All mythologies aside, the most obvious *material* fact about the Left is its overwhelming weakness and its inability to break out of its regional sequestration. Honest people can disagree about the causes, but facts testifying to this weakness are grim, as even the recent elections testify. The Left Front as a whole commands a mere 10 per cent of the seats in the Lok Sabha; within the Front, CPI(M), which carries the main weight and burden, can be credited with 32 (33, if you count an Independent) out of 537; the strength of the Left Front, as well as of CPI(M), in the present Lok Sabha is lower than in the previous one. In the state Assembly elections in its two strongholds, West Bengal and Kerala, the really significant fact is not that the Left Front in Bengal has retained power with a comfortable margin or that the Left Democratic Front in Kerala has returned to power with 80 seats out of 140; the more telling fact is that the margin in West Bengal has been considerably reduced and that in Kerala CPI(M) itself has won only about half of the LDF seats, 41 in a House of 140, or less than one seat out of three. So broad is the alliance in Kerala that, unlike West Bengal where even Forward bloc can be part of a *Left* Front, in Kerala the word 'Democratic' has had to be inserted between 'Left' and 'Front'. These are indicators of *extreme* weakness, the overall triumph in Kerala notwithstanding. It is doubtless true that what has come to be known, justifiably, as CPI(M)'s 'moral authority' is very much far in excess of its numerical strength. However, only idealists would forget material facts in favour of moral leads. The rules of thumb about the exercise of 'moral authority' are two in number. One: moral authority has much more leverage in the making of coalitions before the formation of government, but its utility can diminish with shocking speed if one becomes a Prime Minister simply on the basis of that moral authority with no material force to back it, especially if, owing to the lack of numbers, one has been forced to include rank 'liberalizers', scam-ridden crooks, and representatives of charge-sheeted criminals in one's cabinet. Second: if moral authority is all one has, it is precisely the moral authority that needs to be preserved, instead of being staked, for unpredictable gain and in an odd mixture of panic and euphoria, at the first sign that the mortal battle is about to begin. That, more or less, is what was involved for the CPI(M) in its consideration of the idea that Jyoti Basu be offered as a candidate for the post of Prime Minister.

It was, in any case, in circumstances of unparalleled gravity, and faced with an absolute consensus in favour of 'liberalization' and with the rise of 'saffron' to a position of dominance in political and ideological apparatuses of state, that the Left set out to achieve what seemed impossible: assemble a coalition against this overwhelming force. The wedge to prise open this ruling-class power seemed to lie in the fact that a wide variety of regional parties and groups, who were agreed with the two ruling institutions on the issue of 'liberalization' and all that entails, were nevertheless either openly hostile to 'saffron' or at least indifferent to it. A partial redress of what the ruling institutions had perpetrated could perhaps be attempted by bringing such forces together. CPI(M) was the main instigator and most persevering advocate of the initiative. What it seemed to propose, under the shorthand slogan that has by now become well known – 'Non-Congress, Non-BJP Government of Secular and Democratic Forces' – can perhaps be conceptualized in terms of four concentric circles: (1) the Left Front which was already in place and was more or less reliable; (2) the resurrection of a National Front which already existed but hardly went much beyond the splintered Janata Dal and was thus greatly in need of repair and expansion; (3) a National Front–Left Front (NF–LF) alliance; and, surrounding all that, (4) a loose network of bilateral regional alliances between individual members of the NF–LF and local parties that had not been drawn fully into the NF: altogether, this last and largest of the concentric circles was to be called the Third Force or the Third Front. Prospects were daunting. The refusal of the Bahujan Samaj Party (BSP) to join with the Samajwadi Party (SP) and indeed to continue flirting with BJP meant that no major alternative could be posed against the latter in their UP citadel. Naidu's insurrection, N.T. Rama Rao's overthrow and death, and Laxmi Parvathi's candidacy served to undermine the National Front and bolstered the Congress in Andhra Pradesh. In Bihar, Laloo Prasad failed to stem the formidable force that the combination of the BJP and the Samata Party became, and the two Yadavs[17] found it difficult to overcome local animosities. CPI(M) persisted but, in view of its overall strategy as much as the material constraints imposed by its numerical inferiority, it refused to assume formal leadership of the alliance by offering a Prime Ministerial candidate. The issue of Jyoti Basu's candidacy was debated among parties and in the press for virtually the whole year, but CPI(M) never indicated consent and remained intransigent: guidance, but no formal leadership.

As the election results rolled in, all seemed lost: the BJP increased its tally substantially and emerged both as the dominant force in west and north, the most populous zones of India, and as the largest party in parliament; together with its allies, it gained roughly twice as many seats as the NF alliance, while the rest of what was loosely called the Third Force did well but was not part of the formal alliance. Over the next ten days, two things of great significance happened: the Third Force rapidly came together and transformed itself into a United Front, but the CPI(M), whose brisk guidance made it all possible, refused to spare Basu to lead the government, if and when a government of the United Front (UF) materializes. If the UF holds together and overthrows the BJP government on the floor of the House and takes charge, with the Congress forced to bring up the rear to save its own bloodied skin (but without winning any of its purported conditions), it will have been the greatest feat of organizational skill in recent memory, and most of the credit shall accrue to CPI(M): a government of UF is nothing but a materialization of CPI(M)'s slogan of 'Non-Congress, Non-BJP Government of Secular and Democratic Forces'. That a small battalion of thirty-odd MPs, guiding a ragbag coalition of anti-communist secularists, is about to achieve precisely this end is, to say the least, astonishing. The other decision of the CPI(M) – *not* to field Basu for the premiership – has served to enhance its prestige among outsiders, who are agog at the sight of a political party that still has the moral stamina to refuse the premiership, in the light of its own principles, even when it is offered the opportunity on a platter. It has thus sought to demonstrate in practice that, unlike other parties, it acts not for self-aggrandizement but for the transformation of the social, political, and economic structures of the country.

The Liberal Order and the United Front

There has also been a cluster of beliefs which tended to underwrite the hope, indeed the conviction, that the essentially democratic and secular India shall not give power to the prodigies of the *parivar*. It has been widely believed, first, that the majority of the Indian populace is essentially secular and will not elect a party so rabidly communal; second, that the humanist and tolerant outlooks inherent in Indian traditions of piety shall necessarily refurbish the polity's essentially secular character;[18] and, third, that the upper reaches of the Indian polity – the constitutional covenant, the liberal intelligentsia, the higher judiciary, the constitutional experts, the English-language media, the English-educated cosmopolitan bourgeoisie, Big Business itself – were fundamentally liberal and would abhor an illiberal, irrationalist, religiously irredentist, violence-prone *Hindutva* combine of the *parivar* and the Sena. We were going through very hard times but the deluge, we were assured, was not to be, not in the foreseeable future at any rate. It was some such combination of convictions which helped persuade many of us that the polls which were forecasting that the BJP and allies would emerge as the largest bloc, with 185 to 200 seats, were biased and implausible.

As it turned out, much of this conviction was ill-founded. Whether or not most Indians are secular and tolerant is somewhat beside the point. A majority of the electorate need not vote for a party to come to power. It is well known that fascist regimes of the past have always taken power as minorities in parliament and have always used that power to convert themselves into a majority in what remains of parliament.[19] What is much less understood, thanks precisely to the bourgeois propaganda, is that the association between liberal capitalism and majority rule is itself a myth perpetrated by the bourgeoisie through its legitimation technologies. It is quite frequently the case in the history of constitutional governance that government has not been based on active consent of the majority of the electorate through the exercise of universal suffrage. In a typical capitalist society today, roughly one-third to half of the electorate does not vote; Reagan's landslide, the largest in US history, was ratified by only 27 per cent of registered US voters. From among those who actually bother to vote, a share of 35 to 40 per cent is almost always sufficient to obtain a clear majority of seats; the BJP has just swept UP with less than 35 per cent of the votes actually counted – which comes to well below 20 per cent of the eligible electorate. That the BJP has received 160 seats on the basis of roughly 20 per cent of the votes counted, or that its seats have gone up from 119 to 160 without any appreciable improvement in its share of the vote thanks to the number of candidates fighting against it is a confirmation of this intrinsically aberrant characteristic of bourgeois democracy. The system of proportional representation as Italy until recently had tends somewhat to restrict such aberrations; the 'first past the post' system that we have inherited from our colonial masters tends to accentuate the inherent anarchy of what passes for the bourgeois political order. Be all that as it may, the basic fact is that an *electoral* test to determine whether or not the majority of Indians are secular and tolerant enough to save the Republic from *Hindutva* may never materialize.

But then there is also the matter of the liberal character of the Indian establishment. Here, a minimal clarification of the two different usages of the term 'liberal' is in order. In political parlance, the term 'liberal' refers to free expression of ideas, the right of assembly, the formation of political minorities and majorities, the main principles of electoral politics. It is in keeping with this sense of liberalism that it has been widely argued, and President Sharma has reaffirmed the argument, that in the absence of a clear majority in Parliament the leader of the largest single party and of the largest alliance that went into the elections as a *clearly constituted alliance*[20] must be called upon to form a government. The same principle now requires that in order to remain in government the BJP must prove its majority on the floor of the House, because plurality of seats before Parliament is constituted is not the same as a majority *after* the actual constitution of Parliament.

I have grave doubts about this particular mode of argumentation within liberal politics, and doubts can only increase when this very structure is invoked on behalf of the President when he overlooks the candidacy of Deve Gowda who had commitment of support from well over the majority, on the plea that the largest party, no matter how small in itself, must be invited. This is odd when the President knows full well that the one who is first called to form a government has an inestimable advantage, especially in a city like Delhi where money controls so much of what passes for politics. But the problem of the exigencies of the liberal order extends beyond the President to the intelligentsia committed to this order. Consider the fact, for example, that certified liberals such as Soli Sorabjee and Nani Phalkivala, both eminent constitutional experts, publicly advised the President to invite the BJP to form a government, as did *The Times of India*, heretofore the keeper of the liberal conscience, in two successive editorials in one week.[21] More important, from the standpoint of the Left, is that the commitment to the survival of liberal democracy also put in a quandary a great many others in the 'unorganized Left' whose detestation of the BJP is unquestionable. As a political scientist at Delhi University put it: if you argue that Vajpayee cannot be called to form a government because of his communalism, what stops someone else from saying that Jyoti Basu cannot be called in because he is a Communist, considering especially that, in the electoral arithmetic at hand, CPI(M)'s 32 seats compare rather unfavourably with BJP's 160? It was, in other words, the logic of political liberalism itself, as understood by a wide spectrum of influential opinion, that required that Vajpayee *should be* called; and the logic was so inexorable that even Deve Gowda, an authentic representative of the growing agro-based bourgeoisie, could not be called in *at that stage*. Those who imagine that Basu would have been made Prime Minister because of his personal charm and prestige, and that the Third Force lost the chance because of Gowda's lack of such personal attributes, lend themselves to a theoretical position which sees politics not in terms of structural imperatives but as a game of person-alities – at best a Weberian notion of 'charisma'. There is no *evidence* that the President's own views about constitutional propriety depended on Jyoti Basu's charisma, which is in any case rather stronger for the Left Front, and its friends and the masses in West Bengal, than for others in the rest of the country. It is of course probable that in case Jyoti Basu had acceded to the collective request of his colleagues in the Third Force, he *might* have been called in at the *second* stage, *if* Vajpayee failed to establish a majority and *after* Basu had proved his acceptability to the likes of Rao, Manmohan Singh, and Chidambram.

There is the more crucial meaning of 'liberalism', however, from which the currently powerful euphemism of 'liberalization' is derived. This refers to a freedom of the market in which capital has the unfettered power to deal with commodities, including the crucial commodity of labour, entirely as it pleases; economically liberal states are, as a rule, strongly supportive of capital and repressive towards labour. India has been more or less fully liberal in the former, political sense since Independence; what limits to economic liberalism it had ever set for itself are being shed now with remorseless alacrity and pre-Ricardian zeal. Every shred of available evidence suggests that *this* liberalism is at the heart of ruling-class consensus even though it is flexible on the issue as to which section of its governing caste shall be the one called to implement its policies. The fact that so much of the support of the capitalist class has shifted in favour of the BJP as the Congress becomes less and less capable of retaining its position as the predominant ruling institution of the country demonstrates that the bourgeoisie may well be willing to sacrifice much of its political liberalism, even its secularism (such as it is), at the altar of a rightwing authoritarian regime, so long as the 'shock therapy' of its economic liberalism continues apace.

I have argued that the premiership of Vajpayee has arisen from inside the logics of Indian political liberalism, even though some aspects of his party are at variance with liberal political principles in the broadest sense. I will further argue that this bourgeoisie would have preferred to prolong Congress rule but, given the internal decay of the Congress, the imperatives of economic liberalism required support for the BJP precisely because of the latter's full commitment to multinational companies, the Indian big bourgeoisie, and its representatives in the bureaucracy. The newspaper reports on the first working day that the BJP was in office (18 May) were significant in this regard. For instance, the front page of the Delhi edition of *The Times of India* on that day carried a photograph of Rao and Vajpayee shaking hands and one of Jaswant Singh attending office as the new Finance Minister; the main headline read, 'Government will honour all contractual obligations: FM', addressed obviously to the multinational companies. The layout of the front page in the section 'Business Times' was even more indicative. The photograph above the main text, the only one on the page, was that of Jaswant Singh with Montek Singh Ahluwalia, the Finance Secretary and Manmohan Singh's gift to his successor, looming in the background. Below the photograph one found a boxed and highlighted news item reporting the new Finance Minister's promise that all the high-ranking officials in the Ministry will remain in place and that there will be business as usual. In a side column we were told that with the coming of the BJP government at the centre the Maharashtra government – not Enron itself so much as the Swadeshi government of *Hindutva* – is hopeful that work on the Enron hydro-electric power project shall now begin quickly and in earnest.[22]

Far from saving us from *Hindutva*, it is precisely the political and economic liberalism of the Indian bourgeoisie and its managing committee, the Indian state, that has brought us to this impasse. Which brings us to the matter of Deve Gowda, whom the CPI(M) has supported as Prime Ministerial candidate, with perhaps some sense of irony. He is at the cutting edge of the class offensive of a newly emergent but already very powerful fraction of the Indian big bourgeoisie, namely the agro-based barons, and the revision of the Land Ceilings Act that his government has passed in the Karnathaka state Assembly is the most advanced such measure yet, probably soon to be followed in Maharashtra; it is significant that Gowda's main ally within the Congress is said to be Sharad Pawar. This legislation in Karnathaka is the direct opposite of the land reform programmes of the Left Front government in West Bengal.

This breadth of the alliance is itself dictated by a concern for the religious minorities. Anyone still capable of remembering that the mosque in Ayodhya was demolished, despite the Supreme Court injunction, when the BJP was in power in UP and the Congress at the Centre – not to mention the fact that the Congress government has all these years had in its possession all the evidence necessary for prosecuting the criminals in high places and low, and has not done so – can hardly take exception to the proposition that the minorities are safe with neither party and that the country needs the government of a secular, democratic force which in the present circumstances can only be a broad alliance. The practical possibility of such an alliance's providing a real alternative is greatly weakened, though, by the fact that its government will be crucially dependent on the Congress. Thus, the efforts to put together a UF government are being undertaken from a position of great weakness. It seemed far-fetched, therefore, that such glaring weakness could be turned into strength through a sleight of hand or play at charismatic politics when some two-thirds the Third Force was itself anti-Communist and rightwing, the only virtue of most of them being that they represented a whole range of regional populisms and were not given to spilling the blood of the minorities. In other words, a perception seems to have grown within the CPI(M) that the fifty-odd parliamentarians of the Left Front, well over half of whom CPI(M) itself supplies, could hardly form the nucleus of a government without renouncing all that it stood for; the BJP and Congress from the outside, key members of the alliance such as Chidambram and Gowda from the inside, would have eaten them for breakfast. Indeed, the allies themselves were not proposing, so far as one could tell from their public pronouncements, a government dominated by the CPI(M); they seem to have proposed only that it lend, more or less as a sacrificial lamb, Jyoti Basu as a symbolic figurehead without any agreement on policy – a key distinction which is often forgotten in the heat of debate. This incontrovertible weakness of the Left, the unreliability of allies on most issues, and yet the necessity of a secular and democratic government that would protect the minorities – combined with the very class nature of the Indian state, and restricted within the parameters that the specific forms of Indian liberalism has defined for its state – seem to have dictated the necessity of trying to form a government that would be reasonably acceptable to that liberal order and would yet represent the regional aspirations alongside a firm commitment to the secular covenant. The ultimate choice that the Left made seems to have been that it was better to remain at the very base of the alliance so as to help it form as stable a

government as possible, but also to resist the lure of the Prime Ministerial post so that it would continue to have the moral authority to try
and influence policies of the ensuing government in the interests of the
nation and its people. Shrewd as ever, *The Times of India* commented
editorially on another aspect of this choice: should the CPI(M) remain a
communist party or should it become a social-democratic one? *The
Times* noted that it had chosen to remain what it has been, at least for
now.[23] Despite this refusal to become a social-democratic party at this
important juncture, the stature of the party kept growing in national
politics and even among the ranks of anti-Communists because everyone
could see that neither a firm alliance between JD and SP before the
elections nor the post-election expansion of the NF–LF into a credible
Third Force and then into a fully fledged United Front would have been
possible without the leading role of the CPI(M) and its refusal to enter
into electoral opportunism in order to get the premiership in a short-
lived government – a little place in the sun before the night of the long
knives sets in.

Structures have a way of reasserting themselves, and it can safely be
said that the three political forces that are ranged against each other –
the BJP and its allies, the United Front, and the Congress, with their
respective leaders – reflect the present condition of the Indian liberal
order quite accurately. The landscape is dominated by shades of saffron,
the hard saffron of the BJP which relies heavily on Vajpayee's civilities
for legitimation in the bourgeois order; and the soft saffron of Rao's
Congress which does not even have the guts to get rid of the leader who
has brought it to this impasse. It is only fitting that Vajpayee and Rao,
a would-be poet and an aspiring author of semi-pornographic fiction,
are good friends. But then there is the United Front which may, but for
the power of money and the potential of the Congress to stab it in the
back, yet defeat the BJP on the floor of the House. Its most redeeming
feature is that it is profoundly opposed to saffron, represents a plurali-
zation of regional aspirations and populisms, and is on the whole anti-
Brahminical in its caste politics without the stridencies and caste
opportunisms of a Kanshi Ram.[24] Meanwhile, the UF is also an authentic
expression of the contemporary liberal order of the Indian bourgeoisie,
in that it accurately represents the shift of political gravity towards the
states of the south and towards the capital gravitating and growing
there, in new industries, new information technologies, agro-based
accumulations, and research and development complexes, while to the
west, where similar accumulation processes are also at work, the BJP
holds Gujarat quite firmly and shares Maharashtra with Shiv Sena and
the Congress. It is also quite possible that in the event that the UF
actually comes to power, it will start supervising a transition in Indian
politics from the inherited mechanisms of viceregal centralization to the

American-style negotiations among constituent states as they are represented by regional leaders, racketeers, and strongmen; within the predicates of the liberal order, we could confer on this process the title of 'democratization'.

Barbarians at the Gate

Barbarians are at the gate, but has fascism arrived?

Since that watershed in Indian politics which is symbolized by Ayodhya, the present writer has been in the forefront of those who have argued that *Hindutva* communalism in general and the RSS and Shiv Sena in particular are not expressions of the familiar kind of rightwing politics but the specifically Indian forms of fascism; also that our collective devotion to electoral politics is such that we tend to treat the BJP as a normal political party, like any other but worse than all the others (along with the Sena of course), and not for what it is, namely an electoral front for a sinister, semi-secret, fascist organization whose bid to take power began in the 1920s, a quarter-century before the founding of the Jan Sangh and more than half a century before the BJP was even a gleam in anyone's eye. Most of that argument still remains unwritten though fragments of it are available in sections of three published articles.[25] This is not the place to try to formulate what is yet unwritten, or to recapitulate what has been published already. A couple of salient points may be summarized nevertheless, starting with the global context in which the RSS arose some seventy years ago and the more recent conjuncture in which the BJP, as its parliamentary and relatively benign face, has made its parliamentary mark, greatly aided by more openly fascistic members of the *parivar* such as the VHP, Bajrang Dal, and Durga Vahini, not to speak of the RSS itself which serves as the BJP's think-tank and practical guide, and provides the disciplined core of key leaders in a chaotic and corrupt parliamentary party, without taking any share of direct responsibility.

1. The founding of the RSS in 1925 took place in the first phase of the great upsurge of fascist movements in Europe, and, inspired by the European fascisms, elsewhere in the world. Thus, fascism was a *generalized* phenomenon globally, from Norway to Argentina and from Austria to Japan, even though it took its classical form and established its enduring regime only in Italy alongside the close variant of the Nazi regime in Germany. In at least half of the European countries such movements were very powerful, and a large European zone came to be dominated by them at one time or another. French fascist writers inspired not only the German Nazis but as far-flung a figure as Ali Shariati, the anti-Communist theorizer of the radical side of the Irani

revolution who is much idolized by those Islamicists and their allies who are disgruntled with the turn the Islamic Revolution actually took. Inspired by this European phenomenon, many parties were founded outside Europe, including the Phalange in Lebanon, which simply borrowed its own name from the Spanish fascists, and the Hizb al Ba'th al-'Arabi al-Ishtiraki (for short 'Ba'ath', and in English 'The Party of Arab Socialist Regeneration') which modelled its name on the official designation of the German Nazis, National Socialism.[26] The RSS was part and parcel of this international phenomenon and the founders of *Hindutva* were quite conscious of this connection; they are known to have argued that the German solution of the 'Jewish Question' was a fitting model for the way the 'Muslim Question' could be resolved in India. A telling contrast between the European and non-European fascisms is that while the European ones arose directly in response to massive revolutionary upsurge among the working classes and used a racialistic national ideology more for irrational mobilizations against the Left, fascism in non-European countries, which lacked the sharp class polarization of industrial societies, tended to be structured around ideologies of racialism, religious zealotry, majoritarianism, rightwing cultural nationalism, and millenarian rhetorics of racial and national redemption. Even so, it is important to note that the RSS arose in India partly inspired by the European phenomenon but, concretely, in response to the development of a secular and all-inclusive nationalism as a mass movement after 1919, as well as the very first stirrings of an organized working-class movement in the 1920s; opposition to Gandhi and 'Bolshevism' were early features of the rhetoric, and when the RSS was banned after Gandhi's assassination its imprisoned leaders offered cooperation to the Congress against the then united CPI. It needs to be added also that so pervasive has been the influence of fascist ideas outside Marxist circles that some of these ideas appear simply as 'common sense' or as established truths even in places where the enunciators of such ideas may not even know that they are derived from fascist ideology. This is certainly true of a great many rightwing ideologies, but it can also easily be shown that many of the postmodernist ideas of today are embedded in the unacknowledged and possibly unrealized influence of the fascist philosophical positions against Reason and Modernity. This is the dangerous ground on which our own postmodernists, the subalternist historians and the indigenist social scientists, often tread; hence the phenomenon, both ironic and logical, that individuals who are otherwise opposed to *Hindutva* come to occupy alongside it what Sumit Sarkar has called their 'shared discursive space'.[27]

In our own time, the BJP of course has a specific Indian lineage; but it is today also part of a much wider global turn to the Right, often to the extreme Right, which has witnessed over the past twenty years or so, especially from the mid-1970s onwards, the coming to prominence of irrationalist, racist, fascist, and proto-fascist movements across the globe. Sources for this global trend have been extremely diverse: (1) a reaction against the rise of revolutionary movements and many other kinds of dissent in the period up to the end of the 1970s; (2) the growing stagnation in the advanced capitalist economies, from the early 1970s onwards, and the need for irrationalist and national-chauvinist movements there both to control and to divert the working masses; (3) the crisis of the Soviet model in the COMECON countries and the rise of such movements both to combat socialism and to occupy the political space being vacated by the retreating communist parties; (4) a majoritarian reaction against the global assertion by minorities of their rights as part of the democratic aspirations arising throughout the world; (5) the sexual and generally patriarchal anxieties in traditional households about the increasing participation of women in the professions and the labour force, hence their partial escape from the twenty-four-hour policing by domestic regimes; (6) the crisis of religious and traditionalist orders brought about by the spread of secular ideologies and the irreversible social process of secularization as a necessary accompaniment of modernity, and hence the religious backlash; (7) the burgeoning communitarian bases of organization in diverse countries, especially the poorer ones, to take advantage of electoral politics for social advancement and to organize collectives to fight all the more ferociously over the distribution of limited resources, especially in the context of capitalist rapaciousness and weak working-class movements; (8) the objective necessity for the bourgeois order to displace the terrain of struggle from class conflict to community conflict, and so on. As one can readily see, the new-found power of *Hindutva* from the late 1970s onwards arose at the intersection of many of these trends.

2. The RSS is a unique – and in its own sinister way impressive – *revolutionary* organization of the radical Right. In its organizational structure and tactics of mobilization it owes much to what it has learned from the radical and revolutionary Left, for its own cynical purposes. This too is unsurprising, for, as Régis Debray in his better days once put it, 'Revolution revolutionizes the Counter-revolution.' That is to say, once a revolutionary experience has become part of historical legacy, everyone can draw lessons from that legacy. That is why every revolution has to be original in its organizational form, since the very success of the previous revolution renders it unrepeatable. Counter-revolution draws lessons of two kinds: to prevent more revolutions, but also to imbibe some enduring lessons about organizational work and problems of strategy, so as to define its own originality. Not that the RSS ideologues have become students of Lenin and Gramsci, but they

have imbibed much simply by virtue of their living in a historical period when that kind of experience was gained in some places and was studied the world over, especially by the counter-revolutionaries trained in imperialist academies.[28]

It is very much to be doubted that the RSS has any basic commitment to parliamentary government, but it understands the sturdiness and objective necessity of this form in India. What is remarkable is not that it violates democratic norms repeatedly; that is only to be expected. What is remarkable is that, for an organization of its type, it acts with remarkable discipline and (all things considered) restraint; has a shrewd sense of timing in its offensives and retreats; and is always careful as to how much and how frequently it would overstep the bounds of what is ultimately acceptable within the Indian constitutional setup. To give an extreme example: it built up a massive movement towards the Ayodhya demolition not in a day but through a series of actions and waves of advance and retreat, to test the waters. It eventually demolished the mosque as an act of its own consolidation, having surmised – quite correctly, however bitter it may be to say so – that the act would eventually be acceptable to large parts of society, including its executive, judiciary, armed forces, and even large parts of the intelligentsia. But it also knew how to disperse its forces, how not to press the issue of Mathura and Varanasi at the wrong time.[29] Brutal it is; adventurist it is not. It is very unlikely, therefore, that, even in the worst-case scenario of Vajpayee gaining a majority on the floor, the RSS would try to convert this immediate electoral advantage into the establishment of its own rule. This not because the RSS is not a fascist organization but because it has always had an accurate sense of the balance of forces; it has never been in a hurry; it understands (as we do) that the BJP's actual numerical inferiority and its highly regionalized bases of power as well as problematic relationships in the mosaic of castes and sub-castes forbids too quick a seizure of real state power: it wishes to rule the country, not blow it apart.

3. With the growing erosion of the twin pillars of Nehruvian ideology upon which the Republic was originally founded, 'secularism' in society and 'socialistic planning' in economy, managers of ideology in the emerging dispensation are experiencing a vacuum and must create an alternative coherence, even if it is an irrationalist one. Although a vast machinery has been assembled to dismantle the Nehruvian ideological legacy from the Right, this is not a matter of ideology alone. Rather, it signifies a profound shift in the very nature and purposes of the Indian bourgeoisie as it shifts from demands for protectionism to demands that it be allowed to integrate itself more fully with transnational capital. The ideological complex that has come to be associated in India with the name of Nehru and refers to the formative phase of the Republic under his

stewardship was descended from the ideologies of national Independence and was located in the rationalist discourse of Justice and Rights; what is taking its place, at the highest levels of ideological construction, is an irrationalist discourse of the market as the primary regulator and arbiter of the social good, and an equally irrationalist ideology of majoritarian aggressivity as the rationale for restructuring the state. Notwithstanding the scope of the actual achievements of the Nehru period, which were meagre from the Left standpoint but far more substantial than ideologues of liberalization and postmodernity concede, 'socialistic planning' and 'secularism' were two parts of a single whole; 'secularism' was to control the voraciousness of majoritarianism as 'socialistic planning' was to control the appetites of the private-sector bourgeoisie. Now, with the renunciation of even the pretence of 'socialistic planning', what happens to its necessary accompaniment, 'secularism'? The problem here is that the market ideology may take the place of planning but it cannot resolve inter-denominational disputes. Is secularism compatible with liberalization? Are relations among denominational communities to be determined by majoritarianism, as relations in the market are determined by prior possession of property and levels of accumulation? Is there to be a marriage of majoritarianism and the market? What is the nature of the mass psychology refracted through liberalization?

That is one kind of issue: the mass psychology premised on the idea of infinite competition among unequals. But there is also the attendant problem that while everyone gets caught in the vortex of that competition – as individuals, communities, and denominations – 'liberalization' *per se* can be the ideology, properly speaking, only of the ruling class and those more privileged sections in the upper layers of the propertied and professional petty bourgeoisies who actually benefit from the market. Among the rest, especially among the lower sections of the petty bourgeoisie, it produces a fractured consciousness: a belief in the rhetoric of opportunity but also an anxiety stemming from actual experience of economic and social uncertainty; an actual experience of the fracturing of solidarities based on traditional moral economies, poised against irides-cent promises that communities of caste and denomination shall be reconstituted; loss of dignity in daily life compensated through aggressive acts of symbolic redemption, and so on. In short, the making of a mass hysteria. This desire to compensate for real fractures through symbolic unities mirrors the double movement of the market, which unifies the nation as a single system of exchange and circulation while also fragment-ing it into infinitely competing individuals, firms, communities, and regions. In short, then, the market both unites and fragments the nation in a single motion. It alone cannot hold the nation together, especially in the context of scarcity and of acute maldistribution of what is available within that scarcity, and a society, moreover, which is the world's most heterogeneous in its sociological composition. The ultimate logic of 'liberalization' and the market, if left to its own devices, presses towards disintegration.

In a developing society where the structures of capitalism are fully in place but where processes of state formation are weakly developed and premised on acute unevennesses of region, community, and class, an ideological cement of a nationalist kind is an objective necessity. It therefore follows that if the Left fails to provide that cement, and if ideological traditions descended from the anti-colonial movement begin to collapse, an aggressive kind of rightwing nationalism *will* step into that vacuum to resolve a crisis that is produced by the objective processes of state formation and capitalist development, and further aggravated by today's 'liberalization'.

In the midst of all this, and at a more integrative level, *Hindutva* emerges to offer a rightwing, fascistic redefinition of Indian nationalism, and is attempting to cut across regions, classes, and castes in order to stabilize its claim as the only available unifying force. *Hindutva* is undoubtedly the spontaneous ideology of the socially and professionally dominant upper castes, especially in these times of middle- and lower-caste assertions. Conversely, however, it can be strategically used to incorporate considerable segments of the deprived castes and tribes, with offers of cultural sanskritization and socio-economic upward mobility through political empowerment; the inroads the BJP has made among such castes and tribes in Gujarat, Madhya Pradesh, Bihar, and elsewhere should lay to rest the old thesis that it can only be an upper-caste phenomenon: one has only to look at the terror squads of the Bajrang Dal to see where the shock troops come from. Even in the case of 'minorities', the BJP has had its successes in relation to Sikhs, exploiting the Congress-supervised carnage of 1984 in Delhi and the Congress–Akali electoral contest in Punjab to its own advantage.

For the propertied classes as a whole, the BJP's redefinition of nationalism is extremely useful on at least three counts. First, since the bourgeoisie has itself given up the ideology of economic nationalism in favour of 'liberalization', it would be comfortable enough with an alternate definition of nationalism that fully subscribes to that 'liberalization' and more or less buries the vestiges of anti-colonialism and anti-imperialism. Second, since its own ideology of capitalist rationalization can hardly speak to the masses, the bourgeoisie would welcome an irrationalist movement that shifts the focus of mass attention from the material facts of their own deprivation to imaginary and symbolic issues, such as 'Hindu honour'. Third, every nationalism needs a rhetoric of the strength of the nation-state. The attraction of the BJP is that its rhetoric of the 'strong nation' is not opposed to imperialism, with which the bourgeoisie is ingratiating itself, but is focused on regional dissents, separatist movements, the weaker neighbours, and the right to nuclear capability, all of which promote a mass psychology favouring a strong, more or less militarized state. A state, in other words, that is strong in relation to its people and its immediate neighbours but weak in relation to capital, domestic and foreign: exactly what the bourgeoisie wants. Finally, the capitalist class has no difficulty with those cynical uses of religion that encourage a consumerist, commodified communal life and use religious festivity for a mass purchasing spree; this commodified religion which spreads the consumerist ethic into the lowest depths of the believing community is actually good for capitalism.

The point is not that the capitalist class as a whole has shifted over to the BJP. Much of it has but the whole of it has not, for the simple reason that Congress has been decaying but is far from being dead. It still polls many more votes than the BJP; it remains the only party with the most significant presence in most regions, whose loyalty structure cuts across more castes and denominational communities than any other; and it is the historic ruling institution with old ties to Indian capital. Furthermore, the proliferation of regionally based parties indicates the attempt of regionally based bourgeoisies, especially the agrarian bourgeoisies and the middling layers in both town and country which often intersect with middling and mercantile castes, to have parties of their own in order to negotiate compacts with the big national parties, principally the Congress and now the BJP. In short, then, one is not witnessing some regrouping of the whole of the capitalist class under the BJP banner. Our argument, rather, is that much of capital seems to have shifted to support of the BJP already, and that there is no reason to believe that there is any basic contradiction between *Hindutva* and the capitalist class as a whole, nor to believe that in the case of a definitive decline or irreparable splintering of the Congress, the most powerful segments of this class will not shift its support to *Hindutva*. Indeed, the options of the ruling class are numerous, with not one possible ruling party but two at its disposal, along with the shifting alliances of the smaller parties, among which it can pick and choose. Hence the large area of commonality between the BJP and the Congress (a strong agreement on 'liberalization' and only a degree of difference in the shade of saffron), but also fierce competition for first place in the affections of the bourgeoisie.

Rightwing Authoritarianism

The capitalist state in India is alive and well, facing no crisis, commanding options; there is no objective necessity for a gigantic upheaval in the very structure of the state, which a fully fledged fascist takeover would cause. Continued BJP rule, if such were to come to pass, would more probably take the form, in the foreseeable future, of a rightwing authoritarianism within the liberal order.

Barbarians are surely at the gate. It is also true that the RSS is a fascist organization and the BJP is, in the final analysis, its parliamentary front; a BJP government means that a section of the RSS is at present ensconced in the corridors of the highest power, with presidential consent and constitutional sanction. Even more alarming is the fact that the RSS has won two strategic victories of far-reaching consequence in a matter of four years, first in the form of the immensely violent fascist spectacle of the Ayodhya demolition, in defiance of its constitutional obligation, and now with the right to form a government being conceded to it by a President whose secular and democratic credentials are beyond question but who has nevertheless bestowed the final form of legitimacy on the BJP as a reliable guardian of the Republic.

But has fascism begun? No, it has not. The immediate evidence is that the constitutional order itself sees no threat from it; otherwise, President Sharma, himself a liberal constitutionalist, could have easily invited Deve Gowda to form a government, with 316 parliamentarians pledging support to him, 47 more than was necessary to establish a majority on the floor of the House. That too would have been perfectly constitutional. The President did not fulfil a constitutional requirement against his personal will; he exercised what he took to be his own discretion.

Moreover, there are certain specificities characterizing the current Indian situation. Not only is there no crisis of the state; even the traditional ruling institution, the Congress, is very far from having succumbed. The civilian bureaucracies, the police, the paramilitary forces have been quite obviously penetrated by communalists, and we can assume that similar processes are at work in substantial sections of the armed forces as well; a BJP government must be toppled as soon as possible, because these institutions will be further communalized if they stay. But the institutions themselves, however much they may happily adjust to authoritarian rule, do not give much sign of the kind of restlessness that gets translated into fascistic upheavals; rather, ideologies of representative government and civil freedoms seem to have penetrated much further than communal fascism as such. In society at large, the BJP's inability to expand its electoral base does not signify a rapidly growing consent; the consent for an outright RSS regime is likely to be far narrower. Large regions of the country, notably in the south and the east, are outside their reach as yet; it is not possible to establish fascist rule over half a country without precipitating irreversible separatisms in the other half. Within the areas of their greatest influence, north and west, caste insurgencies forbid an overreaching zeal.

The CPI(M) and 'Moral Authority'

The argument that fascism has come and we should therefore stake all in order to overthrow it before it entrenches itself, and that the CPI(M) has the historic duty and opportunity as well as moral authority to do so, seems to have been a fundamental element in the campaign that suddenly erupted in a section of the Left intelligentsia to press Jyoti Basu to offer himself as candidate to become Prime Minister.

Within the predicates of electoral democracy, the CPI(M) undoubtedly commands, as we have said earlier, a degree of moral authority far exceeding its actual strength. It is somewhat incredible that a party that draws *all* its MPs from only three states in the Union (one relatively large, one small, and one minuscule) should be the central and indispensable force in the making of what has now culminated in a powerful United Front far more representative of regions and social diversities than the Congress itself, which claims the mantle of anti-colonial nationalism, not to speak of the BJP, a culturally monolithic and highly regionalized minority party. The 'moral authority' is undeniable, but what are its sources?

This authority exists because of an odd reversal of roles in 'the world's second largest democracy', in which all the political parties that represent the liberal order are seen as flouting the basic democratic norms and attempting to subvert the Constitution itself, while Communists are seen by large sections of the politically interested public as *accepting* the obligations and prerogatives laid out in the Constitution, even when the exercise of some of those prerogatives works against their interests, as in a thousand forms of direct and indirect interferences that the Centre routinely exercises in relation to the CPI(M)-ruled states, not to speak of the fact that agreeing to form state governments within the republic of the venal bourgeoisie, and scrupulously observing the limits inherent in a constitutional order that vests most authority in the Centre, is itself an act of enormous restraint. And the CPI(M) is seen as *defending* constitutional norms even when its own interests are not at stake, as in the famous instance when Namboodripad forcefully intervened in the tussle between Rajiv Gandhi and Zail Singh that threatened to break those norms. Furthermore, as one judges from whatever glimpse one gets of its internal functioning, the CPI(M)'s 'democratic centralism' seems to offer relatively more inner party democracy than any of the so-called 'democratic parties', notably the Congress, the supposed pillar of Indian democracy.

With regard to the recent controversy surrounding the Jyoti Basu candidacy, rumour has it that (1) some members of the Politburo, including perhaps the party General-Secretary and Jyoti Basu himself, were in favour of the candidacy, and (2) that the issue was hotly debated and eventually decided by a relatively narrow margin in the Central Committee. We have no way of judging the veracity of the rumour. The striking thing, however, is that so many people actually find it credible that an issue of such importance actually gets *debated* and gets decided by a *vote*, in the *second highest* body of the party, which might well have overturned the recommendation of its own General-Secretary. It is *expected* of the CPI(M) that it would function in this fashion; it is judged by its own moral standards when it fails to do so. All this contrasts rather sharply with the utterly conspiratorial and corrupt faction-mongering recently witnessed in the inner workings of the BJP in Gujarat and elsewhere, or the cloak-and-dagger relationship it retains with the RSS, so that not only its role in the country at large but even its functioning in relation to itself is shrouded in secrecy, illegality, loutishness, strong-arm manipulation, and corruption and lumpenization at the highest levels.[30] Roughly the same can be said of the Congress but for two contrasts, one negative and the other positive. The negative contrast is that dissent against the 'supreme ruler' is perhaps even more uncommon in the Congress; but the positive contrast with the BJP, for which we should consider ourselves fortunate, is that there is no equivalent of the RSS behind it. The Congress is lamentably full of thuggery, but it is what it is; it is not the open face of a closed fascist organization.

That, then, is one side of the 'moral authority': the upholding of certain democratic and constitutional norms when no other party of any size or consequence does so. The other side has to do with power and the modalities of its exercise. The CPI(M) is widely seen as a party that does not take power through deals and sleights of hand; that forms governments when and so long as it enjoys the mandate to do so; that takes seriously its promise to implement a certain programme; and – crucially – that invites others to hold it accountable for what happens under its administration. In West Bengal, for example, the cumulative effects of agrarian reforms have begun to show, but we have reason to regret that literacy campaigns have not been equally successful, that schools in the countryside need a very substantial overhaul, that there are instances of corruption at the lower and sometimes even the middle levels of the cadres involved in the Left Front administration, that industrial policy is not as sharply differentiated from the Centre's as it should be – (*Can* the states go against the grain of the Centre in a basic way?) – and that Calcutta is fast becoming a White city in the midst of a Red countryside. All true, but what is also true is that even when it falls short of expectations, which it frequently does, we reserve the right to judge the CPI(M) by certain standards which we no longer apply to other electoral forces. Corruption so massive that an ordinary human mind fails to comprehend its scope are routine in other parts of the country, not to speak of the Centre, which has become a veritable cesspool under Rao; but news of even petty venalities in West Bengal still has the capacity to shock us because they are not supposed to happen. Meanwhile, Jyoti Basu undoubtedly commands immense respect, but the size and longevity of the electoral mandate that the CPI(M) has been receiving in West Bengal cannot be explained away through Weberian devices, as a politics of personal charisma.

Between the conditions in which Basu has ruled in West Bengal and the conditions in which he was being urged to make a bid to become Prime Minister, the contrast could not be sharper. It has to do with the size of the mandate and the kind of company one keeps. In West Bengal, the mandate is such that even now, when it has shrunk in the recent elections, the CPI(M) alone has a clear majority in the Assembly, even without its allies in the Left Front. In Lok Sabha, by contrast, the CPI(M) controls roughly 6 per cent of the seats. Even in West Bengal, some of the allies, notably of the Forward Block, have been an embarrassing liability; even in West Bengal, where he has a massive party at his command and where the civil administration has no choice but to cooperate, the Basu government has hardly been able to keep corruption in check. Yet, because he has a firm grip on the administration thanks to the size of the party and the mandate, West Bengal has, in the Indian Union, a unique achievement to its credit: in a state which witnessed a Partition as bitter as that in Punjab, where conditions for communal riots are more ripe than in Bihar and UP, there have been no such riots, save a brief one in the wake of Ayodhya – which was shocking *because* it happened in West Bengal and happened under the watch of the Left government. Could this performance be duplicated at the centre, where the CPI(M) has no such presence? How does one check corruption when some of the most corrupt politicians in the land hold key ministries in one's cabinet and the huge machinery of national administration is largely beyond one's control because the mandate is so small and tenuous? What would happen, then, to 'moral authority'?

But there is another point to consider, decisive in its own way. The difference between state government and national government is not just a matter of scale but also fundamentally qualitative. Communists can be allowed to form state governments because their authority is so very narrow, and the entire machinery of the bourgeois state is there to ensure that no basic limits are crossed. National government, on the other hand, is both the 'managing committee of the bourgeoisie as a whole' and the condensation of the state's claim to monopoly over instruments of violence. No Communist can be trusted with power over these apparatuses unless there are prior guarantees that he will make no significant moves, and indeed those guarantees can be believed only when the Communist has no power to make such moves; but then why accept responsibility for other people's corruptions, violences, and sundry misdemeanours if one cannot do anything significant? The idea that one can become Prime Minister at will and walk out of the office at will, untarnished and only ennobled by the experience, amounts to believing in a hallowed Robin Hood at the head of a gang of thieves.

One is reminded of a comment Antonio Gramsci made on the urge to make the highest bid so as to overcome one's own dire weaknesses in a single sweep. He writes at one point in the *Prison Notebooks*:

> When you don't have the initiative in the struggle and the struggle itself comes eventually to be identified with a series of defeats, mechanical determinism becomes a tremendous force of moral resistance, of cohesion and of patient and obstinate perseverance. 'I have been defeated for the moment, but the tide of history is working for me in the long term.' Real will takes on the garments of an act of faith in a certain rationality of history and in a primitive and empirical form of impassioned finalism.[31]

There are three key points here: (1) 'a series of defeats' leading to 'mechanical determinism', and this combination of 'defeat' and 'determinism' itself leading to a situation in which 'resistance' comes to be seen mostly in 'moral' terms; (2) 'real will' taking on 'the garments of an act of faith', or, to put it differently but still very much in Gramscian terms: an 'optimism of the will' being practised without its necessary complement, the 'pessimism of the intellect'; and (3) all this leading to an 'impassioned finalism' which, one might add, takes on the contradictory form of a gambler's mentality, in which faith in one's own eventual victory ('history is working for me') is combined with the desperation that all one's resources must be staked on the very next play, or else all shall be lost. Finalism of faith thus comes to complement the finalism of fear.

In the circumstance of a Basu candidacy there were only three possibilities, of which one or the other had to materialize. First, and the most unlikely, was that Jyoti Basu *would* be called in the very first round and that he would have to go very quickly into the situation without any substantive prior agreement about the composition of government or about the price the Congress would extract for support from the outside; then the noose would be tightened. Second, he would be in a situation where he had announced his candidacy but was not called in the first round; as the question of defeating the BJP on the floor of the House became paramount, tough discussions would begin on the same issues that had not been thrashed out earlier, except that Basu would have staked his 'prestige' – now as prisoner of the politics of charisma – and the difficulties of dominating a discussion with 32 MPs out of 269 would begin to tell. The third possibility is that the CPI(M) would acknowledge what pressure it needed to accept in order to capture the Prime Ministership and would in the process make Basu utterly dependent on the Congress (I), on Rao in particular, who would set the policy agenda that Basu would then be invited to implement if he wanted to keep the Congress as an ally and himself stay in the Prime Ministerial chair.

Conclusion

A debate on the 'no confidence' motion is to begin in two days. The BJP will undoubtedly use the occasion as a study circle for the nation; it will expound on the purported nobility of its purposes, the perceived need for a fresh mandate because the alternative is unviable, its putative status as a party destined to rule, its determination either to prove its majority on the floor now or to return to the House in the near future with a full majority, the whole nation united behind it. In the last instance, it may recommend dissolution of Parliament. It has been robbed of the grievance that as the largest party in the House it had the right to be called first and wasn't; President Sharma's indiscretion may yet prove to have an unintended benefit. Under the circumstances, Thakeray's threat of 'civil war' is mere bluster; they will always try to wade through rivers of the blood of minorities to get to power, but a carnage that involves the 'Hindu nation' itself is more than they can muster: *that* would be the surest way to destroy themselves. The moneybags of the BJP–Sena combine have been roaming the streets of Delhi, looking for MPs to whom they could deliver sacks of currency, bags of gold, petrol pumps, flats in the posh areas of the capital. With how many this monetary magic has worked, we shall soon find out. MPs of the UF have smelled power – power of their own – which will give them the chance to make far more money than a one-shot bribe can offer; they, or at least most of them, may be able to resist the BJP. Congress, pushed into a corner, is fighting for survival; it has no objection to its own shade of saffron, but if it accepts becoming the BJP's junior partner, its historic claim to be the natural ruling institution of India, and hence its birthright to first place in the affections of the bourgeoisie, is sealed. If it is to rise yet again, out of its own ashes, it needs time; and for that it has to sit on the Opposition benches:

competitive opposition to the BJP, provisionally cooperative opposition in relation to the UF. It is likely now to lick its wounds and play fast and loose with the UF.

The very swearing-in of a BJP Prime Minister was somewhat like the crossing of a Rubicon. As claimants to power they have *arrived*, and the presidential indiscretion has bestowed upon them a legitimacy that the nation can ill afford. A quick and sharp defeat on the floor of the House will undo some of the damage, but not all. For that, a much longer, determined contestation will be required. Hence my sense that even if the secular forces win this round, they will have earned only a reprieve, not the initiative. The latter remains with the RSS and cannot be wrested from them unless the UF actually becomes a cohesive and permanent force of a kind by means of which the centre of political gravity can be shifted, slowly and gradually, towards the Left. The moral authority that the CPI(M) has saved for itself by resisting the temptation of highest office will be crucial in making that effort for a cumulative and fundamental shift, but the odds at present are, sad to say, against it.

If a United Front government does come to power, it will have four main virtues. For the first time since at least 1980, we shall have a government that poses no threat to any minority and is secular in ways that Congress no longer even dreams of being. Second, a UF government will be far more representative of the regional pluralism, the mosaic of linguistic nationalities and regional and social identities, which India comprises. Third, it will undoubtedly exploit the caste issue but less than the Congress or the BJP, and powerful forces of non- and even anti-brahminical caste configurations will be inside the government, which will then substantially depart from the brahmin–*banya* nexus. Fourth, east and south shall predominate over north and west (the centres of BJP–Sena power), and the forces representing the south shall be substantially different, and better, than the ones that have congregated around the Congress in the past.

Conversely, on the crucial issue of 'liberalisation', business will go on as usual, and the process will indeed deepen. The Left has no leverage in this regard because the entire dominant order is ferociously committed to this transformation; there is no mass movement opposing it; and within the Left Front itself, there are elements that are hard on *Hindutva* but soft on liberalization. Because of all that, the bourgeoisie will have no objection to a UF government and there shall be no class offensive of the bourgeoisie against it; the UF need give no guarantees because it *is* the guarantee. Nor will there be any reduction in corruptions and scams. These are not aberrations of the Indian liberal order; they *are* the order, and nothing, not Basu's most fervent prayers, could have changed that until the structure itself changes, which is far beyond the present capacities of the Left.

The Left, more specifically the CPI(M), has made its choice – a choice, as Achin Vanaik put it in *The Telegraph*, both principled and pragmatic. From the duty of facing up to one's own past defeats and their consequences, from reviewing the causes of those defeats, from fresh thinking on how to break out of one's regional sequestration, from the need to build a mass movement, there is no easy escape – certainly not one that takes you straight into the Prime Minister's chair. What we have here is a reprieve and it should be used, above all, to put one's own house in order, before the Congress, or someone within the UF itself, trips the wire. Because that tripping of the wire too is written into the design of things at hand.

The BJP in Government

I India Goes Nuclear

Thieves in the Night

The Pokhran explosions have brought independent India to a watershed comparable, in its long-term political significance, to the Sino-Indian War, the Emergency, and the destruction of the Babri Masjid. The national equation as well as India's international relations have been altered for the foreseeable future.

From the opening of the propaganda offensive by Defence Minister Fernandes in early April 1998 to Prime Minister Vajpayee's letter to Clinton after the explosions, the BJP government has maintained its focus on China as the strategic adversary that threatens India's security directly and as the main culprit behind Pakistan's nuclear capability, not to speak of the threat it is said to pose through Myanmar. This focus on China is deliberate, as the beginning of a methodical Red-baiting offensive within the country, as the inauguration of an arms race on the Asian continent, and as an appeal to long-term US goals in Asia. What we may be witnessing is the staging of a short-term Indo-US tension as a prelude to a long-term, comprehensive strategic alliance.

It is possible that there was an 'intelligence failure' on the part of the CIA and that the US government was caught unawares, as is being claimed in some US circles. That is possible but not probable, given the American capabilities of global surveillance. Nor would it be the first time in recent history that the United States would claim an 'intelligence failure' when it was necessary to pretend lack of advance information with regard to practices that it condones but is formally committed to opposing. The US government is also bound by its own laws to impose sanctions against countries that undertake such tests. A degree of tension in the short run is inevitable. But the sanctions are likely to be imposed indifferently and will be gradually relaxed in the not too distant future. Multilateral agencies such as the World Bank, and some countries such as Japan, are likely to follow the US lead in imposing while actually circumventing these sanctions.

Meanwhile, the immediate reaction from various Western capitals shows that while the tests are being condemned all around, there is no consensus behind the sanctions, and that the BJP government will be able to ride them out easily. The fact that key countries such as Russia, France, and Britain – three members out of five in the official nuclear club – have not imposed sanctions is as significant as the fact that the United States has done so. This fact will also be cited within the United States as an excuse for relaxing the sanctions, in view of non-cooperation from 'allies' and because American sanctions in the context of this non-cooperation will be portrayed as favourable to European capitals and detrimental to American business interests. This argument can only gain further strength from the breakneck liberalization and privatization that the BJP government is now bound to undertake.

Aside from a possible short-term irritation, the long-term prospect is for a closer anti-China axis between the United States and India. This possibility gains greater credence in the overall context in which these tests have been undertaken. We are witnessing immense intensification of an international campaign on the issue of Tibet. Key members of the Clinton Administration, including senior officials from the Pentagon, visited India immediately after the BJP takeover, explicitly endorsing the regime. This occasion was used to announce, with deliberately high visibility, the impending Indo-US joint exercises in high-altitude combat.

The crash of economies in East and Southeast Asia, from which the advanced capitalist countries have benefited enormously, is a key aspect of changing international and regional environments. In this economic warfare China is the next target, and the United States must greatly welcome military pressure on China. Americans know from long experience that many distortions in and the eventual collapse of the Soviet economy ensued, at least substantially, from the unbearable pressure which that economy had to endure as the Soviet Union sought to retain some degree of military parity with NATO. Today, the United States would like nothing so much as a similar diversion of Chinese resources towards military expenditures in an Asian arms race. Behind the BJP's bogus anti-imperialism and the American sanctions lies this prospect of a far-reaching alliance in a new Cold War.

The deliberate demonstration of multiple technologies through five different tests – especially the thermo-nuclear explosion and the last two tests with the objective of collecting data for further computer simulations – leaves no doubt that this is a step towards actual weaponization, in keeping with the BJP's repeated promises to make the 'bomb'. Although these tests do not yet make India a nuclear power in the definitional sense, the BJP has nevertheless signalled that India will now become a nuclear power in the same sense in which Israel is. In this context, the distinction between testing and weaponization becomes more or less a scholastic eyewash.

The terms of the discussion about the Comprehensive Test Ban Treaty (CTBT) have been changed drastically. Refusing to sign the CTBT on grounds of its discriminatory character when India was not a nuclear power could be reasonably construed as an act of resistance to unreasonable foreign pressure. By contrast, conducting actual tests, becoming a *de facto* nuclear power, and then offering to consider accepting some portions of that treaty will now be presented by the BJP-controlled media as an act of responsible statesmanship in the international arena. The BJP will try to take credit not on one count but on three: for not signing it, for signing it, and for signing it only partially to the extent that Indian national interests are supposedly safeguarded.

This is a sophisticated approach with great propaganda value, and an alternative needs to be developed that is somewhat different from the alternatives being posed, even after these tests, by advocates and opponents of the CTBT. A call to sign it *now* converges alarmingly with what Clinton is demanding and the BJP itself is proposing. A call not to sign it amounts to pious nostalgia for the way the world was before these tests. The BJP can in fact live with either of these options. By not signing it, it keeps open the option for further tests and open weaponization. By signing it, all of it or in part, the BJP manages to diffuse international condemnation, appeases the CTBT activists, carries on perfecting technology for weaponization in laboratories, and paves the way for the Indo-US axis sooner rather than later.

In practice, the BJP will act precisely as it acted on the Ayodhya issue and as it has been acting on the nuclear issue until now. The BJP said openly that it was going to do in Ayodhya what others would shudder even to think. Then, it did what it said it would do, in contravention of all legality, human decency, and its own bogus promises. With that design accomplished, it restrained its allies from immediately going on to similar vandalism in Kashi and Mathura, so as to project for itself an image of relative moderation while keeping that issue alive but simmering only very slowly, for another time, even as the situation on the ground in both those places has been changing radically from one day to the next. The issue of the Ram Mandir itself was largely taken out of public debate while the most meticulous preparations have been made, right under the noses of all the official guardians of Indian secularism, for the building of the Mandir at an opportune time, exactly in the place where the Masjid once stood.

The BJP has acted in the same fashion on the nuclear issue. It, and the Jan Sangh before it, had repeatedly promised weaponization. Upon taking power, it assigned the highest priority to carrying out these tests, without informing either friend or foe, with exactly the kind of covert preparation and lightning strike that it had practised at Ayodhya. Having demonstrated its hawkishness, it will now offer to sign the CTBT but only partially, knowing that the alternative pressures, to sign all of it or sign none of it, will only grow in the coming weeks and months, and that it must allow time for the sense of horror to get routinized and for the passions to subside. Then it will strike again, with yet another surprise, just as it will one day undoubtedly launch the building of the Mandir in the most dramatic way possible.

The CTBT is going to remain an issue in public debate. So, a position has to be taken and the only possible position is that decisions of such far-reaching importance ought not to be used, cynically, as bargaining counters and that the situation therefore must be frozen until the nation has sorted out the very basic parameters of its governance. The point needs to be made that India *has* to have the capability but also *has* to refrain from tests and deployments. The traditional Indian position, which says that India will sign the treaty as soon as the weaponized states have given us a time-bound schedule for the destruction of their own existing weapons, is basically correct. The more crucial point, however, is that, having acted like thieves in a night of long knives, *this* government has lost the moral right to rule and must resign so that a more responsible government can take over.

That a party which commands merely a quarter of the national vote could take an action of this magnitude so secretly and unilaterally, without a national debate, without consultation with senior leaders of the Opposition, without a strategic review it had promised, without informing its own allies in government, raises questions not only about the competence of the BJP to rule but also about the kind of powers that are concentrated in the Prime Minister's Office (PMO). What this event demonstrates most dramatically is not that we need a presidential form of government but that far-reaching reforms are needed to prevent the PMO from acting in so presidential a manner. Moreover, when the PMO itself has been taken over by the semi-secret organization of the RSS, which then brings its own mode of functioning to this high office, the question arises whether or not the PMO alone should continue to have sole authority over decision-making on the nuclear issue. Should there not be an autonomous agency for this critical area of decision-making that is equally answerable to the executive, the legislature, and the judiciary? There needs to be a debate, in Parliament and outside Parliament, as to the kind of mechanisms we require which guarantee operational secrecy but decision-making transparency on such a fundamental issue of the nation's security policy.

Nor can the argument be made that such precipitate action was necessary in view of some immediate foreign provocation. China had taken no steps in recent years and even decades that posed any threat to Indian security. Pakistan had not carried out any nuclear tests, and its 'conventional' intervention in Indian domestic affairs, as in Kashmir and Punjab, should be dealt with through 'conventional' and political means. Meanwhile, India already has enough technology, as the BJP government itself said, to match Pakistan's recent missile test, so that 'Pokhran' simply cannot be presented as a response to 'Ghauri'.

Nor have these tests any element of anti-imperialist nationalism. The BJP has not said that these were designed against the US nuclear threat in the Pacific–Indian Ocean zones. It has targeted neighbours instead. Far from securing us against imperialist threats, this action will lead to an unnecessary, expensive, dangerous, and unethical arms race in Asia, will sabotage the South Asian Association for Regional Cooperation (SAARC) within South Asia, and will negate the process of normalization with China. In so doing, the tests play into the hands of imperialists who are keen to keep Asia divided and have all of us squander our resources on weapons of destruction instead of devoting them to regional cooperation that can free us from imperialist pressure. In *this* sense, of making the people of Asia fight each other, the BJP is acting today in the imperialists' interest just as the RSS, through its communalism, used to undermine the national struggle against British colonialism. This collusion with imperialism, combined with fratricides aimed at fellow Indians and fellow Asians, is the historic vocation of the Sangh *parivar*.

The crucial reason why the BJP government needs to be confronted has to do, however, not so much with external relations as with what these explosions have wrought inside the country. The *combination* of (1) the show of Indian might and independence in decision-making, (2) the inviting and defying of US sanctions, and (3) the ability to act decisively despite coalition constraints, has enabled the BJP to claim that it will safeguard the interest of a 'strong' and independent India against foreign pressure, in the tradition of the National Movement. This is a crucial moment in our history because the issue of anti-imperialism has hounded the RSS throughout its existence. Everyone knows – and therefore the BJP and the United States also know – that defiance of imperialism is a basic ingredient in Indian nationalism. For the BJP to graduate from 'Hindu' nationalism to 'Indian' nationalism, and thus to become a nationally hegemonic power, it too must undergo this baptism of fire. The real fire it will not endure, but such fires can be simulated by organizing mass frenzy in the streets, and on the electronic media. For this to happen, *spectacles* must be staged, just as the destruction of the Babri Masjid was orchestrated essentially as a fascist spectacle.

If that spectacle paved the way for the BJP to emerge as an all-India party and eventually the ruling party, these nuclear fireworks help it cut across the Hindu/secular divide and reach out to claim the mantle of Indian nationalism as such. This *will* unite very broad sections of the Indian middle classes – and not only the middle classes – whatever the immediate behaviour of the stock market might be. The impression will gain ground that the BJP is the only party capable of providing India with a coherent, assertive, visionary leadership. This effect is not going to wear off in days, or weeks, or months. Only a sustained counter-offensive can prevent it from being still there twenty years from now.

The BJP had so far established its leading role in defining Indian *culture* and Hindu *religion*. Now, with nuclear demagoguery, it has made its first massive attempt to capture the high ground of defiance against Western and Chinese nuclear monopoly. In both cases, the appeal is made to atavistic feelings of aggression, in the form of a promise to redeem *honour*. Meanwhile, if the Ayodhya movement redefined the role of Ram in Indian belief systems as an all-India deity and supreme warrior-prince, the Pokhran explosions were deliberately scheduled on Budh Purnima; if Ambedkarites have their anti-caste Buddha, *Hindutva* will have its own Buddha that will bless nuclear weapons for the greater glory of *bharat mata*. These fantastic rewritings of the Indian past must not be dismissed simply as ludicrous, which of course they are. It is precisely the evocative power of this irrationality which is most frightening and dangerous. Such are the raw materials from which fascist victories are moulded.

So powerful in fact is the lure of this mob psychology that the Congress as well as much of what remains of the United Front (UF) have already fallen into line. A story is going the rounds that what Vajpayee accomplished was only what Narasimha Rao had attempted. In his TV appearance, Jaipal Reddy tried hard to make out that the BJP is only taking credit for an event that had been prepared by the United Front government. Deve Gowda, the first UF Prime Minister, has pronounced that the explosions were 'necessary' for Indian security. Gujral, the second UF Prime Minister, has called on us all to speak in 'one voice' with Vajpayee. Arjun Singh, the chief custodian of Congress secularism, has declared that the tests were not at all designed to enhance the political prestige of the BJP. Many more statements of this kind can be expected as time goes by.

In a quick poll in the wake of the tests, *The Hindu* found support for them among 91 per cent of the respondents. The cynics of the Congress and the UF are responding to this jingoistic consensus that the BJP has crafted. In the process, we are witnessing a sea-change in public dis-course. The BJP has in reality departed from the national consensus on nuclear policy as it was first formulated in Nehru's days and was then adjusted in the early 1970s. But the indecent haste of the Congress and

UF stalwarts to take credit for what the BJP has wrought is creating the impression that the Vajpayee government has only implemented what has been Indian policy all along.

These are the most dangerous of times. The whole process of coalition-making that brought the BJP to power has shown that not only is Congress secularism merely pragmatic, but so has been the secularism of a majority of the non-Left political formations in the country. Most of them can easily move into an equally pragmatic communalism, as Trinamool Congress, breakaway faction of the Bengal Congress, is now showing after joining the BJP. Even in that arena the Left is in reality rather isolated, but secularism itself has been such a fundamental value in India that most of these pragmatic communalists dare not confess to their ideological shifts even as they join up with the BJP, as we are witnessing in the case of Chandrababu Naidu. Thanks to this ambiguity, the Left had enjoyed a relatively wider area of manoeuvre in anti-communal politics.

In the wake of these hawkish tests, however, the extent of collaboration among virtually all the bourgeois parties is far greater and much more openly professed. The Left therefore has much less room for manoeuvre now, it is much more squarely in danger of being called 'anti-national' and being made, in the foreseeable future, an object of full-scale repression on the charge that it has 'extra-territorial loyalty'. The spectre of the repressions that took place in the wake of the Sino-Indian war of 1962 now haunts the land, barely two months into the BJP government. And yet, the Left will lose its very *raison d'être* if it does not differentiate itself from the kind of national chauvinism that is represented by the BJP's designs in the nuclear arena, and if it does not define for itself and for the nation a nationalism different – more comprehensive, more fundamentally anti-imperialist – from the kind that the BJP will predictably unleash on the question of US sanctions. The Left has to move with the greatest of caution but move it must.

On the nuclear issue itself, three things need to be done. First, all the secular, anti-communal, and anti-fascist forces should come together on the principle that in acting in a unilateral, irresponsible, and chauvinist manner which threatens regional peace the Vajpayee government has lost the right to rule and must therefore resign.

Second, on the question of sanctions, all patriotic forces have to take the position that no foreigner has the right to threaten us with economic strangulation. But this point has to be made alongside the equally fundamental points that (a) the BJP's irresponsible behaviour has brought upon us not only American sanctions but also ridicule from peace-loving peoples worldwide, and (b) the American sanctions are themselves a bargaining position and a prelude to the formation of a long-term Indo-US axis in Asia.

Thirdly, public discussions and hearings should be organized, in as many places as possible, involving eminent scientists, the more sane military experts, some sensible politicians, social scientists, philosophers, jurists, economists, political activists of various kinds, to consider various issues of nuclear power *in the drastically altered situation that now exists.* The arbitrary nature of the PMO's powers should be part of this discussion. Similarly, we need a nationwide discussion and perhaps even an independent Commission to investigate issues of nuclear safety and the environmental and ecological costs involved in following this nuclear road. After all, the villagers who live in the Pokhran region are no less Indian citizens than the Advanis and the Vajpayees. In the process, the Reds may learn to be a little more Green, and the Greens a bit more Red. Initiatives of this kind can help break the initial isolation that is in the short run inevitable in opposing the BJP's jingoism.

But isolation on the nuclear issue can be broken most effectively only if this issue, for all its gravity, is not addressed in isolation. The connection must be made with the communal agenda, with the fact that a step of this magnitude has been taken purely for the greater glory of the RSS, and that the consensus behind Vajpayee's nuclear policy amounts to a consensus behind *Hindutva*. Equally strongly, the point needs to be made that this act of bogus nationalism is designed to facilitate the ability of the *Hindutva* forces to implement a programme of liberalization and privatization far more drastic than anything Chidambram, Finance Minister in the UF government, was able to implement or even envisage. If the consensus built on nuclear sabrerattling is not broken, public properties will be sold to private capital more or less in the style of Russia, because after a Swadeshi nuclear bomb there need be no other Swadeshi.

Competing Cruelties: Pokhran to Chaghai

The predictable has happened. If the Pokhran explosions signalled a watershed in the history of modern India comparable to the Sino-Indian War and the Declaration of Emergency, the subsequent developments, including most dramatically the Chaghai explosions in Pakistan, have brought our subcontinent, this beloved land of fraternal hatreds and common scars, to the worst crisis we have known since 1971.

In claiming that the Chaghai explosions have only proved that India was always right in claiming that Pakistan is secretly building nuclear weapons, Prime Minister Vajpayee is being at best disingenuous. Everyone has known for a long time that both India and Pakistan had developed nuclear capability. Having exploded a nuclear device in 1974, before Pakistan even assembled its own nuclear programme, India had established an early lead. We also have a much bigger, far more sophisticated science and technology establishment, so that superiority in the nuclear arena, if that is what the policy-makers wanted, was easy to maintain. The assumption, inside the country and abroad, was that such a capacity and manifest superiority could be responsibly managed here, thanks to the sturdy traditions of democratic governance in India, which presume that a national consensus must be built before embarking on drastic shifts on such crucial areas of national policy as the matter of nuclearization obviously is. The Pokhran explosions, coming so soon after the minority government led by the BJP came into power, showed that this faith in the basic values of democratic governance could no longer be taken for granted in today's India.

Pakistan, by contrast, assembled its nuclear programme much later, with a very rudimentary science and technology establishment, a few capable scientists notwithstanding. It proceeded with stealth and subterfuge, making all kinds of shady deals across the world in order to obtain technologies and materials it could not quickly produce on its own. Pakistan also had no consistent tradition of democratic governance and the kind of restraints that such governance requires. The national security apparatuses, including notably the intelligence services, have had far greater power and freedom in making such policies even in the periods when Pakistan was not governed directly by the military. For all these reasons, Pakistan was feared to be far more capable of unilateral action in the nuclear arena and of comparatively more deceitful conduct in international affairs. As democratic traditions now begin to crumble in the face of fascist onslaughts within our own country, India is today, for the first time since the end of British colonialism, even less trustworthy than neighbouring Pakistan, as a democratic polity and as a responsible member of the comity of nations worldwide. This is a grave reversal of roles.

The unilateral action in Pokhran, combined with the kind of jingoistic flourishes which emanated from the government thereafter, proved that assumptions about a stable structure of cautious, progressive, and accountable governance in India were wrong. Those explosions were carried out by a minority government which is said to have wilfully misled foreign diplomats and in any case took no one into its confidence within the nation except for a very small group of people around the Prime Minister. In Pakistan, by contrast, Nawaz Sharif commands more than a two-thirds majority in Parliament, and having been given the gift of bellicosity from the BJP government, he ordered the retaliatory explosions at Chaghai with the full knowledge of everyone inside his country and outside.

It was obvious, in short, that if either side took a unilateral decision to undertake weapons-orientated explosions, the other side would respond. By acting first, India gave Pakistan the opportunity to portray itself as the injured party. Indeed, in a single stroke, the BJP government has succeeded in helping Pakistan come far closer to reaching two of its strategic objectives which it had not been able to achieve through its own efforts over two decades or more. Pakistan has been given the opportunity to present its own nuclear explosion as merely a defensive response to India's unilateral decision. India, it can now credibly claim, seeks 'superiority' and 'hegemony' whereas Pakistan seeks only 'balance' and 'parity'.

Moreover, Pakistani governments have always sought, and sought all the more vigorously over the past decade, to 'internationalize' the Kashmir issue, whereas Indian governments have always argued that this is strictly an internal matter which, purely for the sake of regional peace, we may be willing to discuss with Pakistan but only bilaterally and within a strictly defined agenda. The BJP government's claim after Pokhran that India's new-found nuclear capacity has altered the balance of forces in Kashmir, combined then with Pakistan's swift response, has created an opinion abroad, voiced most clearly by Madeleine Albright's State Department, that the 'Big Powers' should directly undertake to solve the Kashmir problem as the new threat to world peace.

If the public pronouncements of the Defence Minister and the Prime Minister's letter of explanation to Clinton ruined the process of normalization with China that successive Indian governments and diplomats had secured over a decade or more, the post-Pokhran belligerency of other Cabinet ministers, notably that of Mr Advani and Mr Khurana, has helped Pakistan in the pursuit of its main strategic aims. These strategic aims have both short-term and long-term aspects, and even as we launch upon a new arms race in the subcontinent, with fresh and perhaps uncontrollable escalations in Kashmir, it is best to take stock of where we have arrived and the roads that were taken to arrive here.

The long-term dynamic of Pakistan's strategic thinking is traceable to its defeat at India's hands in Bangladesh and the kind of settlement that ensued from that defeat. Neither its settled policies in Punjab and Kashmir, nor its role in Afghanistan, nor its nuclear programme can be fully grasped outside that context. Meanwhile, neither India's ability to roll back Pakistani infiltration in Punjab, nor the relative success in containing the insurgency in Kashmir, nor the lead in nuclear technology should make us complacent about the real dangers of escalation at this juncture.

For example, Pakistan has at its command thousands of the world's most seasoned guerrillas many of whom have gained combat experience in Afghanistan and have successfully fought against the Soviet armies. The BJP leaders are simply wrong in claiming that the Pokhran explosions have shifted the balance of power in Kashmir. Possession of nuclear arms make no difference to hit-and-run combat and mobile warfare through small units, as the Americans in Vietnam and the Soviets in Afghanistan found out.

On the other hand, when Nawaz Sharif warns our Home Minister against any 'misadventure' in Kashmir, he means that he is simply waiting for the actual personnel of the Indian armed forces to cross into Pakistan-occupied Kashmir (POK) so that he may openly send those guerrillas into the Indian side of Kashmir, just as Pakistan waited for the sudden Indian explosions before carrying out its own explosions openly and with prior warning to the world. *That* is what will bring Madeleine Albright flying into Delhi and then taking the Kashmir issue back with her to Washington, New York, Geneva, or wherever.

If India does not wish to 'internationalize' the Kashmir issue, it has to be very cautious on the ground. And, in that, there is no alternative to the patient work of containing infiltration from Pakistan within the bounds of low-intensity warfare and gaining the time to implement a policy in which all the people of Jammu and Kashmir, Hindus as well as Muslims, can see justice.

Settling the Hindu refugees back into their original homes and giving them the wherewithal to rebuild their lives in dignity and safety must be very much a part of that patient work. But so must be not merely safeguarding but actually fortifying Article 370, which guarantees the special status of Jammu and Kashmir, so as to reassure the Muslim segment of the Kashmiri population that the rest of India looks at them as a precious part of this polity. Similarly, the youth of Kashmir have to be given secure and enriching livelihoods. In the best of times, we have treated Kashmir simply as a tourist playground, destroying much of its natural resources, turning the Dal Lake into a silted cesspool, and tying up the livelihood of Kashmiris largely to this demeaning trade. We have to clean up and rebuild a whole economy. Short of that, Kashmir shall remain unwinnable, nuclear toys notwithstanding.

In the larger process, we have to understand what the Pakistani state takes to be its own compulsions, regardless of how we view them on this side of the border. At the end of the Bangladesh war the Pakistani establishment was traumatized but there was also a liberal, progressive opinion that saw the justice of the Bangladeshi struggle. Pakistan had been cut to half its size, while India was not only the much larger power but had also emerged victorious. India should have been magnanimous in victory, as the more sagacious advisors of Mrs Gandhi tried to argue. *That* was the time to settle the Kashmir issue in a way that satisfied the Kashmiris, safeguarded all the Indian interests, but also gave some sense of dignity to the Pakistani side, as Bhutto kept asking. We did not have the requisite foresight and grace, and those who are graceless in victory often live to eat the bitter fruit of that victory.

For better or worse, and I believe very much for the worse, it was then, after the defeat by the Indian forces in Bangladesh, that Pakistan decided its own territorial safety required a forward defence, which then meant that it should define its defence parameters inside the territory of its neighbours. The infiltration in Punjab and Kashmir came out of that calculation, as did the initial involvement in Afghanistan when a government took power there that was expected to push the Pukhtoonistan issue. Then came the first Pokhran explosion in 1974, and Pakistan immediately launched on a reckless drive to obtain matching technologies, through fair means or foul – mostly foul.

These are ugly facts, but we need to take stock of all that if a disaster is now to be averted. Successive Pakistani governments have wanted to carry out an explosion of their own but had never been able to find for such an act of international belligerency an excuse that the world beyond South Asia could find persuasive. The BJP government has provided Pakistan with such an excuse, in two instalments.

First came the Pokhran explosions. Even Mr Gujral, who owes his current seat in the Lok Sabha to allies of the BJP, has said in Parliament, though rather belatedly, that at the time when he handed over the nation's premiership to Mr Vajpayee roughly two months ago, the government of India had perceived neither a nuclear threat to the country nor any other strategic reason for carrying out nuclear tests. There is no evidence that any new threat materialized during the next few weeks.

Any unilateral decision on the part of India to go nuclear was already a gift to the Pakistani hawks who have always wanted to carry out their own explosions. But the manner in which a minority government dramatically changed what the nation and the world had understood to be India's long-standing nuclear policy, combined especially with the unbridled rhetoric that ensued after Pokhran, created the impression, very widely shared across the world by now, that India was ruled, for the first time since Independence, by a government that was not only overtly aggressive in its designs but also impulsive and unreliable in its international conduct. What were the main strains of that rhetoric?

There was, first of all, the scientistic inflation. Not just the government but the whole breadth of the media as well as the loyal Opposition, were euphoric about the 'state-of-the-art' technology that the Indian scientists had achieved in their pursuit of weapons of mass destruction. Nothing Pakistan could now do would be good enough, because we were the new Yankees.

Second, the Prime Minister's letter to Clinton focused on China and retrospectively legitimized the provocations that the Defence Minister had been hurling. This was curious. The Prime Minister did not feel constrained to address the international community, or the progressive and peace-loving peoples of the world, or nations of the Third World that had looked upon India as a force for peace in the world, as a leader in the movement for destruction of nuclear weapons, as the home of Gandhi's moral authority, as the nation-state whose formative years had been linked, in Nehru's era, to the making of a non-aligned world and the promulgation of the Five Principles of Peaceful Co-Existence. No, none was worthy of an explanation, except the President of a country that has, even according to *India Today*,[1] 1,400 nuclear weapons aimed at China, as against the fourteen Chinese weapons all of which are deployed for defence against the United States.

Then came the Prime Minister's statement to the press that India had now become a 'Nuclear Weapons State'. The unmistakable implication was that the Pokhran explosions were no mere 'tests' in pursuit of a future weaponization capability but a 'state-of-the-art' demonstration that India already had such weapons. How many? When did these weapons come into being? Who authorized them? What are the delivery systems? Where the command and control systems? Who will push the button, after what process of deliberation, and with what system of checks? We do not know, because this minority-led government, within two months of the installation of the RSS in the highest offices of the Indian state, does not any longer consider itself answerable to the very people whom it purports to represent. We have, in other words, for the first time in the history of modern India, and in utter disregard of the founding covenants of our nation, a kind of governance that presumes to speak on behalf of the Indian people without either representing us or being accountable to us.

Then came a volley of statements from the Home Minister, the Cabinet Affairs Minster, the highest officials of the ruling party, to the effect that the changed nuclear situation had shifted the balance in Kashmir decisively; that we were now ready for 'hot pursuit' of the infiltrators coming from Pakistan; that India will now pursue a policy to 'vacate' Pakistani aggression in the part of Kashmir it holds. When the Prime Minister tried to distance himself from Mr Khurana's more extreme provocations, L.K. Sharma, a Vice-President of the ruling BJP, reiterated Khurana's position in a lengthy statement, and the Department of Jammu and Kashmir Affairs was shifted from the Prime Minister himself to the Home Minister whose own statement had got going the whole rhetoric on Kashmir.

These rhetorical inflations have had sizeable consequences. Inside Pakistan, Nawaz Sharif was already in a position of extraordinary strength. The Pokhran explosions handed to him a national consensus in Pakistan for immediate nuclear response, the threats from the BJP that the Indian armed forces may cross the Line of Control in Kashmir to get Pakistan to 'vacate' POK has given him the opportunity to declare a state of emergency and thereby throttle what little opposition progressive Pakistanis might have been able to mount there.

Meanwhile, China was irritated by the flourishes of Defence Minister Fernandes, was stunned by the explosions, and was then irrevocably dismayed by Vajpayee's letter to Clinton. For the first time in decades, the Chinese government has used the sharpest language and the Chinese media have dredged up all the claims of 1962. An Asian cold war is already on.

It is very much a welcome sign that the Opposition has finally woken up to the fact that nuclearization and the consequent jingoism can only bring disasters for the country. It is most unfortunate that the BJP's allies in government have not even begun that process. But the need of the hour is for all the patriotic forces together to demand the resignation of this government before it launches some other spectacle for whipping up hysteria in its own favour. Chances are that as the policy of nuclearization begins to backfire, the *parivar* may well decide to try to win popularity by suddenly starting to build the Mandir. On this count too, the greatest vigilance is necessary. Fascist spectacles, of one kind or another, are the very lifeblood of this government. Defeating such spectacles has to be part of the patient work that is required for defeating this government as such.

II The 'Nuclear Flashpoint'

The Many Roads to Kargil

I

The wounds of Kargil are, in some ways, as old and untended as the wounds of the Partition itself. As numerous military experts have reminded us, a battle over the Kargil sector has been a prominent feature of the wars of 1948, 1965, and 1971. Even more recently, limited but constant artillery duels across the Line of Control (LoC) have been a routine feature of life in this sector for many years. In the present crisis, the combination of a mass of irregulars and a smaller number of Pakistan army regulars capturing the heights in a surprise incursion reminds us of a similar move in 1948. India at that time took not forty-eight hours, as Defence Minister Fernandes began by promising us this time, but a year and a half to evict the aggressors. At the time of writing, it is not clear whether India will settle for a longer time frame as a matter of prudence or will risk a wider war by going across the LoC in pursuit of quick results and lower casualties.

At no point in this long and miserable history has either the mainly Shia population of Kargil or the predominantly Sunni population of Drass participated in any appreciable degree of insurgency (as India would call it) or struggle for self-determination and/or independence (as the Pakistan government and the so-called 'mujahideen' would call it). This fact is of crucial importance. For, what this prolonged confrontation between India and Pakistan over Drass, Kargil, and Siachen, in the absence of any popular insurgency, demonstrates is that the unfinished business of the Partition in Jammu and Kashmir (J&K) has not one aspect but two, both of which are a result of the indecent and cruel haste with which the British offered the Partition of India and leaders of the Hindu and Muslim elites accepted it, with little regard for consequences.

In the case of J&K, there is of course the issue of the actual wishes of the people – all the people, Hindu, Muslim, Buddhist, and the rest – which both governments, and their respective allies, have interpreted according to their own objectives. But enveloping this is the larger and bloodier issue of a conventional kind of territorial dispute between the two nation-states that emerged out of an ill-conceived and indifferently implemented Partition. If the sheer scale of insurgency and political unrest in the Valley serves to obscure the fact of the underlying territorial dispute, it is in Kargil and Siachen that the territorial nature of the real dispute comes into full view, since battles here are always fought over the heads of the actual population. The Kashmir problem, as we may call it, has proved to be so very difficult to resolve *politically*, in accordance with the actual wishes and interests of the population, precisely because the territorial dispute between the two nation-states is based on irreconcilable geo-political objectives, is largely unconcerned with those wishes and interests, and therefore precludes the political solution on the ground.

If Pakistan were really interested in issues of self-determination and 'freedom' for the Kashmiris, it could begin by granting these rights to the Kashmiris who live under its control, mostly in what it calls 'Azad Kashmir' (Free Kashmir) and what we call Pakistan-occupied Kashmir (POK). The evidence is that the government of 'Azad Kashmir' in Muzaffarabad is demonstrably less free than the state administration in Srinagar and has always been treated as a puppet. Any movement for regional autonomy there is crushed with impunity and the groups that emerge with that aspiration are sidelined and overshadowed by the ones that are the creation of the Pakistani intelligence services. Over the past ten years of insurgency in J&K itself, which Pakistan too calls Occupied

('Maqbooza') Kashmir, it has again done everything to undermine the autonomous groups and to control the insurgency through groups it sponsors. Indeed, it is arguable that a key reason why the insurgency has been declining more recently is that the population finds itself caught between two national security apparatuses, those of India and Pakistan, and while it may be outraged by the sheer savagery of the counter-terror that India practises, much of it has grown similarly afraid of the Islamicist terror squads coming from across the LoC.

On our part, we have never faced up to a simple question: how is it that over half a century, as one generation gives way to the next, 'infiltrators' have come only from the other side of the LoC, to find more or less fertile ground here, but none has gone from here to the other side to sow the seeds of rebellion there as well? Is it that India does not have the intelligence services to match the Pakistani ones? Or is there something more fundamentally wrong with relations between the Indian government and the Kashmiri people? A promise not kept, a resentment never assuaged?

This is not the place to rehash that complicated history, but a certain gap between the promise and the performance can be indicated. For, *in principle*, Kashmir was to be our showcase of autonomous governance, endowed with a very special status by virtue of Article 370, a model of economic and social development that would demonstrate to the hostile, the sullen, the indifferent elements in the Kashmiri population that the rest of India regarded them as precious partners in the making of a free, democratic, pluralist, prosperous nation. *In practice*, J&K has oscillated between military occupation and cynical manipulations of parliamentary governance, by the central governments as well as the local satraps.

Much of the development funds that were meant to modernize and extend the economy were pocketed by notoriously corrupt administrations and by the political middlemen who helped New Delhi in keeping its grip on a population whose democratic aspirations were exceptionally high, thanks precisely to the promise that was once made but never kept. Whenever the military situation was under control, India's consuming classes converged on Kashmir as if it were a mere playground for the rich who had the birthright to devour its natural resources and turn its crystalline lakes into cesspools of weeds and pollution.

When this decade-old insurgency first began in 1989–90, extensive investigative reporting showed that its main social base was among the educated, unemployed youth who found themselves unrepresented in the political process and felt oppressed by the scale of military presence in the daily life of the state. A number of those who took up the gun then were young men whose political aspirations had been thwarted by corrupt practices during the elections which brought Farooq Abdullah to power in the first place. Meanwhile, those who ruled in Srinagar and those who ruled in Delhi were seen as partners in a game of collaborative competition, guarded as much by Article 370 on one flank, as the much too visible armed forces on the other. This is classically the stuff that separatist nationalisms are made of; Pakistan too has known this brew, in Baluchistan for instance.

Some of this cynicism can be illustrated by the current conduct of the two allies in the caretaker government, the BJP and Farooq Abdullah. At a time when the dissidents in J&K have to be assured that Article 370 is a lasting constitutional guarantee and will be implemented both in the spirit and the letter, and when there has to be a demonstrable movement in political and administrative reform so as to bring the various religious communities closer and to guarantee greater rights of representation for everyone, the actual positions and pronouncements of these rulers are at least very alarming.

It is well known that abolition of Article 370 is something of an article of faith for the RSS confederacy, and key leaders of the BJP itself have often campaigned on this issue. What they promise to Kashmiris is not more autonomy but less; and it is only because they rely on such a large number of allies for governance in Delhi that they have not pressed this issue more vigorously, as they have also provisionally suspended campaigning on the Mandir issue. We know perfectly well what they will do if and when they get the chance. The other side of the coin is of course the statement by Home Minister L.K. Advani on 18 May 1998, in the euphoric aftermath of Pokhran II, that India's new-found status as a nuclear power had 'brought about a qualitative new state in Indo-Pakistan relations, particularly in finding a lasting solution to the Kashmir problem'. We shall come to the significance of Pokhran and Chaghai presently. Suffice it to say here that this mentality, which promises to abridge the existing level of autonomy for J&K and sees the problem essentially as an issue between India and Pakistan that is to be settled by changing the military equation, through nuclear means if necessary, is notable for its contempt for the Kashmiris themselves and for the danger it poses not just to Pakistan but to India as well.

The much needed political and administrative reform is now envisaged in strictly communal terms, not to bring the various religious communities closer but to push them further apart. In a far-reaching but little noted report of 13 April this year, the Regional Autonomy Commission, which clearly has the blessing of Farooq Abdullah as well as Karan Singh, recommended the creation of eight new provinces of various sizes within the state, each corresponding to a distinct religious group, so that the whole becomes a mosaic of exclusive religio-ethnic entities.[2] For decades after the Partition, even as Pakistan-backed insurgents tried to poison relations between Hindus and Muslims in Kashmir, our great boast was that society in J&K was not communalized and that the historic cultural unity of the region will help it survive the attempts at sowing religious discord. During that same period, even the Pakistan-backed groups remained 'Muslim' rather than 'Islamicist'.

The phase of the insurgency that began in 1989–90 was notable for a very considerable shift towards religious fundamentalism and for great efforts to communalize Kashmiri society. Selective but unremitting terror against Kashmiri Hindus, which forced many of them to flee to Jammu and beyond, had the effect of creating a new kind of communal violence in the Valley and, in turn, injecting doses of Hindu communalism into sections of the beleaguered Kashmiri pundit community. If implemented, the politico-administrative reforms that are now being proposed will stabilize and greatly extend the communal boundaries that the Islamicists themselves have sought.

The superb coverage of this episode in *Frontline*, cited above, already points to the fact that the plan is remarkably similar to the one that the United Nations mediator, Owen Dixon, had proposed in 1950, and which has been recently revived by the influential US-based think-tank, the Kashmir Studies Group. It also points out that the lower-level functionaries of not only the National Conference but of the BJP itself have been active in promoting it, as is Karan Singh, the Hindu-revivalist Dogra prince. Two further points need to be added.

One is that Farooq Abdullah supervised and blessed this plan while he was also so loyal a member of the BJP-dominated coalition that he threw his close friend and a Member of Parliament, Professor Saifuddin Soz, out of his party for the sin of having gone against the BJP alliance on the vote of confidence. It is very unlikely that he could have blessed the plan for a politico-administrative overhaul of the state without Vajpayee's explicit approval; Karan Singh's own involvement speaks volumes. At the other end of the globe, Selig Harrison, an influential South Asia expert in the United States who is sympathetic to Indian positions, has endorsed the plan publicly.

That brings us to our second point, pertaining to the role of the United States. We know that a key lesson the United States, and the West generally, learned from the competing lunacies of Pokhran and Chaghai was that the time to find a 'lasting solution' to the Kashmir problem had come. This has led to constant, cryptic position-taking in public and repeated, detailed discussions at very high official levels more obscurely, far from the public gaze. The Kashmir problem has in effect been internationalized, the formal emphasis on bilateral talks notwithstanding, and India has contributed its own share to this internationalizing. The offer by the Secretary-General of the United Nations, Kofi Annan, to send an envoy can be politely turned down, but both Nawaz Sharif and Prime Minister Vajpayee are constantly reporting to and getting advice from Bill Clinton, the supercop of troubled waters across the world.

Similarly, India may make all kinds of noises against 'internationalization', but when it writes to the G-8 heads of state, asking for support against Pakistan and suggesting international pressure, including perhaps economic pressure from such agencies as the IMF, it too is internationalizing the issue in a way that corresponds to the world as we now have it, after Iraq and Yugoslavia, with NATO either dictating to or simply ignoring the United Nations. This new recognition of Bill Clinton as something resembling the head of a unitary world government came immediately after Pokhran II when Mr Vajpayee singled him out as the one man to whom he owed an explanation, and the status of Clinton as guide and mediator has only been enhanced as the wages of Pokhran began to be paid in Kargil.

This grovelling before the United States has its own paradoxical side. The Islamicist guerrillas who earned their laurels in Afghanistan before entering Kashmir are a direct product of the United States which is now expected to save India from them after their network has become much larger, and more autonomous, ambitious, and uncontrollable. That network – extending from the Taliban in Afghanistan to the Lashkar-e-Toyaba in Pakistan to Osama Bin Laden roaming across international frontiers – is, in a sense, the Bhindranwale syndrome – or call it the Frankenstein syndrome, if you will – writ large: the proverbial truth that the monsters you confect to prove your own power and prowess may in the end return to menace you, devour you, become your own nemesis. Part of the reason India is getting more of a sympathetic hearing from the United States is that the latter too is now stalked by the beast it created.

But is Bill Clinton simply switching off the lights and going to sleep after telling Sharif and Vajpayee to get on with 'bilateral talks'? I do not know, but my guess is that there are expert groups in various agencies of the US government putting together solutions that they can share with their clients, and the solutions are likely to be along the lines of those they have been implementing in a variety of places, from Palestine to Yugoslavia: local self-governments, ethno-religious enclaves, etc., balanced with low-intensity warfare, supervised 'bilateral negotiations', and the United States, as the leading light of NATO, taking over from the United Nations as world 'peacekeeper'.

The break-up of Yugoslavia into a mosaic of ethno-religious entities and enclaves, with its concomitant institutionalization of religious hatreds and communal killings, began with the pious rhetoric of 'the national question' encouraged by the NATO countries, notably Germany. And the United States has been deeply involved in these processes from the very start, since well before Kosovo and even Bosnia.

Closer to home, both Benazir Bhutto, the former Prime Minister of Pakistan and a mortal enemy of Nawaz Sharif, and Mushahid Hussain, the unscrupulous Information Minister and close confidant of Nawaz Sharif, have called for a US involvement in Kashmir on the model of Camp David or the Dayton Accords. So, there may be more of a connection than meets the eye between the rhetoric of a 'lasting solution' that is being brandished all around, and the communal plan for reshaping the politico-administrative map of J&K which has been announced – with blessings from so many of the powerful players. It is only to be expected that a government of Hindu communalists and its allies will further intensify, possibly with encouragement from foreign 'experts', that process of communalizing Kashmiri society which Muslim communalists from across the LoC had initiated ten years ago.

II

The Pakistan we are dealing with today was born not once but twice, in 1947 and then again in 1971, first through its own labours, for the most part, and then through the bloody surgery that India so deftly administered. Most Indian writing on the subject has found it difficult to come to terms with 1947; about the consequences of 1971 most analyses emanating from India tend to be too smug to be greatly useful. The emphasis usually is on the psychological side of things: Pakistan's sense of humiliation and a reckless desire for revenge. In reality, Pakistani responses were more complex and took quite a few years and many changes in the world to become fully formed.

There was, first, what one might call a crisis of identity. The founding myth of Pakistan was that it was the second largest Muslim country in the world, after Indonesia, and the patrimonial home of the Muslims of what was once British India. Its founders had not been notably devout, however, and for thirteen years prior to the separation of Bangladesh it had been ruled by modernizing generals who looked to Turkey and Tunisia for reform models and to the Shah of Iran for patronage. The Islam of the Pakistani elites during that phase was mild, reformist, recognizably South Asian, deriving its intellectual ambience from the tradition that ran from Shah Waliullah to Syed Ahmed Khan, and its pietistic current from the Sufi saints of Punjab and Sind. All of that came unstuck in the crucible of 1971.

Pakistan was now the third largest Muslim country on the subcontinent, trailing behind Bangladesh and India. Half the market for its industry was gone, as were two of its three major exports: jute and tea. Worse still for its military-bureaucratic elite, the country it contrived to administer and defend was cut to half the size. It was in the midst of this crisis that the Islamicist vocation of the state was born: if Pakistan was no longer the home of the *majority* of subcontinental Muslims, it had to be the home of the *good* Muslim, the *pious* Muslim. The markets it had lost in East Bengal had to be compensated with markets elsewhere, and new types of exports had to be developed. The answer was 'the Muslim world', especially the socially backward, super-rich, archconservative Gulf kingdoms which needed everything, from onions to bureaucrats, for which they could pay with petrodollars.

A new vision of Pakistan was crafted: it was an extension of the Islamic world of West Asia, rather than an integral part of a multireligious South Asia. The Pakistan army found a new vocation: training the armed personnel of these kingdoms, not to speak of defending the King of Jordan and the parameters of Riyadh, the Saudi capital. Pakistani bankers took to advising the rentier kings of the desert. Doctors, accountants, engineers, teachers, the whole of the professional classes looked forward to making money in what came to be called, euphemistically, 'the Middle East', by which they meant places like Dubai and Bahrain. Instead of jute and tea, Pakistan now had other, more lucrative exportables: fruit and vegetables grown in new kinds of capitalist garden-agriculture, cheap manufactures, the labour power of the working classes, the expertise of the professional elite, the veneer of urbane sophistication that a settled agrarian society of great cultural depth could impart to the newly rich among its patrons.

Nothing worked as magically in restoring the self-confidence of the Pakistani state and its privileged classes as the infusion of petrodollars. But this new sort of money brought with it a new and curiously effective commodity as well: petro-Islam. A hybrid thing, born of centuries of ferocious conservatism so characteristic of the desert, but also of unprecedented levels of newly acquired wealth, the product neither of a settled history nor of accumulated labour but of chance – the black gold happened to lie here rather than elsewhere. It was a curious kind of Islam, equally ferocious in its pieties and its consumerism.

Thanks to the euphoria created by the victory in Bangladesh, few in India cared to notice that something utterly fundamental had changed in the Pakistani state's self-perception. Within a few years of the defeat in 1971, Pakistan began to see itself not as some beleaguered South Asian non-entity, as the Indian establishment was prone to view it, but as a strategically located middle-sized power straddling the two worlds of South and West Asia, uniquely poised to take advantage of a host of geo-political possibilities and enjoying widespread support among the Islamic states. Ironically, the defeat at India's hands had forced Pakistan to find its Islamicist moorings in West Asia, while its own new economic compulsions combined with new financial opportunities in the world of

Arab petrodollars in the heyday of OPEC had made it possible for Pakistan to carve out this new role for itself.

We have so far mentioned the crisis of identity and the successful reorientation of policy, with a focus towards West Asia rather than the subcontinent, as the first major consequence of the loss of East Bengal. The second consequence was even more far-reaching. Having gained the unique, albeit dubious, distinction of becoming the first postcolonial state of any international consequence – ally of the United States as well as China – to be dismembered and cut in half by a combination of a secessionist movement inside the country and a massive, brutal strike by a militarily far more powerful neighbour, Pakistan fell back on the old, tired adage: offence was the best defence. In concrete strategic terms, this meant it was safer to fight all future wars on hostile, alien territory than on one's own, which fact entailed that the defence parameters for Pakistan's security were to be drawn inside the territory of the two neighbours Pakistan considered hostile: India principally, but also to a certain extent Afghanistan. Pakistan's relatively successful role in the insurgencies in Punjab and Kashmir came in the wake of this new strategic doctrine of forward defence because there was fertile ground in those states for Pakistan to exploit.

These shifts in Pakistan's policies and perceptions, including the rise of new kinds of Islamism, were already in place during the Bhutto years, well before General Zia's 1978 coup, even though more simplistic versions would tend to present Bhutto as a secular, modern, Left-orientated autocrat and would date the beginning of Islamization to Zia's rise to power. In fact, Bhutto was ideally suited to conceive and implement these changes. As an acute student of international affairs, he knew that with Egypt's defeat by Israel in 1967, and especially with the death of Nasser which coincided almost perfectly with the break-up of Pakistan, the centre of gravity in the Arab world had shifted from the radical regimes to the monarchical ones, notably from Egypt to Saudi Arabia. He knew also that even though Nasser-style anti-imperialist nationalism had gained a new lease on life in Qaddafi's Libya, the rapid rise in oil incomes had benefited not so much the small producers as the Gulf kingdoms, especially the Saudi and Kuwaiti monarchies. To them he now turned with a whole range of schemes for cooperation.

Islamism of the Middle Eastern variety came to Pakistan during the Bhutto years in several guises. There was the immense popularity of Qaddafi whose main achievement in the ideological sphere was to restate Nasser's secular anti-imperialism in stridently Islamic terms. It was after Qaddafi's speech at the grand new stadium in Lahore, named after him, that wearing the Islamic *chador* became quite the fashion among urban middle-class girls, while a whole battery of quasi-radical intellectuals set out to find revolutionary virtue in Islam, several years before the Irani revolution helped turn religous radicalism into a large-scale industry. But the Bhutto who invited Qaddafi to display his revolutionary eloquence in the cricket stadium also invited King Feisal of Saudi Arabia to lead the Friday prayers in the grand old Badshahi Masjid, with Qaddafi grudgingly but piously in attendance, as Lahore hosted a spectacularly staged session of the Organization of Islamic Countries (OIC).

There was the petro-Islam of social conservatism and consumerist hysteria that came as part of the baggage of the workers and professionals who returned after sojourns of some years in the oil kingdoms. And there was the puritanical Islam of Arab youth squads of the Ikhwan-ul-Muslimun (Muslim Brotherhood) who made their first appearance on the college campuses of Pakistan at this time, as fraternal delegates to the conferences and conventions staged by the student wing of the notorious Jama'at-e-Islami, which was to play such havoc during the Zia years, especially after the onset of the war in Afghanistan. Or, there were the many Islams – the tribal, the academic, the mercantile, what have you – that came from Afghanistan when Bhutto started offering offices and other facilities to the Islamic parties and organizations which left their country after Daoud's coup of 1973, well before the 1978 revolution. One now forgets, for example, that Gulbuddin Hekmetyar, who was to play such a pivotal role in the Islamic insurgency during the Zia period, eventually becoming even the Prime Minister for a brief period before the Taliban took over, was recruited by the Pakistan intelligence services not during that later phase but earlier, in the mid-1970s, when Bhutto's own flirtation with Afghani Islam was at its most intense.

The birth of the nuclear programme in Pakistan was a two-faced affair. The shift in the balance of forces between India and Pakistan after the 1971 war was of such magnitude that Pakistan could no longer even dream of achieving strategic parity in conventional weapons in any foreseeable future. This was not easy to accept immediately after so decisive a defeat, especially if Pakistan was to recover from that defeat through the risky new doctrine of a forward defence. Then came India's first nuclear tests, at Pokhran in 1974, and Pakistan saw itself falling woefully behind not just in conventional weapons but also in nuclear technology. Bhutto now resolved to proceed with a fully fledged nuclear programme at break-neck speed, towards weapons production capability, not only to attain parity in a nuclear field where India had already established a clear lead, but also to overcome through nuclear parity the very sizeable disadvantage Pakistan had in weapons of conventional warfare. In relation to India, Pakistan's nuclear programme was always of a defensive nature, a desperate attempt to catch up with a neighbour that had already slashed it to half its previous size. And this character of the Pakistani nuclear programme as a *response* to an India that was seen as more advanced and aggressive remained right up to Pakistan's own explosions at Chaghai, which came only after Pokhran II.

All this is difficult to comprehend for the bellicose policy-making establishments in India, which suffer from a Great Power syndrome and which reserve for themselves, but deny to Pakistan, the privilege of lunacy that is said to be the birthright of Great Powers alone. This is bad enough. But what is particularly difficult for Indian policy-makers to appreciate, precisely because they insist on viewing Pakistan simply as some illegitimate little backwoods of South Asia, is that part of the motivation for Pakistan's launching on its nuclear programme at the very time when it was trying to shift its historic orientation from South Asia to the Middle East, had little to do with India and everything to do with its ambitions in the so-called 'Islamic World'.

In a nutshell, Pakistan wished to emerge as the only nuclear power in that world, which it saw as its ticket towards dominance there, considering that it had neither oil nor the wealth and clout that comes with it, and it therefore had to make the most of the professional expertise and military capability it possessed, which was greater than any Arab country except, perhaps, Egypt. For the conservative Arab sheikhdoms, a nuclear-capable Pakistan would be the great military power in their midst. To the radical nationalists, of Libya or Palestine for example, a nuclear-capable Pakistan could be presented as a counterweight to Israel. Throughout the Bhutto period, this other aspect of Pakistan's race towards nuclear capability – which the Western media called 'the Islamic bomb' – was predominant, and it is worth remarking that in Bhutto's own view he was being sent to the gallows for the sin of having defied US imperialism and Israeli Zionism on the nuclear issue. In early 1978, weeks before Bhutto was hanged, an aide to the PLO Chairman told me that Arafat himself believed there was much truth in Bhutto's assessment.

Why was Pakistan allowed to carry on with its nuclear programme even after Bhutto's judicially sanctioned assassination? The first reason was precisely that: Bhutto had been despatched, and the man who had despatched him was much more reliable. Zia was possibly the shrewdest ruler Pakistan has ever had, but he was also a pious Muslim of conservative stamp, a man of kulak origins who had risen from an early career in the colonial army to high office in Pakistan's notoriously rightwing armed forces. 'I am a man of the Right', he had exulted soon after consolidating his power, 'and all these liberals better move to the centre.' He was too far to the Right to notice that 'liberals' already were in 'the centre'! If Bhutto had turned to Saudi Arabia for pragmatic reasons and to Afghan Islamic groups for cynical ones, Zia was to do so out of conviction. And if Bhutto was split between a certain variety of Third World nationalism and day-to-day dependence on imperialism, Zia's relationship with the United States was uncomplicated; many in Pakistan noted the fact that he had launched his coup immediately after attending the 4th of July celebrations at the US embassy. He was, in short, trustworthy.

On the nuclear issue, Zia seems to have argued persuasively with his US patrons that (1) Pakistan's geo-political compulsions on the subcontinent required developing this capability since India already had it and was working to improve it; (2) Pakistan would not undertake tests and explosions so long as India did not do so; and (3) Pakistan would never make this capability available to Third World nationalists, Arab radicals, etc. Rhetoric aside, this remained Pakistan's policy for another decade under Benazir as well as under Nawaz Sharif, until the BJP-led government unilaterally changed India's historic position on the nuclear issue by staging Pokhran II.

III

In *Shame*, which is surely the most compact and possibly the best of his novels, Salman Rushdie has a wonderful scene in which Zia – or Raza Hyder, the fictional character that stands in for Zia – hears the news 'that the Russians had sent an army into the country of A' and promptly brings out four prayer mats so that he and his cronies can 'give thanks, pronto, fut-a-fut, for this blessing that had been bestowed on them by God', while one of those cronies begins 'to fantasize about five billion dollars' worth of new military equipment, the latest stuff at last, missiles that could fly sideways without starving their engines of oxygen'. We are still living with the consequences of that 'blessing'. At least one of the roads that has now reached Kargil originated in Kabul some twenty years ago. It was at the Khyber Pass that Professor Brzezinski, President Carter's National Security Advisor, had stood, an American-made gun in hand, promising his hired mujahideen that this gun would enable Islam to prevail against the godless communists. Osama Bin Laden is only one of the hundreds of thousands who came out of the barrel of that gun; he simply has more money than most others of his kind.

What did the war in Afghanistan mean for Pakistan?

In the nuclear arena itself, the great dependence of the United States upon Pakistan for the conduct of the war meant that Pakistani intelligence services were free to beg, buy, and steal nuclear technologies from the best laboratories of the Western world without getting punished, even as the United States continued to blame China and North Korea for transferring this technology to Pakistan; the Americans had to swallow hard as Pakistan developed its weapons capability.

Then there was the money. Quite aside from the countless billions that came from the United States and the Gulf monarchies, the illegal drug trade alone, which American secret services helped organize for the Afghan mujahideen to finance part of their operations, was said to be bringing in over two billion dollars annually during the early 1980s. A side-effect for Pakistan was that for a decade or so drug addiction grew in Karachi faster than in any other city in the world, and Karachi became a major hub for gun-running by drug-trafficking mafias; it was in those years that social and political life in the city was first massively criminalized. And the cancer of course spread far and wide.

In other parts of the country, in the Northwest Frontier Province particularly, but also in Baluchistan and Punjab, over three million Afghan refugees poured in, altering the social fabric itself in the regions where they were concentrated; one-third to one-half are said to be there still. Many of the leaders of Afghan Islamic organizations had migrated to Pakistan during the Bhutto period, and the bulk of the ruling class, minus the ones who went straight to Western countries or went to Iran instead, now also converged there. The refugee camps, where military training and Islamic education of the most arcane kind were dispensed in equal measure, became the source of virtually infinite recruitment for the war inside Afghanistan. The combination of military expertise and extreme religious conservatism that the Taliban has displayed is a direct reflection of the lethal brew first stirred up in those camps. We might add that the seven-party alliance that was recognized by Pakistan and the United States as the legitimate soldiers of God, who then fought over the spoils after the Soviet withdrawal until the Taliban threw them out, was only slightly less conservative than today's Taliban and surely no less brutal. The same applies to the Pakistanis who joined them in increasing numbers and the ones who came from a variety of other countries, from the Sudan to the United Kingdom. Many of those who have tasted blood are now looking to other sources for the same ghastly nourishment.

In the process, Pakistan's own Islamicist organizations, such as the Jama'at-e-Islami, which had remained politically marginal and militarily inconsequential, have made spectacular progress in terms of money, arms, men, and expertise. There has also been an immense proliferation of other such outfits. Furthermore, there is still a huge pool of human beings, not only in Afghanistan but also in Pakistan, not only army regulars and controlled irregulars but also freelance seekers after martyrdom, from among whom guerrillas for covert wars can still be recruited. Equally dangerous, perhaps, is the fact that many are men of shifting loyalties and fierce egotism, under no one's control and largely footloose. Weapons of all sorts and of all levels of sophistication, right up to a handful of Stinger missiles, are spread across Pakistan and among the Afghan irregulars; no effort to disarm this marauding mass can wholly succeed.

Not only has Pakistan's social and political culture become very much more Islamized, but the character of the armed forces has also changed dramatically, so that the numbers who subscribe to an extreme form of political Islam are now so great that it may destabilize the inner unity of the military itself. An eventuality may yet arise in which the most extreme wing stages a coup against both the civilian authorities and their own less piously inclined colleagues, to join up with extremist political organizations in the civilian arena and to establish in Pakistan the type of Islamicist state, suitably modified for Pakistani conditions, that the Sudan and Afghanistan have already known, or the kind that may yet arise in Algeria. This is not by any means fated but it is a distinct possibility.

As the war in Afghanistan progressed, the national security apparatus in Pakistan grew in scope and ambition. The doctrine of forward defence that had initially conceived of defence parameters being drawn some kilometres into neighbours' territories came now to include the whole of Afghanistan as a neighbouring state that could be turned into a permanent dependency and, as a legitimate sphere of influence, the states that have arisen out of Soviet Central Asia. By the time the Soviet troops were withdrawn, another, brand new self-image of the military-bureaucratic state emerged: Pakistan was especially chosen by the Lord to become the country that was to beat the Soviet Union out of Afghanistan, out of the Cold War, out of existence. Pakistani military officers are known to have joked that they would have done the same to Vietnam if the Americans had had the sense to deploy Pakistani troops instead of their own. A third-rate military machine that is intoxicated by so dazzling a self-image is a dangerous machine.

This is the tiger Nawaz Sharif is trying to ride.

IV

There are powerful currents of opinion about Pakistan among academic experts, think-tanks, and policy-makers in India which make too much, even when it comes to foreign policy and military strategy, of the distinction between civilian and military governments and among various centres of power in Pakistan. Defence Minister Fernandes' statement that the Kargil operation was an undertaking of the Pakistan army in which the Inter Services Intelligence (ISI) was not involved and which did not have the sanction of Prime Minister Nawaz Sharif was of course exceptionally foolish, but it comes precisely out of that mechanistic sense of how Pakistan is governed or makes its policies.

We speak of the Pakistani ISI these days as we once used to speak of the American CIA, as something not only transcendentally diabolical but also as some sort of a super-government that does as it wishes. It is surely the case that the relationship between the intelligence agencies and the GHQ in Pakistan became especially complex in the course of the Afghanistan war and thereafter. Nevertheless, the ISI is a department of the armed forces in which the chain of command remains, in the final analysis, intact. The Kargil operation was prepared in elaborate secrecy, on a scale that is yet not clear even after a month and a half of fighting. It is inconceivable that any of the key intelligence services would remain uninvolved. By the same token, what task is assigned to the ISI, SSG (Special Services Group), or any other such agency would necessarily be determined by the chief commanders of the armed forces, who are not obliged to reveal to their subordinates their actual war plans. The sort of distinction between the Pakistan army and the ISI that Mr Fernandes wishes to observe is simply fanciful.

What about Nawaz Sharif? Unlike Mr Vajpayee, whose party commands less than a third of the national vote and who has been unable to retain the confidence of the House for the coalition of motley groups that made him Prime Minister, Nawaz Sharif commands enough strength in his Parliament to change even the Constitution if he so desires. He has used this power to get rid of the President, the Supreme Court Chief Justice, as well as the army Chief of Staff who dared to differ with him. It is inconceivable that the current army chief, General Musharraf, whom Sharif is said to have especially favoured because he has no independent personal base among the key commanders, would launch so large an operation without seeking permission from his Prime Minister.

The assumption that the Chief of Staff could, even in the conditions currently obtaining, defy his own Prime Minister to such an extent, rests on three misconceptions: (1) that the various centres of power in Pakistan are so autonomous and so much at odds with each other that each pursues its own discrete objectives; (2) that the army, in particular, pursues a foreign policy of its own; and (3) that the Kargil operation is so irreconcilable with the undertakings Pakistan gave when Mr Vajpayee's bus lurched into Lahore that the operation must be seen either as Sharif's perfidy or as an adventure launched behind his back. The fallacy that governs each of these misconceptions is that Pakistan does not have a coherent state authority capable of pursuing fixed, long-term objectives.

It is undoubtedly true that the army has a much bigger role in the Pakistani polity than is the case in India and that this inordinately large role remains whether a general or a civilian heads the government; even the census in Pakistan is taken by the army, and it is the army that takes over the elaborate machinery of the Water and Development Authority (WAPDA) when that institution pushes itself close to bankruptcy. The army even took over the task of invigilation during the recent examinations at Peshawar University to prevent cheating. All that is true. That does not mean, however, that there is some fundamental cleavage between the civilian and military authorities over national interest, foreign policy, and military strategy. Our own argument would suggest, by contrast, that there are of course ideological shifts, as governments come and go, and dramatic new forces emerge with the passage of time and in response to events inside and outside the country; nevertheless, a basic continuity persists in definitions of the national interest and strategies to prosecute it.

Contrast this with the hallowed fantasies that now surround the Lahore Declaration and which are largely of our own making. After Pokhran II and Chaghai tremendous pressure was exerted by the NATO countries, principally the United States, to undertake tangible action to resolve or at least diffuse the Kashmir crisis because Kashmir had become, as they put it, a 'nuclear flashpoint'. Unwilling and even unable to come up with creative, substantive new thinking, Mr Vajpayee opted for a politics of naive gesture symbolized by what came to be called the 'bus diplomacy'. Nawaz Sharif simply obliged, though he did not go so far as to disturb his own routine and come to Delhi.

We are a sentimental people, and even the progressive and liberal commentators fell for Mr Vajpayee's short-lived atmospherics. Not Sartaj Aziz, Pakistan's Foreign Minister! On the eve of the bus trip, when Mr Vajpayee was already overcommitted, Aziz delivered much publicized and hard-hitting speeches, saying bluntly that the atmospherics must not be seen as making any fundamental difference to Pakistan's settled positions on Kashmir. When *The News*, an English-language daily published by the Jung group, organized a meeting of Pakistani and Indian parliamentarians, where a great deal of poetry and sentiment also flowed, a group of unidentified men broke into the compound of the house of Imtiaz Alam, the editor who had played a prominent role in organizing the event, and set his new and expensive car on fire. Later, when Najam Sethi, a veteran Pakistani publisher and commentator, shared with the BBC some information on the corruptions of the Sharif family, the Pakistani government waited until he had expressed on Indian soil the dissent he routinely expresses in his own newspaper, *The Friday Times*, and arrested him, with the complicity of the Pakistani High Commissioner in Delhi, on the improbable charge that Sethi was a RAW (Research and Development Wing) agent.[3] The government of India contrived to notice not much of it and continued to speak of the Lahore Declaration, a veritable pack of cosmetics, as if some new chapter in subcontinental history had been opened.

Drunk on his own rhetoric, Mr Vajpayee went to Minar-e-Pakistan, which stands in Lahore at the spot where the historic Pakistan Resolution of 1940 was passed, and spoke of India and Pakistan as 'separate nations'. Our media saw fit to characterize this gesture as a historic turn where India – or was it the RSS? – had finally accepted the Partition. Pakistanis were barely amused. Hardly anyone there believes that it is for India – or for the RSS – to issue certificates of legitimate birth, and thereby accept or reject the reality of Pakistan, over half a century after the event. Those who make policy in Pakistan politely waited for Mr Vajpayee to depart.

What went wrong? The media hype of 'bus diplomacy' was the other face of the Pokhran lunacy. Having committed an act of extraordinary hawkishness and belligerence, which had dismayed people round the world, raising the suspicion that the government of India was losing its capacity for responsible action, Mr Vajpayee desperately needed to reincarnate himself as a man of peace. No one approved of Pakistan's nuclear blasts, but most had concluded that it was an unpleasant, if predictable, response to Indian irresponsibility. Mr Vajpayee had to take a unilateral initiative in going to Lahore because he had taken the unilateral initiative on the nuclear issue. A comedy of penance was sold to the media as if it were the arrival of a flock of doves. He had to move fast, before the international pressure for 'internationalizing' the Kashmir issue became unbearable.

And there lies the rub: the gesture's haste. When Kissinger journeyed to Beijing in the dead of night, he had done so after prolonged and extremely careful preparations for rapprochement, which itself became possible only after historic shifts had taken place within China in its attitude towards the United States, the Soviet Union, Vietnam, and itself. Similarly, when Sadat made his dramatic visit to Jerusalem, it was only after months and years of careful preparation and only when the transformed relations between Egypt and Israel had been agreed upon, between the two governments, inside each of the polities and in collaboration with their common patron saint in the United States.

No such preparations preceded the trip to Lahore; not even the glimmer of a thought actually to resolve the Kashmir issue went into Mr Vajpayee's journey. It is possible that RSS now believes too much in the effectiveness of spectacles – not the real but the hyper-real, as the postmodernists would say – and that Mr Vajpayee made himself believe that his alighting from a garishly decked-out bus on the other side of the Wagha border could change the shape of international diplomacy as Mr Advani's *rath yatra* had altered the fortunes of the RSS within the country.

At some level, the bus diplomacy turned out to be as inept as most of this government's other initiatives. More fundamentally, the BJP-led government misconstrues what Pokhran and Chaghai signify. On 18 May last year, Mr Advani had claimed that Pokhran II had strengthened India's hand in Kashmir. Writing in *Frontline* at the time,[4] I had suggested that our blustering Home Minister did not seem to understand that nuclear weapons have little bearing on guerrilla actions and localized, low-intensity warfare. Now, a year later, one needs to go a step further.

Pokhran was a gift to Sharif, just as the Afghan war had been to Zia. Since 1971, Pakistan had been trying, unsuccessfully, to overcome its strategic inferiority in conventional warfare. By opening the way for nuclear parity and competitive weaponization, the Vajpayee government handed to Pakistan a strategic equivalence it could not otherwise achieve. To the extent that the possession of nuclear weapons capability on both sides tends to put serious constraints on a full-scale conventional war, to that same extent it facilitates the institutionalization of low-intensity, localized wars. The more the two countries move towards weaponization, the more Kargils we shall have. In this sense, the present reality in Kargil is not only the other face of the rhetoric of Lahore, it is also a precise, necessary, repeatable consequence of Pokhran.

Mediation by Any Other Name

The President of the United States went to work on the 4th of July, cancelling a part of the customary holiday on America's holiest day. Mindful of the sensitivities of the BJP-led government in New Delhi, the White House claimed that a meeting had been hastily arranged in response to Pakistan Prime Minister Nawaz Sharif's urgent request. Facts indicate otherwise.

The weekend of 26–27 June appears to have been decisive. It was then, at the end of the week, that the Pakistan Army's Chief of Staff, General Pervez Musharraf, had casually told a press conference in Karachi that Sharif would soon be meeting Clinton. He had just concluded intense negotiations with General Anthony Zinni, Commander-in-Chief, US General Command, and the Deputy Asssistant Secretary of State Gibson Lanpher who had been in Islamabad since 23 June, and therefore had reason to know. On that same day, 27 June, the *Sunday Telegraph* in London reported that the mechanics of a negotiated withdrawal by Pakistan-inspired forces occupying the heights of Tiger Hill, Marpo La, and Batalik were a topic of conversation between Zinni and Musharraf. In Karachi, where Musharraf himself was to make that statement, *Dawn*, the oldest of the English-language dailies in Pakistan, went further and wrote:

Pakistan had insisted on reciprocity. For example, a promise by the Indians for time-bound discussions on Kashmir in return for assisting the Mujahideen to home bases. Pakistan, on its part, would be prepared to consider as part of the permanent solution the inclusion of the entire Valley and the Muslim parts of Jammu in the Azad Kashmir territory – a settlement on the line of the Owen Dixon plan.

That 'the Owen Dixon plan' is very much in the air these days has been reported in *Frontline* previously,[5] and we shall return to the matter presently. That 'the Valley and the Muslim parts of Jammu' should be included 'in the Azad Kashmir territory' is of course Pakistan's *maximum* demand, which India is most unlikely to concede. But that some variant of this solution, interim and much softer, is being prepared seems beyond doubt, as we can surmise from the contours of the plan for reorganization of Jammu and Kashmir that Farooq Abdullah's Regional Autonomy Commission had released already, on 13 April, as well as the carefully prepared proposal that Benazir Bhutto, former Prime Minister of Pakistan, published on the Op-Ed page of the *New York Times* on 8 June under the significant title 'Camp David for Kashmir'.

We shall return to this key document later. Two things may be noted immediately, however. One is that what happened in Washington on the 4th of July was itself a miniaturized Camp David, with Pakistani and American specialist groups sitting across the table, yet again, to hammer out the final wording of the joint statement; the US National Security Advisor Sandy Berger clearing the wording with his Indian counterpart Brijesh Mishra on the telephone; and Prime Minister Vajpayee available and waiting at the other end of another telephone line while Sharif and Clinton met in person. The latter is known to have called Vajpayee in the middle of that meeting. Clinton's 'personal interest in encouraging an expeditious resumption and intensification' of bilateral efforts that the joint statement promises seems to hold at least a faint promise of a more comprehensive and prolonged 'Camp David' through other means. In any case, the phrasing does come very close to what *Dawn* had indicated on 27 June as Pakistan's basic negotiating position: withdrawal of the mujahideen in lieu of a promise for time-bound discussion on Kashmir. Natwar Singh, seasoned diplomat that he is, was actually stating less than the truth when he charged that the phrase 'personal interest' amounted to third-party intervention.

The other curiosity is that the ink on the joint statement was barely dry when Benazir Bhutto announced her imminent return to Pakistan. As if on cue, her party has promised a massive welcome rally, on the model of 1986, warning the government not to act in haste. Now, the reason why she has been cooling her heels abroad is that she and her husband have both been sentenced on corruption charges, and husband Zardari is not only held in prison but is alleged to have been gruesomely tortured quite recently. Cruelty comes more or less naturally to Sharif. What assurances has Benazir received, and from whom, to contemplate a spectacular return? After all, she was similarly cooling her heels in foreign countries more than a decade ago when Zia's body went up in a ball of fire over Bahawalpur in an air crash that has never been adequately explained. Then, too, the Americans had arranged for her to return and go straight into an election that she was bound to win. It is too early to say whether or not they would be able or even wholly willing to stage her second coming. They would in any case like to indicate to Sharif that they have options.

When Musharraf told the press of Sharif's impending meeting with Clinton, over a week before the event, too many people thought he had spoken out of turn. Not so. He seems to have by then worked out with General Zinni not just the politics of Kargil, for which Lanpher was at least equally suitable, but the great technical details involved in the proposed withdrawal, in the contemplated 'restoration' of the 'sanctity' of the Line of Control (LoC), and in the radical disagreement between Pakistan and India over the implications of the fact that the LoC does not extend to Siachen even on the maps, beyond the point that is known as NJ9842, even though the 1949 agreement records a summary verbal reference that beyond that point the line went 'north to the glaciers'. He knew what he had offered Zinni on all these counts, and what the latter thought of it.

By then Lanpher and Niaz Nayak, the retired Foreign Secretary of Pakistan and a trusted advisor of Nawaz Sharif, had spent the whole weekend in Delhi, conferring with Brijesh Mishra and Vajpayee, who also now knew what Zinni had been offered and what Washington's view was going to be. Nayak returned to Pakistan on the 27th, the day Musharraf announced the Sharif visit; the latter, in turn, cut short his visit to China on the 28th, in view of his impending visit to Washington, after he had concluded his meetings with all the key Chinese leaders. Clinton modified his vacation plans to satisfy not only the Pakistan Prime Minister but Mr Vajpayee as well, as we shall see.

Why the urgency? It is worth recalling, I think, that a large number of intruders have been routinely crossing the LoC from the Pakistan side, year after year, for over a decade now, trained and armed for organizing insurrection on Indian territory, leading to great and constant tragedies in the Valley as well as Jammu. It has been a long time since either side has treated the LoC with any sense of 'sanctity'. Why was respect for the 'sanctity' of the LoC now so urgently affirmed by all and sundry? Part of the reason undoubtedly is that the Kargil operation was of a different order. Musharraf himself has said that between 1,500 and 2,000 fighters from the Pakistani side were involved; reports in the Indian media suggest that they were spread across roughly 1,000 square kilometres, including the majestic heights. As of 8 July, the Indian official claim was that 643 intruders and 321 Indian men, including 23 officers, had died. We can safely assume that Indian casualties have been substantially higher; nor does the figure include the maimed and the injured.

So, we have a curious situation that speaks volumes about the mentality of ruling circles around the world. The 'sanctity' of the LoC meant little for a decade while the terrorized populations of the Valley and Jammu were involved, but restoration of this 'sanctity' became a serious issue when fixed bases on stretches of territory were at stake; in war, territory is always more important than the people who live there. By now, it has also become clear that Pakistan started preparing this operation soon after the nuclear blasts last summer; by October, some reports had appeared to that effect in sections of the British press. The United States, meanwhile, had greatly intensified surveillance over the whole length of the Indo-Pakistan border, including the LoC and the Siachen triangle where the boundaries of India, Pakistan, and China meet in glacial silence. It seems improbable that the United States did not know of the movements of men and material. There is no public record suggesting that it shared this information with India or urged Pakistan to abandon the project.

Clinton's first calls to Sharif and Vajpayee came on 14 and 15 June, after three weeks of a 'war-like situation', as Mr Vajpayee carefully described it. Some ground must by then have been prepared, for such calls to be meaningful. Then, over the next two weeks, things moved at dizzying speed until Musharraf announced the prospect of a Clinton–Sharif meeting, which took place a week later. Why such an urgency that the US President was found at Blair House on the 4th of July?

By then, the real scale of the Pakistani operation had become quite clear. That Pakistan had established fixed bases meant it expected to come under attack, suffer casualties, move when absolutely necessary, regroup elsewhere, and so on, until one of three things happened: (1) the Indian response would be so restrained that at least a goodly number of the intruders would be able to hold on until the winter set in; or (2) Indian determination to conclude the operation before September would be so great that casualties would mount, the armed forces would start clamouring to cross the LoC, and the threat of a larger war would help focus everyone's mind; or, (3) India would seek international mediation and the Great Powers would oblige so that Pakistan could then extract at least minimal promises, threatening more hostilities in other places and at other times.

By mid-June, a combination of (2) and (3) had come to pass, and even (1) could not be entirely ruled out. That Pakistan would be approaching NATO countries for mediation was part of its plan. What now changed was that India too started imploring the NATO countries to step in, competing with Pakistan for attention and sympathy. Well before

Clinton and Sharif agreed that 'concret steps' would be taken to respect the LoC in accordance with the Shimla Agreement, India had been requesting G-8 countries to take such 'concrete steps' as blocking economic assistance to Pakistan from the IMF and other multilateral agencies. It seems quite clear by now that Vajpayee's letter to Clinton, handed over to Sandy Berger by Brijesh Mishra on the eve of the G-8 meeting in Cologne, essentially said that India would soon have to make the decision on crossing the LoC and time was running out for G-8 countries to act. By 26 June, when Zinni returned to the United States and Lanpher and Nayak appeared more or less simultaneously in Delhi, the Indian army chief General Malik was indicating that he would go to the Union Cabinet for permission to cross the LoC. The moment for drastic action was at hand.

Easier said than done, though. Everyone knew that Pakistan had by then concentrated enough forces on its side of the LoC to engage India in a limited battle within Kashmir, but also that any significant escalation would also mean that the Kashmir issue would return to the Security Council. The main favour Clinton did India was to take into his own hands the problem Kofi Annan had sought at one point to mediate, and he moved quickly enough. It is ironic that India and the United States have now become partners in sidelining the United Nations as a dangerous institution that may actually respond to the interests of *all* its members, while direct Great Power mediation is what we are actively seeking.

The United States of course did not go so far as to try and block financial assistance from any quarter at all. On 29 June, well before Sharif's visit was officially announced in America, State Department spokesman James Rubin said that the United States had no plans to influence the IMF. During that same week, and obviously well before the Clinton–Sharif statement, France assured Pakistan that supplies of the most sophisticated weapons for the latter's navy and air force would be delivered on schedule, in July and thereafter, while the operation in Kargil continued. Before Sharif had concluded his visit to Beijing, China and Pakistan signed a fresh agreement to establish, in Pakistan with Chinese assistance, a new factory for the manufacture of aircraft for the Pakistani air force. In remarks quoted in the *People's Daily*, Prime Minsiter Zhu Rongji referred to Kashmir as 'a historic problem involving territorial, religious, ethnic and other elements'. The Organization of Islamic Countries (OIC) quickly passed the Pakistani resolution affirming the right of Kashmiri people to self-determination.

The Indian media reported it all, but in small print as it were, refusing to draw the conclusion that in virtually every resepect and in all the usual quarters it was business as usual, and that Pakistan's great 'isolation' in the 'international community' was restricted to the scale of its operation in Kargil beyond the LoC, which of course even the Pakistan government must have anticipated before launching the operation. For them, the question had always been: how far will the condemnation go, in material terms, and what else, other than condemnation, could they earn?

If General Musharraf was the first to announce Sharif's projected visit, he also affirmed the army's support for the outcome of the visit with remarkable alacrity. He was the first within Pakistan to use the language that the Foreign Office spokesman Tariq Altaf was to use in Washington even before Sharif's delegation left the United States: that Pakistan 'will appeal and use its influence' with the mujahideen. The Urdu daily, *Jung*, reported Musharraf as saying that '[t]he Mujahideen will be asked to change their position. It remains to be seen how they will respond.' Saying that there was 'complete understanding' between the army and the civilian government, he went on to praise the Sharif–Clinton agreement because, as he put it, it recognized 'the need to address the current volatile situation in Kargil within the context of the larger Kashmir situation'. This is exactly what Foreign Minister Sartaj Aziz was to say in his much publicized interviews in London, on his way back to Pakistan. By the time Sharif got up to present to the nation the position arrived at during the session of the Defence Council, the high powered military–civilian committee, that language had become the official line of the government of Pakistan.

My guess is that the language had been developed before Sharif went to Washington and that Clinton knew of it, in general terms, before he signed the joint statement. What the United States actually expects and what undertakings Pakistan has actually offered are still shrouded in mystery, all the public posturing in various quarters notwithstanding. At no point has this diplomatic process been even remotely transparent, and there is no reason to believe that it has become so in the wake of a single statement. The Indian position that there can be no ceasefire until after the Kargil intrusion has been withdrawn has certainly been upheld; nothing short of that could be tenable. Similarly, it goes largely in India's favour that the statement calls for 'the restoration of the Line of Control in accordance with the Shimla Agreement'.

On the other hand, the 'forces' that are to return have not been identified as personnel of the Pakistan army, and Pakistan has won at least three further concessions: that Kashmir is indeed an issue between India and Pakistan that is yet to be 'resolved'; that the LoC is to be respected by 'both' sides; and that it is Clinton who will ensure 'expeditious resumption and intensification' of talks to resolve these issues, including Kashmir.

Four actions from the Pakistan side can now be expected. First, having held its positions in Kargil long enough to have forced India to seek mediation, it will withdraw all or most of its personnel from the positions the Indian armed forces have not yet overrun, and the muja-hideen will now regroup, to survive elsewhere in the area and periodi-cally to carry out small actions, mostly on a level that does not threaten the overall process but still keeps the pot simmering. Second, Pakistan seems to have used the cover of the Kargil operation to infiltrate a large number of terrorists into the Valley and the Poonch–Rajouri sector, and killings there will revive, as appears to be happening already; the emphasis will be shifted from 'occupation' to 'insurgency'. Third, Pakistan will remind the United States that it has always regarded the 1984 Indian occupation of Siachen as a 'gross violation' of the Shimla Agreement and that the seven meetings that have taken place between Pakistan and India over this issue have failed to produce an agreement, the last one having broken down in November 1998, just about the time when Pakistan seems to have begun the Kargil operation in earnest.

All this will be used to argue that India is not respecting the LoC either and that while Pakistan will take 'concrete steps' to defuse the crisis, none of these problems can be resolved without addressing the main issue of Kashmir, once and for all. We can undoubtedly show that the LoC never covered Siachen, but that only proves it is yet to be demarcated there; it does not automatically endorse our claim to Siachen, which is itself based on successfully grabbing it and on the further claim that the whole of J&K – PoK included – is ours in any case. Furthermore, Pakistan can be labelled the aggressive party on most immediate counts; the key fact remains, however, that there is no international consensus in favour of the Indian position that J&K – even the *whole* of J&K – is non-negotiable Indian territory. The language of the joint statement itself describes it as an issue yet to be resolved, which is the crux of the international consensus.

To the extent that the Kargil situation gets defused, to that same extent will pressure on India increase to resolve the Kashmir issue. The test will probably not come until after the September election. However, once the new government is in place and Clinton begins to prepare his projected trip to South Asia, pressure will mount for 'expeditious resumption and intensification' of the process to show him something tangible when he arrives. We may not call it mediation, but we are certainly in the middle of it.

We need to be soberly sceptical regarding the dominant interpretation in India, that the joint statement is some unalloyed victory for us; that a new watershed has been reached in Indo-American relations; that Paki-stan is henceforth isolated in the community of nations; that Sharif is similarly isolated within Pakistan; that the civilian government is paying for the blunders of the Pakistan army, etc. Just as the army high command was careful to inform Nawaz Sharif and obtain his permission before launching the Kargil operation, Sharif has been careful in not just informing but directly involving his Chief of Staff in the whole of the diplomatic process. The key negotiations took place not between Sharif and Clinton, not even between Sartaj Aziz and Talbot, but between Musharraf and Zinni. If Sharif loses office over this issue then Musharraf too will go, and, under the circumstances, he can only be replaced by far more rabidly Islamicist generals. The Americans know it and they could hardly have participated in a process that would yield such a dire result. Their position is likely to be much closer to the plan that Benazir published in the *New York Times* on 8 June.

Before discussing that plan, a couple of things should be clarified. The first is that precisely because she is currently not holding any office in Pakistan, Benazir is free to spell out in public the contours of a future settlement that Sharif, carrying the weight of Prime Ministerial office, cannot. And, because of her freedom, she is the right person for Americans to employ to send up the trial balloons, with proposals that are not exactly on the table but very much in the air, ready to land in Prime Ministerial laps. Second, Z.A. Bhutto built his entire career on an extremely frenzied anti-India hysteria, which his daughter also fully exploited when she herself was Prime Minister; it is unlikely that she went through so radical a change of heart just because she met Shimon Peres, as she so disingenuously claims. The plan has come from sources, perhaps a conjunction of several sources, which we do not know. Most importantly, she and Nawaz Sharif may be mortal enemies, but Benazir still aspires to return as Prime Minister, and it is most unlikely that she would publicly present a plan for which she has not already obtained some considerable support from policy-making institutions in Pakistan as a whole. As I have emphasized previously, it is simply foolish to think that Pakistan lacks a coherent state authority, beyond the personalities, that sets long-term objectives.

The general principle she proposes is what she calls 'deliberate, incremental advance', so that the hardest decisions are left to an indefinite future. The plan itself has five components:

1. 'The two sections of Kashmir should have porous and open borders. Both sections would be demilitarized and patrolled by either an international peacekeeping force or a joint Indian-Pakistani peacekeeping force.'
2. 'Both legislative councils would continue to meet separately and on occasion jointly', but 'none of these steps would prejudice or prejudge the position of both countries on the disputed areas'.
3. '[T]he borders . . . would be opened for unrestricted trade, cultural cooperation and exchange', leading to 'the creation of a South Asian Free Market zone'.

4. 'Only after all of these confidence-building measures' and a 'significant set period of time (Camp David called for a five-year transition), would the parties commence discussions on a formal and final resolution to the Kashmir problem.'

She ends her short piece with words of warning: 'The clock is ticking. The time to act is now.' It is plausible that the Pakistan army staged the Kargil action so that the ticking of the clock would become loud enough for all to hear. This, too, is paradoxical. By the middle of summer 1998, insurgency in Kashmir had come substantially under India's control. Pakistan, the inferior military power, had no means to expedite the pace. Then we gifted them Pokhran II, nuclear parity, competitive weaponization. When Kargil exploded, the world sat up to listen to their case on Kashmir in a way it had not done in a long time. And we were the ones who had to run for cover, begging the superpower to intervene on our behalf and feeling grateful that it had been even-handed in doing so.

We do not know the behind-the-scenes secrets, but there is no public evidence of any major tension between the army and the civilian government in Pakistan. Second, a lot of war hysteria had been whipped up in Pakistan, as if the time to liberate Kashmir had come, but outside the rabid Islamicist circles there was little enthusiasm for the Kargil venture. So long as the inner unity of the armed forces remains intact, the government will successfully contain the immediate agitations from the Islamicist extremists; they are powerful but they cannot succeed without a split in the army, which does not seem to be at hand. Once the dust settles, the government will prevail in arguing that the Kargil operation has helped 'internationalize' the Kashmir issue, bringing the day of 'liberation' closer. Even the Islamicists will have to come along, just as the BJP has been able to silence the VHP, the Bajrang Dal, etc. by assuring them that the day of the building of the Ram Mandir in Ayodhya is drawing nearer.

Pakistani society has not become notably more rightwing or less attached to democratic values because of the Kargil crisis; these deficits in Pakistan came earlier. Ours has! There is now a widespread consensus that the government should not be criticized while the fighting lasts, as if democratic dissent were a peacetime indulgence. Israel feels more beleaguered than any other nation on earth, and yet it has not been involved in a single military action over the past thirty years without being challenged, by one group or another and for one reason or another, on the streets of Tel Aviv. In India, by contrast, we do not get a decent protest from the Press Council of India, for example, when the government denies us the right to watch Pakistani TV or read a Pakistani newspaper. A government that has lost confidence in the lower house refuses to call into session the upper house, but the opposition parties which had defeated this government on the floor are reduced to mere pleading for the favour of being listened to. Kapil Dev and Ajay Jadeja mouth what Thakeray was preaching last year, and receive accolades from across the country, including Mr Raj Singh Dungarpur, President of the Board of Control for Cricket in India, whose offices had been attacked by Thakeray's goons.[6] Meanwhile, an extraordinary consensus develops, all the way from Mr L.K. Advani, against whom charges are about to be framed for his role in the Ayodhya demolition, to Mr Rajiv Dhavan, a lawyer of impeccable liberal credentials and well-deserved repute, that Pakistan was a 'rogue state', 'terrorist state', etc., forgetting that no one demanded that India be declared a 'rogue state' when a government here was supporting the LTTE or when a Prime Minister colluded in letting Bhindranwale loose upon the country itself. The BJP's own allies seem to have retreated into the background so much that it has effectively become the government of the BJP plus Fernandes alone. It is difficult to foresee the consequences of such subservience for the evolution of the polity.

Meanwhile, the clock will go on ticking, louder and louder, because it now has nuclear energy powering it.

III Rightwing Politics and the Cultures of Cruelty: Some Notes on the BJP in Government

Since forming the government in New Delhi in February 1998, through its political arm, the BJP, the Sangh *parivar* has conducted an unremitting low-intensity warfare against the minorities, most especially the Christian minority. This campaign went into high gear in Gujarat during the closing week of 1998, and then momentarily spun out of control with the burning of Graham Staines and his two sons in Orissa on 23 January this year [1999]. This brutal killing of an Australian missionary and his children has served to focus the nation's attention in a way that raping of Indian nuns, assaults on Indian pastors, and burning Indian churches could not. We are, as usual, deeply concerned about our image in Western countries.

Staines devoted his life to serving people afflicted with leprosy, whom caste Hindus in particular and the Indian middle classes in general would not dream of touching. But then, in his death too, he has taught us a lesson we are in dire need of learning. The lesson is simply this: there has been flowing, for some decades now, a wide and meandering river of blood in this country that joins the burning of this kindly

Australian with the assassination of Mahatma Gandhi. The perpetrators are of the same lineage.

For now, at least a section of the BJP seems to be on the defensive on the communal issue. But it is a party that made huge capital out of the demolition of the Babri Masjid. It will try to accumulate more capital out of the deaths of a few dozen, perhaps a few hundred, Christians. And there are similarities. As we know, top BJP leaders were present and vocal at the demolition but then blamed the demolition on a 'mob' that had supposedly got out of hand. That the 'mob' comprised the BJP, Vishwa Hindu Parishad (VHP), Shiv Sena, and the Bajrang Dal, which had openly vowed to demolish the Masjid and had rehearsed the event beforehand, was not something Mr Advani, President of the BJP at that time, and his colleagues were willing to grant.

This time around, the response has been even more brazen. Against documented evidence of punctual participation of the same *Hindutva* brigade, not to speak of the freshly muscled Hindu Jagran Munch (HJM), the same Mr Advani, now the Home Minister of India, has issued a clean chit to the Bajrang Dal and to the Sangh *parivar* in general. Instead, we are being told of a dark 'international conspiracy', not just by Keshubhai Patel, the Gujarat Chief Minister and a veteran of the RSS, but also by the BJP President, Kushabhau Thakre, as well as the Defence Minister of India, George Fernandes, who seems to have carved out for himself a place somewhat to the right of Murli Manohar Joshi, the latter probably not much more communal than Mr Advani but surely less suave. In a brief interview, Mr Thakre alleged a vast and improbable conspiracy that included the Left parties, the Congress (I), Pakistan, and perhaps even some unnamed Western powers. If these gentlemen are to be believed, the Christians are burning their own churches and Bibles simply to defame the BJP; in this scenario, then, the torching of Staines is just another attempt at defaming the ruling party. Meanwhile Mr Vajpayee plays, as he has played for a quarter-century, the role of reluctant saffronite and sad warrior. These role assignments, with Mr Advani and company breathing fire while the Prime Minister and his men speak of regret and atonement, have also become by now much too familiar. It was only to be expected that even though the involvement of the Bajrang Dal, a veritable terror squad of the RSS, has been reported widely in the media and suspected by the Orissa police, the Home Minister, himself a veteran of the RSS, would certify the Dal as 'good nationalists'.

Nor has the campaign of violence against Christians entirely abated in the aftermath of the Staines burning. Within the next ten days or so, reports of such violence were coming from states as far-flung as Kerala, Uttar Pradesh, and Orissa, including the alleged rape of a nun. And the

VHP's Dharm Sansad (religious parliament), which met in the midst of it all, demanded a white paper on 'conversions' and confirmed, as if on cue, that these 'conversions' were high on its agenda. On the issue of temple-building in Ayodhya, this crafty parliament of the pious spoke with a forked tongue: offering reprieve and 'postponement' in one sentence, promising to shift from preparation to construction in the next.

Most commentaries have emphasized the fact that this campaign of hate and violence has been centred on the state of Gujarat, where the BJP is the most secure and powerful and where the Christian community is small, insecure, and mostly scattered in the rural and forest areas. It has also been pointed out that the anti-Christian campaign, with its emphases on foreign funding and the foreignness of the religion itself, is also connected with the rise of Sonia Gandhi, born of a Catholic Italian family, to active leadership of the Congress. The threat from her has become especially palpable since the stunning defeat of the BJP by large margins, and the attendant resurgence of the Congress, in the recent Assembly elections in Madhya Pradesh, Rajasthan, and Delhi.

These circumstantial connections are undoubtedly there. What is striking about the overall pattern of this violence, however, is that while much of it is of course concentrated in Gujarat, it is also extremely widespread across the country. Aside from Uttar Pradesh, Kerala, and Orissa which we have already mentioned, murder, rape, burning of churches and Bibles, and many other violences of various kinds have also occurred in several other states, including Maharashtra, Karnataka, Tamil Nadu, Madhya Pradesh, West Bengal, Bihar, Delhi, and Haryana. Acts of this kind against Muslims have occurred in Jammu and Kashmir during these same months. And we of course know that various arms of the RSS have been extremely active in states of the northeast, even though we know of no acts of documented violence there in recent months.

Intensity may be lesser or greater in this state or that, in one region or another; we are clearly looking at the map of the whole country, however. I have called this low-intensity warfare and it is likely to continue for a prolonged period. The government's embarrassment at the murder of Staines, a white foreigner, and at the reaction from Western countries, especially the United States, to that murder, will probably serve to limit the intensity in the foreseeable future. By the same token, if and when the BJP and its parent organization so decide, the violence is likely to be ratcheted up. In any case, the national scope of this hate campaign reminds one, despite its currently low level, of the map of more spectacular communal violence that used to be drawn in India at the time of the various *yatras*, setting out from various corners of the country, when Muslims were the main target and when violence would erupt all along the routes of the *yatras*, eventually enveloping most parts of the country.

This similarity is not accidental. Rather, it would appear to be a part of the design. The RSS uses violence methodically, to define certain issues in certain ways, to focus everyone's attention on those issues, to try to build a national consensus and a widespread common sense along the lines defined by the RSS. At one time or another, they concentrate their power where they feel strongest. But a *national* consensus cannot be built in one corner of the country. For that, the net has to be spread wide. Through decades of experience, they have learned how to concentrate their forces and how to disperse them. And the numerical strength of those forces has kept growing, precisely through a politics of unremitting violence. Bajrang Dal alone, by its own confession, now has over two hundred centres in the country where it trains what amounts to a phalanx of stormtroopers. In the coming years, we are likely to see a quantum leap in the scale of attacks.

The calculations of the RSS are sinister, calm, shrewd. They know that the Indian middle classes, like middle classes everywhere, dislike too much outright violence. In order to be at length accepted by these classes that have a liberal self-image, incidents have to be sporadic and carefully calibrated. These middle classes get very perturbed while the violence is going on; numerous anti-communal groups crop up during such times, like clusters of seasonal mushrooms. When the violence subsides, most such groups decrease in size, and the thankless, colourless task of keeping some anti-communal work going again becomes restricted to a few untiring individuals, a handful of dedicated and imaginative groups such as Sahmat, or just the Left parties. It is in such times – times of calm *after* the storm – that the broad opinion actually shifts and what the RSS had proposed before the violence becomes part of the prevailing common sense. Thus it is that what in the 1950s would have been considered communal ideas are now a substantial part of liberal common sense, certainly in the northern and western states in India, but not only in these regions. In other words, RSS reaps the benefits of violence not while the violence is going on but afterwards, when much of the urban privileged classes accommodate themselves to their agenda.

Few liberals would approve, in retrospect, the demolition of the Babri Masjid, especially the manner of its destruction. But there is also a sense of great relief that the episode is behind us. And there are many more Indians in the urban middle classes than was the case some decades ago who believe that religion is central and constitutive in determining one's cultural identity; that Indian culture is in some primary way a Hindu culture; that Muslims and Christians do not really accept that culture;

and that in order to become 'true' Indians these religious minorities must join the so-called 'national mainstream'. This much the demolition, and the campaign that preceded and surrounded it, has achieved. The centre of ideological gravity has shifted, so that even the Congress (I) is, in its inimitably cynical fashion, constrained to say that Hinduism is the best guarantee of secularism in India. Those of us who are not Hindus, who believe in other religions or believe in none, are apparently not a part of this best guarantee. The *Organiser*, mouthpiece of the RSS, quite correctly pointed out that this has been the position of the RSS all along. With such parties at the helm, no one needs a weatherman to tell which way the wind blows.

After a few nuns have been raped, a few pastors attacked or murdered, a number of churches burned and Bibles defiled, while the country is also treated to scenes of 'reconversions' where at least some of those souls who have strayed into Christianity or Islam will rediscover their true Hindu identity, the country may seriously settle down, as Mr Vajpayee has proposed, to debate whether or not conversions from Hinduism to any other religion should be allowed, and under what conditions. (Conversions from other religions to Hinduism will always be allowed because that only reaffirms our national-religious ethos.) What Mr Vajpayee neglects to note is that this systematic violence is itself a form of debate, though one-sided and though with weapons quite different from words. For the RSS, it is simply a form of consciousness-raising for the nation as a whole. A few rapes and a few murders don't really matter, so long as the consciousness does get raised.

What consciousness? In a country like India, nationalism is an objective necessity. National unity against imperialism is the only rational basis for this nationalism. So, those who do not want to fight imperialist domination must invent some other basis for their nationalism. Inevitably they will claim a nationalism of 'blood and belonging'. They will promise to unify the nation in the name of race and religion, but they will only end up fragmenting it because race has no meaning in India, even though the founders of the RSS were much given to speaking of the 'Hindu race' very much on the Nazi model of the Aryan race; and because we have belief systems so very numerous as to defy categorization. For this reason, therefore, this RSS nationalism of blood, belonging, and culture wars has to be even more fictive and hysterical than would be the case in less heterogeneous societies. Only those of us who are committed to an anti-imperialist nationalism actually need a culture of broad religious tolerance because without such basic recognition of our internal diversities we cannot unify the nation against foreign capital. Those who need no such anti-imperialist unity can happily carry out orgies of violence.

One way of putting the matter is that the Hindu Jagran Munch

(HJM) exists because the Swadeshi Jagran Munch (SJM) is a fake through and through.[7] If you do not wish to fight imperialism you fight your own cousin and kin, in pursuit of an impossible purification. There was a time when adherents of Swadeshi used to burn foreign cloth. Now we burn our Christian fellow citizens because they are presumed to believe in a 'foreign' religion. Even the slogans become more bizarre: *Garv se kaho hum Hindu hain* (Say with pride that we are Hindus) becomes *Garv se kaho mein Campa Cola peeta hoon* (Say with pride that I drink Campa Cola), while the heights of the food-processing industry in reality get handed over to the likes of Pepsi, and human beings as well as crosses are burned in order to draw the imaginary line between *swadeshi* and *videshi*.[8]

Such brutal tactics have worked in the past. They may also work in the future. So one must ask: why does the RSS succeed, and succeed so spectacularly, through this politics of hate? One answer simply is: all rightwing extremists and religious zealots create a culture of cruelty and irrationality – a culture of racial or religious or national bigotries – which makes violence against minorities – or, more generally, 'internal enemies' – a permanent and defining element in obtaining a hysterical kind of unity of the purported religious majority under the banner of that bigotry. In conditions of crisis in which large sections of the population are resentful of the conditions in which they live, this resentment of the lumpen and the vagrant, especially among the poor and the petty bourgeois, can be mobilized to recruit the stormtroopers. That indeed is the basic profile of members of the Bajrang Dal, the Hindu Jagran Munch, and the like. And when the possessing classes have delusions of grandeur but live in conditions of misery typical of backward capitalist societies, far too many of them get attracted to a politics of blame; there must be internal enemies – religious minorities, secularists, Nehruvians, communists – who are preventing them from finding their own place in the sun. The RSS undoubtedly draws on all these resentments.

But there is something else that too is equally fundamental. A culture of communal cruelties finds its place in society at least partly because a broad and generalized culture of cruelties already exists. A little reflection on events of the past month, the first of this year, should clarify this point. The very day that Staines and his two little sons were burned in Orissa, a young and promising woman journalist, Shivani Bhatnagar, was killed in her Delhi flat, apparently by someone who knew her. The cause of the murder is not known, nor do we know for sure the identity of the men who had raped Anjana Mishra on the night of 9 January on a lonely road in Orissa, though one can be reasonably sure that the rapists had their orders from and were protected by the mighty in the state. For the argument at hand, the relevant point is that there are certain kinds of violence that are committed only against women, that they are committed routinely, and that their frequency makes it easier for others to practise the same kind of violence for communal reasons.

The month that saw the torching of Staines in Orissa also saw, in New Delhi, the killing of six individuals by a bunch of upper-class boys driving an unregistered BMW, imported into the country illegally, who then absconded from the scene of the crime and were caught only through the diligence of a lone police officer. These criminals are still arguing for a novel kind of plea bargain whereby they would be let off with little punishment in lieu of payments to the family members of the deceased; boys who can play around in cars worth 70 lakhs can clearly pay a great deal as 'blood money'. In the pages of *Frontline*, Praful Bidwai has correctly called this a 'class crime', symptomatic of the ethos of the super-rich spawned by the kind of capitalism we have been practising for a while.

The same month also witnessed, in Bihar, the gunning down of twenty-one *dalits*, several of them women and children, by the marauding goons of upper-caste landowners. On the day that these lines are being written, newspapers have reported the burning of a *dalit* woman, also in Bihar, by a man to whom she owed some money. It is very much to President Narayanan's credit that he denounced not only the Staines burning in Orissa but also the crime of the Ranbir Sena[9] in Bihar. The point, in any case, is that caste violence is at least as common as communal violence, and that this particular *dalit* could be burned all the more easily because she was a woman.

Finally, there is the steep decline in the civic ethos that underlies the conduct of our politics. The BJP rules with the cooperation of rather a large number of allies, which include everyone from Farooq Abdullah, the purported leader of Kashmiri Muslims, to the Akalis, the puported leaders of Sikhs. These allies have witnessed almost a year of this violence without protest, let alone dissociating themselves from the coalition. Now that national as well as international pressure is picking up, these allies have adopted an astonishing posture: they demand that the BJP distance itself from its parent organization – the RSS, which BJP leaders like Vajpayee and Advani call their *mata* (mother) – but they are not willing to leave the coalition government themselves. It is like the Pakistan army during the Bangladesh carnage; every officer knew what was going on but none ever resigned on the issue. Our two countries indeed have a great deal in common.

Gender, class, caste. These are the perennial and fundamental sources of violence in our society. Communal violence is a particular social pathology which is being practised on a large and escalating scale for reasons strictly of political power, by a fraternity of organizations that includes the ruling party. In that sense, it has a unique salience for us all. However, such organizations can continue to command prestige in society, even to the extent of becoming the governing party, because those other kinds of brutality make communal violence seem part of the normal patterns of life.

The politics of hate that sets the political agenda today, as the RSS targets minorities, is as venerable as the century-old process that has gone into the making of modern India. It is more influential today than ever. In most instances of such politics, religious extremism plays the same role that racialism has played in the history of European fascisms. Indeed, religion itself is viewed in such tendencies primarily not as spiritual faith or a system of beliefs but as racial particularity and civilizational essence.

For Savarkar, the revered forefather of this extremism who was not even notably devout, what all Hindus share is 'common blood'. According to him, then, those Indians for whom India is undeniably a *janm-bhoomi* (birthplace) but who subscribe to other religions have fallen out of this mainstream of blood and belonging. They have thus lost their rights as equal members of this nation and should therefore be prepared for repression or even extermination. As he eloquently put it:

> Germany has also shown how well nigh impossible it is for Races and cultures, having differences going to the root, to be assimilated into one united whole, a good lesson for us in Hindustan to learn and profit by.

It is worth emphasizing, though, that unlike Hitler, for whom the crossing over from one race to another was simply impossible, Savarkar does offer to non-Hindu 'races' an alternative: namely, that they can rejoin this mainstream if they convert to Hinduism and bring up their children as Hindus. Biologistic racialism is here, straight out of the Nazi ideology, but subordinated to a far more determining majoritarian culturalism; culture indeed functions, more or less, *as* biology.[10]

This demand, made some eighty years ago by one of the illustrious founders of *Hindutva*, sheds a rather interesting light not only on the VHP's ongoing terror campaign against hapless Christians in Gujarat, precisely on the issue of conversions, but also on the proposition advocated by Prime Minister Vajpayee, an old veteran of the Savarkar-inspired RSS, that there should be a national debate on this issue. 'Conversion' has been central to the very ethos of RSS extremism, as bogey, as project, and as threat.

They begin with a semantic sleight of hand. Opting out of Hinduism for some other religion is called 'conversion'; opting out of some other religion in favour of Hinduism is called '*re*-conversion'. The dominant media just take up this vocabulary and assist in creating a sort of common sense that anyone who is converting to Christianity or Islam is doing something out of the ordinary, possibly something anti-national as well (the famous 'foreign hand'!), whereas anyone converting to Hinduism is only returning to his or her true essence.

If a Christian mission, after having been in the area for a hundred years or more, manages to convert some 25,000 souls whom we, in our infinite wisdom, continue to call 'tribal' and/or 'untouchable', because these damned of this earth see in even the most miserable form of Christianity a way out of the filth of a caste-ridden society, that is said to be emergency enough for the nation solemnly to 'debate' the matter, while the various offspring of the RSS carry out their campaigns to kill and burn. But if a functionary of the BJP announces an explicit plan to convert a hundred thousand or more to Hinduism within a year, he is supposed to be doing only the natural thing, the right thing, because he has the rights of the twice-born: born first as Hindu and therefore, logically, as the 'true' Indian as well. And the rights of this variety of the twice-born include their ability to hold out the threat that those who do not 're-convert' shall be treated as pariahs, even non-citizens.

It was well before the Partition of 1947, when over a quarter of the Indian population belonged to organized religions other than 'Hinduism' even in its broadest definition, that Hindu extremism – the RSS, the Hindu Mahasabha, and the rest – adopted Savarkar's notion that only a Hindu was a 'true' Indian, and that the rest could be treated as 'true' Indians only if they converted to Hinduism. In claiming that a quarter or more of the population should convert to a particular religion or else be denied equal status in society, Savarkar's was undoubtedly the most ambitious plan in pursuit of conversions that modern India has known. Neither the Christian missions nor the Tabligh movement spawned by the Muslim clergy can offer anything even vaguely comparable in scope or ambition.

But for the power and devotion of the RSS to the pursuit of this design, one would dismiss the Savarkar project as one of those crackpot ideas that extremists think up. Given the power and the devotion, however, one has to take stock of the long-term implications of the project, and in doing that one has to understand what is unique about the RSS and the way in which it organizes this project, quite beyond the electoral calculus.

Since its inception during the 1920s, the RSS has been primarily interested, from the side of the extreme Right, in what Gramsci once called a 'war of position'. It has been aimed, in other words, not at short-term electoral power but at long-term historical change. For this reason, then, it is really not possible to gauge the power of the RSS from the electoral fortunes of the BJP, especially if we do not sufficiently appreciate that the design for historic change may go on even as electoral fortunes fluctuate. In that larger project of historical change, RSS has always calculated, I believe correctly, that if they can continue successfully to engineer fundamental cultural change, dividends in the electoral arena may come later but will then come more reliably and enduringly.

A second and crucial element, a secondary layer as it were, was added during the 1950s and has been a part of their design ever since, for reasons very palpable. Once the republic of the bourgeoisie emerged as the primary form of rule in independent India, the RSS understood, after some floundering, as everyone else in India also understood, also after some floundering, that the electoral process would be the one through which governments would now rise and fall, in any foreseeable future. This process the RSS has sought to address, and has so far addressed with impressive success, first through the Jan Sangh, which culminated in its central role in the Janata government that emerged after the Emergency, and then through the BJP, an extremely sophisticated political machinery in charge of a government these days which is run strictly by veterans of the RSS; there is hardly any significant leader of the BJP who is not such a veteran.

This game, too, the RSS has played with dexterity. Ordinarily, in mature bourgeois democracies, there are very sharp constraints within which any political force is permitted to propagate its politics of hate. In Germany or Italy, for example, where stable democracy is not much older than in India and where neo-Nazis and neo-fascists have a fairly strong presence, the politics of hate in the postwar period has so far been contained on the margins of society. In India, by contrast, and through much trial and error over virtually half a century, the RSS has understood that the constraints are much less operative, but also that some do exist. The BJP is there to test the limits of those constraints so as constantly to expand the scope for irrationalist politics, but also to capture governmental power within the general framework of those constraints, however brittle they may be.

The main objective of the RSS is not parliamentary politics, however, but the politics of hate. It seeks to undo the traditions of secularism, democracy, and socialism that have been embedded so powerfully in at least a substantial part of modern India, and to remake the whole of India in its own image. Most of that project it pursues not through the BJP, the parliamentary front, but through the other fronts, such as the VHP and the Bajrang Dal, designed more specifically for those purposes. A mark of their great success is that they have convinced the liberal media, and perhaps many beyond even the liberal media, that the distinction between BJP and VHP is not merely procedural but real, and that what we are witnessing is not a division of labour within a cluster of fraternal groupings but a fundamental political difference among fronts of the RSS itself.

Some of that basic project of uniting a majority of Hindus the RSS pursues through the BJP as well, however, and it is a sad comment on the nature of our polity that the BJP has benefited so spectacularly from campaigns of hate. This too we find difficult to concede. It is thought best not to recall, for example, that in the elections of 1989, which marked the resurgence of the BJP that is not yet over, 47 of the 88 constituencies it captured were ones which had experienced the most virulent forms of communal violence during the preceding year.

Nor is it comfortable for us to contemplate the possibility that this politics of hate may actually be popular among key sectors of the Indian polity, notably the professional middle classes and the trading bourgeoisie in northern India. Thus, for example, a MARG opinion poll conducted soon after the destruction of Babri Masjid and in the midst of the massive communal violence that ensued, showed that 52.6 per cent of those interviewed in the north approved of the demolition (as against 16.7 per cent in the south, it must be added).

That this is a derangement especially common among the well-off becomes refreshingly obvious, however, if we consider yet another statistic from roughly the same time: a survey conducted in Delhi and western Uttar Pradesh showed that while 60 per cent of the white collar professionals and 62 per cent of the traders approved of the demolition, among workers the support fell to 28 per cent.

The point in citing these statistics is not to suggest that the politics of hate has some inexorable logic in our society, equally among all classes and regions in the country. The point is to say, rather, that it is much more popular among the beneficiaries of the system than among its victims, and that it is most effective among the social segments and in regions which have been much more influenced by rightwing politics in general.

Having said that, it is also the case that the consent it commands is very widespread in society, especially among the politically powerful and influential segments; and that this consent has been very much on the increase. What accounts for this power of the politics of hate in a society where at least the urban intelligentsia cultivates for itself and for the country an image of liberal tolerance, benign spirituality, etc.?

The first reason can be traced, I believe, to the earliest period of our modernity, and to the colonial character of this modernity. The very sense of history of the first generations of the Bengali intelligentsia, for example, was deeply marked by the colonially propagated ideologies of Aryan identity, Vedic purity, and 'Muslim tyranny', which criss-crossed with beliefs of the Hindu upper castes themselves; Orientalist knowledge of that kind was born in something of a symbiosis with certain basic properties of the brahminical world-view. The typical reform movements of the late nineteenth century were markedly revivalist in character, except when they were explicitly of the downtrodden castes and therefore anti-brahmincial as such. Based as they were among the beneficiaries of traditional systems of caste and property, the reformers frequently had a vested interest in propagating a romantic notion of the cultures of the upper castes to which they themselves belonged and which were now presented as the very essence of being 'Indian' and 'Hindu'.

Precisely at the time, during the closing years of the nineteenth century and the opening years of the twentieth, when representatives of Indian economic nationalism were formulating analytic procedures for explaining colonial exploitations, some of the most influential figures in the literary and cultural fields were deeply attracted by a cultural nationalism that was distinctly revivalist in character and religiously exclusivist by implication. Neither Bankim nor Aurobindo, neither the Swadeshi Movement in Bengal nor the Shivaji cult propagated in Maharashtra by such icons of Indian nationalism as Tilak himself, were entirely untainted by that kind of revivalist fervour. Indeed, so powerful was the revivalist culture of the upper castes that when anti-brahminical movements surfaced in Maharashtra, whether under Phule or Ambedkar, it was the extremity of the backlash of the upper castes in that region that gave us the RSS in the first place.

This is not to say that either Tilak or Aurobindo would be quite approving of what the *Hindutva* of our own day is and does. And yet there is enough there for a common sense to prevail today among sections of the urban upper castes and middle classes, in various parts of India, especially the northern and the western, and for them to be persuaded that the social vision and cultural idiom of this modern-day *Hindutva* is descended from that general ambience of our 'renaissance' and 'awakening'.

The potentials of that kind of revivalism were so pernicious that Tagore was to warn at length, already in the second decade of this century, that there was only a short step from revivalist zealotry to communal frenzy. In two of his major novels, *Gora* and *Home and the World*, whatever their shortcomings, Tagore was to portray with great sensitivity and acumen how revivalist politics and communal closures may be particularly tempting to the socially insecure and the upwardly mobile.

That, then, is the first point: the sheer persistence of brahminical revivalisms at the very heart of what were expected to be structures of our modernity and which never did give us any kind of modernity, precisely because of the authorization and sustenance they received from the colonial and brahminical representations of Indian history and thanks to their own interest in representing their caste cultures as our 'national culture'. Needless to add, this was a two-way traffic, in the sense that colonial representations of Indian history and Hindu religion relied crucially on what they learned from their interpreters, translators, and native informants, who themselves were drawn, as a rule, from among the upper castes. Modern-day *Hindutva* has derived much comfort from those earlier revivalisms.

One could also say that since the advent of mass politics in India during roughly the 1920s, there have been essentially three alternative visions competing for dominance here. There is of course the vision represented by the communists as well as the independent Left, which has been committed to creating a modern, civil, secular, democratic culture and which has held that such a culture cannot come into being, in the specific conditions prevailing in India, without also building a genuinely socialist society: socialist in a sense far more radical than the Nehruvian. Second, more widespread and powerful, has been what one might call the vision of national independence together with social reform, industrial capitalism, and a political democracy – in short, a modern bourgeois order. That, in essence, was Nehru's dream. Finally, there has been the conservative, caste-based elitism which came eventually to be monopolized by the RSS, with considerable fuel from the Hindu Mahasabha, which had itself come into being in opposition to both the communist and the bourgeois-nationalist movements.

If the communist movement was inspired by Marxism, Hindu extremism was undoubtedly inspired by fascism, as the direct links between Italian Fascists and such leaders of this extremism as Moonje and Shyama Prasad Mukerjee would testify.[11] The conflict between the two visions was inevitable because they represented radically opposed visions, both on the national and the international scales. Within the country, though, the second vision, that of capitalist democracy in the framework of an independent polity, was by far the dominant one. Whether a culture of civic virtues or a culture of hate and cruelty prevails in our country has depended, in general, on the actual balance of forces among these competing visions, which we could also describe as visions associated with the Left, the Centre, and the Right, respectively. Whether or not the Right can be contained will depend, in other words, on whether or not the Centre will hold and incline, for its own survival if not anything else, towards the Left.

The politics of hate has been both the moment of birth and the chief instrument of expansion for the RSS, considering that it was founded in the aftermath of the Nagpur riots of 1923 and was already playing a role in the later riots of 1927 in the same city. Then, before Independence, the RSS had two brief moments of growth: between 1939 and 1942, with the outbreak of the Second World War and the 'Quit India' movement, when the National Movement was very much on the defensive and the colonial state was assisting all kinds of communal forces; and again during the 1946–48 period, when the RSS had much room for action in the midst of the communal holocaust that accompanied the Partition. Its involvement in the assassination of Mahatma Gandhi put an end to all that, however, even though Sardar Patel, the powerful Home Minister of that time who was also a rival of Nehru from the side of the Right within the Congress, did get the RSS off the hook by legalizing it again after a brief ban which followed that assassination.

The astonishing fact about communal violence in India is that it was at its lowest level of intensity during the first decade after Independence, when the memory of the Partition and the attendant slaughter was sharpest; and that the intensity of this violence has increased with every succeeding decade even though the Partition, which is said to explain this virulence in northern India, keeps getting more distant in time.

Although Nehru was relatively isolated even within the Congress, he and his associates seem to have been successful in stemming the communal tide during the 1950s. Political discourse in the nation was preoccupied with issues of land reform, planned development, and India's place among the newly decolonized states and in the anti-imperialist movement of the non-aligned. The Communist Party was the main opposition, and the contest therefore was between what we have described as visions of the Left and the Centre. The Right – the RSS with its newly formed parliamentary front of the Jan Sangh – was simply sidelined.

What began to happen thereafter is that the Centre, or what could have been the Centre, kept collapsing. Powerful elements of the ruling class in northern India, from the former ruling families of the princely states to sundry Marwari capitalists, patronized the RSS with a vengeance; Vajpayee's own early parliamentary career from Gwalior is inconceivable without the key patronage of the Scindias, the local royalty who kept one foot in the Congress and the other in the RSS. Then there was the political elite, some of whom came from the upper classes while others didn't. The roll call of those who were associated with the RSS in one way or another is embarrassing for all those who believe in some essential secularism or even civic decency of this elite. From Patel to Gulzarilal Nanda, with Jayaprakash Narayan and the whole Sarvodaya crowd in between, not to speak of myriads such as Dr Karan Singh, the Dogra prince from J&K, large sections of this elite, so polite and liberal otherwise, trusted and cooperated with the RSS quite happily.

But then there were at least two other features of politics in India during the period after the 1960s, as communal violence began to escalate, which contributed to giving us a more generalized culture of cruelty. One was the routine participation of large numbers of police and paramilitary personnel in communal violence, almost always on the side of Hindu communalism and across a wide territory from, let us say, Meerut and Moradabad in Uttar Pradesh to Ahmedabad or Surat in Gujarat or Bombay in Maharashtra, without fear of any severe punishment from the ruling party of the day. The second was the propensity of the Congress itself to play what was quaintly called 'the communal card', so that one was faced with a macabre field of competing communalisms practised unequally but fervently by what were once conceived of as the 'Centre' and the 'Right', and it became difficult to differentiate between the pragmatic and the programmatic communalisms of the respective parties.

It is in this larger context, then, that images of those burned houses and torched crosses can be flashed into the living-rooms of the affluent across the country, and nothing really happens in response. This kind of indifference to communal violence is made all the more possible because the victims are poor and, even as Christians, at the lowest possible rung of the caste society. It is only the cynicism of the VHP which can terrorize them on the one hand and urge them, in the same breath, to return to a Hindu fold that was never very keen on them in the first place. Communal violence is combined here with that of caste and class. What has become more marked in independent India with each passing decade is not just a vortex of communal hatreds but a much wider culture of cruelty in which polarization of castes and classes has been quite as bloody as conflicts between religious or denominational communities that are so methodically engineered by the far Right and often have the character of pogroms carried out by its disciplined cadres.

A culture of cruelties serves at least two broad functions for the dominant classes and social strata as well as the fascist core of the RSS. On the one hand, its sheer scale and persistence promotes certain types of moral numbness, amnesia, and schizophrenia, while also maintaining a rigid wall that separates the powerful from the powerless. Knowledgeable journalists who have studied the situation on the ground, such as P. Sainath, have estimated that in the not so populous state of Rajasthan alone, *dalit* women get raped by men of the upper castes at an average of one every three days; the total number of such cases registered across the country has in some years exceeded 26,000. Estimates published in *India Today* claim that in the country as a whole women face a dowry death every 1 hour and 42 minutes, a rape every 54 minutes, a molestation every 26 minutes. Class and caste violence intersects with this gender-based violence in countless ways, so that the permanent structure of cruelties in society is in fact immeasurably greater than even these statistics suggest.

Now, it is not possible for a society to reproduce itself on such a basis without regarding violence against women, against dominated castes and the working classes, as something reprehensible and yet inevitable, as if it was in the order of nature itself. Nor is it possible, for those who are themselves liberal in social views, compassionate in family life but not much involved in political mobilization on such issues, to live with facts of this order without developing a very elaborate mechanism of forgetfulness, to treat each event of cruelty as if it were unique, out of the ordinary, an affair of fringe criminality, not a social pathology that might involve themselves; in order to treat today's cruelty in that manner, one must constantly forget the sheer persistence of such cruelties one has known from the past. One must also cultivate a certain degree of schizophrenia if one is to live daily in the midst of mass cruelty in one's real life, while at the same time maintaining, at some level of ideality, that India has some unique civilizational mission in the annals of the world, which runs, in some pristine purity, from Buddha to Mahatma Gandhi.

Such moral numbness, amnesia, and schizophrenia promote extraordinary brutality against a broad range of the powerless and the despised, and help create what one might call the mass psychology of fascism. In this context, then, the killing of a few Christians or a few Muslims here and there loses its capacity to shock – beyond the day, the week, the month – those who are not affected or victimized by it. They learn to think of it as deplorable, but strange, remote, a product of some local resentment against the Christian missionaries or – as more and more learn to argue – an expression of the 'Hindu hurt' at the memory of India once having been conquered by invaders who subscribed to Islam.

This passive acceptance of communal violence, alongside other forms of violence, by broad sections of society is one consequence of what I have called a culture of cruelty. But it also facilitates the acceptance, frequently through indifference, of the more extreme forms of politically motivated – indeed, politically *organized* – violence of the far Right, as it sets out to redefine Indian nationalism in a fascistic direction. Here, too, all kinds of amnesia and evasion are at work. Everyone knows that the RSS is classically an organization of fascist inspiration; that the BJP is a parliamentary front that the RSS utilizes with the specific purpose of capturing governmental power; that the Hindu Jagran Munch (HJM) is another front of the RSS, specifically designed for mass propaganda in favour of a hysterical kind of Hindu extremism; that the VHP, Durga Vahini, Bajrang Dal, and several other fronts are organized precisely on the model of fascist terror squads, also by the RSS; and that all these fronts, together with perhaps fifty or more other secret and not so secret fronts, proudly proclaim themselves to be members of a single family (*parivar*) headed by the RSS itself. All this is very well known and surfaces, by fits and starts, in the scholarship and media coverage related to these organizations. And yet, the politics of evasion and amnesia requires that in the normal course of events, whenever the level of violence returns from the spectacular to the routine, the liberal scholars and media personalities themselves would portray the BJP simply as a normal party, very much like the Congress, a bit further to the Right but also more efficient, and not a child, really, of the RSS; that the liberal media would similarly report the cruelties of the Bajrang Dal as something entirely separable from the settled objectives of the BJP; that every time the BJP promises to suspend any aspect of its extremist programme, the media would follow with the suggestion that the more power accrues to the BJP the more liberal it would become; that Mr Vajpayee, who has been a member of the RSS for almost sixty years, be punctually portrayed as a man of great liberal sagacity; and so on.

This politics of evasion and amnesia among liberal scholars and media persons corresponds, then, to the politics of opportunism among the organized parties. With the exception of the Left parties, there is none that would not make deals with the BJP if and when the occasion arises. In 1996, when the BJP first emerged as the largest party in Parliament, it was unable to find a single ally among the dozen or so others. We persuaded ourselves that this isolation of the BJP resulted from the sturdiness of our secular traditions. The simple fact was that the BJP had fallen much too short of the majority and none of the smaller parties joined it in coalition because the alternative coalition, which came to be called the National Front (NF), had many more seats and a greater chance of forming a reasonably durable government, with the support of the Congress (I). As the National Front began to unravel over the next year and a half, the BJP's isolation also ended, and one party after another started joining its electoral coalition, until the elections of 1998 produced the government of a BJP-led coalition comprising eighteen parties, including Farooq Abdullah's National Conference with all its special claims to represent Kashmiri Muslims. By the time this coalition came to face the vote of confidence in Parliament on 17 April 1999, when it lost the support of Ms Jayalalitha and her contingent of eighteen MPs, Dravida Munnetra Kazhagam (DMK) of Tamil Nadu, which once had its roots in the legendary traditions of rationalism and secularism in the Tamil Nadu of yesteryears, joined the BJP coalition, for reasons of purely cynical electoral calculation for the future, even as the coalition in fact lost the vote of confidence. As I prepare the final draft of the present text, the media are rife with news stories of a broad spectrum of former socialists, including some who rose to prominence as leaders of *dalits* or the insurgent middle castes and have had long careers in opposition to the BJP, that are coming together in a new configuration intending to contest the impending general elections in alliance with the BJP. The number of forces that have moved from centrist and anti-BJP positions into a full-scale coalition with it is now so large that a BJP-led alliance is likely to emerge as a durable ruling coalition; if they managed to rule for merely thirteen days in the first round and then for thirteen months in the second before losing on the vote of confidence, the short period they have spent as a defeated but caretaker government has seen them garner enough support to rule for perhaps the full five-year term in the third round. That's when they will complete their 'long march through the institutions' and the centre of gravity will then have shifted decisively in favour of the RSS. That appears to be the logic at work at least for the present, and this logic reinforces the historic fact that the far Right has hardly ever come to command a parliamentary majority on its own until after substantive forces from the liberal centre have wandered into its camp.

A widespread culture of cruelty at the base in society at large, rampant opportunism in the political superstructure, an evasive liberal intelligentsia to negotiate the space between the society and its political superstructure – such is the combination that is making the task of the far Right so much easier. Mr Vajpayee, the darling of the liberal media, is the friendly face of this creeping fascism.

I have alternately used different terms: fascism, far Right, rightwing authoritarianism, and so on. Meanwhile, much ink has been spilt in Indian academic discourse to determine whether or not it is permissible to speak of fascism in this context. The favoured term that has emerged is 'Hindu nationalism' or, more generically and vaguely, 'ethno-religious nationalism'. Such alternative terms have their uses, I suppose, but they beg the question on at least six counts. First, this is clearly not the way the majority of Hindus in India have expressed their nationalism; what purpose is served by dignifying RSS extremism with the term 'Hindu nationalism', if not unwittingly to concede the RSS thesis that Hindus who do not subscribe to this extremism are not true to their nation, which is not secular Indian but specifically Hindu? Second, nationalisms are of various kinds. What kind of nationalism is it that arises in a multireligious society, identifies itself with a particular religious entity, bars the rest from this nationalism, so that religion comes to function here more or less as a racism? The fact that boundaries between race, religion, and culture are blurred only highlights the fact that in a great many ideologies of the far Right – and not only the far Right – in these postmodern times, 'culture' frequently functions pretty much the way 'race' used to serve in those other ideologies of the far Right that were decended more directly from nineteenth-century biologism, evolution-ism, and the conjunction of these pseudo-scientific ideas with imperialist ideologies in general.

Third, all fascisms include a pathological kind of nationalism as a key component of their ideologies; one can surely be both a fascist and a 'Hindu nationalist' just as one can be both a Nazi as well as a devout believer in the superiority of the Aryan race, German destiny, Semitic subversion of that destiny, and so on. Fourth, different nationalisms – all the way from the fascist to the communist – are undoubtedly distinguishable from each other in terms of their ideology, their organi-zational forms, their objectives, their mobilizational techniques, the social composition of their mass base, etc.; aside from being 'Hindu', what is the nature of this 'nationalism' in relation to all those other characteristics? Fifth, 'nationalism' was not some empty terrain in India before this 'Hindu nationalism' arose to occupy it, so that there are historical geneses to be accounted for; what has been the relationship between the nationalism which first created the Republic in independent India and this latter-day 'Hindu nationalism' which now wishes to restructure it so very radically? And, finally, no two fascisms in history have ever been identical. The real question is not whether or not a movement can be called 'fascist' even if it does not fully correspond to its historical predecessor in Italy; much more interesting is to ask what fascism would look like if it were ever to come to India.

In 1996, when the BJP first formed a government – for thirteen days before resigning for lack of strength in the House – there was much fear expressed that fascism had finally come to India. I had then argued that a distinction must always be made between the parent organization, namely the RSS which was undoubtedly fascist, and its parliamentary front, the BJP, whose function was to play strictly by the rules of constitutional democracy, gather more and more support for its own projects and thus pave the way for a *future* government of the RSS itself, in the real sense; a government led by the BJP but including a wide range of allies was likely to be a transitional government of rightwing authoritarianism which, under the given circumstances, was not likely to last for long.[12]

That the BJP government was at that time so quickly defeated was undoubtedly a great blessing, but that it was able to form government at all actually strengthened it a great deal; polls taken at that time seemed to suggest that the fact of forming the government had expanded its electoral base by roughly 4 per cent. This, combined with the inner erosion of the National Front and especially the perfidy of Congress (I), which summarily withdrew support from the NF government for spurious reasons, greatly contributed to the BJP's ability to gather coalition partners and form a more durable government after the elections of 1998. That government has now lost the confidence of the House, is functioning as only a caretaker, and will face fresh elections in September 1999. However, the disarray in the ranks of the Opposition, the fact that the BJP was the government in power at the time of the fighting in Kargil and would therefore be the main beneficiary of the patriotic fervour which arose in response, and the very fact that it ruled for over a year with the help of a broad coalition, would suggest that it is likely to return with an enlarged mandate.

The fact that the BJP at the Centre led so diverse a coalition meant that it could not function even as a transitional regime in its own right and had to modify greatly even its minimum programme. But it did manage to install a regime that was itself transitional towards the kind of transition it hopes to make if and when it comes to power with a clear majority. How so? First, the degree of consent it managed to elicit from its allies. It is significant that all the communal killings carried out by the RSS confederacy which we discussed earlier did not lead to the threat of withdrawal of support from even one of its seventeen allies. This consent has been taken so much for granted that George Fernandes of the Samata Party seems to have been the only one among the allies who has been consulted in any of the major policy initiatives, and even he was kept in the dark at the time of the momentous decision to undertake nuclear explosions, though he was the Defence Minister. It is a characteristic feature of the politics of opportunism we mentioned earlier that the BJP bought off its motley group of allies by conceding their sectional demands – such as protecting them from prosecution for corruption – while they ceded to the BJP full control over governance.

This relatively free hand for the BJP, even though it is yet to form a government exclusively of its own, without relying on powerful allies with a mind of their own, has meant that it has also been free to use the governmental machinery to consolidate even further its relations with the bourgeoisie, diversely, at all levels of property, as well as to conduct what I have earlier called a long march through the institutions, that is to say, appointing numerous personnel of its own at all levels of military and civilian bureaucracies, educational and cultural organizations, planning and policy establishments, etc., and to penetrate even the autonomous institutions in civil society by channelling government funds in one direction rather than another. This last element – the long march through the institutions – is, I believe, crucial. I have argued previously that once it became quite clear that parliamentary democracy was here to stay and enduring power in India could not be gained through frontal attacks and *coups d'état*, the RSS settled for something resembling a 'war of position'. This had three prongs. One, mass work, by the RSS itself and its numerous fronts, branches (*shakhas*), network of schools (*shishu mandirs*) and so on, so as to create an alternative ideological and cultural climate among various strata of society as well as to recruit cadres and active sympathizers. Second, parliamentary politics, through first the Jan Sangh and then the BJP, methodically supplemented by the other mass organizations as well as the stormtroopers of the VHP, etc., by combining the legal with the extralegal in mass mobilizations. And third, penetration of the liberal professions and the state apparatuses. As has been the case in the individual states where the BJP has formed government in the past, the BJP-led government at the Centre has now been an important instrument in greatly accelerating the process of change at all three levels, even though the BJP itself has yet to form a government of its own, which it is now all the more likely to do in the foreseeable future. It is in this sense that one can say that a real transition is yet to begin but that we are witnessing a transition to that transition.[13]

The fundamental premise of my argument here is that India is at present undergoing a revolutionary process. We do not recognize it as such because it is a revolution not of the Left but of the far Right. Whether this revolution will fail or succeed is far from clear, nor is it at all clear that even the simple territorial unity of the country will survive the fires that this offensive has lit. The cultures of cruelty spreading all around us are a part of this far Right revolutionary offensive because values of democratic, secular civility must be made to crumble from the inside. And structures that correspond to those values must be eroded from the inside because, in the conditions of electoral and parliamentary democracy prevailing in India today, what the far Right visualizes and prepares for is not a frontal seizure of power but a hurricane from below, carried out by a widespread and pliable mass of the wretched of this earth led by a well-disciplined counter-revolutionary elite.

I have written elsewhere, more or less polemically, that every country gets the fascism that it deserves, by which I simply mean that the specific form that a fascist movement takes shall always depend on the social physiognomy of that country: that is to say, the economic, political, philosophical, aesthetic, religious, cultural, and ideological forms specific to that country.[14] India is no exception to this rule, and to identify the forms specific to our experience we have to look downwards and inwards. But the Indian experience cannot be extricated from the experience of the modern world as a whole. So we need a very firm sense of our unique particularity within which certain types of politics are organized, but also some holistic and comparatist knowledges of what are, after all, global trends. It is in order to locate the broad phenomenon that has come to be associated with the idea of 'fascism' in this larger story that one needs to be mindful of the actual origins of this kind of politics in the late nineteenth century, in France and

Germany notably. I should also want to offer a certain principle of periodization for our experience of this kind of politics during the present century, which is based on a contrast that runs as follows.

The politics of the far Right, which always includes lesser or greater degrees of fascistic content, has of course remained a punctual though not usually the dominant political tendency throughout the whole of the imperialist period. However, there have been two quite different historical moments when the epidemic of such movements has become particularly widespread, for somewhat different structural reasons. Thus, we might say that the fascisms of the inter-war period corresponded to the crises of accumulation brought about by the maturing of imperialism itself as it made a fuller transition from the competitive to the monopoly structure of capital. This is an explanation that Baran and Sweezy, among others, and Poulantzas in his own way, have accepted; and I would add that whereas movements of this kind were particularly strong in the core countries of Europe, their influence spread through much of the world, from Japan to Iraq, Syria and Lebanon, and from Argentina to India. By contrast, the end-of-the-century politics of the far Right, including its fascistic component, corresponds to the late imperial period of full globalization of the capitalist mode, in which capitalism has already triumphed over communist states but faces internal crises of stagnation in the core countries and unmanageable social tensions in the less industrialized countries, brought about in part by that imperialist globalization and in part by the defeat or decay of the socialist, democratic, and secular-nationalist projects within the imperialized countries.

This principle of periodization seems useful on three counts. First, it clarifies the point that since today's insurgencies of the far Right belong in an entirely novel period of modern history, they cannot repeat the experience and the forms of an earlier and very different period. They have to be understood both in terms of their lineage as well as their originality. Second, the characterization of the later, more contemporary phase helps us understand a certain reversal: whereas the scale of violence in such malignant movements has so far been quite manageable for the constitutional governments of Western Europe, they have erupted with far greater ferocity in the peripheries of the system where conditions of crisis are more advanced, especially in some central European and Asian zones including, notably, India. Whether Russia will go the way of Serbia is not yet clear. Third, this sense of the scope of malignancy also clarifies that what we are dealing with here is not some kind of Indian exceptionalism – a mere 'Hindu nationalism' – but a generalized experience of our time that is taking specific forms in our own country.

Of Dictators and Democrats:
Indo-Pakistan Politics in the Year 2000

As a military takeover in Pakistan coincided almost perfectly with the announcement of the latest election results in India, political equations in South Asia changed dramatically in the second week of October 1999. This chapter, drafted in March 2000, will attempt to summarize the main features of the Indian elections as well as the takeover in Pakistan, but with the aim of looking at these developments not separately but in conjunction, to clarify what all this might portend for Indo-Pakistan politics as a whole in the foreseeable future. The essential contention here is that the extreme and dangerous volatility that India introduced into subcontinental politics with the Pokhran explosions, and which Pakistan then escalated with the Kargil adventure, continues and has become worse in a framework where a government led by a political party, the BJP, that doubles as the primary parliamentary front of the RSS, has emerged stronger than ever in India. Domestically, this formation of the far Right has succeeded in gathering around itself a formidable coalition of allies and has armed itself with a new doctrine of 'credible minimum nuclear deterrent' and of a 'limited war' facilitated by that deterrent and underwritten by huge increases in military expenditures. Externally, it has acquired a brand new 'strategic partnership' with the United States which includes cooperation over 'anti-terrorist' activities against 'Islamic fundamentalism' across national frontiers. This extraordinary conjunction of domestic strengths and external alliances, in the midst of a war hysteria fed by the insurgency in Kashmir, constitutes the main danger to peace in the subcontinent. General Parvez Musharraf's military takeover in Pakistan is, by comparison, tame, defensive, and beleaguered.

I

Though they did mark a new watershed in modern Indian politics, the election results of October 1999 were on the whole unsurprising. When the BJP was first invited to form the government in 1996, without a single ally in Parliament, its government had lasted for barely thirteen days but the media exposure it thus received, combined with the very idea that it *could* emerge as the ruling party, is estimated to have added 4 per cent to its electoral base at that time. This new eminence then meant that a number of the smaller, regional parties that had previously found it impossible to entertain the idea of aligning with the BJP now began gravitating towards such an alliance; a fundamental taboo of Indian politics had been broken. The BJP had acquired quite a few such allies by the time the elections of 1998 came around and then gained several more after the elections, as power seemed within reach. With a motley crowd of these allies, it ruled for thirteen months this time, and then for another few months as a caretaker government, before the 1999 elections, when the Opposition that had defeated the BJP-led government in a vote of confidence on the floor of Parliament failed to form a government of its own.

The BJP, then, went into the elections with several advantages. Heading a precarious coalition, it had ruled for just over a year but the Opposition had simply fallen apart. The BJP was increasingly seen as the natural party of rule, a strong successor to Congress (I), and was thus able to gain support from a broad coalition among the erstwhile secular-centrist parties, houses of business and industry, media barons, etc. It went into the polls this time heading a much more formidable alliance of parties, and although the BJP itself failed to increase the number of its own seats in Parliament while its share of the national vote actually fell by two percentage points, the National Democratic Alliance (NDA) which it had put together won with a comfortable majority in Parliament while the disarray of the Opposition reached newer depths. Congress (I)'s share of parliamentary seats fell to the lowest number that it has commanded at any time since Independence, and the same was true for the Left Front even though it slightly improved its share of the vote. It also became clear that, with the exception of the Congress and the Left, every other party was now quite willing to align itself with the BJP if its regional and sectional interests so required. This strategy of alliances paid high dividends on several counts. Even though the BJP itself polled only 23.7 per cent of the vote the allies together accounted for another 17.1 per cent and well over a third of the seats that the coalition had won; these allies actually occupied more seats in Parliament than did Congress (I). The allies thus make the BJP look much bigger than it is.

The BJP's own historic base is overwhelmingly in the upper castes and urban middle classes, but alliances with such formations as Dravida Munnetra Kazhgam (DMK), Telugu Desam Party (TDP), and Janata Dal (United), which are regional parties based mainly among middle castes, meant that the alliance included formidable sections of these castes. Similarly, the about-turn of *dalit* (formerly 'untouchable') leaders such as Ram Vilas Paswan from militantly anti-brahminical and secular positions into the BJP camp gave the alliance a considerable proportion of the low-caste vote as well; in the crucial state of Bihar, for example, the BJP-led alliance won 33 per cent of the *dalit* and 41 per cent of the so-called 'Other Backward Castes' (OBCs) – those at the lowest rung in the caste hierarchy, though above the outright 'untouchables'. Indeed, such alliances served to give the BJP access to population groups and political platforms that had remained inaccessible to it in the past and to 'normalize' its presence where it had been previously seen as an unacceptable intruder. It is now poised to expand at the expense of its own present allies. The scope of the alliance then also meant that although Congress (I) still remains the one political party with a considerable presence in all regions and states of the country, the BJP-led coalition now has the most widespread bases of power, so that the BJP can no longer be considered a party restricted to particular regions. Meanwhile, the BJP has displayed a remarkable capacity to forge a complex strategy whereby it concedes to its allies their local and sectional interests but treats them, with their acquiescence, as irrelevant so far as formulation of national policies is concerned. This gives the BJP, with less than a quarter of the parliamentary vote, extraordinary powers to speed up the march of the RSS through the whole range of institutions of the Indian state, through appointments and fundings and internal structural transformation, even as it leads the government of a broad alliance.

In a post-election poll, it was revealed that 46 per cent of the voters had never heard of the nuclear explosions and only 15 per cent said that their vote had been affected by the fighting in Kargil. So one cannot say that these events had moved the mass of the electorate to any considerable degree. However, 'the bomb' as well as the military performance in Kargil under the BJP government undoubtedly served to consolidate support for the BJP among the hawkish urban middle classes, within its own regular support bases across the country, and among all those most intensely exposed to the media, creating among these strata an image of the BJP as a purposeful, determined force working for a 'strong' India. This then is combined with the consequences of liberalization at home and abroad, which have become clearer only during the period of BJP rule. The consumerist hysteria of the urban middle classes is being catered to through imported consumer goods and the production of foreign brands under licence within India. Statistics show that poverty, especially rural poverty, has increased throughout the decade of liberalization, but the consuming classes have never had it so good and there is a massive elite consensus behind these policies which cuts across parties but benefits the party in power which is *seen* to be implementing them. Alongside this opening up of the Indian markets, including financial markets, to foreign capital, there is now an evolving 'strategic relationship' with the United States which holds out the promise to those same classes that India will now replace Pakistan, their 'enemy', in American affections. And anti-Muslim sentiments of Hindu communalism at home and the increasingly Islamicist thrust of the insurgents in Kashmir have coincided with the growing American focus on 'Islamic fundamentalism', Afghanistan, Osama Bin Laden and so on. So, India under the BJP is fast emerging as America's 'most allied ally' in this crusade against 'fundamentalism'; high-level meetings to coordinate Afghanistan policies are becoming routine, and joint working groups are being formed to make a shared war against 'terrorism' a key part of the new 'strategic partnership'. For the first time since the mid-1970s, the urban middle classes are perceiving India as again able to strut on the world scene and large sections of the heretofore liberal intelligentsia are moving over to the BJP on this score alone. That India executes this strutting not as an independent leader of the non-aligned movement but as America's junior ally does not bother these liberal sections because that is precisely what they want.

The transformations that have emerged in recent months, especially since the elections, are thus decisive but unsurprising. The writing on the wall has been clear for quite some time and we are witnessing the consolidation of existing long-term trends. In a sense, these trends in Indian politics only confirm the historic experience across the world that a regime of the far Right emerges in conditions where the Left is too weak to stem the tide and the liberal centre collapses in such a way that a part of it declines absolutely while the other part links itself up with the Right. Nor is it surprising that the BJP has used this new consolidation to somewhat speed up its own agenda, as indicated, for instance, by its attempt to legalize the induction of RSS cadres into the police force, its promulgation of a new doctrine of 'limited war', its enormous increases in the military budget, or its across-the-board attacks on democratic and progressive expressions on the scholarly and cultural fronts.

All this only confirms the analyses presented in the preceding chapters and need not detain us here. What has happened in Pakistan during these same months actually constitutes the real novelty – something bordering on a rupture – even though the situation there is still unclear and may well prove to be merely transitional. Furthermore, the rhetoric that surrounds the issues of democracy and dictatorship these days is so simplistic and yet so compelling that there is a perennial temptation to celebrate India, even as it nestles in the embrace of the RSS, as 'the largest democracy in the world' while the multiple crises of Pakistan's polity are submerged under the unitary focus on the civilian–military dichotomy. The real situation would appear to be somewhat more complex.

II

The military takeover in Pakistan is by no means the cause but a symptom – in some basic ways a consequence – of crises that the new regime has inherited, however reluctantly. Let us summarize a few.

There is, first of all, the sheer size of the Islamicist establishment. The coalescence of Zia's own systematic attempts to Islamicize Pakistan and the enormous American organization and funding of the Islamicist rebellion against the Soviet-aligned regime of the People's Democratic Party of Afghanistan (PDPA) had been crucial in the making of this establishment. The Inter-Intelligence Services (ISI) directorate which is run by military officers who are functionally independent of the military high command was created for the express purpose of organizing the Afghan rebellion strictly under the CIA's own control. This outfit not only took control of the Islamicist jehad in Afghanistan but became so powerful that, for example, two military officers assigned to ISI duty came to be stationed in every district in the country; others wove themselves into the Islamicist organizations of various sorts, in Pakistan as well as Afghanistan, which grew at dizzying speed. At its height, the ISI produced such luminaries as Generals Hamid Gul and Javed Nasir, former chiefs of the agency and currently influential leaders in the world of militant Islam. Khaled Ahmed, possibly the most perceptive Pakistani commentator on the issue, speaks of a 'reverse indoctrination' whereby ISI operatives who had gone to organize Islamic militias for American-sponsored crusades themselves came to be infected with the most archaic and crusading ideas so common among the militants. This fitted perfectly with Zia's own efforts to Islamicize the armed forces and civilian life alike, and the interface between well-trained military personnel and devout youth coming out of the Islamic seminaries which were sprouting all over the country has given to Islamic militias a fighting capacity quite the equal of any informal army in the world, probably much greater than in the Algerian case, and a symbiosis with tens of thousands of serving personnel at all levels of the armed forces which is quite unprecedented in countries not already under Islamicist rule. Estimates of the Taliban who arose out of Pakistani seminaries and went to fight for the jehad in Afghanistan hover around 100,000, while the seminaries themselves, with their numbers running into tens of thousands, underwent the most radical changes. This complex is then enveloped by a much larger social force which may not be part of the Islamicist insurgency yet, but which will undoubtedly serve as a great reservoir in any situation of massive and enduring social conflict in pursuit of an Islamic revolution. The annual conference of the Tablighi Jama'at, for instance, draws some two million people in a congregation that is estimated to be the second largest in the Islamic world, next only to the Mecca pilgrimage. And this does not even include the Jama'at-e-Islami, the most sophisticated Islamico-political force in the country, or the Dawat al-Irshad, the most tightly organized of such groups and the parent of Lashkar-e-Toyeba. At the highest level of army and government, meanwhile, Musharraf is currently flanked by this fire-eating Islam in the shape of General Aziz, his Chief of General Staff, and Rafiq Tarar, the President he has inherited from Nawaz Sharif.

This whole establishment used to be enthusiastically pro-American while the Soviet armies were fighting in Afghanistan and the CIA was organizing funds for them as well as supplies of weapons on a scale that is still shrouded in secrecy but which is estimated to have run into tens of billions of dollars. Then, with the Soviet withdrawal and the final collapse of the PDPA, the Americans began to lose interest in them, leaving Pakistan free to shape most further developments, including the government of the Taliban which came into being with American approval and Pakistan's active involvement in all aspects of the fighting that brought them to power. Funds from the United States had dried up by this time anyway, even though outright American hostility towards the Taliban came somewhat later. Drunk on their success against Soviet troops, and perhaps not quite appreciating how much of their military success was itself owed to American funds and weaponry, the jehadi groups began seeing themselves as being at the cutting edge of an Islamicist revolution across national frontiers, spilling not only into Kashmir but also southwestern China, the Central Asian republics that were formerly a part of the Soviet Union, and even as far as Chechnya, not to speak of establishing centres in the United Kingdom and flirting with the idea of Islamic revolutionary terror on US soil itself. Having been dropped by the Americans, they too turned anti-American; mutual hostilities grew with each new step. Something of the same happened with the Pakistan army itself. During the Afghan war, Americans had supplied virtually unlimited funds and state-of-the-art weapons to that army. Then, after the Soviet withdrawal, those supplies began drying up, so that the Pakistan army has received hardly any hardware from the United States over the past decade or so.

This was mirrored in the economic sphere as well. During the Afghan war, Pakistan was the third largest recipient of American aid, after Israel and Egypt. Indirect funding, such as through the drug trade or third-party transfers, was additional. Then the Americans suddenly discovered that they could no longer live with Pakistan's nuclear programme which they had ignored when Pakistan was needed for the war in Afghanistan, and economic assistance also started disappearing. As luck would have it, remittances from Pakistanis working in the Gulf countries began dwindling just about then, as the IMF and the World Bank also became more serious about their 'conditionalities'. An overblown, profligate state which had never believed that funds would start disappearing so fast, entered into a serious financial crisis, while General Zia's death and the advent of electoral democracy in Pakistan brought to power two of the most corrupt regimes in Pakistan's history; Nawaz Sharif's is said to have been one of the most corrupt regimes in the world, comparable to the Nigerian, and the best that one could say in Benazir's favour is that she was not quite in the same league. Now, after the recent rescheduling of some debts, Pakistan faces an economic future where its external payments for debt servicing for 2001 will amount to $5 billion, which is more than all the expected foreign-exchange earnings that year. Whether or not Pakistan will default at that point is a decision that will be made not in Islamabad but in Washington – and Washington is likely to demand a heavy price for a favourable decision. This dire economic situation also raises some questions about Pakistan's resolve to match India in the nuclear field. Such a nuclear policy, leading to weaponization and development of new delivery systems, may be not only morally reprehensible but also economically unfeasible, draining resources that the country does not actually have.

Having had its finest hour during the Afghan war, which lasted for over a decade and misled Pakistani rulers into believing that the glory was permanent, Pakistan's more recent experience in its foreign relations has been rather traumatic. There is, first, the historic shift in its relations with the United States; a client for fifty years, which rose into the most intimate of embraces during the Afghan episode, has fallen from favour to such an extent that its greatest success with its former benefactor is that it has not yet been declared a 'rogue' and a 'terrorist'. India grabbed Siachen, then promised as long ago as 1989 to demilitarize it but never kept the promise. In September 1997 India promised to set up a 'working group' on Kashmir; instead, in May 1998 it unilaterally carried out nuclear tests, with no prior warning. Pakistan tried to save its face with Chaghai, but its nuclear technology was shown to be much more primitive. After waiting ten years for a mutual settlement on Siachen, it organized its own adventure in Kargil but was humiliated, militarily and diplomatically. As the Indian media portrayed Clinton's impending visit as if Solomon was coming to visit Sheba, Pakistan begged for a brief stopover of a few hours; Clinton demanded – and got – the right to address the Pakistani populace – on dictatorship, extremism, etc., no doubt! The worst, however, has been the long-term fallout of the Afghan policy itself. Within Afghanistan it has thrown in its lot exclusively with the Taliban, and the most the Pakistan government is now able to do to placate the other forces is to restrict the number of the Taliban travelling from inside Pakistan to fight for their colleagues and counterparts against the Northern Alliance. The rabid anti-Shia ideology and activity of the Afghani Taliban and the Pakistani Sunni militias are such that Pakistan's alliance with the Taliban has isolated it from Iran as well, and it is only with very great difficulty that Musharraf is now mending those fences. As the Taliban and Pakistani jehadis set out to infiltrate other states, Pakistan's corresponding isolation from a variety of countries, from Tajikistan to Russia, is increasing rapidly.

Almost the most vexing aspect of these foreign-policy dilemmas for Pakistan is that it may lose the secure place it has occupied alongside its historic friend, China, and in the Islamic world. China's refusal to veto the UN sanctions against the Taliban government probably signifies its concerns about the incursion of Islamic jehadis into its own Muslim population, which would in turn make it hostile towards the Islamic militias within Pakistan. The anti-Shia activities of the Taliban and the Deobandi–Wahabi crowd in Pakistan, which has included the killing of Irani personnel, severely tests the good relations between the governments of Iran and Afghanistan, which in turn affects Iran's project to build an oil pipeline to India through Pakistani territory. Given the extent of Shi'ism in Kashmir itself, it is not at all clear what the future holds for Kashmiri Shias as militants committed to a highly sectarian form of Sunni'ism enter the Valley in large numbers. Pakistan's Afghan policy, which once earned it such acclaim in many capitals, from Washington to Beijing, has become its greatest problem, but that policy is profoundly linked now to the issue of the existence of armed Islamicist militias in Pakistani civilian life and the divisions within the army between its secularist and Islamicist wings. Those Islamicist militias, with massive networks of seminaries and pietistic organizations such as the Tablighi Jama'at or the Jama'at-e-Islami, cannot even begin to be controlled without a united effort and great determination on the part of the armed forces, but it is precisely that lack of unity within the armed forces which renders effective actions against them impossible. Jehangir Karamat, the Chief of the Army Staff (COAS), whom Sharif sacked, and Musharraf, the COAS who overthrew the Sharif government, are both men of the more liberal, secular wing: officers of the old stamp. But it may already be too late for such as them. There are others, of a different persuasion, waiting in the wings to overwhelm them.

It is not at all clear whether or not Musharraf will be willing to undertake the daunting and risky task of harnessing these Islamicist insurgents. The signals he has so far given have been contradictory and vacillating . Giving him the benefit of doubt, though, let us assume that such signals are indicative not of a lack of intent but show him to be playing a game in which the dice are loaded against him. If so, the least that can be said is that he cannot fundamentally alter the Afghan policy unless he can restrain and disarm – really disarm – the Islamicists at home, and that he cannot even begin to do so unless he can show some real progress on the Kashmir issue – the one issue on which all liberalist projects in Pakistan have always come to grief, being defeated by the bellicose and the rabid. For that, the key lies rather less with him and rather more with governments in India and Washington. India should show some flexibility here not because the insurgents have succeeded in their mission but because it is only by making some progress on the issue that the subcontinent can be saved from constant bloodletting, not to speak of a possible war that may not remain 'limited'.

Unfortunately, the current Indian policy does not appear to be designed for de-escalation and the myopic US actions do not augur well either. In order to grasp what is at stake, the Indian intelligentsia needs to properly understand just what is going on in the 'enemy' country, instead of simply contrasting Indian 'democracy' with Pakistani 'dictatorship'.

III

Now that General Musharraf has emerged as the 'Chief Executive' in Pakistan, it would be useful to find out why and under whose prompting, in those first few confusing days of the Kargil operation, Defence Minister Fernandes went out of his way to certify that neither the Sharif government nor the ISI were involved and that the operation was exclusively a design of the Pakistan army. As if on cue, Musharraf's close-up photograph suddenly appeared on the cover of a national weekly with the provocative caption 'Know Your Enemy'. The Defence Minister's statement was soon to be dismissed as extravagant, much as an earlier statement by him that China was India's real enemy was also once dismissed as a personal idiosyncrasy. A certain indelible image had been created, however, with deliberate precision. The current conduct of Indian policy towards Pakistan receives such support from most of the liberal media today thanks to this image of Musharraf as an Islamicist fanatic who singlehandedly authored Kargil and then staged a coup, to hide his sins, against an elected Prime Minister of Pakistan who had given us the Lahore Declaration. We cannot grapple with the irresponsible nature of India's own current policy without interrogating that image.

The first thing to be said about General Musharraf's takeover of 12 October 1999 is that it was not a coup but, as Musharraf himself was to later call it, a 'counter-coup'. All available accounts seem to suggest that it was a reluctant takeover. Musharraf seems to have anticipated that something decisive was afoot and had prepared his military forces for the eventuality, but it was a reactive strategy and therefore unclear as to what comes next. Even the Provisional Constitutional Order that sought to give the action some legitimacy retroactively came two days later. Real coup-makers normally carry such things in their hip pockets.

The drama began on 20 September when the US State Department issued an unusual warning, addressed to 'political and military actors' in Pakistan, against a coup. Later reports revealed that the head of the Pakistan ISI, Lt. Gen. Ziauddin, had arrived in Washington the day before, to join Sharif's brother Shahbaz (the then governor of Punjab) who had been there for three or four days already. Ziauddin was actually reported to have been a guest of the CIA, at Langley, just outside Washington, and is reported to have stayed there for almost a week which included briefings for committees of the US Congress as well as officials at the CIA and the State Department on Afghanistan-related issues. The American press later reported that the visitors informed their hosts of the action that was soon to be taken against Musharraf. The hosts are not known to have demurred.

Sharif had earlier fired another COAS, Jehangir Karamat, an officer of impeccable propriety. Then, at least a modicum of protocol had been observed. So Karamat chose to obey civilian authority and left. Morale in the army plummeted nevertheless, since that dismissal was part of a series of actions which included the sacking of the President and storming of the Supreme Court by goons loyal to Sharif, ouster of the Chief Justice, and exoneration of the goons by that same Supreme Court. Sharif had wanted to appoint Ziauddin, not Musharraf, in place of Karamat even then. Prevented by the opinion of the corps commanders at the time, he then prepared a coup against the new Chief of Staff. In the event, the military brass stood behind their chief because they saw it as an attack not just on Musharraf's position but on the unity of the army itself and because they perceive the army as the last remaining institution in the country to give it some semblance of coherence.

That a showdown was imminent had become clear by 8 October when Musharraf sacked the Quetta Corps commander Tariq Parvez for holding an unauthorized meeting with Sharif. It also became clear soon after the coup and counter-coup that Sharif was actually trying to split the army, when it was found that he intended to dismiss not only Musharraf but also some other corps commanders, such as Lt. Gen. Mahmud Ahmed whom Musharraf later chose to replace Ziauddin at the ISI. It was in this context, then, that two days after the coup and the counter-coup Mr Justice (retd) Fakhruddin G. Ibrahim, one of the very few judges who had refused to take an oath of office under Zia's Martial Law, welcomed the 1999 Provisional Constitutional Order (PCO), promulgated by General Musharraf, as having been made inevitable by Sharif's attempt to split the army, and as one that was preserving civil law, civil liberties, etc. It is not clear whether the Sharif–Ziauddin combine, had it succeeded, would have allowed even the degree of civil liberties that still exist in Musharraf's Pakistan.

On 17 October, five days after the conspiratorial attempt to sack Musharraf, Ardeshir Cowasjee, a determinedly outspoken critic of the Pakistani rulers, wrote in *Dawn*, Pakistan's oldest and most prestigious English-language daily:

> Nawaz planned a coup. On October 11, to maintain secrecy and cover his tracks, he and his co-conspirators, Inter-Services maestro Lt. Gen. Ziauddin, Supreme Court stormer Mushtaq Tahirkheli, information wizard Mushahid Hussain, PTV boss Parvez Rashid, won-over journalist-turned speech writer Nazir Naji – flew to Abu Dhabi to finalize the coup programme.

We know the rest of the story: the diversion of the aircraft, the attempted arrest and probable assassination of the Chief of Staff, troops loyal to the ISI chief surrounding PTV and spilling on to the streets of Islamabad, and so on. Toward the end of his column, Cowasji said of Musharraf:

> He is a man who opposes the belief that the preservation or gaining of any territory is worth the nuclear destruction of even one city. We and the world should now feel safer knowing the nuclear button is in his hands rather than those of unpredictable, untrustworthy, unthinking politicians such as 'democrats' Benazir Bhutto and Nawaz Sharif.

It is also instructive to recall the column of Ayaz Amir in the same newspaper two days earlier, on 15 October. Amir is now one of the most outspoken and virtually abusive critics of Musharraf on the grounds that the Army Chief has outstayed his welcome. Indeed, as early as 22 October he was to observe: 'the army action should have fitted the provocation and not exceeded it as it obviously has done.' Barely three days after the coup and the counter-coup, though, he had written: 'The army's hand was forced. If it had not done what it did it would have stood condemned before the bar of history.' He also went on to say: 'the Sharifs, as their internal difficulties mounted, had started clinging to America's coat-tails, in the process becoming the greatest lackeys of the Americans that we have ever had ... No wonder the Americans seem unhappy with the coup. This is not what they were banking on.'

We still do not know what had been worked out at Langley that the Americans 'were banking on'. It is reasonable to surmise, though, that when the US State Department warned against a coup in Pakistan some three weeks before it happened, it was something of a veiled instruction to Musharraf to go quietly into the night, making way for the trusted ISI chief to take over military command. The IMF cut-offs and the strong-arm American condemnations that came later were already implicit in that instruction. The instruction came, however, in a situation where the Pakistan army has been getting very little hardware from the United States for a decade or more, and it is likely that a section of the Pakistan army is growing increasingly disenchanted with the Americans on that score as well. This comes out vividly, for example, in Tariq Ali's article in the *Guardian* of 14 October where he quotes an army general as saying 'Pakistan was the condom that Americans wanted to enter Afghanistan. We have served our purpose and they think we can just be flushed down the toilet.' This rage is something that Indian policy-makers need to take into account as they begin nursing the ardent wish to turn India into such a 'condom', hoping that the Americans will resolve for us problems we are unwilling to resolve for ourselves.

It is important to recall that all this occurred in a climate of opinion in India in which most national dailies are becoming indistinguishable from government handouts, while the BJP-led government whips up a hysteria of gigantic proportions. We are routinely treated to the most lurid accounts of the ISI being active in every nook and corner of India, but no one pauses to think that Musharraf's counter-coup was designed precisely to prevent an ISI chief from taking command of the army itself, in a covert operation that the chief shared with the most corrupt politician Pakistan has ever known, whom, too, we now remember neither for Chaghai nor for Kargil but, nostalgically, for the exhibition-ism of the 'bus diplomacy'.

We contrive to believe that Musharraf's absence at Waghah when Mr Vajpayee alighted from his bus was an act of hostility, but we are not willing to listen to him when he says to the editor of *The Hindu* that uniformed men have no place alongside the civilian Prime Minister on occasions of that kind, and that the three military chiefs did meet the Indian Prime Minister as soon as the latter arrived in Lahore. We continue to portray Musharraf, in the footsteps of George Fernandes, as the sole 'architect of Kargil', to such an extent that both the German and American envoys in Pakistan have had to go on record saying that that is simply not the case; the whole of the Pakistani establishment, led by Sharif, was involved and no special responsibility attaches to Mushar-raf. Indeed, soon after Sharif returned from Washington, Mirza Aslam Beg, a former Chief of Staff, revealed that well before Kargil actually happened Sharif had been extensively briefed, both at the Army GHQ and at the ISI headquarters, about the details of the contemplated operation which was prepared and executed with his prime ministerial authority. That Aslam Beg would be particularly incensed by Sharif's attempt to deny his own responsibility in the matter and by the latter's indecent haste in rushing off to Washington is also understandable. He was the Chief of the Army Staff in Pakistan in 1991 at the time of the Gulf War and had advised Sharif to condemn the US bombings, for which he was sacked.

As for the Lahore Declaration, Musharraf has made no bones about the fact that the service chiefs had some reservations. What is becoming clear now is that senior civil servants in Pakistan were also opposed to diplomacy being turned into a TV show, and that the final wording was decided upon at the very last minute when Brajesh Mishra pressed Sharif and the latter responded by pressing his own team of experts, on a matter that he understood little.[1] It somewhat boggles the mind that an event as spectacular as the Indian Prime Minister showing up in Lahore to signal a 'historic' turn in relations between the two countries was staged with no prior understanding as to what they were going to commit themselves to at the end, before the TV cameras were switched off. Abdul Sattar, a retired diplomat and the current Foreign Minister of Pakistan, stated the view of his senior colleagues succinctly when he said that Sharif was as impulsive in Lahore as in Kargil, and as impulsive in going into Kargil as in getting out of it. One might add that Sattar has not acquired some new hawkishness after joining Musharraf's cabinet. While Sharif was still very much in power, Sattar had joined Agha Shahi, a former Foreign Minister, and Air Marshal (retd) Zulfiqar Ali Khan, in drafting a key policy document, 'Responding to India's nuclear doctrine', which advocated that even if Pakistan were to sign the CTBT it should reserve the right to limited weaponization. The report had pointed out that 'in August 1999, India [had] released a draft nuclear doctrine which envisages, in the guise of "credible minimum nuclear deterrence" a massive expansion of strategic as well as conventional forces'. The document that Sattar co-authored advocated that 'the nuclear threshold should be maintained at a high level' in response to the Indian doctrine. If some recent speeches are anything to go by, Sattar seems to have adopted a softer line on nuclear issues since emerging as Musharraf's Foreign Minister. All this would again suggest that Pakistan's positions have not notably hardened on such issues as Kashmir or the nuclear policy after Sharif's ouster. That ouster has been welcomed in most political circles in Pakistan not because Sharif was perceived as a friend of India but because he is seen as having been a corrupt, inept, authoritarian, impulsive leader; those who oppose Musharraf's takeover do so not for foreign-policy considerations but on the issue of electoral democracy. The takeover itself was welcomed across the political spectrum; what has disconcerted a large number of his supporters is his failure to put in place mechanisms for holding free and fair elections in the foreseeable future.

The Indian government deals with monarchs and dictators around the world but scuttles the SAARC meeting that was scheduled to be held in Kathmandu on 26–28 November, on the grounds that Pakistan has a military government, thus deliberately letting go a chance, as Musharraf was to point out to Karan Thapar on Indian national television, for the two heads of government to meet informally, without preconditions or prior agenda. This too is odd. General Zia-ur-Rehman of Bangladesh was one of the early promoters of the SAARC idea and General Zia-ul-Haq was the one who signed the founding document for Pakistan; Rajiv Gandhi seems not to have had any difficulty with working on regional cooperation with whoever happened to be leader in neighbouring countries. Now Vajpayee scuttles the chance to meet and try to defuse tensions, but when Musharraf says that Kashmir cannot be avoided in any serious discussion of outstanding disputes because it is the only real dispute while all else are, as he puts it, easily resolvable 'irritants', the BJP government contrived to see in it not a restatement of Pakistan's historic position in its relations with India but a new hardening and a departure from previous positions, and it demands that any future talks be unconditional. We only have to look up the hard-hitting speeches that Sartaj Aziz, the then Foreign Minister of Pakistan, delivered on the eve of Mr Vajpayee's visit to see that Musharraf is simply restating something that has been said all along, even as the 'bus diplomacy' was being choreographed on television.

The Indian government says that Musharraf's emphasis on Kashmir hardens the Pakistani position. Mr Vajpayee feels free, however, to announce – and then go on repeating – that the only thing to discuss is the modality for the return of Pakistan-occupied Kashmir to India. As some commentators have pertinently asked: is this what Mr Vajpayee told Sharif? Or, is Indian policy on this key issue just drifting from one extreme to the next? This demand for unconditional talks from Pakistan, while India puts forth an impossible condition, we do not see as the hardest of all hardenings. By contrast, Musharraf in his interview had the flexibility, at least, to say that he could offer no final solutions because that is precisely what needs to be discussed. Our irrepressible Defence Minister, the hawk of all hawks, meanwhile announces a fresh new 'doctrine' of 'limited war' and the BJP's loyal ally in Kashmir, Farooq Abdullah, spells out what that means: 'War might bring friendship', he says. 'After destruction there is always construction. Maybe the next war will see India taking Pakistan-occupied Kashmir and then there will be no Kashmir problem.'[2] No wonder that Farooq stood next to Vajpayee at Jullunder when the latter threatened a pre-emptive nuclear strike and announced that India would not talk to Pakistan until after it has returned the part of Kashmir it occupies.

IV

In this reckless atmosphere, then, the word 'democracy' is brandished as a fetish. The same Americans who can ruin the lives of millions of Iraqis in order to restore the retrograde Kuwaiti monarchy to its previous splendour can brandish this fetish whenever it suits them, while Indian rulers and media managers simply ape this habit because it suits them too. The new Vajpayee government in India and that of Musharraf in Pakistan emerged more or less simultaneously. In one case, we have a non-elected 'chief executive' whose actual policies are no less democratic than those of the elected head of government whom he replaced. In the other case, we have a coalition headed by a political party which is itself only a front for a semi-secret organization whose fraternity of fronts reminds one of the Nazis. Who is to say which of these regimes is worse, for the respective countries and for our two fraternal peoples together? Sharif got his 80 per cent majority with barely a 25 per cent turnout and proceeded to wreck every major institution in civil society that came his way. It was in his time and in response to his Islamicist demagoguery that the Supreme Court of Pakistan committed the outrage of admitting a petition which asked for the unseating of a sitting judge of that same Court on the grounds that he was a non-Muslim. As some Pakistani journalists pointed out, two of the only three Supreme Court judges who have had a decent record of unassailable integrity in the whole wretched history of that country have been non-Muslims. Did Sharif have the guts to get up and say so when the attempt was made to remove a sitting judge for not being a Muslim? With such men Mr Vajpayee can happily do business, perhaps because they are of a kind. But when Sharif himself fell out with the Chief Justice, he sent goons to attack the Supreme Court and had the attackers garlanded by his partymen, on the lawns of the Court itself. Whose democracy, then, and how, and for whom?

Our newspapers portray Musharraf as a 'fundamentalist', a catch-all designation which means nothing. In the American lexicon, which we have inherited, Osama Bin Laden, a product of the CIA who has turned anti-American, is a fundamentalist, but the Saudi monarchy and its religious establishment, whom Bin Laden opposes, are not. Every account of Musharraf that we possess, formally and informally, portrays him as being a liberal Muslim. He is said to enjoy his whisky in private and he publicly declares Kemal Ataturk, an enemy of 'fundamentalism', as his hero. The chief of the Jama'at-e-Islami denounces him and he calls upon religious leaders to come forward and rescue Pakistani Islam from bigotry. Najam Sethi, the Pakistani journalist who was framed by the Pakistani High Commissioner in India, upon instructions from Sharif and his gang, has said in his newspaper, *Friday Times*, that among all the men of authority – some eight or ten of them – to whom Mr Qazi's infamous letter about him was sent, Musharraf was the only one who asked to see a copy of his actual speech and then refused to let the Pakistan Army Intelligence categorize Sethi a spy. Who, in this macabre world, is the 'democrat': the elected Prime Minister who gets an innocent journalist framed on false charges, or the Chief of Army Staff who refuses to subscribe to the frame-up?

Compare this with India, where the leading lights of government – Vajpayee, Advani, Murli Manohar Joshi- – as well as their would-be successors – Pramod Mahajan, Govidacharya, Uma Bharati – are all members of the RSS. Musharraf has as yet done no damage to Pakistani civil society that compares with the stunning amalgamation of the police force and the RSS that is afoot here under BJP's dispensation. It is possible that Musharraf will want to restrain outfits such as the Lashkar-e-Toyeba but will be too weak to do so; that remains to be seen. But what also remains to be seen, in the fairly near future, in our own case, is whether or not we shall have a veritable GESTAPO, in every sense of that historic acronym, when members of a communal-fascist organiz-ation that stands above the government, as its 'soul' and guide, appear in police uniform at the doors of citizens. Thanks to the courage of such ordinary citizens as the beleaguered journalists, the human-rights activ-ists, members of the women's organizations, and those working for dialogue and peace in the subcontinent, Pakistani civil society seems to be going through the birth pangs of democratic institutions. Meanwhile, liberal democracy in India appears to be entering something of a twilight, with far-reaching consequences for the social fabric, not to speak of the minorities, whose status must always be the yardstick to judge any democracy – and not to speak of the Constitution itself, the chief glory of this republic, which is now in for a battering. Pakistan never had sturdy democratic institutions; we did. Many on that side of the border are trying to build some, we are destroying ours. No members of the Islamicist Right sit in the current Pakistani cabinet; members of the Hindu Right are at the helm of affairs in India. Nor is it at all clear why being a member of the armed forces, in the case of Musharraf, is said to be so much worse than being members of the RSS, as are all the key rulers of India today.

Musharraf is no saviour. The record since 12 October suggests that he is a man of liberal intentions, weak will, considerable love of power, and no vision for what his country should become. As soon as he took over, the Indian government and liberal media started to single him out as a spokesman for the jehadi groups, specifically of Lashkar-e-Toyeba. That's unlikely. Sharif's own cynical Islamism was much more danger-ous. It is also the case, however, that large sections of the Pakistan army are too closely identified with those groups and Musharraf will probably not defy them; if pushed too far, he may even join them for his own survival. He speaks grandly of why he will not give up power until he has set things right, but all he talks about is punishing the defaulters on bank loans and streamlining the district-level administration; he speaks of taking away the unlicensed weapons of the militias but seems powerless to make his own administration move to implement his promise. Noble enough, but not enough in times of danger. Most of the advisors he has chosen are safe and dim; the younger ones are well-meaning but with little authority in society at large. There's a drift, and the danger in drifting in hard times is that one gets overpowered by superior forces. In Pakistan, there would appear to be two: the Islamicist Right in civilian life, and the more determined generals – probably very much to his Right and more doggedly Islamicist. This may well be a time of transition – not to the sturdy civil society which the decent citizens of Pakistan are striving for but to a government of the Islamicist Right.

The present writer is hardly the only one saying so. Numerous liberals and progressive Pakistanis have said much the same, loudly enough for this to appear on front pages of India's national media. Why does the Indian government not adopt a policy that responds to this fact? Indian national interest requires that we not help create a situation where the Islamicist Right takes over in Pakistan. To that end, India must deal with Musharraf not as a general but as the only head of government that the country currently has, just as Pakistan must deal with Mr Vajpayee as the Prime Minister of India irrespective of his life-long RSS credentials. Why has India then adopted a posture that insists that nothing but bilateral talks would solve the problem but also that we shall not talk until after Pakistan returns what we call PoK and they call 'Azad Kashmir'? Why is the Indian Defence Minister expounding a doctrine of 'limited war' directly in relation to Pakistan, if not to hold out the threat that India now reserves the right to send its troops across the LoC? And why is Mr Vajpayee so keen to deploy his characteristically cynical double speak where he says in one breath that Indian nuclear policy abjures the right of first strike and, in the very next breath, that India is 'not going to wait'?

These men are neither inexperienced nor dimwitted. Where, then, lies the method in this madness? First, our rulers have yet to overcome the delirium caused by the Pokhran lunacy. Never in the past fifty years have threats of actual use of nuclear weapons been traded so frequently and irresponsibly as during the less than two years since this delirium first set in. The RSS mouthpiece, *Panchjanya*, demanded the use of nuclear weapons at the height of the Kargil crisis, while only a little less strident threats were made by Pakistan's Foreign Secretary, Shamshad

Ahmed, and by the Indian naval chief, Sushil Kumar. Second, we are more or less intoxicated now by the prospect of a 'strategic relationship' with the United States, hoping that the messiah will bring hard cash and help us bully our neighbours, in the name of Indo-US cooperation against terrorism, quite forgetting that the plight Pakistan is in today is in considerable measure a product of the 'strategic relationship' that *Pakistan* used to have with that same country. We wish to be where Pakistan was until quite recently, unmindful of the fact that in consequence of this change of roles we shall one day be where Pakistan is today. The hope in India, before the rise of the RSS to power, was that Pakistan, authoritarian at home and a US client in foreign relations, will one day follow in the footsteps of a non-aligned and democratic India; the result of the RSS coming to power is that India is following in the footsteps of Pakistan, authoritarian at home and begging the sole superpower for a smile and a wink.

Third, though, behind this show of cockiness there's also a real panic. Even in the dead of winter the insurgents have struck with great impunity at any target in Kashmir or Jammu that they have chosen; what will happen when the summer comes? Shall we know how to control that much bigger insurgency, if it really materializes, when we have not known how to control this more limited one? And, if that larger insurgency really explodes, the BJP-led government could still control the domestic situation but could it go on resisting the external pressure to 'internationalize' the Kashmir issue? The panic, combined with the intoxication on the prospect of hosting Clinton, expresses itself in the swagger, the rhetoric, the threat of crossing the LoC, teaching Pakistan a lesson, dropping a nuclear bomb if necessary.

Fourth, the bluster is meant to conceal the reality of India's quite considerable diplomatic isolation which too we are unwilling to acknowledge. The Western countries, upon whom India has come to rely so exclusively, do not approve of Pakistan's sponsorship of terrorism or its deployment of its own troops beyond the LoC. Those same powers, though, regard Kashmir as a 'disputed territory' and, even more significantly, are not willing to brand all Pakistani involvement in Kashmir as 'terrorism'. They wish to restrain Pakistan in some important ways but they also want India to respond; hence the emphasis on 'bilateral talks' but also, as high up as Clinton himself, the offer to 'mediate' – 'if asked'. Has the 'mediation' actually begun, and is that why the Indian government is protesting its innocence so very much? We don't really know, for example, the actual extent of the Talbot–Jaswant talks, ten rounds of them, mostly in a 'third' country. The line between 'mediation' and 'consultation' is always thin until high-profile 'mediation', based on extensive prior 'consultation' , really begins.

But there is also a larger problem that no one ever talks about, which has to do with India's relative isolation in the very environment in which Pakistan lives and where India once had much greater presence and influence than Pakistan then did, namely the so-called 'Islamic World'. When that world was dominated by anti–imperialist radical nationalism of the Nasserist vintage, non-aligned India spoke to them in a shared language, as Pakistan could not. That not-so-distant past we have thoroughly abandoned, so that Arab nationalists are now bewildered as to what happened to their Indian friends. Neither during that phase nor in the more recent one, when the shadow of Islamism over that world grew taller, did India ever seriously claim the status within the so-called 'Islamic world' that historically belongs to us. Bluntly put, India has the third largest concentration of Muslims in the world, larger than Pakistan's. India could justifiably demand, but it would also have to properly live up to, a status within the world of Islam that would be commensurate with this fact.

However, the idea that India is really a 'Hindu' country with a Muslim 'minority' is now so deeply ingrained in the Indian political elite that no one is capable of credibly making the *claim* that India has an important place in the world of Islam. And this utter inability, which immediately translates into unwillingness, to represent the Indian Muslims on the platforms of the world as their *authentic* representatives then means that no one abroad is willing to recognize India's right to do so. The Indian state finds it difficult enough to represent the generality of Indian Muslims at home (except its own clients among them). It doesn't even try to represent them abroad, except in such politically inconsequential matters as arranging for the pilgrimage to Mecca. In the context at hand, then, what all this means is that Pakistan does live within its own environment and, despite the current tensions with Iran, it could speak to us through intermediaries, from Saudi Arabia to Egypt to Turkey to Algeria, not to speak of the Palestinians, but we now have very little relationship with that world and we think it beneath our dignity to deal with such riff-raff, so that 'mediation' for us always means 'Americans'. We clearly suffer from delusions of grandeur, thanks to demography and the size of the market that we can offer to advanced capital. And, thanks to these delusions, we are unwilling to acknowledge how isolated we actually are in the world of Asia, and therefore in the world of small and medium-scale powers in the region that we, objectively, share with Pakistan.

In the environment in which India and Pakistan actually live China, a traditional friend of Pakistan, is actually the key country. Could we ever dream of using China's good offices for the 'secret diplomacy' that belligerent opponents in times of danger so desperately need? China undoubtedly has the kind of clout with Pakistan to guarantee any understanding that Pakistan gives, but we ourselves don't have that kind of relationship with the one major (nuclear) power that lives within our own environment. And we cannot. Against whom is this 'strategic partnership' of India with the United States being formed? When the United States had that kind of relationship with Pakistan, friends and enemies were well known, on both sides: Pakistan always refused to be used against China, always offered to do its bit in defending the oil sheikhdoms against popular insurgencies, always offered itself against the Soviet Union, and finally found its moment of glory in the American crusade in Afghanistan; that glory is now proving to be its undoing. What is the nature of India's 'strategic partnership' with the United States today? Against whom? Why is India conducting naval exercises with France? Why are Indian naval ships showing up in US waters? And so on. Is India now getting ready to be the Asian junior partner of NATO, much as Pakistan, as a member of both CENTO and SEATO, was once expected to guarantee US interests from Turkey to the Philippines? Who is the enemy in Asia, for NATO, but then also for India?

V

But the real method behind New Delhi's move to a hard line on all issues pertaining to Pakistan – no talks until PoK is returned; 'limited war'; pre-emptive nuclear strike; and so on – may actually lie elsewhere: in the calculation that a bigger, more highly visible insurgency in Kashmir, combined with a Pakistan ruled by the Islamic extremists, whether of the military or the jehadi wing, would in fact help RSS build the kind of national-security state of the Hindu Right that it aims to do, as well as to emerge as the US's great ally in the containment of 'fundamentalism' – implicitly a counterweight against China as well. Full-scale Islamization of Pakistan is thus expected to make saffroniza-tion of India that much easier, re-enforcing the chorus for a 'strong' state and redefining India's role in Asia as a whole. Jehadi groups becoming the official paramilitary units of the state in Pakistan would help further justify the integration of the Indian police forces with the RSS and the emergence of the Bajrang Dal as the Patriotic Youth of India, so certified by the state itself.

Seen from this perspective, foreign policy emerges yet again as an extension of domestic policy, facilitated by a dramatic shift in the balance of forces at home. That process had begun already in 1998 and thereafter when the BJP was able to forge a broad alliance that included a variety of erstwhile 'secular' parties which went merrily along while Christian homes and churches were burnt down in Gujarat and an Australian missionary and his two sons were burnt alive in Orissa. The shift became really unmistakable in mid-1999, however, when the Opposition failed to form a government after the BJP had lost the vote of confidence. Three things then happened. First, it became clear that the BJP was now the dominant centre towards which the lesser formations would in the foreseeable future gravitate. The failure of the Congress and Samajwadi Party to come together to form an alternative government showed, if proof was still needed, that virtually no one outside the Left was willing to compromise sectional interests in order to build an enduring platform against the RSS. The unity of the Left Front itself received in the process a final and not so decent burial, with two of the four parties in the Left Front government in Bengal refusing to accept the policies of CPI(M) and CPI, on the formation of an alternative government, and the CPI itself adopting a neutral position between the BJP and the Rashtriya Janata Dal (RJD) of Laloo Prasad Yadav while CPI(M) supported the latter during the more recent state elections in Bihar.

Second, and thanks very much to this disarray among its erstwhile opponents and the unconditional support it received from its allies, the BJP not only stayed on as a 'caretaker' government to supervise the next elections, in August–September 1999, but also managed to appear as the normal party of rule when it got the chance to stage the budget session on its own terms during those days of mere caretaking. Third, when the Kargil war broke out during those same months before the elections, it was the Opposition that floundered while the BJP remained secure in its commanding position, as it deliberately conducted itself in a manner which treated the Opposition contemptuously while showing that the allies did not really matter and could therefore be taken for granted. It is indicative of the steep decline in the politics of Opposition in India that in the Kargil affair, as on the hijacking issue more recently, every party in the Opposition sought to occupy the high ground of patriotism by accusing the BJP of not being hard enough in its military resolve. When it comes to Pakistan, no political party of any consequence, including the Left parties, seems able to speak in any language other that of the national-security apparatus. Every one wants to teach Pakistan a tougher lesson, and none dares say that there is in Kashmir, quite aside from the Pakistan-sponsored terror squads, a genuine home-grown insurgency which needs to be addressed not militarily but politically. It is on the basis of this prior consensus, this deafening silence of the lambs, that the BJP feels free to pursue its extremism.

While the Congress went into the elections of 1999 on the hollow ground of going it alone, thus refusing to face up to its own crisis and decline, the BJP gathered around itself a formidable alliance that guaranteed it a comfortable majority in the ensuing Parliament. Knowing that electoral programmes in Indian democracy mean rather little, it conceded to its allies in the newly formed National Democratic Alliance (NDA) a document that was muted on its favourite *Hindutva* plank. Knowing also the supine character of its allies, and confident that it would be able to dictate its terms once the new government was formed, it conceded to them a complex pattern of seat-sharing that reduced the number of constituencies it contested for itself but increased the chances that the alliance would have a larger aggregate of seats in Parliament. The formula of governance was simple: concede to the allies their sectional and regional interests so as to get from them a free hand in setting the whole range of policies on the national level.

Predictably, the formula worked. The Akalis, the Naidus, the Farooqs have remained loyal allies as the BJP moved, especially after its national meeting in Chennai, to implement its so-called 'hidden' agenda across a number of fronts. Starting with Gujarat, BJP-ruled states are being turned into laboratories of what India may look like as the *parivar* extends its grip on the land. In West Bengal, the erstwhile secular Mamata Bannerji has become the agent for expansion of the RSS throughout the state. In Kerala, the RSS is on a rampage of selective murder. From Varanasi to Kanpur to Bhopal, the terror squads of the VHP and the Bajrang Dal are out to intimidate teenagers and filmmakers and political opponents alike, teaching them fine and bloody lessons in RSS-style 'Indian culture'. Having remade the cultural and education organizations of the state in its own image, the ruling party uses institutions like the Indian Council of Historical Research (ICHR) to suppress volumes assembled by two of the country's leading historians and already in advanced stages of printing at the Oxford University Press. As soon as an archaeological expedition finds remains of Hindu and Jain temples in Fatehpur Sikri, the magnificent capital that Emperor Akbar built and then abandoned, the new head of the ICHR, Mr Grover, declares, as reported in the *Indian Express*, that Aurangzeb was behind the destruction; never mind that many of the finds date back to the fourth and fifth centuries.

The Chief Minister of Uttar Pradesh openly says that he will not obstruct the impending construction of the temple in Ayodhya, whatever the court verdicts. By contrast, when the President speaks up to restrain the attacks on the Constitution which he is duty-bound to defend, the organs of the ruling party itself attack him for being anti-BJP and soft on the Congress; in the speech that the BJP then wrote for the President as he inaugurated the Budget Session, he was forced to compromise on the question of reviewing the Constitution. The group that has been appointed to undertake this review, against the wishes of the Opposition though with no objection from the BJP's own allies, includes individuals who have no expertise in constitutional law. There is no white paper, no guidelines or charter of reference, no sanction by

Parliament itself, even though Parliament alone is empowered to amend the Constitution. The executive branch does as it wishes on constitutional matters. On the foreign-policy front, we are being treated to the extraordinary spectacle of regular sessions of strategic talks between the Foreign Minster and officials of the United States with no public accountability, in Parliament or outside, as to the contents of these talks.

The radical shift in India's posture towards Pakistan is part of this larger pattern. The 'limited war' doctrine of Mr Fernandes is the external aspect of the gangs of self-appointed defenders of Indian culture at home. The demand that Pakistan return the PoK before India sits down to talk is to declare that the BJP government intends not to resolve but to intensify the conflict, so as to institutionalize a permanent war psychosis which can be used to constitute a right-wing consensus at home. As the RSS chief declares that the release of three prisoners in exchange for the Kanadhar hostages was a sign of 'Hindu weakness', the Prime Minister feels constrained to brandish nuclear weapons as if these were mere equivalents of the *trishuls* in Bajrang Dal's arsenals. This particular government is not even five months old, and it is already becoming difficult to say just where these politics of violence, hysteria, and spectacle are taking the country. Indian polity is in any case not in much better shape than is Pakistan's.

Notes

Preface

1. The texts omitted from the present edition are as follows: 'Imperialism and Progress', 'Class, Nation, and State: Intermediate Classes in Peripheral Societies', 'Structure and Ideology in Italian Fascism', 'Reconciling Derrida: "Spectres of Marx" and Deconstructive Politics', and 'Culture, Nationalism, and the Role of Intellectuals: An Interview'.

2. Aijaz Ahmad, *Ghazals of Ghalib* (New York, Columbia University Press, 1971; Delhi, Oxford University Press, 1994).

3. See 'Introduction: Literature among the Signs of Our Time', in Aijaz Ahmad, *In Theory: Classes, Nations, Literatures* (London, Verso, 1992), pp. 1–42.

Chapter 1

1. On this episode, see Bipan Chandra, 'Nehru and the Capitalist Class, 1936', in *Nationalism and Communalism in Modern India* (Delhi, Orient Longman, 1979).

Chapter 2

1. *Pakistan Newsletter*, 1 (March 1977). I drafted these words for a short-lived and anonymously produced émigré journal.

2. For a contrary view, see *MERIP Reports*, 58 (June 1977).

3. On the political plane, the destabilization campaign was conducted by the Pakistan National Alliance (PNA), a coalition of nine political parties. Of these only the National Democratic Party (NDP) and Tehrik could be considered secular, although they too had accepted the Islamicist programme of the PNA as a whole. The NDP and JUI are discussed below, in notes 12 and 13; the Jama'at has been given a whole section later (pp. 42–8). The Muslim League, a political organization of semi-feudal landlords and their hangers-on, is not a religious fundamentalist party as such, but (a) its present chief, Pir of Pagaro, is head of the biggest religious grouping in Sindh, and (b) ML is a close ally of the religious parties.

4. Tehrik is a peculiar construct. Initially, it was built around the maverick

personality of Asghar Khan, a retired air marshal, who started making a bid for popular support during the anti-Ayub movement of 1968–69. Through him, Tehrik is connected with segments, though not necessarily the dominant faction, of the armed forces; his open letter, at the height of the destabilization campaign, inciting military officers to mutiny, and Bhutto's inability to do anything about it, shows the extent of the protection Asghar Khan has enjoyed. Through a number of its officials, Tehrik appears to be well connected with monopoly houses (e.g. Musheer Pesh Imam, a banker and advisor to monopolists), metropolitan institutions (e.g. Wazir Ali, a retired World Bank official), and plain old subversion (e.g. Nawab Bugti, the most retrograde chieftain of Baluchistan, widely believed to be on the CIA payroll). Thanks to its close alliance with Jami'at-e-Ulema-e-Pakistan (JUP), Tehrik also enjoys the support of the merchant capital located in Karachi. Its liberal image, based as it is on a predominantly secularist outlook and a populist agrarian programme, is itself owed to the fact that Tehrik represents segments of the urban propertied classes, and its landlordist faction is small and 'modernist' in outlook. We classify it as an ultra-Right party nevertheless, because of its connection with Karachi-based capital, with sections of the armed forces, and with imperialism, and because of its putschist stance throughout the destabilization campaign.

5. See *Pakistan Forum*, Karachi, February 1978.

6. *Al-Fatah*, Karachi, 6 January 1980.

7. An analysis of the mass movement of 1968–69 is beyond the scope of this article. Certain contrasts between that and the so-called 'Democratic Movement' of 1977 are, however, quite obvious. That earlier movement was largely spontaneous; was based primarily among the enlightened segments of the petty bourgeoisie and their allied strata among workers and the urban poor; adopted 'socialism' as its ideology, counterposing it against both militarism and religious fundamentalism; obtained the only free and fair general elections ever held in Pakistan; produced an overwhelming victory for leftist democratic parties throughout Pakistan; and established the principle that Pakistan, as a multinational state, should be a federation based upon a constitutional covenant agreed to by representatives of the various nationalities. By sharp contrast, the so-called 'Movement' of 1977 was instigated by the ultra-Right from the very outset; was based upon retrograde sections of the petty bourgeoisie and the urban lumpen elements; adopted 'Islamism' as its ideology; led to the dissolution of the federal principle and replacement of it by a highly centralized state; led also to the indefinite postponement of general elections; gave ascendancy to the ultra-rightist parties, at the expense of the leftist elements and without reference to the electoral process. Thus, the mere fact that large numbers of people were mobilized in both instances does not establish identity, or even commonality, of purpose in the two events. Rather, we can say that the so-called 'Movement' of 1977 was organized with the precise purpose of annulling the gains of the mass movement of 1968–69.

8. The Left inside the PPP was itself an amorphous entity. The leftist strain in it was best represented by men like Mairaj Muhammad Khan, who briefly served as a minister in Bhutto's first Cabinet and was then ousted and imprisoned for close to four years, losing much of his eyesight in the process. Mubashir Hasan, the Secretary-General of the PPP, an engineer by training,

and Bhutto's Finance Minister for over two years, is also a self-professed Socialist of a liberal-humanist kind. J.A. Rahim and M.A. Kasuri, a senior diplomat and a famous lawyer respectively, who both became ministers in Bhutto's first Cabinet, can be described as elder statesmen of social democracy in Pakistan; Rahim was beaten up by PPP goons after being ousted from the Cabinet. And there were others in important places, e.g. Sheikh Rashid. With the exception of Rashid, all these men were purged at various stages – though, admittedly, many new elements of the radical Left joined the PPP in later years, always on a local or intermediate level. These elements later played the key role in the movement against the martial law regime which reached its height between 18 September 1977 and 4 January 1978. However, the PPP could not sustain that movement precisely because the previous purges had weakened the party irrevocably.

9. Of the four provinces in Pakistan, the PPP had a negligible following in Sarhad (NWFP) and Baluchistan when it formed the government at the centre (December 1971). In Punjab, too, the biggest landlords – the main force of semi-feudal power in Pakistan – had stayed out of the PPP until then; later, of course, many joined. In Sindh, by contrast, some of the biggest landlords, at odds with the previous regime, had joined the PPP almost at its birth. After the provincial governments of Baluchistan and Sarhad were dismissed, the landlord class in those two provinces experienced something of a split, with many of the most powerful landowners and tribal chiefs staying in opposition, but many of the leading landlords either joining the PPP or cooperating closely with it. In Punjab, the shift in the class base was persistent but gradual; by 1977, however, the landlords were clearly in charge of the party machine there as well. Thanks to the even more openly reactionary character of the opposition parties, however, most peasants in Punjab and Sindh continued to support the PPP. This electoral support was further consolidated with the announcement of land reforms in January 1977.

10. Men like G.M. Khar, Nawab Kureishi, Sherpao, Jatoi, and Mumtaz Bhuttoo constituted the leadership of the landlords' group. Nawab Bugti was a close ally in Baluchistan, though he never joined the PPP formally.

11. After the coup of 5 July, Tikka Khan submitted an affidavit in the Supreme Court justifying and taking full responsibility for the counter-insurgency operation in Baluchistan during the Bhutto period. Bhutto's own affidavit offered no self-criticism for the Baluchistan policy, which was portrayed as a valiant attempt to defend the territorial integrity of Pakistan. In an unrelated development, Tikka Khan was later arrested by the military authorities, for leading a 'violent' demonstration for the release of Bhutto.

12. The National Awami Party (NAP) has a chequered history, which is tied, moreover, to the little-known history of the Communist Party of Pakistan (CPP). After the CPP was banned in 1951, it adopted the policy of sending its cadres in the main opposition party of that time, the Awami League (AL), to do mass work and to unite with its left faction. The theory was that *if* the left faction could become dominant in the AL, and *if* the AL could become the dominant party of the country, Pakistan could enter a phase of 'national democracy', which would in turn permit the CPP to resume legal existence (and its interrupted revolutionary tasks). In the event, the AL did briefly form

the government, but under the dominance of its right wing, led by Suhrawardy, and took Pakistan deeper into the imperialist orbit. Maulana Bhashani then led the left faction, along with its Communist component, out of the AL and founded NAP, which immediately became a mass party in East Pakistan but remained rather small in West Pakistan, where NAP was further weakened after the next split (1967–68) when the pro-Chinese Communists began to depart, along with their supporters, to form a number of Maoist parties, at least one of which quickly became larger than the CPP itself. Thereafter, NAP became predominantly an alliance of the pro-Soviet Communists (the underground CPP) and the reformist landlords of Sarhad and Baluchistan, while both these groupings had some bases among the petty bourgeoisie. In Baluchistan, however, NAP did become a kind of umbrella organization for the Baluch national movement as a whole, and its leftist component there included more than the traditional CPP. After NAP was banned in 1975, it was resurrected again under the rubric of the National Democratic Party (NDP), under the leadership of Sher Baz Mazari, one of the most notorious landlords in Punjab; subsequently, CPP cadres were expelled from the NDP, along with their sympathizers, and most of the Baluch nationalists have refrained from joining it. Thus, in its latest reincarnation, NAP/NDP is more clearly landlordist than ever before, with a much narrower social and political base.

13. Jami'at-e-Ulema-e-Islam (JUI), led by Mufti Mahmud, is a regional political formation, based in some districts of Sarhad and in some elements of the Pashtun population of Baluchistan and Karachi. In its social composition, JUI represents the regional interests of the middle and rich peasantries, including their pauperized sections now located in urban areas. Its programme thus usually includes an anti-feudal nuance as well as puritanical denunciations of the monopolist bourgeoisie. In its rightwing radicalism, JUI is similar to some sections of the Muslim Brotherhood in Egypt. However, it has moved consistently towards the other, much less radical rightwing parties for some years now, especially since the elections of 1970.

14. Foreign commentators, even some very perceptive ones, seem to believe almost universally that NAP had won the elections of 1970 in Sarhad. Actually, it had polled only 18 per cent of the vote. NAP was able to join the provincial government because of its electoral alliance with JUI.

15. In spring 1975, for example, 35,000 workers were reportedly laid off in the textile industry alone, in the Karachi–Hyderabad zone.

16. The key weakness of these struggles was that they neither originated nor culminated – thanks to the factionalism of the organized Left – in the creation of a cohesive political party, or even a united front of workers' organizations. The actual struggles thereby remained confined to spontaneous rebellions, localism, and a fundamental economism.

17. See *Report of the Land Reform Commission* (Lahore, 1959).

18. *Pakistan Economic Survey, 1975–76*, Finance Division, Government of Pakistan.

19. Ibid.

20. 'Semi-feudal landlords' and 'capitalization of agriculture', do not refer to two altogether exclusive and competing sectors of the economy. Typically, capitalist inputs are used, on a part of their farms, by the same big landlords

whose cultivators – sharecroppers, tenants, wage workers, etc. – suffer the most obvious semi-feudal relations of social and economic dependency. Schematically speaking, the term 'semi-feudal' refers to social relations of production which facilitate the coercive appropriation of (a large part of) the direct producers' surplus by the dominant landlord class, whereas 'capitalization of agriculture' refers mainly to the instruments of production, the expansion of the money economy and commodity production, the rise of rural credit as a major incentive for the transformation of the factors of production, etc. It is a common practice among these big landowners to use a part of their land for highly mechanized capital-intensive farming while leaving all the rest for very traditional forms of sharecropping.

21. This section summarizes an argument, along with supportive data, from my recent monograph in Urdu, *Halya Boharan Ki Ma'ashi Jarein: 1977* (Lahore: Punjabi Adabi Markaz). Some statistics are taken from: *Recent Trends and Development Prospects*, a World Bank Report, No. 1023 PAK, dated 1 March 1976; *Pakistan Economic Survey, 1976–77* and *1977–78*, as well as *Estimates of Foreign Assistance, 1976–77*, issued by the Finance Division, Government of Pakistan; *Banking Statistics of Pakistan, 1972–73* and the *Annual Report 1977*, issued by the State Bank of Pakistan; and the *Annual Report, 1973–74*, issued by the Board of Industrial Management.

22. *Pakistan Economic Survey, 1975–76*, pp. 178–9.

23. (a) In 1972, the International Monetary Fund (IMF) forced the Bhutto government to lift the import ban on over three hundred commodity items, as a precondition for approval of loans. The annulment of this protectionist measure, coupled with a 130 per cent devaluation which came as part of the same package, boosted the import of foreign consumer goods and industrial raw materials at the expense of domestic products, thereby aggravating the crisis of domestic industry. (b) According to Stephen R. Lewis, in *Economic Policy and Industrial Growth in Pakistan* (London, 1969), up to 76 per cent of Pakistani manufacturing in the 1960s relied heavily on protection, and some manufactures were sold at prices as much as 150 per cent higher than those prevailing on the world market. With the liberalization of import policies in 1972, the bottom simply fell out of this type of manufacturing.

24. General Habibullah, a close relative of Ayub Khan and one of those representatives of the monopolistic bourgeoisie whom Bhutto had once ordered to be handcuffed for television display, reemerged immediately after the coup as an advisor to Zia on industrial policy. The Nawab of Hoti, the only really big landlord who ever managed to transform himself into a monopolistic bourgeois, came out of the woodwork to serve briefly as Minister of Education in Zia's first, quasi-civilian cabinet. The Habibs and the Saigols, the proprietors of the largest commercial banks nationalized during the Bhutto period, are known to have been negotiating with the regime for licences to reestablish private banks. Zia himself has spoken of returning industry and commerce to the 'golden era' of the Ayub dictatorship. Meanwhile, it is an open secret that elaborate plans have been drawn up already for full denationalization of those industries that had been taken over. Those plans have not been implemented so far only because the bourgeoisie is reluctant to resume private control over the industrial plant since it is apparently uncertain about (a) political repercus-

sions, particularly among the working class itself; (b) the ability of banks to finance the private sector on the requisite scale, considering the preexisting crisis of liquidity and the increased demands of the state upon the same banking system; and (c) the ability of the present regime to survive, and hence the long-range prospects for the policy of denationalization as such.

25. Sher Baz Mazari, President of the NDP; Pir Pagaro, President of the Muslim League; and Nawab Bugti, a key figure in Tehrik, are among the representatives of this reactionary and openly pro-imperialist top stratum of the landlord class.

26. The Jama'at is of course the characteristic political formation of this class segment, but elements of the reactionary petty bourgeoisie play a significant role in all parties of the PNA. Most significantly perhaps, this class segment predominates, in numbers and outlook, in the institutions of the state, the armed forces in particular. The close collaboration between the Jama'at and many of the leading elements in the officers' corps should be seen not as an accident, nor only as a conspiracy (although the conspiratorial aspect is not negligible), but as a structural class conjunction.

27. In Pakistan, where the public sector has always been very limited, the bureaucratic bourgeoisie is also numerically very small and structurally very weak, as compared, for example, with the state bourgeoisie in Nasserite Egypt or in Boumédienne's Algeria. And, thanks to its own weakness, it acts in conjunction with, not in fundamental opposition to, private capital.

28. The regional origin and predominantly kulak background of the officer corps only partly explains the solidly reactionary outlook and conduct of Pakistan's armed forces. In fact, their whole genesis, rooted as it is in the colonial past, is conditioned by repressive purposes. After Independence in 1947, 5,000 British personnel stayed back to reorganize and prepare these armed forces for the neocolonial era; 2,000 were still there in 1951. Then, Pakistan signed a Bilateral Military Pact with the United States (1954), and joined SEATO (1954) and CENTO (1955 – named 'Baghdad Pact' at the time), the notorious military alliances sponsored by imperialism, headed by the United States. Since then, the entire elite of the officer corps has been trained by North Americans. In turn, Pakistani troops have been used for massacring the Palestinians in Jordan as well as against the Dhofar Revolution, not to mention the extensive role they play in maintenance, training, and even active duty in all the oil kingdoms of the Gulf (especially in the UAE). More recently, Pakistan has come to rely heavily on these same kingdoms for military credits and 'third-party transfers' of weapons originating in the United States. This new dependency is also reflected in the political and ideological outlook of the armed forces.

29. The main tradition of Islam among the peasantries of Pakistan is one of heterodoxy. Orthodox, fundamentalist Islam is popular only among small sections of the peasants, mainly among Pashtun peasants, and of course a very vocal but actually rather small cross-section of the urban petty bourgeoisie. This explains why political parties of religious orthodoxy have never been able to take root among the peasants, with the exception of JUI among a section of the Pashtun peasantry – and here too, one suspects, the kulak-based populism of JUI is perhaps at least as important as its fundamentalism in religious

matters. Thus, in the elections of 1970, for example, the three fundamentalist parties together polled less than 15 per cent of the vote and obtained half that percentage of seats, primarily through petty bourgeois support.

Chapter 3

1. I use the awkward phrase 'nationalist Muslims as they were represented in the Indian National Congress' in more or less the same sense in which Mushirul Hasan uses the simple term 'Congress Muslims' in, for example, his *Nationalism and Communal Politics in India 1835–1930* (Delhi, Manohar, 1991). The longer phrase is used here for a certain emphasis. There were also a great many *nationalist* Muslims who did not join the Congress. Many more worked primarily in or around the Communist Party than is generally recognized; some others went into smaller parties of various types; an incalculable number did not join any party because of more or less equal discomfort with League policies and the presence of substantial Hindu communalist forces inside the Congress. The vast majority of Muslims – indeed, of all Indians – neither belonged to any political party nor had any opportunity, until after Independence, for electoral expression of their will, thanks to the extremely restricted nature of the franchise, even in 1946.

2. For the text of the Address, see Malik Ram (ed.), *Khutbaat-e-Azad* (Delhi, Sahitya Akademi, 1974). The significance of the Address will be discussed below.

3. See, for a fuller discussion of this point, Fazlur Rahman, *Islam and Modernity: Transformation of an Intellectual Tradition* (Chicago, University of Chicago Press, 1982).

4. In this 'period' I include all his writings between the founding of *Al-Hilal* itself and the writing of *Qaul-e-Faisal*, thus including *Al-Balagh*, *Tazkira*, and the articles and addresses of the Khilafat Movement.

5. Publishing houses in Karachi and Lahore, like Maqbool Academy and Daata Publishers, have brought out literally dozens of collections of Azad's essays, culled from *Al-Hilal*, *Al-Balagh*, and sundry lesser-known journals, as well as numerous editions of *Tazkira* and *Masala-e-Khilafat*. It is also significant that the full file of *Al-Hilal* was reprinted in a modern, multi-volume, well-bound edition in Pakistan well before the Indian reprint.

6. See Qazi Javed, *Sir Syed se Iqbal tak* (Lahore, Book Traders), 1975.

7. No adequate translation of the term, *umma-wahida*, is really possible. Azad later took to translating it into Urdu simply as *muttahida qaumiyat*, with the emphasis falling both on nationalism and on *ittehad*, meaning 'unity'. But that is something of an interpolation. The translation of *umma* as 'nation' is of course in keeping with the exigencies of the modern nation-state, but 'people' – even in the generic sense of 'human species' – would be closer to the etymological root; in the strictly religious discourse of Islam, meanwhile, the term connotes a sense of 'community', mainly of shared belief, as in *Ummat-e-Rasul*, i.e. Community of the Faithful held together by a shared belief in the Prophethood of Mohammad. *Wahida*, meanwhile, carries the literal sense of 'united', but Azad cites the case of a *treaty* between Muslims and non-Muslims,

concluded by the Prophet of Islam, as the basis of his conception. The 'unity' implied in the term, then, has the sense of an 'alliance'. The context, usage, and consequences of this conception shall be discussed presently, in the main body of this text.

8. I.H. Qureshi, the late doyen of rightwing historiography in Pakistan, is notable for having emphasized the break between Azad's earlier period and the latter, locating it, as I do, in 1922. But his reading is almost exactly the opposite of mine, for he sees the latter period of Azad's life in terms of a betrayal of Indian Muslims. See I.H. Qureshi, *The Muslim Community of the Indo-Pakistan Subcontinent, 610–1947* (The Hague, Mouton, 1962).

9. See, for characteristic examples of this trend among very diverse writers, Abdur Razzaq Malihabadi, *Zikr-e-Azad* (Calcutta, 1959, reprinted Delhi, Maktab-e-Isha'at-e-Quran, 1965); Humayun Kabir, *Muslim Politics, 1906–47* (Calcutta, 1969); M. Mujeeb, *The Indian Muslims* (London, Allen and Unwin, 1967, and Delhi, 1985); Malik Ram, *Kuch Abul Kalam Azad Ke Bare Main* (Delhi, 1989); the chapter on Azad in Rajmohan Gandhi, *Understanding the Muslim Mind* (Delhi, Penguin, 1987); or the latest and in some ways the best – though far too unquestioning – biography of Azad by V.N. Datta, *Maulana Azad* (Delhi, Manohar, 1990).

10. Ian Douglas is critical and contentious, and he might have provided a refreshing contrast to the kind of hagiography one often gets in the name of biography, but he is unable, finally, to deal sympathetically with Azad's religious ideas, possibly because of his own prior location in Christian theology and the preoccupations that follow from that location. See I.H. Douglas, *Abul Kalam Azad: An Intellectual and Religious Biography*, ed. Gail Minault and C.W. Troll (Delhi, Oxford University Press, 1988).

11. The main liturgical formulation, the *Kalima Tayyaba*, without which none is considered by the pious as a Muslim, runs as follows in English: 'I give witness that there is no God but Allah, and that Mohammad is Allah's Prophet.' Pressed in Aurangzeb's court to recite the Kalima on pain of death, Sarmad uttered the opening phrase: 'I give witness that there is no God . . .', then stopped. Threatened again with beheading, he simply said: 'I have reached the first stage only, that of negation; let those who have seen what cannot be seen speak the rest.' Then he bowed his head for the sword to fall, and composed the following magnificent couplet:

> shor-e-shud wa az khwab-e adam chashm kishudem
> Didem ki baqi ast shab-e-fitna, ghunudem

The sword of course fell.

As one reads Azad's lyrical and passionate account of this episode in the 1910 essay, one is scarcely prepared for the extremist piety that surfaces soon thereafter, in the *Al-Hilal* decade.

12. His early adoption of the pseudonym 'Abul Kalam' (literally, 'Father of Theology') – which he had taken already in 1903, when he brought out the very first issue of *Lisan-al-Sidq* – is significant in relation to this ambition of composing, before the age of thirty, a master treatise of sweeping proportions. Then, in November 1915, *Al-Balagh* first announced the impending publication of the *Tarjuman* along with two other multi-volume works – *al-Bayaunfi al-*

Maqasid Al-Quran and *Muqaddama-e-Tafsir* – for which immediate subscriptions were sought. In the event, the last two works were simply dropped. There were all kinds of stories about the *Tarjuman*'s having been started, half completed, fully finished at various points, and parts of it destroyed by the police or lost by unreliable assistants. It is likely that there actually were some unfortunate incidents at the time of Azad's internment in Ranchi and subsequent imprisonment at the height of the Khilafat Movement; it is also likely that some stories of the work having been done at an earlier date are exaggerated. The two published volumes which eventually came in the 1930s offer translation and somewhat unsystematic commentary on roughly half of the Quran.

13. Azad is said to have written a favourable treatise of indeterminable length on Sirhindi during his internment days in Ranchi, at just about the time he wrote *Tazkira*. There is in fact a very long list of Azad's writings in that internment period which are said to have disappeared when his trusted lieutenant of those days, Fazluddin Ahmad, the man chiefly responsible for the writing and publication of *Tazkira*, precipitately left Calcutta. There had apparently been a falling out. The alternative version is that the police kept taking away and returning his papers throughout that internment and the subsequent imprisonment, with much writing getting lost in the process. Given the ambiguity surrounding the many writings of Azad that do exist in print, one can never be entirely sure of details.

14. The scheme was at best the product of an overactive imagination; Azad was then barely thirty years old, with no major work of either *fiqh* or *kalaam* to his credit. Nor did he belong to any of the major seminaries (e.g. Deoband, Firangi Mahal, Nadva). In the Khilafat Movement itself, he was only *one* of several leaders (e.g. Ansari, Ajmal Khan, the Ali brothers, Maulana Mahmud Hasan himself who was still alive until 1920). This is quite apart from the fact that Indian Islam since at least the early Mughals had had no institutions of that kind, nor could there be one. The rule of the Muslim dynasties in India was absolutist but non-theocratic, i.e. they never had a ruling order of clergy on the pattern of either medieval Christendom or even the *mevleviat* (organized under the office of *Shaikh-al-Islam*) in Osmanli Turkey. Broad diversity of sects and seminarian traditions among Indian Muslims, including principally the Shia–Sunni divide, made such an institution inconceivable.

15. It is curious that Azad's life as a journalist never quite took shape, even though much of his fame as a writer and thinker rests on his work in *Al-Hilal* and *Al-Balagh*. All in all, he was associated in an editorial capacity with no fewer than twelve journals during the twenty-five years between 1903 and 1928, usually for a very few months, never for as much as three years. This is in sharp contrast with Gandhi whose journalistic writings, in both English and Gujarati, were continuous and prodigious, even though he was hardly ever seen as a journalist.

16. In his biography, V.N. Datta makes the point that the reason why Azad did not revive his projected work on the *Tarjuman* during the Ahmednagar years was that he needed a great many scholarly references which he could not obtain in prison. The point is well taken. But we still do not know why volume III which was scheduled for publication in 1937 never appeared; why Azad

never even tried to return to that work, in or out of prison; why in all the letters of *Ghubar-e-Khatir* he never expresses the desire to resume that work or any regrets at being unable to do so. Azad had the reputation of a great scholar. It is significant that his most enduring work of Urdu prose, undertaken in the years of his maturity and accomplished over two years, is an exercise in the epistolary art, a minor genre.

17. *India Wins Freedom*, The Complete Version (Delhi, Orient Longman, 1988), p. 248.

18. Nehru is said to have rendered the Ramgarh Address into English and Azad wrote him a letter thanking him for the accuracy. The curious thing about the Urdu text as we find it in the definitive edition, however, is that there are entire passages in it, especially some of the ones summarized in our own text here, which simply lack the characteristic voice and inflection that a knowledgeable reader would normally associate with Azad's own prose. Such passages actually read much more like a very competent translation of Nehru's English. The exact relationship between Azad's and Nehru's voices, as these voices are embedded in the texture of the Urdu prose of this Address, is far from clear.

19. In his introduction to *Tazkira*, Malik Ram states the matter with the greatest delicacy: the whole book is written as he puts it, as if 'he [Azad] is getting ready to assert a very special claim'. What Malik Ram means of course is that the whole majestic narration of his ancestors' great courtly eminence as key theologians and educators under the Mughals was implicitly to demonstrate that Azad was eminently deserving, even by lineage, of being declared the *Imam-al-Hind* by common consent. In this context, the closing pages on his own life of 'drunkenness and sexual excess' carry a very different kind of significance. Sulaiman Nadwi, a well-known theologian and an associate of Azad during the *Al-Hilal* days, had already made public his knowledge of Azad's more profane pleasures. The concluding pages, acknowledging all that without conceding any point of actual fact, were designed to consign all that to the past and to preempt hostile attacks.

20. See, for the violence of Azad's language during this period, 'Masala-e-Islam' and other essays selected from *Al-Balagh* and reprinted in *Nigarishat-e Azad* and *Mazaameen-e-al-Balagh* (Lahore, Maqbool Academy, n.d.).

21. *Mazameen-e-al-Balagh*, p. 143.

22. Ibid., p. 177.

23. Hasan, *Nationalism and Communal Politics in India*, p. 119.

24. Some of these developments will be discussed below, in section V.

25. Mr Advani was the President of the BJP when in 1990 he undertook a *yatra* (pilgrimage) from the famous temple of Somnath to Ayodhya – some 1,500 miles in all – in a Toyota truck decked out like the Lord Krishna's mythic chariot in a Bollywood movie, with Lord Shiva's *trishul* (trident) prominently displayed among the artefacts of Hindu spirituality decorating the Toyota, all in the service of Ram and with the promise of bringing about the *ram rajya*.

26. The two sets of terms here refer to the two major currents in medieval devotional theisms, Bhakti and Sufism.

27. Azad's own account of his family lineage in *Tazkira* portrays his

ancestors coming from Herat in the early days of the Mughal Empire and living uninterruptedly in Delhi until his grandfather (mother's uncle) and father set out for Mecca via Bhopal. There is reason to believe, however, that his grandfather had moved to Delhi from Qasur, a township near Lahore, to join the pietistic circle around Shah Abdul Aziz, the son of Shah Waliullah, who had done the first Urdu translation of the Quran. When Azad announced the imminent publication of the *Tarjuman* in 1915, he specifically cited Shah Abdul Aziz as the Quranic scholar and translator whose work his own was going to supersede – a rather large claim to make, within the traditions of Islamic piety, for someone without any significant work of Quranic scholarship to his name – but he never mentioned that his own grandfather was the disciple of that same man.

28. This is the reason he gives for the adoption of the pen-name 'Azad' in *India Wins Freedom*, recounting his life in such a way that the decision appears to have been taken in the years of his 'doubt' *after* he had come across the works of Sir Syed and had, according to him, started reading English. This dating is patently false. It is also significant that (a) the 'Prospectus' in this book mentions Azad's discovery of Syed Ahmed Khan's work but not his repudiation of it during the *Al-Hilal* decade and beyond, and (b) he mentions sectarian differences among Muslims as the only direct cause of his 'doubt' and 'crisis'. Even *Tazkira* and *Ghubar-e-Khatir* had been less misleading. Sir Syed had been directly blamed there for the 'crisis' because it was his writings which had created the doubts and the doubts had led to virtual renunciation of religion; the *Ilhad* of the Aligarh school was, as we know, one of main themes of the *Al-Hilal* period. Meanwhile, the crisis, which according to epistle 11 of *Ghubar-e-Khatir* lasted for a decade between the ages of fourteen and twenty-four, is related in both the Urdu books not to frustration at sectarian differences but much more directly to his surrender to all kinds of earthly pleasures, presumably love, sex, wine, and so on.

29. Malihabadi attributes this point to Azad himself. See *Azad ki Kahani*, p. 240. Other biographers have also remarked on this practice and Azad's adoption of the pen-name for that reason.

30. For what it is worth, the Malihabadi text portrays Azad's mother actively disliking the Urdu langauge and the Indian people generally.

31. The accounts of this refusal to inherit the status of *pir* are unclear, though. There is reason to believe that the country-wide travels which Azad undertook between 1902 and 1906, *after* the age of fifteen, in connection with his journalistic work, were connected also with visiting the circles of his father's *murids* in different parts of the country, as son and possible successor of the *pir*. That he rejected the pressure to assume that position in 1909 is unquestionable. However, with the launching of *Al-Hilal*, the establishment of *Dar-al-Irshad*, the aborted attempt to create a country-wide network under the organizational name of 'Hizb-e-lslami', the despatch of emissaries to various parts of the country to obtain Bait (the *murid's* vow), and the culmination of all this in the bid to get accepted by congregations of the *ulema* as *Imam-al-Hind*, it seems that the local pressures of 1909 were resisted but then revived on a much larger scale.

32. Ram (ed.), *Khutbaat-e-Azad*, pp. 262–3.

33. Some of the biographical accounts are simply careless. Mustafa Kamil was a charismatic Egyptian leader and founder of the first major political party there in the aftermath of the Occupation of 1882, bourgeois and mildly nationalist and in dire competition with the Islamic formations which eventually coalesced around Rashid Rida and his *Salaffiya* Movement. Azad mentions having met some of Kamil's followers. Since the name of Mustafa Kemal, the Turkish leader, is better known in India, however, some biographers have sometimes collapsed the two names.

34. Datta, *Maulana Azad*, p. 23.

35. This too is problematic, however. On the same page of *Tazkira* Azad says that the 'episode' occurred nine years before the date of the writing. According to Fazluddin Ahmad Mirza, who was responsible for the whole venture of the writing and publication of the book, *Tazkira* was written between June and October of 1916. That would suggest that the 'episode' occurred in 1907. It is possible, of course, that the rhapsodic account of the 'episode' was written two years after the drafting of the rest of the book, in 1918, but there is no firm evidence of that either. Difficulties of this kind only go to show how impossible it is to speak of 'facts' about this whole phase of Azad's life.

36. In *India Wins Freedom* Azad suggests that he had learned enough English in his middle teens, very much on his own, to start reading books. Hasrat Mohani's testimony claims that he first learned English much later, in Alipur prison. The actual extent of this knowledge is unknown, the many suggestions of enthusiastic biographers notwithstanding. Mahadev Desai's *Maulana Abul Kalam Azad: A Biographical Memoir* (2nd edn, Agra, 1946), is characteristically misleading on this count.

37. In his *Al-Balagh* articles and then throughout the Khilafat Movement, Azad had consistently countered criticisms by saying – and quoting Imam Ghazali to the effect – that life under the worst kind of oppressive Califsh is better than a single night without a Califsh.

38. Literature on developments in modern Turkey, is truly vast. The following may be consulted for general information: Feroz Ahmed, *The Young Turks* (London, Oxford University Press, 1969), and *The Making of Modern Turkey* (London, Routledge, 1993); Niyazi Berkes, *The Development of Secularism in Turkey* (Montreal, 1964); Nikkie R. Keddie, *Sayyid Jamal-ad-Din al-Afghani* (Berkeley and Los Angeles, University of California Press, 1972); Bernard Lewis, *The Emergence of Modern Turkey* (London, Oxford University Press, 1968); S. Merdin, *The Genesis of the Young Ottoman Thought* (Princeton, Princeton University Press, 1962); Binnaz Sayari (Toprak), *Islam and Political Development in Turkey* (Leiden, Brill, 1981). Among individual articles, the following may be particularly useful: Serif Mardin, 'Religion in Modern Turkey', *International Social Science Journal*, 29:2 (1977); D.A. Rustow, 'Politics and Islam in Turkey', in R.N. Frye (ed.), *Islam and the West* (The Hague, 1957); and A.L. Tibawi, 'Islam and Secularism in Turkey Today', *Quarterly Review* (London, 1956).

39. Rida's influence on Azad's intellectual formation seems to have been decisive and lasted far beyond the *Al-Hilal* decade, since the philosophical

influence of Rida's unfinished *Tafsir*, which covers rather less than half of the Quran, can be seen in the *Tarjuman* itself, which covers rather more than half.

40. Literature on these Arab developments is, if anything, even more vast than on Turkey. For the problem at hand one could consult Albert Hourani's classic *Arabic Thought in the Liberal Age, 1798–1939* (London, Oxford University Press, 1962), and go on to the useful *Modern Islamic Political Thought* by Hamid Enayat (London, Macmillan, 1982). Supplementary readings might include Ali H. Dessouki and Alexander Qudsi (eds), *Islam and Power* (New York, Random House, 1981); Samir Amin, *The Arab Nation* (London, Zed Books, 1978); Georges Antonius, *The Arab Awakening* (London, 1936); Michael Gilsenan, *Recognizing Islam: Religion and Society in the Modern Arab World* (New York, Pantheon, 1982); Nikkie R. Keddie (ed.), *Scholars, Saints and Sufis* (Los Angeles, University of California Press, 1972); R.P. Mitchel, *The Society of Muslim Brothers* (London, Oxford University Press, 1969); Maxime Rodinson, *Marxism and the Muslim World* (New York, Monthly Review Press, 1981); Hisham Sharabi, *Arab Intellectuals and the West* (Baltimore, Johns Hopkins University Press, 1970); J.H. Thompson and R.D. Reischauer (eds), *Five Tracts of Hassan al-Banna, 1906–1949* (Berkeley, University of California Press, 1978).

41. In his *Al-Balagh* articles in particular, Azad spoke at length and with definite pride about his own absolute Pan-Islamism, using the term in declarative, triumphalist tones, and asserting with characteristic aplomb that *not* to be a Pan-Islamicist would be contrary to Quranic injunction and Prophetic *Hadith*, therefore amounting to heresy. It was only in the post-Khilafat days that he quietly dropped the whole rhetoric.

42. M.K. Gandhi, *An Autobiography: The Story of My Experiments with Truth* (Boston, Beacon Hill, 1957).

43. Ibid., p. 449.

44. *Maqalaat-e Sir Syed* (Lahore, 1962), vol. 4, pp. 260–71.

45. Azad's essay on 'The proposed Shia College' makes remarkable reading, in the context of this tie between his anti-colonialist passion on the one hand and, on the other, his fundamentalist fury against religious liberality at Aligarh.

46. See, for some interesting comments on this issue, Sumit Sarkar's essay 'The Pattern and Structure of Early Nationalist Activitsm in Bengal', in his *Critique of Colonial India* (Calcutta, Papyrus, 1985).

47. Aziz Beg, *Jinnah and His Times*, cited in Datta, *Maulana Azad*, p. 136.

Chapter 4

1. This essay was first drafted for a Conference on 'India, the First Decade: 1947–57', organized jointly by the Nehru Memorial Museum and Library, the University of Oxford, and the University of Texas (Austin), with three sessions held at the respective venues, in 1991–92. A revised version was delivered as lectures at the Indian Institute of Advanced Study, Shimla, 1993.

2. The obvious invocation of European modernism in this case is misleading. Some writers in this tendency, notably Miraji, were at least vaguely familiar

with European modernist currents but most were not. Considering that Urdu literature had nothing in its past comparable to rationalism, Romanticism, or realism, in the European sense, literary 'modernity' here was a weak, vague and imitative affair, defining itself simply in opposition to 'tradition' and that too mainly in terms of literary *form*, blank verse instead of the *ghazal*. But, then, 'progressives' were also experimenting with form and their opposition to traditional *society* was far more sweeping. So, the main difference between 'progressives' and 'modernists' turned out to be political. Ideologically anti-Communist and politically quietists, the 'modernists' found themselves isolated in a culture passing through a mass anti-colonial movement and were able to muster a major cultural impact only after the Partition had broken up those reading and writing communities.

3. See Saadat Hasan Manto, *Partition: Sketches and Stories* (New Delhi, Viking, 1991), for a rough approximation of the text of *Siyah Hashye*. Khalid Hasan's editing is at best lamentable, and even his translations are not entirely reliable. He changes words, sentence structure, even titles of stories without any explanation whatever.

4. The title *Khuda ki Basti*, roughly translatable into English as 'God's Hamlet', has the enraged and ironic meaning of having been *abandoned* by God and state alike, which the English phrase simply does not communicate.

5. Sajjad Hayder was a civil servant in the imperial government, hence unable to participate in the Freedom Movement, but his sympathies were well known. Like a great many Muslim nationalist intellectuals of the period, he was also a Turkophile and had adopted the Turkish pen-name Yildrim. Qurratul 'Ain's mother, Nazar Sajjad Hayder, was also a writer of fiction, but unfortunately of a very sentimentalist variety.

6. For an instance of the communal position surfacing in otherwise liberal discourse, the following from the concluding paragraphs of Amrit Rai's informative book, *A House Divided* (Delhi, Oxford University Press, 1984), should suffice:

> ... what I must stoutly contest is Urdu's claim to being a common language of the Hindus and the Muslims ... modern Urdu acquired its present character by deliberately throwing out words of Indian origin, i.e Sanskrit words and their derivatives, from the naturally growing common language of the Hindus and the Muslims, and by substituting them, as far as possible, exclusively with Persian and Arabic words. (p. 288)

That Urdu has been the language of the minority of Muslims and of even a smaller minority of Hindus is undoubtedly true, even though Amrit Rai is not willing to grant even that. The claim, however, that Urdu is the language of no Hindus at all is an extraordinary claim, especially from Amrit Rai, a native of Allahabad, the city that has given to Urdu its greatest novelist of the twentieth century, in the figure of Premchand, as well as Firaq, arguably the best writer of Urdu *ghazals* in this century – both so recognized not only in India but also in Pakistan. His other claim, that modern Urdu has thrown out 'words of Indian origin' is simply fantastic, worthy of the late Girilal Jain. It is certainly true that Urdu draws its *technical* vocabulary largely from Farsi and Arabic, but, as I shall detail presently, all the root words and some three-fourths of the entire Urdu lexicon is known to have been derived from that same Prakrit–Apbharansa base that is also the base for Hindi. But then Amrit Rai simply equates 'words of Indian origin' with 'Sanskrit words'. This sanskritizing impulse has not always been salutary for modern academic Hindi itself. On a related matter, I also think that Urdu needs to recover its connection with Sanskrit in the formation of its technical vocabulary, not by purging itself of Persian (or English) words but by making use of all the resources, past and present, that are available to people of north India.

7. *Dawn* (Karachi), 26 February 1948.

8. I use the term 'Urdu-speaker' here in the sense given to it by *Linguistic Surveys*, to indicate the so-called 'mother tongue'.

9. This notion of colonial scientificity is also taken whole by Amrit Rai in his invocation of the 'national interest' in denying that any region can have more than one language: 'The regional language, in each case, must be paramount, and nothing that in any way undermines or splits its authority can be desirable' (p. 209). I fail to see, Grierson and Amrit Rai notwithstanding, why the 'region' of Kashmir should not recognize the further 'regional' specificity of Jammu and Ladakh or why Kashmiri and Urdu cannot coexist in a shared cultural space.

10. See Ashish Bose, 'Some Aspects of the Linguistic Demography of India', in *Language and Society in India: Proceedings of a Seminar* (Simla: Indian Institute of Advanced Study, 1969), pp. 37–51. The interpretation of statistics is entirely my own.

11. Mohan Singh Diwana, 'Indian Socio-linguistic Background', in *Language and Society in India*, pp. 73–4. See, for more detailed treatment of this issue of multi-linguality in Indian literature, the chapter 'Indian Literature: Notes towards the Definition of a Category', in my *In Theory: Classes, Nations, Literatures* (London, Verso, 1992).

12. What I mean here by phrases like 'pro-Pakistani in sentiment' is hard to describe. I have in mind a particular grid: the idea that Pakistan is the 'homeland' of subcontinental Muslims, or that the Muslims of the subcontinent constitute a nation; that Partition was a good thing, despite the accompanying human carnage; that Pakistan needs to be defended against India; that Pakistan offers a secure future to the Muslims. We find such ideas routinely in the school of historiography perpetrated by I.H. Qureshi, in the cultural analyses of influential writers like Jameel Jalibi; even in the kind of literary criticism that Muhammed Hasan Askari, in his youth a member of the Progressive Movement, began writing in the latter part of his life when he became an obscurantist Muslim of the Thana Bhavan School. It is the presence of such ideas in a variety of other writings in Pakistan after the 1960s which makes the utter absence of these ideas in the literary documents – poetry and fiction of the earlier generation – so very striking.

13. Muhammed Safdar Meer, 'Sialkot ki Faseel'. Safdar Meer represents a particular kind of pattern in Pakistan. A graduate of Government College, Lahore, he had travelled to Bombay in the 1940s to join the Communist Party. In that he failed and returned to Lahore, at the time of the Partition, joined the staff of the same college, where he was dismissed in the course of the large-scale purges of the Left which occurred in the mid-1950s. After some years of

personal adversity, he re-emerged as an influential journalist, having made his peace with the Ayub regime. The poem was composed in the midst of the war, and Safdar Meer recited it from loudspeakers fitted on military jeeps which roamed through the city of Lahore. It was later published in the 'war number' of the Pakistani journal, *Naqsh*.

14. Rafiq Khawar's long poem *Gandhinama* was a notable attempt to tell the achievements of the Mahatma in an epic mould. Unfortunately Khawar's abilities fell far short of the techniques he tried to imbibe from Homer, Milton, the *Mahabharata*, Meer Anis, and so on. After the war, Khawar too went the way of Safdar Meer, writing in the Pakistani journal *Barg-e-Gul* ('Mujahid' number, 1966) that Pakistani poetry had finally found a worthy theme: war and national defence.

15. 'Generations of Grief' is not quite an exact translation of the phrase *Udas Naslain*, but 'Sad Generations' – or, 'Aggrieved', instead of 'Sad' – sounds sentimental and peevish in English.

Chapter 5

1. This is a revised version of the Amal Bhattacharji Memorial Lecture, delivered at the Centre for European Studies, Calcutta, on 27 December 1992.

2. Page numbers embedded within the text refer to the following collections of Gramsci's writings: *Selections from Cultural Writings* (London: Lawrence and Wishart, 1985) (henceforth abbreviated as SCW); *Selections from the Prison Notebooks* (New York, International Publishers, 1971) (henceforth, SPN); and *Letters from Prison*, edited by Lynne Lawner (New York, Harper and Row, 1973) (henceforth, LP).

3. *Anandamath*, a famous novel by Bankim Chandra Chatterjee, is a viciously anti-Muslim, communal, and Hindu-revivalist text; one of the more significant points of intersection betweeen traditions of Indian liberalism and Hindu revivalism. *Bande Mataram* ('Hymn to the Mother[land]') is the famous song from the novel, a version of which the Indian Republic uses as its national anthem.

4. Pier Paolo Pasolini, 'Gramsci's Language', in Anne Showstack Sassoon (ed.), *Approaches to Gramsci* (London: Writers and Readers, 1982).

Chapter 6

1. This essay was written initially for the workshop on 'Culture, Community, and Nation' organized by the Deccan Development Society on 6–9 December 1993 in Hyderabad, to commemorate the first anniversary of the destruction of the Ayodhya mosque. Revised versions and new sections were developed later for talks at SNDT Women's University in Bombay, University of Poona in Pune, and Miranda House in Delhi. Here I extend, with specific reference to contemporary India, the argument I began formulating, more obliquely, in 'Fascism and National Culture: Reading Gramsci in the days of *Hindutva*' (also published in the present volume).

2. Prabhat Patnaik and Sumit Sarkar were among those who spoke of fascism in that context. See Prabhat Patnaik, 'The Fascism of Our Times', *Social Scientist* (March–April 1993), 238–9, and Sumit Sarkar, 'The Fascism of the Sangh Parivar', *Economic and Political Weekly*, 28 (30 January 1993), 5. Sarkar seems to have partially distanced himself from that position. See his 'The Anti-secularist Critique of *Hindutva*: Problems of a Shared Discursive Space', in *Germinal*, 1 (1994), p. 108, footnote 2.

3. This lecture is reprinted here as chapter 5.

4. The Sangh *parivar* is also discussed in chapters 7 and 8.

5. For a brief summation of these mobilizations, see K.N. Panikkar, 'Religious Symbols and Political Mobilization: The Agitation for a Mandir in Ayodhya', *Social Scientist*, 242–3 (July–August 1993).

6. Articles and even book-length studies on the RSS, its affiliates, activities, and allies – and on communalism in general – are too numerous for quick citation. Few, however, attempt a rounded account of the entire period of this cancerous growth. Among such general narratives, two might be mentioned. A succinct and politically reliable account is to be found in Tapan Basu, Pradip Datta, Sumit Sarkar, Tanika Sarkar, and Sambuddha Sen, *Khaki Shorts, Saffron Flags*, Tracts of the Times/1 (Delhi, Orient Longman, 1993). Walter K. Andersen and Shridhar D. Damle, *The Brotherhood in Saffron: The Rashtriya Swayamsevak Sangh and Hindu Revivalism* (New Delhi, Vistaar Publications, 1987), traces the history of the RSS and its affiliates up to 1982 with a wealth of detail, and from a position sympathetic to the Saffron brigade. Christophe Jeffrelot, *The Hindu Nationalist Movement in India* (Delhi, Penguin India, 1996; French original 1993), is more recent and carefully researched.

7. Jayaprakash Narayan (JP) had personally and publicly denied that the RSS was fascist and had praised it, instead, for its democratic struggles and, pointedly, for its role in the struggle against corruption and in favour of the poor against the rich. Upon his arrest, JP invited Nana Deshmakh, a well-known *pracharak* and key leader of the RSS, to take charge of his movement. This leadership role was later taken over, in November 1976, by D.B. Thengadi, a former *pracharak* who was then serving as the general secretary of the *parivar*'s labour front, the Bharatiya Mazdoor Sangh.

8. The desperation of these ex-Congressmen was well grounded. In the elections of March 1977 which brought the Janata Party to power with 298 seats out of the 542 in Lok Sabha, the Jana Sangh commanded the largest component, with 93 seats, so that three RSS members – Vajpayee, Advani, and Brij Lal Vohra – became central ministers. After the assembly elections of June the same year, RSS members presided over governments in the three states of Himachal, Rajasthan, and Madhya Pradesh, and in the union territory of Delhi. It was on the coat-tails of illustrious ex-Congressmen, such as Jayaprakash and Morarji Desai, that the RSS first arrived in the halls of power.

9. The state, the bourgeoisie, the dominant media have been far more preoccupied over the past three years with the single incident of the Bombay blasts precisely because the criminal gang that is said to have engineered those blasts are Muslim; by the end of 1995, the Central Bureau of Investigations (CBI) had produced 170 chargesheets related to that lone incident, while the media have kept the memory of those blasts open like a wound. No such alacrity

or alarm has been shown regarding either the destruction of the Babri mosque or the rivers of blood that have flowed in all parts of India since the *rath yatra* of 1991, instigated and carried out by the *Hindutva* forces, even though far more substantial evidence is available about the culprits in those cases.

10. What is offered here is a *generalization* pertaining to a global trend. Such a broad, macro-historical generalization does not seek to explain developments in each region and country. Patterns of economic growth and political form in the East Asian region or in the oil-producing countries, for example, are obvious exceptions to these general trends.

11. In some other countries, such as Indonesia or Ghana, that kind of state had been dismantled through *coups d'état*. Latin America witnessed similar reversals, culminating in the coup against Allende's socialist government in Chile, which had a decisive impact globally.

12. The literature on the rise of Islamicist radicalism since the late 1960s is vast. For the points raised here, the following may be useful: Samir Amin, 'Culture and Ideology in the Contemporary Arab World', *Rethinking Marxism*, Fall 1993; Fanny Colonna, 'Cultural Resistance and Religious Legitimacy in Colonial Algeria', *Economy and Society*, 3: 3 (1974); John Howe, 'The Crisis of Algerian Nationalism and the Rise of Islamic Integralism', *New Left Review*, November–December 1992; and Saad Eddin Ibrahim, 'Anatomy of Egypt's Militant Islamic Groups', *International Journal of Middle Eastern Studies*, 12 (December 1980).

13. Andersen and Damle, *The Brotherhood in Saffron*, p. 50.

14. Ibid., p. 215. According to the same authors, the RSS was claiming a *shakha* in every one of about 5,000 villages of Kerala by 1981, which has not yet made BJP a major political force in the state but has transformed the communal situation in Kerala dramatically even though the claim itself seems to have been somewhat extravagant.

15. The next two paragraphs summarize an argument that has been presented at much greater length in 'Structure and Ideology in Italian Fascism', in *Lineages of the Present* (Delhi, Tulika, 196). This essay has been omitted from the present edition.

16. The revolution in Iran has spawned a veritable industry for analyses of it. The following may be consulted more fruitfully: Ervand Abrahamian, *Iran: Between Two Revolutions* (Princeton, Princeton University Press, 1982), and *Khomeinism* (London, I.B. Tauris, 1993); Shahrough Akhavi, *Religion and Politics in Contemporary Iran* (Albany, State University of New York, 1980); Hamid Algar (ed.), *Islam and Revolution: Writings and Statements of Imam Khomeini* (Berkley, Mizan Press, 1981); Michael Fischer, *Iran from Religious Dispute to Revolution*, (Cambridge, Mass., Harvard University Press, 1980), and 'Islam and the Revolt of the Petit Bourgeoisie', *Daedalus*, Winter 1982; Azar Tabari, 'Role of Shi'i Clergy in Modern Iranian Politics', in *Khamsin 9* (n. d.); Sami Zubaida, *Islam, the People, and the State* (London, Routledge, 1989). Nikkie R. Keddie has also authored and edited work of exceptional acumen. For a succinct comment on the disorientations of Islamic revivalisms, see Aziz Al-Azmeh, *Islams and Modernities* (London, Verso, 1993).

17. This broad agreement is signified by routine invocation of the rightwing indigenist positions of such social scientists as T.N. Madan, Ashish Nandy, and

Veena Das by such subalternists as Gyanendra Pandey, Partha Chatterjee, and Dipesh Chakrabarty. Virulent attacks on secular politics are part of the shared perspective of these overlapping tendencies as they constantly seek to stage the premodern as the postmodern solution to the problems of modernity. See, for example, T.N. Madan, 'Secularism in its Place', *Journal of Asian Studies*, 46 (1987), 4; Ashish Nandy, 'An Anti-secularist Manifesto', *Seminar* (1985), 314; Partha Chatterjee, 'Secularism and Toleration', *Economic and Political Weekly*, 29 (9 July 1994), 28; and Gyanendra Pandey, *The Construction of Communalism in Colonial North India* (New Delhi, Oxford University Press, 1990), chapter 1.

18. That anti-modernist indigenism relies heavily on the most mundane of Euro-American thought is so obvious as hardly to need documentation. For illustration, though, we may cite an essay of Ashis Nandy which is a special favourite of the subalternists: 'The Politics of Secularism and the Recovery of Religious Tolerance', in Veena Das (ed.), *Mirrors of Violence: Communities, Riots and Survivors in South Asia* (New Delhi, Oxford University Press, 1992), pp. 69–93. By the time we get to section three of the essay, 'The heart of darkness', Nandy begins with a full-blown chart in the manner of modern statisticians and behavioural psychologists, and offers an explanation of contemporary communal violence without any reference to the actual political projects of *Hindutva*, without any reference to the actual events of that violence, but purely in terms of the clichés of the wholly secular, wholly Western, and modern ego psychology, overlaid, for good effect, with reference to Bogardus, Erich Fromm, Adorno, Bettelheim, someone called Milton Rokeach, and, most approvingly, Hannah Arendt and Herbert Marcuse – all of this in less than five pages.

19. See, for instance, Margaret C. Jacob, *The Radical Enlightenment: Pantheists, Freemasons and Republicans* (London, George Allen and Unwin, 1981), which also includes a most useful bibliographical essay on the subject. In his work on the eighteenth century, and more recently in his book on Blake – *Witness against the Beast: William Blake and the Moral Law* (Cambridge, Cambridge University Press, 1993) – E.P. Thompson points out time and again the extreme complexity of an 'Enlightenment' that came to be identified only retrospectively, by the middle of the nineteenth century, with 'rationalism'.

20. Needless to add that Locke's social contract did not envisage rights of representation for women and the propertyless, and that Mill's radical individualism, verging on libertarianism, excluded the colonized. 'Despotism', he says, 'is a legitimate [form] of government when dealing with barbarians' – meaning of course, the non-European and the colonized.

21. Mary Wollstonecraft and others were to soon enquire: what, then, is the gender of 'Citizen'? Thus began that productive dialogue between feminism and the Enlightenment that is yet to be concluded.

22. For a brilliant and closely argued text on this theme, though with emphases rather different from the ones I have briefly picked up on here, see Etienne Balibar, 'Citizen Subject', in Eduardo Cadava *et al.* (eds), *Who Comes after the Subject?* (New York, Routledge, 1991). See also chapters 2 and 9 in Etienne Balibar, *Masses, Classes, Ideas: Studies on Politics and Philosophy before and after Marx* (London, Routledge, 1993).

23. As he puts it in *Emile*: 'He who wishes to keep the first place in the civil order for the feelings of nature does not know what he wants . . . he can never be either man or citizen. He can be no good to himself, or to others.'

24. In Rousseau's own words, 'you are undone if you once forget that the fruits of the earth belong to us all, and the earth itself to nobody'.

25. Colletti argues convincingly that despite all the emphasis on the priority of the social over the individual, Rousseau's thought finally remains within the confines of individualism. See the closing pages of his careful treatment of this subject in Lucio Colletti, *From Rousseau to Lenin* (New York, Monthly Review Press, 1972).

Chapter 7

1. Between 1951 and 1977, Bharatiya Jana Sangh (BJS) functioned as the parliamentary front of the RSS, as the Bharatiya Janata Party (BJP) does now. When Indira Gandhi announced fresh elections towards the end of the Emergency, a large number of political formations, ranging all the way from the Socialists to the BJS, renounced their separate status as distinct parties and came together in a new party called the Janata Party, which went on to win 295 out of the 542 seats in Parliament, thus ousting Mrs Gandhi and forming a government with Morarji Desai as Prime Minister. The segment that had come into the Janata from BJS captured 93 of these seats, emerging as the largest contingent within the ruling party. Mr Vajpayee served as External Affairs Minister in that government. A point of discomfiture for their colleagues was that the BJS itself had indeed been dissolved but its former members who were now in Janata retained their membership in the RSS. This issue of 'dual membership' became especially explosive after the Janata government collapsed and the party failed miserably in the elections of 1980, in which Mrs Gandhi swept back into power. Forced to choose between their two allegiances, the former members of the BJS, led by Vajpayee, refused to leave the RSS, left the Janata Party instead, and founded the BJP.

2. Narasimha Rao became Prime Minister in 1991 when Congress (I) won the elections, though with a narrow margin, in the wake of Rajiv Gandhi's assassination. Manmohan Singh was his Finance Minster and put in place a well-integrated plan for privatization and 'liberalization' that had been taking place for some time anyway, though without much public fanfare in terms of ideological pronouncements.

3. Vishwanath Pratap Singh (popularly known as 'V.P.') first rose to prominence as a minister in Rajiv Gandhi's government. He broke with Rajiv in 1987, accusing him of corruption, formed his own party (Janata Dal), and became Prime Minister at the head of a minority government supported by the Communists from the left and the BJP from the Right. The government fell when the BJP withdrew its support in retaliation against his stand in favour of the oppressed castes and his opposition to the BJP's own communal mobilizations.

4. Ram Manohar Lohia, founder of the Socialist Party in 1955, who had a visceral hatred of Nehru, had built a sizeable base for himself, especially in UP, with a combination of a broadly populist programme and extreme linguistic-

cultural chauvinism in support of Hindi as the national language. The Socialists often allied with the BJS in elections, as for example in 1962, and found it easy to join them in forming a single party when Janata was born in 1977. Jayaprakash Narayan ('J.P.') had been a veteran Congress Socialist since the 1930s but came to oppose Nehru as one who had marginalized the Gandhians after the latter's death, as J.P. himself drew closer to the latter-day Gandhians such as Vinoba Bhave, while also cooperating with the RSS in their social-work projects. In 1974 he agreed to lead a mass movement, which increasingly looked like a full-scale insurrection, with the help of the Socialists and especially the RSS, against Indira Gandhi. It was his call to the army to revolt against Mrs Gandhi's 'authoritarianism' which led to the Declaration of the Emergency. Mulayam Singh Yadav in UP, and both Laloo Yadav and Sharad Yadav in Bihar, emerged out of that movement and benefited greatly from the subsequent electoral upsurge of the relatively more affluent sections of the middle castes, especially in north India.

5. I italicize the word *forge* because both its meanings are here intended: as in 'forgery', knowingly making a counterfeit of some original, bluff, a smile at poker; and 'forging in a smithy', the world of ironmongering, production, creating the yet uncreated. What is recalled here is that magnificent irony at the end of James Joyce's *A Portrait of the Artist as a Young Man*, when Stephen speaks about the resolve to 'forge in the smithy of my soul the uncreated conscience of my race'. It is much to be emphasized that secularism in India is not the recovery or reformulation of a past piety; it is an effort to create the yet uncreated. For the Left the project of secularism in India is inseparable from the struggle for socialism to which, however, its allies in the Third Force are deeply hostile. This hostility in turn renders the alliance unstable and highly contingent.

6. For a shorthand narrative of this period, the statement of the 'triangular contest' argument, and some comments on the contradictory role of the Soviet Union in the contest, see 'Introduction' and chapter 8 in Aijaz Ahmad, *In Theory: Classes, Nations, Literatures* (London, Verso, 1992; Delhi, Oxford University Press, 1994).

7. Jyoti Basu, an old leader of the CPI(M), has been the Chief Minister of West Bengal for over two decades, heading the government of the Left Front coalition.

8. Surjeet is the General Secretary of CPI(M). Chidambram, a great enthusiast of neo-liberalism, was Commerce Minister in the Congress (I) government of Narasimha Rao and then became the Finance Minister in the United Front (UF) government that emerged after the present article had been drafted.

9. A significant conclusion of the remarkably accurate exit poll conducted by Yogendra Yadav and reported in *India Today* is that 'only the BJP does well with the young and new voters' and is overwhelmingly the most popular party among the well-educated, upwardly mobile, urban, Hindu males in the populous zones of northern and western India. *India Today*, 31 May 1996.

10. Kalyan Singh was at that time the BJP Chief Minister of UP.

11. Mulayam Singh Yadav, who has been Chief Minister of India and was to serve as Defence Minister in the United Front (UF) government that

emerged after the publication of the present article, is head of the Samajwadi Party (SP), which itself came out of the fragmentation of Lohia's original Socialist Party. Mayawati is one of the two main leaders of Bahujan Samaj Party (BSP), a party predominantly of *dalits* and other oppressed castes and tribes, though it does claim to be the party of all non-upper castes, including Muslims. The BSP's main numerical power is concentrated in UP. It is a party of shifting alliances, going first with the SP and then the BJP; with the latter's support, Mayawati also served as the Chief Minister of the state.

12. *Manuwadi* refers to someone who observes the caste-based practices of the Brahminical order as laid down in, or derived from, the classical Sanskrit text *ManuSmriti* (Laws of Manu). *Dalit* activists use this term for upper castes in general. OBCs ('Other Backward Castes') are those which are a notch above the *dalits* but still low in the caste order and for whom Indian law also provides reservations in government jobs, educational institutions, etc. Some sections of the OBCs have emerged as owners of property and social power in the agrarian structure.

13. Prabhat Patnaik, 'The Fascism of Our Times', in *Social Scientist*, 238–9 (March–April 1993).

14. After her return to power in the early 1980s, Indira Gandhi turned to religio-communal tactics, in order to fight back against parties to her Right, including the BJP. She would frequent holy sites regularly, visiting a dozen temples all over India within the first six weeks of returning to power. In Jammu and Kashmir (J&K) she utilized frenzied appeals to Hindu communal sentiment in order to undermine her main opposition, the National Conference. Her son Sanjay was credited with having created the monster of Khalistani terrorism by inciting Bhindranwale against the Akalis, who were the main opposition to the Congress in Punjab. As Prime Minister, Rajiv Gandhi first surrendered to Muslim communalists by blocking a divorced Muslim woman's legal attempt to get a settlement according to civil law instead of the Special Muslim Personal Law, and then appeased the Hindu communalists through a large number of his actions, including the order to unlock the Ayodhya mosque and thus rekindle the controversy there.

15. Shiv Sena has undergone many incarnations: as anti-communist goon squads; as sons of the soil and self-styled representatives of the Maratha community in Maharashtra, saving the homeland from migrants from other parts of India; and as rabid Hindu communalists. In all its guises, it has been deeply involved with the crime underworld of Bombay and devoted to terror as a means to power. The Sena–BJP alliance currently rules Maharashtra.

16. *Hawala* is slang for certain types of illegal transactions in exchange of foreign and domestic currencies.

17. Mulayam Singh Yadav in UP, Laloo Prasad Yadav in Bihar.

18. In such arguments, the word 'Indian' tends to imply 'Hindu'. This kind of slippage occurs even in the writings of historians whose own commitment to secularism and hatred of *Hindutva* is beyond the smallest shadow of doubt, and who may personally not even subscribe to any religion at all. Thus, for example, when such historians as Romila Thapar and Ravinder Kumar bemoan the 'semitization' of Hinduism, they are unwittingly bemoaning the idea that

Hinduism is becoming more like Islam and Christianity, implying that this evolution of Hinduism is much to be regretted, and the further idea that the difference between these religions is fundamentally racial in character. What is merely an unwitting slippage here of course has a far more pernicious genealogy in the writings of many whose own intentions are very far from being noble.

19. There are significant and ominous lessons here. Mussolini was appointed Prime Minster by the King when his party commanded less than 10 per cent of the seats in Parliament, thanks to the threat of Fascist violence, sympathy for Fascism among army officers and civil servants, pressures from a section of the big bourgeoisie, and advice from military leaders. He first formed a *coalition* government with the Liberals, the historic ruling institution in post-Risorgimento Italy. Even more significant from today's vantage point is that Hitler first became Chancellor of Germany without a majority in Parliament but as the leader of the largest party, so that President Hindenberg, by no means a Nazi himself, invited him to form a government on perfectly constitutional grounds.

20. The phrase 'clearly constituted alliance' here is crucial for the argument as it evolved, because those who favoured calling in the BJP and its allies argued that only the core parties of the NF–LF were a real alliance, whereas other constituents of the Third Force were not (DMK, for instance, was allied with CPI but not CPI(M) and thus not with the Left Front), and that the assurance from the Congress that it will support the Third Force in Parliament did not matter because it had fought elections against the constituents of the NF–LF. It was a flimsy argument but it received the President's approval.

21. Sorabjee, otherwise known as a liberal lawyer of considerable eminence, of course went further. Writing in *The Times* on 17 May, he opined: 'Atalji has been sworn in as Prime Minister. There can be no question about his personal fitness for the post . . . The happiest part is the induction of Ram Jethmalani in the Cabinet, a position unfairly denied to him in 1977 and 1989.' Between these two sentences, he ridiculed what he took to be the alternate list of Prime Ministerial aspirants, from 'the Marxist octogenarian Jyoti Basu' to 'Phoolan Devi, the Bandit Queen'. Then came the liberal turn, with a strange twist: 'Will the BJP government last? . . . How sincere will it be in the fight against communalism, casteism and corruption?' This presumes, of course, that 'communalism' is something outside the BJP which it has the 'sincere' intention to 'fight', and what needed to be seen was the *degree* of its sincerity. All this is a fair indication of what the temperature of the liberal discourse might have been if the CPI(M) (not just Jyoti Basu as detached individual) had indeed sought to lead the government.

22. By the time the Lok Sabha actually met for the swearing-in of the MPs, the BJP's position had eroded so much and the dominant media, ecstatic at Vajpayee's swearing-in, was in such disarray, that *The Times* of 23 May reported the inaugural session of the Lok Sabha on p. 11, kept the front page clear of such irrelevancies, and gave space to two anti-*Hindutva* articles on its editorial page, just to cover up what it had been doing on the previous days.

23. 'CPM Flags Red', lead editorial in *The Times of India*, 15 May 1996.

24. The BSP chief.

25. See chapters 5 and 6 above, and 'Structure and Ideology in Italian Fascism', which was included in the earlier version of the present volume published in India (Delhi, Tulika, 1996), but has been omitted here.

26. Factions of the Ba'ath, much decayed now, of course continue to rule in Syria and Iraq.

27. Sumit Sarkar, 'The Anti-Secularist Critique of *Hindutva*: Problems of a Shared Discursive Space', *Germinal*, 1 (1994).

28. See chapter 6, section V for more discussion of this question

29. The RSS and its affiliates have compiled a very extensive list of the mosques which they say have been built by Muslim rulers after demolishing the Hindu temples that stood there previously. The Muslim populations of today are expected to atone for those sins and give up their places of worship for demolition. The Ayodhya demolition was the first such action for the redemption of Hindu honour. The mosques at Mathura and Varanasi, also in Uttar Pradesh, are under threat next. However, the RSS and its affiliates understood very quickly that there was no real support for such actions among large sections of the population where they wish to build their constituencies and have therefore backed off at least for now.

30. The most recent demonstration of this routine behaviour in the BJP, which the corporate media like to portray as 'the party with a difference', was summarized by Siddharth Varadarajan in a fine piece in *The Times of India*, 23 May 1996:

A day after the PM's national broadcast, the BJP exposed itself again, this time in Gandhinagar. Within minutes of Mr Vajpayee's leaving a *janasabha* celebrating his coronation, BJP activists stripped one of its own senior ministers and gave him a severe beating. The attack was carried out in full view of other BJP bigwigs and the police reportedly took their time to intervene. The Minister, Mr Atmaram Patel (who is 70), belongs to the state BJP's 'rebel' faction of Mr Shankarsinh Vaghela. The systematic manner in which the cadres went after him and then destroyed the cars of other prominent dissidents (news reports say that they were armed with a list of number plates) suggests the attacks were pre-planned . . .

31. Selections from the *Prison Notebooks* (New York, International Publishers, 1971), p. 337.

Chapter 8

1. *India Today*, 1 June 1998, p. 57.

2. See 'Broadening the Base', *Frontline*, 18 June 1999.

3. RAW is India's secret-service charged with foreign intelligence and espionage.

4. 'Subcontinental Crisis', *Frontline*, 19 June 1998, an earlier version of which is the section 'Competing Cruelties', pp. 247–53 above.

5. 'Broadening the Base'; 'The Many Roads to Kargil', *Frontline*, 16 July 1999, reprinted here at pp. 253–70 above.

6. Shiv Sena has mounted violent agitations to try to prevent India from

playing cricket with Pakistan and has been viewed as a lunatic fringe. The novelty now was that Kapil Dev, a former captain and current manager of the Indian team, as well as Jadeja, an aspirant for captaincy, also joined their chorus.

7. The Hindu Jagran Munch (HJM, or, in rough English, 'Front for Hindu Awakening') is a broad ideological front of the RSS to propagate ideas of religiously defined nationhood, communal interpretation of Indian history and society, etc., and to encourage the people whom it influences to join other, more strictly defined fronts, such as the BJP or VHP. The Swadeshi Jagran Munch (SJM, or, in rough English, 'Front for the Awakening of National Self-Reliance') draws upon the memory of those strands in the anti-colonial movement which preached economic nationalism. This is not the place to discuss the way in which that earlier Swadeshi Movement combined anti-colonial mobilizations with rhetorics of Hindu revivalism. Suffice it to say that SJM's indigenist rhetoric is merely gestural, since the RSS has never been an anti-imperialist organization. This lack of substantive anti-imperialism is what the rhetoric of culturalism and cultural nationalism seeks to obscure.

8. Literally, *swadeshi* means 'indigenous' and *videshi* means 'foreign'.

9. Ranbir Sena is the most notorious and murderous of the private armies kept by upper-caste landowners in Bihar.

10. Not only is religion here collapsed wholly into 'culture', but considering the traditonalist taboo against inter-caste and inter-religious marriages as forms of biologistic pollution, one might suggest that cultural boundaries are in any case policed by maintaining restrictions on biological reproduction and/or 'miscegenation'. Some variant of exclusivist marriage networks exists in most societies even in the reproduction of classes, but one might say, without invoking some comparative anthropological judgement, that prior existence of such boundaries makes it all the more possible for Savarkar's kind of rhetoric to be received simply as common sense.

11. See Marcia Cabolari, 'Hindutra's foreign tie-ups in the 1930s: Archival Evidence' in *Economic and Political Weekly*, 22 January 2000.

12. See chapter 7 in this volume.

13. For systematic exposition of this argument, see chapter 6 in this volume.

14. Aijaz Ahmad, 'Structure and Ideology in Italian Fascism', in *Lineages of the Present*, Delhi, Tulika, 1996. This essay has been excluded from the present book.

Chapter 9

1. K.K. Katyal, *The Hindu*, 21 February 2000.
2. *India Today*, 7 February 2000.

Acknowledgements

' "Tryst with Destiny": Free and Divided' was first published in *The Hindu*, August 1997.

'Democracy and Dictatorship in Pakistan' was first published in *Journal of Contemporary Asia*, 8:4 (1978), pp. 477–512, and then reprinted with a postscript in H. Gardezi and J. Rashid (eds), *Pakistan: The Roots of Dictatorship*, London, Zed Press, 1983, pp. 94–147.

'Azad's Careers: Roads Taken and Not Taken' was first published as an Occasional Paper by the Centre for Contemporary Studies, New Delhi, and then reprinted in Mushirul Hasan (ed.), *Islam and Indian Nationalism: Reflections on Abul Kalam Azad*, New Delhi, Manohar, 1992.

'In the Mirror of Urdu: Recompositions of Nation and Community, 1947–65' reproduces the text of a set of lectures delivered at the Indian Institution of Advanced Study, Shimla, and issued from there as *Lectures 102–105*, in 1993.

'Fascism and National Culture: Reading Gramsci in the days of *Hindutva*' is the revised text of the Amal Bhattacharji Memorial Lecture, delivered at the Centre for European Studies, Calcutta, 27 December 1993, and published in *Social Scientist*, 21:3–4 (March–April 1993).

'On the Ruins of Ayodhya: Communalist Offensive and Recovery of the Secular' is a revised version of 'Culture, Community and Nation: On the Ruins of Ayodhya', delivered as the keynote address at a Conference on 'Culture, Community, Nation' at the Deccan Development Society, Hyderabad, 7 December 1993; and was first published in *Social Scientist*, 21:7–8 (July–August 1993).

A lengthier version of 'In the Eye of the Storm: The Left Chooses' was first published in *Economic and Political Weekly*, June 1996.

'Thieves in the Night' was first published in *Frontline*, 5 June 1998.

'Competing Cruelties' is the earlier version of an essay published under the title 'Subcontinental Crisis' in *Frontline*, 19 June 1998.

'The Many Roads to Kargil' was first published in *Frontline*, 16 July 1999.

'Mediation by Any Other Name' was first published in *Frontline*, 30 July 1999.

'Rightwing Politics and the Cultures of Cruelty' is a composite text drawn from 'The Politics of Hate', *Frontline*, 12 February 1999; 'A Culture of Cruelty', *Frontline*, 12 March 1999; and 'Right-Wing Politics, and the Culture of Cruelty', *Social Scientist*, 304–5 (September–October 1998).

'Of Democrats and Dictators: Indo-Pakistan Politics in the Year 2000' appeared in *Frontline*, March 17 2000, in a much shorter version.

The author and publisher gratefully acknowledge permission to publish these essays in this volume.

Index